DISCOURSE, DEBATE AND DEMOCRACY:

Readings from *Controversia: An International Journal of Debate and Democratic Renewal*

൧൧

Edited by David Cratis Williams and
Marilyn J. Young

international debate education association

New York • Amsterdam • Brussels

Published by:
International Debate Education Association
400 West 59th Street
New York, NY 10019

Library of Congress Cataloging-in-Publication Data

Discourse, debate and democracy : readings from controversia : an international journal of debate and democratic renewal / edited by David Cratis Williams, Marilyn J. Young.
     p. cm.
 ISBN 978-1-932716-48-1
 1. Debates and debating. 2. Democracy. I. Williams, David Cratis, 1955- II. Young, Marilyn J., 1942-
 PN4181.D55 2008
 808.53—dc22

                              2008040815

Design by Hernán Bonomo
Printed in the USA

 IDEBATE PRESS

DISCOURSE, DEBATE AND DEMOCRACY

Introduction

David Cratis Williams and Marilyn J. Young

This volume is composed of selected articles from the first three years of the semi-annual journal, *Controversia: An International Journal of Debate and Democratic Renewal.* Perhaps the best way to introduce this volume is to first introduce the reader to *Controversia* and then to frame the specific articles from the journal that are reprinted herein. And perhaps the best way to introduce the journal is to revisit our initial "Introducing *Controversia*" from volume one, number one (2002). Following that, we will layout the articles reprinted in this book.

I. From "Introducing *Controversia*"

Controversia: An International Journal of Debate and Democratic Renewal is the semi-annual academic journal of the International Debate Education Association (IDEA); IDEA's mission—premised on the recognition that "free and open discussion is essential to the establishment and preservation of open and democratic societies" —is "to offer students and teachers the opportunity to examine issues affecting their lives and their communities; to create broad and inclusive debate clubs that encourage participation by all segments of the population, including ethnic minorities; and to establish independent national debate associations to promote, organize and sustain debate activities in each country."[1] Classroom experience in debates on issues of contemporary relevance, as well as perhaps more extensive training in debate through debate clubs and teams, are a vital step in the creation and renewal of free and open discussion in an open society, but the training in argumentation, analysis, refutation, and advocacy engendered through debate pedagogy cannot stop at the schoolhouse walls. Rather, debate and engagement in the public issues of one's time must infuse public practices and the public consciousness before a society can sustain genuine openness and a functioning democracy. As an academic journal, *Controversia* is dedicated to the scholarly examination of theoretical, historical, critical, and practical concerns relative to the furtherance of cultures of democratic communication and the ideals of open societies.

Perspectives of the Editors

On vital theoretical and pragmatic levels, we believe "democracy" must be understood as a culturally engrained communication system premised upon the competence of rhetors and audiences, as well as on guarantees of fundamental political freedoms. Viewing democracy as a "communication system," we start from perspectives about the nature of human communication and move forward toward social instantiation of these dynamics about communication in the political structure (rather than starting with assumptions about the political structure and working backward to the communication "requisites" that would sustain such a structure). Our orientation toward democracy as a communication system evolves from a dialectical perspective on communication; more specifically, as stated by Kenneth Burke, we "take democracy to be a device for institutionalizing the dialectical process, by setting up a political structure that gives full opportunity for the use of competition to a cooperative end."[2]

The paradox of competition toward cooperative ends frames the communication tenets of democracy. That is, "democracy" is a not a static term, concept, or practice; rather it is a process of opening, questioning, advocating, refuting, persuading, debating, deciding, and changing. It is, when performed well, an engagement in the process of dialectics: informed citizens operate under the sign of "reason" to freely and openly arrive at judgments of past actions for the collective sense of justice and to negotiate future courses of action for the collective good. But even at its "best," democracy is rarely efficient, and it is always contentious. In *Counter-Statement*, Burke maintains that "democracy" is "a system of government based upon the fear that central authority becomes bad authority—democracy, organized distrust, 'protest made easy,' a babble of discordant voices, a colossal getting in one's own way—democracy, now endangered by the apostles of hope who would attack it for its 'inefficiency,' whereas inefficiency is the one thing it has in its favor."[3] The "inefficiency" of democracy keeps the political system "open," just as the persistent presence of "otherness" in Burke's linguistic construction of the dialectic maintains the indeterminacy of meaning. That is, for Burke, dialectic does not lead ultimately to resolution: a static, stable, peaceful, silent end is never attained, even in theory. Rather, the dialectic in language never ceases, and meaning is never totalized.[4] By extension, democracy is never "finished"; change (reversal and transformation) is not only systemic and inevitable, but also undetermined and indeterminate. Nor is democracy ever univocal: when society becomes univocal, it ceases to be a "democracy."

We view democracy as the institutionalization of dialectics—the institutionalized argumentative interplay of differences; when opposition is silenced, when public controversy ceases, when dialectical difference is stamped into the sameness expressed in Burke's notion of "pure identification,"[5] democracy dies.

As a dialectical process, democracy is always active; it requires the engagement of opinions and options through public voices, within public hearing, and under public scrutiny. It is filled with sincere opposition, characterized by compromise, and sustained by controversy. It can be acrimonious and strife-filled; at times, it embraces logomachy. Moreover, it requires constant renewal always and everywhere because, without renewal, the entrenched social, cultural, political, economic, and religious orthodoxies may ultimately silence meaningful public expressions of difference. Democracy may or may not require certain economic prerequisites such as a viable middle-class; it may or may not have necessary implication in specific economic formulations, such as free market capitalism; it may or may not be characterized by specific constitutional, governmental, or non-governmental institutions; it may or may not require certain voting procedures, representational practices, or party formulations. But it *always* requires controversy, and *Controversia* is dedicated to the study of controversy.

II. Article Selections for *Discourse Debate and Democracy*

The articles contained in this volume are drawn from the first three years of publication of *Controversia*. This is not a "best of" *Controversia*: these articles were selected not merely because they are solid essays, representing quality scholarship (although they are, and they do), but rather because they speak to the central issues of the roles of discourse and debate in democracies.

The current volume is divided into two parts. Part One looks at the relationships among argumentation, debate, and democracy. Part Two offers case studies of public argument in both "(possibly) renewing" democracies as well as "(possibly) emerging" democracies.

In Part One the selected essays focus on the application of argumentation to democratic practice. William Rehg discusses the notion of deliberative democracy and the ways in which argumentation theorists can influence the quality of public deliberation. To this end, Rehg argues for a pedagogy that helps students develop critical thinking skills that might "transfer" from the classroom to the public arena. Frans van Eemeren echoes this perspective, arguing in his essay that dialectical procedures for public discourse need to be developed; more specifically, he argues that certain critical discussion rules from the pragma-dialectical theory of argumentation might profitably be applied to public discourse.

In examining the Postmodern turn, M. Lane Bruner focuses on Aristotle's notion of practical wisdom or *phronesis*. Noting that the concept has been complicated by postmodern theories, Bruner reconstructs *phronesis* as political wisdom, thus linking Aristotle's idea to deliberative practice. By teaching a contemporary ideal of *phronesis*, argumentation educators might better equip students to become more effective—and wiser—citizens. Christopher Tindale continues this tradition by examining the argumentative situation to explore ways that argumentation can promote cooperation rather than confrontation.

Gordon Mitchell, et. al., turn the lens of argumentation on a specific situation, studying the political impact of student-driven public deliberation. The authors look at Southeastern Europe as it transitions from communism to democracy; specifically, they examine the impact on subsequent political activities of the Southeast European Youth Leadership Institute (SEEYLI) and the public debate projects it sponsored.

Part Two of this volume looks at specific instances of public argument as they relate to policy and democratization. Carol Winkler explores the ways in which international arguments about US treatment of detainees at Guantanamo Bay negotiates argumentative rules and presumptions. Winkler argues that the Bush Administration places the doctrine of "manifest destiny" into the global arena, altering long-agreed-upon rules for international policy disputes.

Robert Newman examines the way in which American hubris played out in hypocritical efforts to "democratize" other nations through force and manipulation. Gordon Stables examines the way Islamic audiences were conceived by the Bush Administration in their efforts to communicate to those audiences. Stables argues that these conceptions were driven by western notions of civil society rather than by a fully considered understanding of Islamic society.

James Janack moves our consideration of democratization from the Middle East to Russia, studying Boris Yeltsin's 1993 speeches on the Russian Constitution and 1996 campaign speeches to explicate the discrepancies between the Constitution as proposed by Yeltsin and as ultimately adopted. Janack argues that Yeltsin conceived of democracy as a function of a successful market economy rather than a product of constitutional guarantees. Janack extends his consideration of Russian political discourse in his study of Vladimir Zhirinovsky, the leader of the Liberal Democratic Party of Russia. Here Janack argues that Zhirinovsky enhanced his appeal as a protest candidate by emphasizing the carnival aspect of his outrageous rhetoric and bizarre behavior. In this way, Zhirinovsky was able to characterize himself as opposed to the dominant socio-political system, even though that system was not entrenched, but was in a period of instability and transition. We conclude Part Two and this volume with a review essay by David Cheshier in which he examines six studies of the role of public deliberation in the Arab world.

It is our belief that the essays included in this volume provide a foundation for consideration of the roles of argumentation, debate, rhetoric, and critical pedagogy in democracy and democratization. All too often democracy and political discourse are seen as exercises in politics, not as systems of communication. Yet, if one views democracy as we advocate in this introduction, as a system of communication, the elements of communication are revealed as intrinsic and essential to successful exercise of public discourse. This work is one step in the direction of that realization.

NOTES

1. International Debate Education Association, "Mission." http://idebate.org/about.html , 5/16/01.

2. Kenneth Burke, The Philosophy of Literary Form. 3rd Ed. (Berkeley: University of California Press, 1941; rpt. 1973), 444.

3. Kenneth Burke, Counter-Statement (Berkeley: University of California Press, 1931; rpt. 1968), 114.

4. Kenneth Burke, A Grammar of Motives (Berkeley: University of California Press, 1945; rpt. 1969), esp. 21-29.

5. Kenneth Burke, A Rhetoric of Motives (Berkeley: University of California Press, 1950; rpt. 1969), esp. 19-23.

PART ONE: Argumentation, Debate, and Democracy

The Argumentation Theorist in Deliberative Democracy

William Rehg

Abstract

Proponents of "deliberative democracy" hold that legitimate political decisions should issue from a process of public discourse or dialogue in which citizens, adopting a civic standpoint oriented toward the common good, assess the arguments for and against various political proposals. In this article I address the question of how argumentation theorists can positively influence the quality of public deliberation. I propose that higher education provides a broader opportunity for such influence than the highly demanding role of public intellectual. To achieve influence as educators, however, argumentation theorists must aim to impart skills or habits that transfer beyond the classroom. Drawing on comprehensive models of argumentation, I sketch such a pedagogy, specifically one that aims at a habit of comprehensive attentiveness and a capacity to raise some key critical questions. I then specify the kind of deliberative role that theorists achieve when citizens actually use the theorists' models.

Introduction

In the last decades democratic theorists have shown a growing interest in the deliberative features of democratic decision-making. This interest represents a further development of the concern with public participation that, at least in the United States, was revived by the social movements of the 1960s. In any case, the topic of political deliberation brings with it pressing questions about the rational or reasonable character of such deliberation. These are just the kinds of questions in which argumentation theorists and students of public debate specialize. Do not argumentation theorists thus have an important political responsibility—a role to play in deliberative democracies? I think they do. In this essay I bring together recent developments in both democratic theory and argumentation theory to propose one way of conceiving this role and its feasible exercise. I use the term "argumentation theorists" quite broadly, as including anyone involved in the study or teaching of argumentation and its evaluation: formal and informal logicians, philosophers, communication theorists, teachers of composition, debate, rhetoric, and so on. How can this group of theorists have a positive influence on the practice of democratic deliberation?

In section I, I explain the idea of deliberative democracy and the sense in which it presupposes that citizens and decision-makers have some understanding of what reasonable argumentation involves. I then turn, in section II, to the influence that argumentation theorists can exercise as educators; here I sketch a pedagogical approach that promises to impart transferable critical skills. Finally, in section III I specify more precisely the particular status that theorist-educators have when they achieve this kind of influence.

I: The Idea of Deliberative Democracy

If theories of democracy generally agree in according citizens a role in the process of governance, they differ in how they conceive that role and its relation to political legitimacy. Taken in a broad sense, deliberative theories hold that democratic lawmaking should flow from the public, reasonable deliberation of informed citizens. This idea goes back at least to ancient Greece; in the nineteenth century John Stuart Mill was one of its staunchest proponents. However, the rise of fascism in Europe, skepticism about the possibility of a common good in pluralistic societies, and discouraging sociological findings about the political ignorance and apathy of the public led political theorists in the twentieth century to take a rather dim view of democratic forms of popular participation. Elitist and economic theories of democracy (e.g., Schumpeter 1950, chaps. 22-23; Downs 1957) limited citizen participation to voting as an aggregative mechanism for evicting incumbent parties that failed to satisfy majority interests. These pessimistic models are elitist in that they restrict substantive policy deliberation to government leaders, experts, and bureaucrats. As an economic approach to democracy, they apply rational choice theory to the political process, for example they liken voters to consumers who make rational choices among political programs according to individual or group preferences.[1] Although bargaining among parties and interest blocks may occur, there is no conception of the common good at stake in the political process (beyond the aggregation of interests, that is). The reduction of politics to the competition and balancing of particular interests has led some theorists to dub such approaches "strategic" models of democracy (e.g., Michelman 1989; Estlund 1993).

With the revival of the civic-republican tradition at mid-century (e.g., Arendt 1958; Mansbridge 1980), popular participation oriented toward the common good regained respectability. Most at home in the small city-states of classical Greece or other small, relatively homogeneous polities, civic republicanism emphasizes the capacity of public-minded citizens to participate in political decision-making based on shared values (Held 1987; Michelman 1986). Deliberative democratic theory, in the specific sense I will employ that term here, attempts to make civic republicanism service-able for complex, pluralistic societies in which substantive value consensus and direct participation are much less likely. To meet the contemporary challenges of pluralism and complexity, a number of deliberative democrats have turned to Kantian and procedural conceptions of public reason (Rawls 1971; 1996; Habermas 1996; Michelman 1988). These theorists strive to avoid simplistic conceptions of the common good and an over-reliance on the civic virtues of individual citizens; Jürgen Habermas, for example, acknowledges the important role of competing interests, bargaining and compromise, and representative institutions in the deliberative process. At the same time, deliberative theorists insist that legitimate political outcomes depend in significant measure on the quality of the deliberative process, which is to say, on how well the lawmaking procedures allow citizens and legislators to go beyond particular interests and discuss matters from a civic or public perspective.

As a model of decision making, "deliberation as discussion" offers a number of advantages over the mere aggregation of interests by voting (Fearon 1998). But as a conception of citizenship and legitimacy, two considerations provide the most straightforward motivation for a delibera-tive approach. Negatively, one can cite the failure of strategic models since Hobbes to solve the problem of social order. Positively, one can insist that political life involves a solidaristic dimension oriented toward a common good and that therefore some political problems can be adequately addressed only if citizens strive to reach an understanding based on public reasons. To be sure, pessimistic appraisals are not hard to find (e.g., Friedman 1998; Sanders 1997); nor do I claim that deliberative theorists have dealt with all the obstacles facing public deliberation (cf. Johnson 1998; Knight and John-son 1994). Of these obstacles—social inequalities and power asymmetries, media distortions, social choice problems, and so on—public ignorance presents one of the most daunting challenges to the feasibility of deliberative models. Although the ongoing debates over this issue indicate that the fea-sibility question remains unsettled, one cannot simply dismiss the extensive empirical findings on the ignorance of citizens regarding not only issues and candidates but also government structures in general (Somin 1998).[2] Consequently, some deliberative theorists have retreated to very modest positions, admitting that genuinely democratic politics is "extraordinary," or only occasionally "breaks out" of the usual power-ridden political routines (Ackerman 1991; Habermas 1996, chap. 8; Blaug 1999, chaps. 7-8). But if such outbreaks of democracy can and have occurred, then deliberative democracy is not a mere chimera—as Cohen (1999, 410) puts it, such occasional democratic "disruptions suffice as proof of possibility." In what follows I assume that complete pessimism is not warranted. This opens the door for the argumentation theorist.

Deliberative theorists conceive public reason and political legitimacy in somewhat different ways. Specifically, theorists differ in the relative importance they accord to core principles such as fairness and equality, in whether or not they consider deliberation an "epistemic" process oriented toward "correct" outcomes, in the role they accord to consensus, in how they conceive the relation between basic constitutional rights and democracy, and so on (see Bohman and Rehg 1997; Dryzek 2000). However, the importance of public reason for each of these variants—the idea that deliberation involves the dialogical exchange of reasons, or reaching some understanding about what counts as a public reason—means that argumentation must play some role in each approach. If we assume that the civic standpoint is defined by an orientation toward justice or the common good—and that one cannot reduce this perspective to the calculation and balancing of competing interests—then citizens, legislators, and other civil servants who adopt this perspective when they propose a prospective policy or law must make a case before a critical audience. In other words, they must present public arguments in a cooperative, dialogical spirit. Consequently, the deliberative theorist must acknowledge that, at least on some issues, the *quality of arguments and of the argumentative process* makes a difference in our assessment of the outcome.

To be precise, my analysis in what follows proceeds on the basis of the following assumptions regarding deliberation and argument:

> (A1) Political deliberation has a cognitive (or "epistemic") dimension insofar as it aims to answer questions about how the polity ought to resolve social conflicts or deal with common problems. An adequate answer to such questions depends on knowledge of various facts, an accurate perception of needs and interests, reliable forecasts of future consequences, and so on.

Consequently, a deliberative outcome is reasonable insofar as the arguments that justify it take into consideration the relevant aspects of the issue at stake.

(A2) Political outcomes with a cognitive dimension are subject to a normative standard of substantive legitimacy that goes beyond mere procedural legitimacy. An outcome is procedurally legitimate insofar as it is reached according to proper procedure (e.g., as specified in a constitution). But citizens should, insofar as possible, strive for outcomes that are also substantively legitimate because they issue from reasonable public deliberation.[3]

(A3) Therefore, insofar as deliberation involves argumentation, normatively legitimate outcomes must satisfy standards of reasonable argumentation.

These assumptions are ambitious but hardly novel in democratic theory. In any case, they strike me as the most straightforward way of defining the context in which argumentation theorists can play a positive role in deliberative democracy.

Now, to say that a public deliberative process should satisfy standards of argumentative reasonableness is not yet to say that individual participants must, *as individuals,* satisfy such standards. It may be that the standards are achieved only collectively, or only in virtue of institutional design. In fact, I believe that the most plausible normative account of reasonableness lies somewhere between purely individualist and purely collectivist models. I thus assume further:

(A4) Because deliberative reasonableness is a collective product, its achievement presupposes individual participants with *some* capacity to contribute to reasonable argumentation and the reasonable assessment of argumentative cogency.

This assumption seems plausible for those arenas in which the outcome is reached through a vote of some sort. In casting a vote, a citizen takes personal responsibility for an assessment of the issue in light of the arguments and counterarguments that were put forth in the preceding deliberation.[4] Hence deliberation presupposes a certain capacity on the part of the individual participants (whether it overburdens the competence of citizens I take up below). Although the reasonableness of the final outcome is a cooperative result, it depends on each individual's partial contribution and capacity to assess cogency. As I conceive this, no individual is the final arbiter of what counts as publicly cogent, yet each must make as intelligent a contribution as possible to the collective assessment.

The foregoing assumptions define a context in which it makes sense for argumentation theorists to articulate standards of reasonable argumentation. They might also have an educational task, according to A4—more on that in the next section. But first note how modestly I conceive the theoretical task. At least in the narrow sense of this task of articulation, argumentation theorists (a) do not aim to provide a full-blown theory of social conflict resolution, even if argumentation involves conflict (Crosswhite 1996, chap. 4); (b) they do not assume that argumentation by itself can resolve *any* social conflict; and (c) they do not assume that argumentation is always appropriate as a method of conflict resolution. According to this narrow construal of their task, argumentation theorists assume that institutional mechanisms for reaching closure on decisions are already in place; the question then is how deliberative argumentation can improve the substantive reasonableness of those decisions. As a number of political theorists have pointed out, one should not define the normative standard here in terms of idealized consensus on the single right answer (Warnke 1999; McCarthy 1998; Gutmann and Thompson 1996; Rehg and Bohman 1996). I thus make the following assumption:

> (A5) An outcome is substantively legitimate, in a minimal sense, if the preceding public deliberation has exposed and eliminated blatantly *un*reasonable viewpoints, so that citizens can consider the outcome as not unreasonable, even if they do not fully agree with the substantive outcome (Rehg 1997b; cf. McMahon 2001, 100-02).

Substantive legitimacy thus presupposes, at the very least, a minimal conception of "reasonable assessment" that imposes less burdensome cognitive demands on the competence of citizens than the fuller notion of reasonableness in A1. Thus one can think of substantive legitimacy and reasonableness as matters of degree. The argument that follows in section II depends primarily on the minimal conception.

On this modest conception of argumentation theory, then, one begins with a given procedure that has prima facie legitimacy—say one in which the decision is made by majority rule—and then asks how the deliberation that precedes the decision can lead to a more (or less) reasonable outcome. To be sure, one must know something about the particular legal-political context, the decision-making procedure, and how reasonable deliberation connects with that procedure in such a context. Conversely, one's argumentation-theoretic analysis may have implications for procedural design. Thus the narrower undertaking cannot, in the end, be fully separated from a broader interdisciplinary analysis in which argumentation theory is tested against findings from other disciplines such as political economy.

II: The Influence of the Argumentation Theorist as Educator: Achieving Transfer

The foregoing analysis of deliberative democracy opens up the space in which one can meaningfully ask about the role of the argumentation theorist. If argumentatively reasonable public deliberation can occur—even if only rarely—and if even small local improvements in the quality of public discourse are worth pursuing, then the argumentation theorist has a positive role to play in deliberative democracy.

To specify this role more precisely, I assume that argumentation theorists work by and large in higher education, which in the United States means: in two- and four-year colleges and in universities.[5] On this assumption, the question of the public impact of argumentation theorists depends first of all on the more general question of how academics can influence democratic deliberation at all. One approach to this question highlights the role of the public intellectual. Although I don't deny the possibility or desirability of argumentation theorists writing and speaking as public intellectuals, that role imposes a demanding double task on educators. They must meet both the teaching and scholarly demands of their discipline and find time to write popular essays, or somehow connect with social movements (e.g., Flack 1991). Consequently, I want to explore an alternative path of public influence, that of undergraduate education.

Thus I am not so concerned here with theorists' ability to make substantive and publicly influential interventions on this or that topic of political debate—the kind of thing one expects from prominent public intellectuals. Rather, I am concerned simply with the possibility of influencing public deliberation by educating citizens to become better participants in deliberation. The argumentation theorist is particularly well placed in the educational system to influence the people who (we hope) deliberate, or will deliberate, either as citizens faced with voting decisions about candidates and issues, or in some cases as public officials who play a more direct role in lawmaking and policy-formation. Many colleges and universities require their students to take courses in composition, critical thinking, philosophy, and the like. And such are the courses that argumentation theorists typically teach; texts for such courses are the books that argumentation theorists typically write; standards and strategies for such courses are the worries that typically occupy argumentation theorists at conferences. In sum, argumentation theorists have presumably developed a kind of expertise—exactly what kind of expertise I will say more about later—and they have access to close and extended interaction with successive groups of student-citizens. At the very least, we have at hand the raw materials for some kind of influence on public deliberation via influence on those who deliberate.

If we take education as a primary site from which argumentation theorists can make a positive contribution to public deliberation, then the teaching of so-called "critical thinking/reasoning" skills—often understood in terms of argumentation theory—becomes an obvious venue through which such educational influence is exercised. This raises the much-debated problem of the transfer of such skills beyond the classroom (Ennis 1962; Siegel 1988; McPeck 1990; Talaska 1992; Brown 1998). If the teaching of argumentation skills is to have an impact on public discourse, then it seems that students must be able to transfer what they've learned in the classroom to other areas of reflection. This problem is most acute if one defines critical thinking in terms of certain general analytical tools. In that case, "transfer" refers to the ability to analyze and assess public arguments in terms of formal logic, or a list of fallacies, or tree diagrams, and the like.[6] One should not be surprised by pessimistic findings regarding the transfer of such abstract formal skills. Even the less formalistic methods of argument assessment (e.g., Toulmin's model, tree diagrams) tend to be unwieldy and time-consuming to employ on actual full-length arguments (Fulkerson 2001). Empirical studies of writing education tend to confirm such pessimism: Crosswhite (1996, chap. 9), for example, has noted the difficulties students have with the transfer of grammatical skills, when these are conceived and taught in formal terms.[7]

The difficulties associated with the transfer of formal analytical skills have important implications for how composition, critical thinking, and argumentation courses are taught. Methods of analysis and evaluation must be feasible to employ by ordinary reasoners who want to assess everyday arguments of the sort that appear in newspapers and magazines, on television and the Internet. And the skills involved must be learned in such a way that students are continually transferring them to such real contexts. Thus, to achieve transfer means that students must acquire not only a set of competences, but also something like a "critical spirit" or habit of mind (Siegel 1988, chaps. 2-3). In what follows I indicate how a comprehensive approach to argumentation might respond to the problem of transfer. I intend the sketch that follows more as a suggestive illustration of the basic approach than a definitive account that would exclude alternative ways of capturing the various aspects of argumentative practices. Although the pedagogical goals I propose are relevant to course design, I do not intend to propose a specific design.

Suppose, to begin, that our aim is the modest one of educating citizens to be more reflective participants in public deliberation, where "participation" has at least the minimal sense of being a member of the audience to which written and spoken political discourse is addressed. If "reflective participants" are those who deliberate and vote on the basis of reasonable arguments, and if deliberative outcomes are reasonable in the minimal sense that unreasonable positions have been publicly recognized as such and rejected, then our educational aim is to produce citizens who can spot those blatantly unreasonable positions that would undermine the quality of deliberation. According to comprehensive approaches, in order to spot unreason one must attend to a range of dimensions or aspects of argumentation (Wenzel 1990; Rehg 1997a; Tindale 1999).

The areas covered by Aristotle's *Organon* –logic, dialectic, and rhetoric—provides one of the most common starting points for a comprehensive account of the dimensions of argumentation. On one interpretation of Aristotle, "good arguments" should be (a) logically constructed on the basis of (b) dialectically plausible premises and (c) presented in a rhetorically persuasive manner that is (d) appropriate to the specific institutional setting (court of law, legislature, etc). Contemporary theorists also distinguish the process of argumentation from the argument-products that issue from that process; one can, accordingly, develop standards of reasonableness for both the process and the product. Some have linked this contemporary map with the Aristotelian framework by distinguishing logical product, dialectical procedure, and rhetorical process (e.g., Habermas 1984, 25-26; Wenzel 1990). A theory of democratic deliberation must then embed these general features of argumentation in the variety of institutional and social contexts that bear on democratic lawmaking and policy formation.

However, the simple alignment of product, procedure, and process with Aristotle's three perspectives is too quick. If we think of the product of argumentation as the written or spoken conclusion supported by reasons,

17

then there seems to be no reason not to approach the product from all three of Aristotle's perspectives. In that case, the differences between the perspectives, as applied to a given argument-product, correspond to the degree of contextualization. Thus, in assessing an argument for logical validity, one focuses on the internal semantic and syntactic relationships among the sentences that make up the product as a set of reasons leading to a conclusion. In such logical assessments one largely disregards the broader argumentative context—though to be sure one must bring in some contextual considerations simply to interpret the sentences and identify the kind of argument at issue. Richer contextual awareness enters in as soon as one considers the product as a pragmatic result, as the outcome of a particular practice of argumentation. In that case, assessment requires one to examine the product's "dialectical tier," that is its responsiveness to counterarguments, objections and further questions, and the like (see Johnson 2000; Goldman 1994). Here one situates the argument in the context of other arguments. Finally, one can assess the argument rhetorically—thus in relation to the audience context—by examining its use of ethos, pathos, and so on (e.g., Tindale 1999, chap. 5). The analysis would presume some familiarity with the institutional context, but I set that aside for now.

If we demand that reflective audience members be able to fully assess argument-products from all three perspectives, that is to employ the full set of standards that have been developed for these perspectives, then transferability would be in question once again. The comprehensive approach will certainly not help with transfer if all we do is multiply standards of reasonableness. What can transfer, I suggest, is first of all *the awareness that such a range of dimensions exists and deserves critical attention*. According to comprehensive models, reasonable democratic deliberation involves a range of argumentative dimensions, and to the extent that participants have a truncated or overly narrow model of deliberative reasonableness, they are more likely to miss flaws in the reasonableness of their political deliberations. Positively construed, the idea is that participants become more reflective insofar as they are aware of, and thus capable of attending to, the full range of dimensions of political argumentation.

The first pedagogical aim, then, is to educate student-citizens into *a comprehensive critical attentiveness to the general aspects of reasonable argumentation*. To render this general habit of attentiveness effective for evaluation, however, one needs a heuristic—a set of critical questions that open one's eyes to each dimension of argumentation. The second pedagogical aim, then, is not a detailed knowledge of formal rules or standards but *a capacity for raising a few critical questions.* Although these simple questions naturally lead one into finer-grained evaluations based on more detailed methods of analysis and appraisal, they have a critical power of their own to uncover blatantly unreasonable positions.

One can unfold the educational task by starting with the idea of dialectical awareness.[8] To inculcate dialectical awareness, one teaches students to regard arguments in their dialectical context. Thus, in contrast to most logic and reasoning textbooks, which focus on the assessment of single arguments in isolation, one would teach students always to assess *sets of arguments,* that is arguments and counterarguments. Here Crosswhite's (1996, 285-88) recommendation to use a textbook that provides students with a "mini-library" on selected topics is exactly on target. Such a textbook gives students a range of perspectives on issues.[9] Moreover, it encourages students to move beyond simple yes/no oppositions—in the context of democratic deliberation, dialectical argumentation is best conceived, after all, as a cooperative process and not simply as a competitive debate one strives to "win."

The basic critical question for such a dialectical assessment is, what is the appropriate burden of proof in the given deliberative context and how well have the arguments met it (cf. Rescher 1977)? Following Johnson (2000, 207-08), we might expand this basic question into the following three questions: (D1) How well have the arguments responded to, or taken account of, the standard objections and further questions? (D2) How well does each argument address alternative positions? (D3) How well does each argument deal with consequences and implications of its thesis? One can become aware of these questions and objections, alternatives and consequences simply by attending to the ongoing debate on an issue: the public arguers—politicians, intellectuals, and so on—supply the reflective citizen with the dialectical context, as well as with many of the dialectically relevant critical questions. To this extent the quality of the citizen's reflection depends on the quality of the media and public sphere—an issue that leads to some further critical questions regarding the process, which I take up below. My assumption here is that insofar as citizens simply *attend to* the full range of positions, arguments, questions and objections, it is less likely that blatantly unreasonable positions will escape critique. Indeed, one hallmark of an unreasonable position is that it simply ignores further questions and standard objections. Insofar as argumentation theorists can inculcate this simple habit of attention, then, they can enhance the quality of deliberation.

Dialectical awareness naturally leads into the logical and rhetorical assessment of argument-products. On the one hand, assessing the relative plausibility of competing claims requires one to assess particular argument-products from an internal logical perspective, more or less apart from the concrete social context. On the other hand, assessment also requires some attention to the rhetorical context of argumentation. Let me briefly explain my understanding of each aspect in relation to the question of transfer.

Logical assessment requires that one first identify and interpret the specific reasons adduced in support of a particular conclusion. Appraisal then turns not so much on deductive validity as on the relative plausibility of the premises and their degree of support for the conclusion—after all, most natural language arguments are not deductive. Johnson (1992; 2001, 189-206), for example, invokes four simple criteria: the supporting reasons must each be relevant, acceptable, and true, and together provide sufficient support for the conclusion. In my opinion, the crucial critical questions for logical assessment boil down to three: (L1) Are the relevant reasons adduced in support of the position plausible? (L2) Given the burden of proof and kind of argument being made, do the reasons plausibly support the conclusion? (L3) Is there an obvious contradiction or equivocation?[10] One should not restrict this assessment to the primary arguments for a position—what Johnson has termed the "illative core"—but extend it to the responses to objections and so on, the "dialectical tier" (Rehg 2001). These questions articulate what most arguers intuitively know in any case, and one does not need any particular technical expertise simply to raise such broad critical questions.

To be sure, *answering* such questions may well involve technical knowledge and skills. That is what I meant when I said the questions lead into more detailed, finer-grained appraisals, which demand greater assessment skills. Even aside from the technicalities of deductive validity, informal logical standards for the assessment of non-deductive arguments (analogies, inductive inferences, statistical reasoning, and so on) can be quite involved. For example, the kinds of statistical and probabilistic arguments that enter into political issues—in particular when the question depends on scientific findings, epidemiological studies, or social surveys—require some knowledge of technicalities. Hence the logical level poses the greatest challenge to full engagement by citizens in deliberation. I suspect that the ongoing worries of political theorists regarding the capacity of citizens for deliberation stem primarily from the demands imposed by the logical assessments that are necessary for comparing arguments dialectically (e.g., Dewey 1956; Willard 1996). However, such worries often involve inadequately differentiated conceptions of expertise or a failure to appreciate the cognitive division of labor (see Turner 2001; Bohman 1999; 1996, 166-70). Moreover, one should not underestimate the ability of interested citizens to educate themselves, nor their ability to scrutinize competing expert opinions, particularly with the help of counter-experts, citizen organizations and non-governmental organizations (see Gusterson 2001; 1996, chaps. 7-8; Kleinman 2000; Bohman 1999; Fabj and Sobnosky 1995).

In any case, the pedagogical aims that matter for transfer lie at a less sophisticated level of appraisal. If one does supply students with detailed lists of fallacies, valid argument forms, standards specific to different types of arguments, and so on, the first educational goal should be simply *to make students aware* that such dimensions of assessment exist. Second, the broad critical questions I have proposed (L1-L3) are formulated so that citizens can use them "on the fly" as it were—as one reads or reflects on an editorial for example, without the help of paper and pencil, tree diagrams, and the like. As designed for the minimal standard of reflective participation (A5), these questions target blatantly unreasonable positions, which involve more easily spotted implausibilities, equivocations, and unjustified leaps. Using such questions critically is thus less cognitively demanding—and more within the competence of a lay public—than comparing the relative strength of two more-or-less reasonably argued positions.

The rhetorical assessment of arguments is likewise oriented toward uncovering significant deficits in reasonableness. Here one evaluates the argument as the product of a social process in a concrete context—that is, a context in which particular speakers/writers are striving to affect the beliefs of particular audiences. Again, the primary transferable skill is a habit of attention to the presence of such contextual features in the argument-product. The specific critical questions are, at the very least, these: (R1) How is the issue being framed in the argument? and (R2) how is the arguer trying to affect us as members of the audience? Of all the questions involved in a comprehensive assessment, these two demand the most self-reflection. R1 asks one to uncover the background assumptions that shape the dialectical context and thus have been insinuated into one's own thinking (cf. Rescher 1998), whereas R2 asks one to attend to how the argument moves one's affect in specific ways—how the argument appeals to our emotions, instills trust in certain authorities and distrust for others, and so on. The habit of asking these two simple questions can, by itself, enhance reflective participation by leading one to further, more specific questions, such as whether an appeal to authority, or to emotion, is reasonable or not (see Walton 1989). To be sure, these two questions do not exhaust rhetorical analysis. One can ask, more broadly, what different audiences an argument is intended to address and how it tailors different argumentative techniques to each audience (cf. Tindale 1999, chap. 5; Perelman 1982). Again, I assume that blatantly unreasonable positions will display their rhetorically manipulative character more readily to those who, guided by these critical questions, simply pay attention.

The foregoing remarks have focused on some transferable skills—habits of attention and a few broad critical questions—that pertain to the assessment of the argument-products that politically interested citizens find in various public venues. But notice that in the context of democratic deliberation, the dialectical assessment of arguments also leads one to ask critical questions about the *process as such* (in contrast to the questions addressed to the argument precisely *as a product* of the process). These questions concern above all the democratic character of the process: whether the deliberation has been structured in such a way as to ensure that all the relevant considerations and the concerns of those affected by the issue at hand have been adequately voiced. Drawing on Alexy (1990), Habermas (1990b, 87-92) has spelled out the key requirements as a set of idealized "pragmatic presuppositions" of rational argumentation motivated purely by the search for the better argument. Although Habermas has linked such presuppositions to the rhetorical dimension, the specific requirements—that argumentation is open to all those affected, that everyone has equal opportunities to argue, and that no one is coerced by external constraints or internal psychological pressures—seem designed to enhance the dialectical quality of arguments by ensuring that all the relevant considerations have been voiced.[11] In any case, it is at this level, I suggest, that citizens must critically examine the quality of public discussion as it occurs in formal legislative bodies, in citizen groups and other informal arenas, and through the various media outlets that structure the public sphere. The basic critical questions boil down to these: (P1) have all those affected by an issue been included, and given an adequate opportunity to voice their concerns, make their arguments, reply to questions, and so on? (P2) are various social and economic forces/circumstances seriously distorting the presentation of topics and arguments?

P1 and P2 are not such difficult questions to raise, even if answering them fully would require more effort than most citizens care to invest. In fact, answers are not beyond the capacity of citizens, given the amount of information available on such issues in public venues (newspapers, magazines, the Internet, etc.). James Bohman, for example, has further specified a potentially transferable standard for identifying blatant exclusions: his minimal empirical indicator of deliberative capacity is "whether or not citizens or groups of citizens are able to initiate public deliberation about their concerns" (Bohman 1996, 126; 1997). The currently high level of public dissatisfaction in the United States with the legislative process—the post-9/11 patriotic fervor notwithstanding— suggests that citizens have indeed asked such questions and arrived at disheartening answers. At any rate, transfer occurs here insofar as citizens can identify egregious distortions and exclusions in public deliberation— the kind that would seriously undermine its substantive reasonableness.

To summarize my argument in this section then, I have tried to show how a comprehensive approach involves, first, a set of habits of atten- tion to the different aspects of argumentation and, second, a set of broad critical questions. The habits of attention should be transferable inas- much as citizens can learn simply to notice broad aspects or dimensions of argumentation, whereas the critical questions should be transferable because they are less technical than the more detailed standards one finds in critical thinking and logic textbooks. My working assumption is that simply attending to the different aspects of deliberation and raising these critical questions enhances the reflective capacity of participants and makes them less likely to accept blatantly unreasonable positions, even if fully answering the questions would overtax many citizens. Thus, even if the list of questions is incomplete and open to improvement, I hope that the general aim is clear: to provide a set of usable questions that readily stimulate the critical faculties and lead one into the more detailed ques- tions and standards. To be sure, these critical capacities on the part of citizens will enhance deliberation in a way that is effective for outcomes only if citizen organizations, the public sphere, and lawmaking institu- tions are relatively healthy, not disabled by socioeconomic forces or other distortions. This is a far from trivial assumption, which takes us beyond argumentation theory proper into the interdisciplinary investigations to which I alluded earlier.

III: The Status of the Argumentation Theorist: Expert Authority or Vicarious Participant?

So far I have sketched one way that argumentation theorists, precisely as educators, can positively influence public deliberation, namely by educating student-citizens in habits of comprehensive attentiveness and critical questioning. By defining influence in terms of these broad pedagogical aims, I hope to avoid the difficulties connected with more detailed models of reasonable argumentation. The latter are not only more difficult for citizens to transfer and apply in political deliberation; they are also subject to greater dispute among theorists. The potential of such theoretical disputes to undermine the educational influence of theorists is lessened insofar as the broadly defined goals, together with the minimal notion of reasonableness (A5 above), depend more on the ability to spot blatantly unreasonable positions than on finer-grained appraisals. For theorists are less likely to disagree on egregious violations of reasonableness. To be sure, some intractable political disputes may involve disagreements even at the level of what counts as blatantly unreasonable (see Pearce and Littlejohn 1997)—but then I do not claim that argumentation can help to settle every social conflict. In some cases other forms of conflict resolution may be necessary.

In this concluding section, I further specify the kind of influence that fits with the sketch in section II. I am concerned now more with the mode of influence than with its pedagogical path. The question of mode turns on the status of theorist-educators and their proposals vis-à-vis public deliberation. More specifically, I want to ask whether argumentation theorists, when they set forth argumentative standards in their teaching and writing, speak and write as expert authorities on argumentation.

As a classroom instructor, the argumentation theorist is an expert vis-à-vis students in the sense that he or she is certified as the competent authority regarding course material and objectives, evaluation of student work, and so forth. By itself this expert status does not yet relate to public deliberation, indeed classroom expertise is irrelevant to democratic politics if students fail to transfer what they have learned beyond the classroom. However, if students do achieve transfer, what does that imply about the status of their instructor's expertise, that is, the status of the knowledge they have gained from their instructor? And if the argumentation theorist in this setting acts as an expert with cognitive authority, then do the students take (and employ) such knowledge on the basis of trust in this authority? To answer such questions, we must say something more about expert authority in general.

Broadly speaking, an expert is someone who has mastered some area or domain of specialized knowledge beyond the ken of the average person. According to Turner (2001, 129-30), expertise involves cognitive authority that is recognized by members of a relevant audience. The expertise of a quantum physicist, for example, involves not only a mastery of a specialized domain of knowledge but in addition the recognition of such mastery by the relevant sub-community of physicists. The knowledge at issue here is technical in the sense that it is acquired only through specialized training—it is not readily accessible to the average layperson. Thus the cognitive authority of scientists, insofar as they speak about matters of science before a lay public, presupposes a certain amount of trust on the part of the latter—which in general need not be unreasonable (Stich and Nisbett 1984). Moreover, as Turner (2001, 130) points out, the layperson's trust in scientific expertise is not a blind faith, for it also rests on the evident success of the technological applications of science. In any case, trust plays an essential role even *within* communities of experts; most of the knowledge that scientists employ, for example, they acquire through trust in other scientists (Shapin 1994).

In the model of science dominant throughout much of the twentieth century, this kind of cognitive authority went hand-in-glove with the social autonomy of science—the idea that the institutional pursuit of "pure science" is governed best when governed by scientists themselves (Polanyi 1951; Merton 1973; Greenberg 1999). To be sure, this traditional understanding of science in society is currently in transition (Fuller 2000; Gibbons 1999; Greenberg 2001; Nowotny et al. 2001), but it provides a useful starting point for our reflections.

If argumentation theorists enjoy an expertise akin to that of natural scientists—call it *technical expertise*—then we find it most clearly displayed in the finer-grained, counterintuitive methods employed in mathematical logic, statistical reasoning, and the like. But this is just the sort of knowledge that, I have assumed, is less likely to transfer and thus less likely to put argumentation theorists in a position to influence democratic deliberation. However, if we look beyond the classroom setting—if we consider "extracurricular" forms of education and involvement, as it were—then we can see some ways in which such technical expertise can influence deliberation. I mention some of these briefly.

To start with the most obvious avenue of influence, theorists can employ their expertise to organize public discussions that are civil, fair, and effective. A mediator or discussion leader with suitable training and experience can make a significant difference to the quality of actual deliberations. Discussion leaders deploy a kind of technical knowledge when they use non-obvious methods to enhance the openness and civility of discourse (cf. Lasker 1949, chap. 9). Argumentation experts can also influence deliberation in the role of consultants to officials who are faced with questions of procedural and institutional design. Or they may hook up with non-governmental organizations and movements that aim to foster public deliberation (e.g., the national forum movement in the U.S. at mid-twentieth century; see Lasker 1949). Contributing to the design of computer-assisted argumentation systems opens yet another path of influence for technical expertise. Although I cannot go into details here (see Rehg, McBurney, and Parsons, forthcoming), such systems employ computer programs (perhaps made accessible via the Internet) for structuring public discussion and deliberation. Dialectical approaches have provided attractive models here. For example, the Zeno Argumentation Framework (Gordon and Karacapilidis 1997; Karacapilidis et al., 1997) employs a "dialectical graph" for mapping out discussions of public issues; the developers of Zeno hope to employ such a framework in mediation systems, accessible to the public via the World-Wide Web, to enhance democratic deliberation.[12] McBurney and Parsons (2001a; 2001b) have developed a detailed dialectical formalism for deliberating on such issues as risk assessment and environmental regulation. Such initiatives clearly involve a technical expertise, and if successful they would put such expertise to use in actual deliberation.

Such systems will not succeed, however, unless users accept them and employ them properly. Citizens themselves, that is, must perceive the argumentation frameworks as both fair and effective in context (Rehg, McBurney, and Parsons, forthcoming). The same is true for the other types of influence mentioned in the paragraph above. Behind this rather obvious condition lies a deeper point about the status of argumentation theorists and their theoretical models, namely that *the validity of such models partly depends on their reception by users in specific contexts.* If this is the case, then the expert status of theorists is derivative: it depends on what we might call their "vicarious participation" in deliberation.

What I call "vicarious participation" differs from the "virtual" participation that Habermas (1984, 116f, 120f; 1990a, 29-32) has associated with the observer/reader who tries to interpret social interactions and texts without directly engaging the participants or author. According to Habermas, such interpreters—he has social scientists primarily in mind—cannot understand the social situations and interactions they observe unless they implicitly evaluate the various claims the actors are making. The observer thereby participates in the interaction "virtually."

Vicarious participation, on the other hand, represents a further development in the position of argumentation theorists as they strive to spell out—or as Habermas (1990a) puts it, "reconstruct"—the more intuitive standards of reasonable argumentation, such as the pragmatic presuppositions of rational discourse (recall the process idealizations summarized in P1 and P2 in section II). In doing so, theorists aim to articulate the intuitive know-how of competent language users. Thus one strives to elaborate the perspective of a participant in argumentation, and for this one must draw upon one's own everyday know-how and experience in discourse. This orientation to everyday communicative competence has a peculiar effect on the status of the theorist. On the one hand, reconstruction is in the first instance a theoretical exercise addressed to other theorists—a philosophical attempt to justify communicative practices by articulating their implicit normative structures. To this extent, theorists enjoy a philosophical expertise in virtue of their mastery of a certain literature and method of analysis. Insofar as theorists engage in this philosophical enterprise, they enjoy a degree of institutional autonomy in their research, which for present purposes I assume is legitimately governed by disciplinary standards. On the other hand, such expertise differs in an important way from the technical expertise of the scientist or logician. In contrast to technical expertise, the philosophical expertise of "reconstructive" theorists has an internal relation to the know-how of lay people, for that is just what such theorists strive to reconstruct or articulate. That is, in their attempts to articulate pre-theoretical know-how implicit in everyday practices of argumentation, theorists are beholden to lay knowledge: lay participants should be able to recognize their own discursive ideals in the theorist's articulated standards. Argumentation theorists' philosophical expertise rests primarily on the fact that they've simply devoted more time and thought to communicative practices with which socially adept laypersons are familiar.

The development from philosophical expertise into *vicarious participation* involves a more practical relation to lay know-how. That is, philosophical experts become vicarious participants insofar as they connect with citizens engaged in actual public deliberations. I call such participation "vicarious" because it is indirect—the theorist influences deliberation through someone else who has knowledge of the theorist's proposals for good argument and employs that knowledge as a citizen. As educators, for example, argumentation theorists become vicarious participants in public deliberation by virtue of the indirect effect they have on the quality of deliberation through the students who transfer their education in argument evaluation to the public sphere. Similarly, as a scholarly theorist, one becomes a vicarious participant insofar as citizens are influenced by one's philosophical views on argumentation. This transition involves a shift in the internal relationship between expertise and lay knowledge: vicarious expertise is primarily established not in a research setting but in actual practices of discourse and deliberation. This connection modifies the status of the argumentation theorist's philosophical expertise, which now counts as expertise only insofar as lay participants can make it relevant and usable in contexts of public discussion and argument. Thus the theorist's proposals are subject here to a different kind of test from those that establish philosophical expertise. That is, for argumentation theorists who hope to influence the practice of citizens through education, whether curricular or extracurricular, one's models and formulations prove themselves only insofar as they demonstrate their relevance for the participants themselves—which is to say, only insofar as participants in actual conflicts can pick them up and contextualize them in the conflict situation. Proposals that fail to transfer in *this practical sense* fail precisely as theoretical proposals.

Vicarious participation changes the status of technical expertise as well. Argumentation theorists become vicarious participants through their technical expertise when students manage to transfer technical skills to contexts of political argumentation (rare as this might be), or when they (i.e., the theorists) contribute to the design of deliberative forums, computer-assisted argumentation systems, and the like. (By contrast, actually leading a public discussion or mediating a deliberation would involve a direct, "non-vicarious" form of participation.) Again, the transition from technical expert to vicarious participant involves an important shift in context that imposes additional demands on the validation of expertise. Within a discipline, one's technical expertise is validated by other specialists with the requisite training—the intra-disciplinary knowledge and standing of the technical expert is normally not subject to lay judgment, at least on the standard view. However, the technical expertise of argumentation theorists can influence public deliberation in a way that contributes to political legitimacy only if lay participants accept it in context—only if citizens find such knowledge conducive to what they consider fair and effective public discourse. Thus technical experts must be accountable both to their own peers and to a broader public (Willard 1996, 308-11).

This shift in the status of expert knowledge seems to be a general phenomenon at the turn of the millennium, affecting the sciences and medicine generally. Scientific knowledge must now be "socially robust," proving itself not only inside the laboratory before specialists, but also outside the laboratory before interested lay publics.[13] Socially robust knowledge thus involves a shift in the nature of trust as well. Citizens who deliberate will trust the expertise of argumentation theorists—will accord them a certain cognitive authority in deliberative contexts—only if the latter's knowledge proves itself in the eyes of the citizens themselves. This holds for argumentation theory not only insofar as it articulates lay know-how; but also for its technical aspects. The authority that experts enjoy so long as they remain inside the classroom or within their discipline becomes subject to lay judgment and approval once they step into the public sphere and propose standards for public argumentation.

Notice that the ways in which citizens contextualize and employ argumentation theorists' proposals will vary according to the specific proposals and deliberative context. The critical questions outlined in section II most readily apply to the *ex post* evaluation of arguments and argumentative processes—the kind of activity that deliberative democrats expect of citizens and legislators before they cast their vote as conscientious individuals. The *ex ante* design of deliberative forums and procedures typically requires more detailed technical knowledge than contained in these broad questions. An interesting topic of further study, beyond the scope of this essay, concerns the use to which citizens put argumentative models, critical questions, rhetorical techniques and the like when they engage in direct argumentation themselves, actively constructing arguments, rebutting criticisms, innovating to reconcile oppositions, and so on. In contrast to the role of audience member who must make critical "spectator judgments," this more directly engaged role depends on a fluid capacity for making "active artistic judgments" about how to innovate conceptually so as to reconcile differences and persuasively resolve conflicts (Heidlebaugh 2001). Exactly how participants in this active role contextualize the various theoretical recommendations may involve a good deal of ad hoc innovation—unanticipated by theorists—in which opposing theories are creatively combined into novel responses to otherwise impossible conflicts.[14]

In conclusion, argumentation theorists can, as educators and theorists, vicariously influence public deliberation for the better insofar as their proposals are designed in the reflexive awareness that citizens must be able to contextualize and employ such proposals in actual deliberative situations. Successful theoretical proposals of this sort should provide heuristic frameworks that not only enhance the participants' attentiveness to the multidimensional character of argumentation, but also equip them with critical questions that provoke further reflection on the quality of competing positions. If, by virtue of the argumentation theorists' proposals, citizens are better armed against blatantly unreasonable views, then theorists—including those not in the position of public intellectuals—will have made a positive contribution to democratic deliberation.

NOTES

1. As Dryzek (2000, 30-31) explains, rational choice theory assumes that each individual comes to the political process with a fixed set of preferences and chooses the candidates, coalitions, or policies that are most likely to maximize the satisfaction of those preferences; for an introduction and critique, see Heath (2001, chaps. 2, 4). Pluralist theory extends this model by conceiving political competition as one among different interest groups (thus drawing upon James Madison's approach in Federalist Papers no. 10); see, e.g., Dahl (1956).

2. The pessimistic findings should not lead us to forget that citizens are also capable of educating themselves (perhaps with the aid of issue-oriented political groups). A well-known case is the debate over AIDS treatment (see Epstein 2000; Fabj and Sobnosky 1995); according to Gusterson (2001), non-governmental organizations can improve the quality of public participation in policy debates over nuclear issues. For a response to social-choice pessimism, see Grofman (1993); Dryzek (2000, chap. 2); regarding the media and deliberation, see Page (1996).

3. For further elaboration and contrast with the similar models of Habermas (1996) and Estlund (1997), see Rehg (1997b). I suspect that procedural legitimacy suffices for establishing a prima facie political obligation on most issues. If one defines legitimacy in terms of such obligation and construes substantive reasonableness as simply increased satisfaction with outcome, then my approach reduces to David Estlund's "epistemic proceduralism," which ties legitimacy, not to deliberation per se, but to the fairness (impartiality) of a procedure that has deliberative features (see Estlund 1997, 1993). McMahon (2001, chap. 4) seems to have a view similar to Estlund's.

4. Cf. McMahon (2001, chap. 5). The assertion of such responsibility must be qualified for legislators in those contexts in which party discipline and bound mandates (which oblige the legislator to vote according to the will of the constituency) limit the scope of individual discretion.

5. One might extend the analysis to people involved in high-school debating programs, but then additional issues arise beyond the scope of this paper.

6. For a range of approaches to the transfer problem, see Talaska (1992); insofar as we are concerned with the transfer of skills to political life, the problem involves both transfer across contexts (from classroom to public discourse) and the generalizability of standards across subject domains (insofar as political issues range across various topics)(cf. Brown 1998, 28).

7. The transfer of debating skills raises a different set of questions: I suspect the chief obstacle resides in the competitive character of debate formats and the competitive ethos of debate, which could work against the kind of cooperation required for democratic deliberation.

8. In developing the educational task from the standpoint of dialectic, I am not disputing the idea that rhetoric is the most encompassing perspective on argumentation as a social practice (see Crosswhite 1996; Tindale 1999).

9. The book Crosswhite suggests is M. Kiriny and M. Rose, Critical Strategies for Academic Thinking and Writing, 2nd ed. (Boston: St. Martin's, 1993).

10. I cannot defend this particular list here, but L1 and L2 capture the gist of my analysis of Johnson's four criteria for good arguments (see Rehg 2001); I add L3 here because it summarizes the core idea behind logical assessment, and thus opens up on more detailed methods of appraisal.

11. See Wenzel 1979; 1987. Other theorists have referred to similar requirements as dialectical (e.g., Walton 1992; Eemeren and Grootendorst 1992).

12. For a sense of how computer-assisted deliberation might unfold, see the "Scenario" available at the DEMOS website:<http://www.demos-project.org/.>

13. See Gibbons 1999; Nowotny 2001; for an example see Morgan (1993), who notes the importance of local lay knowledge for effective risk management.

14. The point here is also supported by ethnographic and in particular ethnomethodological studies (Garfinkel 1967; Heritage 1984), which show that the contextualizing moves by which competent members of society "apply" general ideas and principles to their local situations involve a good deal of creativity and social negotiation. General strategies and theoretical proposals remain vague and indeterminate until participants actually employ them in situ as tools for managing concrete circumstances whose contingencies and complexity always surpass what theorists can anticipate. In fact, as Tindale (1999, 8-12, 17-18) points out, this contextualizing activity is also required of the spectator judge as well, who must, for example, fill in the context assumed by enthymematic arguments.

BIBLIOGRAPHY

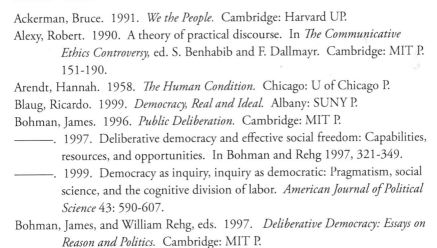

Ackerman, Bruce. 1991. *We the People.* Cambridge: Harvard UP.

Alexy, Robert. 1990. A theory of practical discourse. In *The Communicative Ethics Controversy,* ed. S. Benhabib and F. Dallmayr. Cambridge: MIT P. 151-190.

Arendt, Hannah. 1958. *The Human Condition.* Chicago: U of Chicago P.

Blaug, Ricardo. 1999. *Democracy, Real and Ideal.* Albany: SUNY P.

Bohman, James. 1996. *Public Deliberation.* Cambridge: MIT P.

———. 1997. Deliberative democracy and effective social freedom: Capabilities, resources, and opportunities. In Bohman and Rehg 1997, 321-349.

———. 1999. Democracy as inquiry, inquiry as democratic: Pragmatism, social science, and the cognitive division of labor. *American Journal of Political Science* 43: 590-607.

Bohman, James, and William Rehg, eds. 1997. *Deliberative Democracy: Essays on Reason and Politics.* Cambridge: MIT P.

Brown, Ken. 1998. *Education, Culture and Critical Thinking.* Aldershot: Ashgate.

Cohen, Joshua. 1999. Reflections on Habermas on democracy. *Ratio Juris* 12: 385-416.

Crosswhite, James. 1996. *The Rhetoric of Reason.* Madison: U of Wisconsin P.

Dahl, Robert A. 1956. *A Preface to Democratic Theory.* Chicago: U of Chicago P.

Dewey, John. 1954. *The Public and Its Problems.* Athens, OH: Swallow.

Downes, Anthony. 1957. *An Economic Theory of Democracy.* New York: Harper.

Dryzek, John S. 2000. *Deliberative Democracy and Beyond.* Oxford: Oxford UP.

Elster, Jon, ed. 1998. *Deliberative Democracy.* Cambridge: Cambridge UP.

Eemeren, F. H. van, and R. Grootendorst. 1992. *Argumentation, Communication, and Fallacies.* Hillsdale, NJ: Erlbaum.

Ennis, Robert H. 1962. A concept of critical thinking. *Harvard Educational Review* 32: 81-111.

Epstein, Steven. 2000. Democracy, expertise, and AIDS treatment activism. In Kleinman 2000, 15-32.

Estlund, David. 1993. Who's afraid of deliberative democracy? On the strategic/deliberative dichotomy in recent constitutional jurisprudence. *Texas Law Review* 71: 1437-1477.

———. 1997. Beyond fairness and deliberation: The epistemic dimension of democratic authority. In Bohman and Rehg 1997, 173-204.

Fabj, Valeria, and Matthew J. Sobnosky. 1995. AIDS activism and the rejuvenation of the public sphere. *Argumentation and Advocacy* 31: 163-184.

Fearon, James D. 1998. Deliberation as discussion. In Elster 1998, 44-68.

Flack, Dick. 1991. Making history and making theory: Notes on how intellectuals seek relevance. In *Intellectuals and Politics,* ed. C. C. Lemert. Newbury Park: Sage. 3-18.

Friedman, Jeffrey, ed. 1998. *Public Ignorance and Democracy.* Special Issue of *Critical Review* 12/4: 397-584.

Fulkerson, Richard. 2001. Problems in systematic analysis of "full-length" arguments: The unfortunate limits of textbook advice. Meeting of the Ontario Society for the Study of Argumentation. May 17-19, 2001. Windsor, Ontario.

Fuller, Steve. 2000. *The Governance of Science.* Philadelphia: Open UP.

Garfinkel, Harold. 1967. *Studies in Ethnomethodology.* Englewood Cliffs, NJ: Prentice-Hall.

Gibbons, Michael. 1999. Science's new social contract with society. *Nature* 402 supplement (Dec. 2, 1999): C81-C84.

Goldman, Alvin I. 1994. Argumentation and social epistemology. *Journal of Philosophy* 91: 27-49.

Gordon, Thomas F., and Nikos Karacapilidis. 1997. The Zeno Argumentation Framework. In *Proceedings of the Sixth International Conference on AI and Law.* New York: ACM. 10-18.

Greenberg, Daniel S. 1999. *The Politics of Pure Science.* New ed. Chicago: U of Chicago P.

———. 2001. *Science, Money, and Politics.* Chicago: U of Chicago P

Grofman, Bernard. 1993. Public choice, civic republicanism, and American politics: Perspectives of a "reasonable choice" modeler. *Texas Law Review* 71: 1541-1587.

Gusterson, Hugh. 1996. *Nuclear Rites: A Weapons Laboratory at the End of the Cold War.* Berkeley: U of California P.

———. 2001. Science, democracy, and nuclear weapons. 25th Anniversary Symposium, MIT Program in Science, Technology, and Society. Cambridge, Mass.. Oct. 31, 2001.

Gutmann, Amy, and Dennis Thompson. 1996. *Democracy and Disagreement.* Cambridge: Harvard UP.

Habermas, Jürgen. 1984. *The Theory of Communicative Action.* Vol. 1. Trans. T. McCarthy. Boston: Beacon.

———. 1990a. Reconstruction and interpretation in the social sciences. In *Moral Consciousness and Communicative Action.* Trans. C. Lenhardt and S. W. Nicholsen. Cambridge: MIT P. 21-42.

———. 1990b. Discourse ethics: Notes on a program philosophical justification. In *Moral Consciousness and Communicative Action.* Trans. C. Lenhardt and S. W. Nicholsen. Cambridge: MIT P. 43-115.

———. 1996. *Between Facts and Norms.* Trans. W. Rehg. Cambridge: MIT P.

Heath, Joseph. 2001. *Communicative Action and Rational Choice.* Cambridge: MIT P.

Heidlebaugh, Nola J. 2001. *Judgment, Rhetoric, and the Problem of Incommensurability.* Columbia: U of South Carolina P.

Held, David. 1987. *Models of Democracy.* Stanford: Stanford UP.

Heritage, John. 1984. *Garfinkel and Ethnomethodology.* Cambridge: Polity.

Johnson, James. 1998. Arguing for deliberation: Some skeptical considerations. In Elster 1998, 161-184.

Johnson, Ralph H. 1992. Critical reasoning and informal logic. In Talaska 1992, 69-88.

———. 2000. *Manifest Rationality: A Pragmatic Theory of Argument.* Mahwah, NJ: Erlbaum.

Karacapilidis, Nikos, Dimitris Papadias, Thomas Gordon, and Hans Voss. 1997. Collaborative environmental planning with GeoMed. *European Journal of Operational Research* 102: 335-346.

Kleinman, Daniel Lee, ed. 2000. *Science, Technology, and Democracy.* Albany: SUNY P.

Knight, Jack, and James Johnson. 1994. Aggregation and deliberation: On the possibility of democratic legitimacy. *Political Theory* 22: 277-297.

Lasker, Bruno. 1949. *Democracy Through Discussion.* New York: H. W. Wilson.

Mansbridge, Jane J. 1980. *Beyond Adversary Democracy.* New York: Basic.

McBurney, Peter, and Simon Parsons. 2001a. Intelligent systems to support deliberative democracy in environmental regulation. *Information and Communications Technology Law* 10/1: 33-43.

———. 2001b. Representing epistemic uncertainty by means of dialectical argumentation. *Annals of Mathematics and Artificial Intelligence,* in press.

McCarthy, Thomas. 1998. Legitimacy and diversity: Dialectical reflections on analytical distinctions. In *Habermas on Law and Democracy,* ed. M. Rosenfeld and A. Arato. Berkeley: U of California P. 115-153.

McMahon, Christopher. 2001. *Collective Rationality and Collective Reasoning.* Cambridge: Cambridge UP.

McPeck, John E. 1990. *Teaching Critical Thinking: Dialogue and Dialectic.* New York: Routledge.

Merton, Robert K. 1973. *The Sociology of Science.* Chicago: U of Chicago P.

Michelman, Frank. 1986. The Supreme Court 1985 term—Forward: Traces of self-government. *Harvard Law Review* 100: 4-77.

———. 1988. Law's republic. *Yale Law Journal* 97: 1493-1537.

———. 1989. Conceptions of democracy in American constitutional argument: The case of pornography regulation. *Tennessee Law Review* 56: 291-319.

Morgan, M. Granger. 1993. Risk Analysis and risk management. *Scientific American.* July 1993: 32-41.

Nowotny, Helga, Peter Scott, and Michael Gibbons. 2001. *Re-Thinking Science: Knowledge and the Public in an Age of Uncertainty.* Cambridge, UK: Polity.

Page, Benjamin I. 1996. *Who Deliberates? Mass Media in Modern Democracy.* Chicago: U of Chicago P.

Pearce, W. Barnett, and Stephen W. Littlejohn. 1997. *Moral Conflict.* Thousand Oaks, CA: Sage.

Perelman, Chaim. 1982. *The Realm of Rhetoric.* Trans. W. Kluback. Notre Dame: U of Notre Dame P.

Polanyi, Michael. 1951. *The Logic of Liberty.* Chicago: U of Chicago P.

Rawls, John. 1971. *A Theory of Justice.* Cambridge: Harvard UP.

———. 1996. *Political Liberalism.* 2nd ed. New York: Columbia UP.

Rehg, William. 1997a. Reason and rhetoric in Habermas's theory of argumentation. In *Rhetoric and Hermeneutics in Our Time,* ed. W. Jost and M. J. Hyde. New Haven: Yale UP. 358-377.

———. 1997b. Legitimacy and deliberation in epistemic conceptions of democracy: Between Habermas and Estlund. *The Modern Schoolman* 74: 355-374.

———. 2001. Toward a Pragmatic Theory of Argument. *The Modern Schoolman* (in press).

Rehg, William, and James Bohman. 1996. Discourse and democracy: The formal and informal bases of legitimacy in *Faktizität und Geltung*. *Journal of Political Philosophy* 4: 79-99.

Rehg, William, Peter McBurney, and Simon Parsons. Forthcoming. Computer decision-support systems for public argumentation: Criteria for assessment. In *Proceedings of the Fourth Biennial Conference of the Ontario Society for the Study of Argumentation*, ed. H. V. Hansen, C. W. Tindale, J. A. Blair, and R. H. Johnson. CD-ROM.

Rescher, Nicolas. 1977. *Dialectics*. Albany: SUNY P.

————. 1998. The role of rhetoric in rational argumentation. *Argumentation* 12: 315-323.

Sanders, Lynn M. 1997. Against deliberation. *Political Theory* 25: 347-376.

Schumpeter, Joseph. 1950. *Capitalism, Socialism, and Democracy*. New York: Harper.

Shapin, Steven. 1994. *A Social History of Trust*. Chicago: U of Chicago P.

Siegel, Harvey. 1988. *Educating Reason: Rationality, Critical Thinking, and Education*. New York: Routledge.

Somin, Ilya. 1998. Voter ignorance and the democratic ideal. *Critical Review* 12: 413-458.

Stich, Stephen P., and Richard E. Nisbett. 1984. Expertise, justification, and the psychology of inductive reasoning. In *The Authority of Experts*, ed. T. L. Haskell. Bloomington: Indiana UP. 226-241.

Talaska, Richard A., ed. 1992. *Critical Reasoning in Contemporary Culture*. Albany: SUNY P.

Tindale, Christopher W. 1999. *Acts of Arguing: A Rhetorical Model of Argument*. Albany: SUNY P.

Turner, Stephen. 2001. What is the problem with experts? *Social Studies of Science* 31: 123-149.

Walton, Douglas N. 1989. *Informal Logic: A Handbook for Critical Argumentation*. Cambridge: Cambridge UP.

————. 1992. Types of dialogue, dialectical shifts and fallacies. In *Argumentation Illuminated*, ed. F. H. van Eemeren and R. Grootendorst. Amsterdam: Sic-Sac. 133-147.

Warnke, Georgia. 1999. *Legitimate Differences*. Berkeley: U of California P.

Wenzel, Joseph. 1979. Jürgen Habermas and the dialectical perspective on argumentation. *Journal of the American Forensic Association* 16: 83-94.

————. 1987. The rhetorical perspective on argument. In *Argumentation: Across the Lines of Disciplines*, ed. F. H. van Eemeren et al. Dordrecht: Foris. 101-109.

———. 1990. Three perspectives on argument. In *Perspectives on Argumentation: Essays in Honor of Wayne Brockriede,* ed. R. Trapp and J. Schuetz. Prospect Heights, Ill.: Waveland. 9-26.

Willard, Charles Arthur. 1996. *Liberalism and the Problem of Knowledge.* Chicago: U of Chicago P.

Democracy and Argumentation

Frans H. van Eemeren

Abstract

The problems of young democracies can be confronted only with a more participatory democracy. Still, participation will only work if adequate dialectical procedures for public discourses can be developed, allowing for a methodical critical discussion. Whether differences can be resolved by means of argument also depends on people's attitudes and competences and the realization of certain social and political principles.

Argumentation in the Political Context of Democracy

Speaking in Fulton Missouri at the same place and from the same oaken lectern used by Winston Churchill to make his historic "Iron Curtain" speech 46 years earlier, on May 6th 1992 the former Soviet leader Mikhail Gorbachev delivered a warning that mankind faced "the most difficult transition in its history." According to the British newspaper *The Independent* of May 7th 1992, Gorbachev urged "a new system of global government anchored to the United Nations." The Dutch newspaper *De Volkskrant* reported on the same day that Gorbachev announced "a new era of worldwide democracy."

My contribution to the discussion about democracy is aimed at providing some background from the perspective of argumentation theory.[1] Because I am not an elder statesman, let alone a world leader, I am not in the position to enlighten my views of democracy with such visionary declarations or sweeping statements as I have just quoted. There are, in fact, even more reasons why I cannot be as bold in my pronouncements as I ought to be. My modesty is primarily inspired by the fact that I am not even a social scientist—neither a political scientist nor a sociologist. In discussing what role argumentation can play in the political context of democracy I am going to lean for a large part on the intellectual keystones erected by others.

Developments Towards Democracy

I am not so sure about Gorbachev's predictions about the future, but he was, of course, right about the past. As far as democracy is concerned, in the decade before he made his speech the situation in the world had changed dramatically. There had been a semi-mondial movement from various kinds of right and left wing totalitarianism and authoritarianism towards "economic rationality" and "political democracy." The radical transitions that were taking place in Eastern Europe, where a closed and monolithic communist bloc seemed to be transforming into an (ever-increasing) assemblage of market-oriented democracies, are a perfect illustration.

The rebellion against communist totalitarianism started openly with the events in Poland in 1976. Of course, it could only effectively succeed after the crucial Gorbachev revolution in the Soviet Union. Now we all know, what some of us at the time suspected, and only insiders really knew, that before that it was mainly the fear of physical force, be it from within the country or from outsiders, that had kept the system going for such a long time. From the late 1950s, ideology was no longer the cement, to use Gramsci's expression, that held these societies together. According to Adam Przeworski (1991), what had developed was "an implicit social pact in which ruling elites offered the prospect of material welfare in exchange for silence."[2]

In *Democracy and the Market*, Przeworski cites a Soviet joke—a so-called "anecdote"—that expresses the same point very nicely. A man is distributing leaflets in Red Square. He is stopped by a policeman, who confiscates the leaflets, only to discover that they are blank. "What are you spreading? They are blank. Nothing is written!" the surprised guardian of order exclaims. "Why write?" is the answer. "Everybody knows ...."

It is often observed that in the communist world speech had become a ritual—or else it was dangerous.

The Eastern European Syllogism

The premise of what Przeworski calls "the Eastern European syllogism" is: "If it had not been for 'the system,' we would have been like the West." But what warrant do we have to complete the syllogism, that is: to believe that now, once "the system" is gone, Eastern Europe will find its path to "democracy, markets, and Europe"—to the West? Half of the world's population lives in countries that are capitalist, poor, and ruled by intermittent outbursts of organized violence.

In the mid 1970s transitions to democracy were inaugurated in Southern Europe (in Greece, Portugal, and Spain), in the early mid 1980s in Latin America and during the "Autumn of the People" of 1989 in Eastern Europe.

When thinking about how democracy will develop in Eastern Europe it is tempting to look at Spain for a model because Spain has been so successful, politically as well as economically. But put Poland in the place of Argentina, Hungary in the place of Uruguay and you will see states weak as organizations; political parties and other associations that are ineffectual in representing and mobilizing; economies that are monopolistic, overprotected, and overregulated; agricultures that cannot feed their own people; public bureaucracies that are overgrown; welfare services that are fragmentary and rudimentary.

The main reason to have some confidence that Eastern Europe will escape the politics, the economics, and the culture of poor capitalism, and that it will soon join the West, is geography. The central premise of the Eastern European syllogism is in fact: "There is only one Europe"—the European civilization of which Eastern European countries have been traditional members. Yet will geography be enough to shape economic and political futures? Whether the location of Eastern Europe is such that it will attract flows of investment is still an open question.

Przeworski rightly warned us that it was naive to think that a change in system is enough. Democracy (in any form) may be a necessary condition for economic growth, but it is by no means a sufficient condition, let alone that it is a sufficient condition for complete happiness. Of course, we knew that all the time, but when reflecting on the role of argumentation in democratic social change it is certainly worth remembering that the success, and even the durability, of a new democracy not only depends on its ideological starting points and institutional structure but to a large extent on its economic performance.

Democracy as "Organised Uncertainty"

Even if it were crystal-clear what kind of economic system should be aimed for, the road to it is not an easy one. This may sound pessimistic—but do the Poles not say that pessimism is merely informed optimism? Transitional effects of reforms are likely to include inflation, unemployment, allocative inefficiencies, and volatile changes. Unfortunately, this prediction has recently again come true in several countries—not least in Russia. It is hard to tell whether the unavoidable transitional costs will be tolerated politically in the end. In a period of major change and economic collapse there are inevitably authoritarian temptations.

Against this background, the question arises what kind of democracy will be the strongest in actual practice. What kind of democracy is not only fair and effective but also the most likely to last? A democracy, of course, that has the quality to cope with the problems of a changing society. Oddly enough, the first prime minister of modern Spain, our model of a successful democracy, Adolfo Suárez, regarded it as a quintessential feature of any democratic process that the outcomes are uncertain: indeterminate *ex ante*. In a democracy it is "the people," political forces competing to promote their interests and values, who determine what these outcomes will be. In spite of politicians often being in error but never in doubt, democracy amounts to *organised uncertainty* or, as Juan Linz (1990) puts it, government *pro tempore*.

The crucial moment in any passage from authoritarian to democratic rule is the crossing of the threshhold beyond which no one can intervene to reverse the outcome of the formal political process. Democratization is an act of *institutionalising uncertainty*: of subjecting all interests to competition. It is inside the institutional framework for processing conflicts offered by democracy that multiple forces compete. Although the outcome depends on what participants do, no single force controls what occurs. Here lies the decisive step towards democracy: in the devolution of power from a group of people to a set of rules.[3]

In a democracy, conflicts are ended under established rules. They are, according to Lewis Coser (1959), "terminated," temporarily suspended rather than resolved definitively. Ultimately, voting—majority rule—is the only arbiter. Pertinent here is Jules Coleman's observation that "consenting to a process is not the same thing as consenting to the outcomes of the process" (1989: 197). Jürgen Habermas (1975) distinguishes in *Legitimation crises* between "legality"—*ex ante* acceptance of rules—and "legitimacy"— (for him) the *ex post* evaluation. He and Seymour Martin Lipset (1960) agree that *ex post* evaluations modify the *ex ante* commitments.

The Modern Conception of Democracy

Whether we like it or not, compliance with democratic decisions is not self-evident.[4] How does it happen that political forces that lose in contestation comply with the outcomes and continue to participate rather than subvert democratic institutions?[5] Is their compliance due to the fact that democracy automatically leads to the good? To Joseph Schumpeter (1950), by far the most influential of modern theoreticians of democracy, democracy is not an end in itself. To make this clear, he proposed a "mental experiment." Imagine a country which, democratically, persecuted Jews, witches and Christians. It is not a sufficient ground to approve of these practices just because they had been decided upon democratically.[6]

In his book *Capitalism, Socialism and Democracy*, Schumpeter (1950) defines democracy as "a political *method*, [...] a certain type of institutional arrangement for arriving at political—legislative and administrative—decisions" (1943: 242). The democratic element in the method is the periodic competition of leaders (élites) for the votes of the electorate in free elections.[7] This competition for leadership is the distinctive feature of the modern political method: "That institutional arrangement for arriving at political decisions in which individuals *acquire the power* to decide by means of a competitive struggle for the people's vote" (p. 269, my italics).

Elections are crucial, because it is through elections that the majority can exercise control over their leaders. "Political equality" refers in modern theory of democracy to one man one vote. To be able to maintain such a *representative* system of democracy, the electorate and the political parties must be clearly stratified into leaders and followers. Compliance with the democratic system is only to be expected provided the leaders of the losers of an election can convince their followers that they stand a realistic chance of doing better at the next election, so that eventually they may gain power. Political forces comply with present defeats because they believe that the institutional framework that organizes the democratic competition will permit them to advance their interests in the future.

Conspicuously, modern theory of democracy is presented as a "value-free," empirically-based sociological theory, but Carole Pateman (1990) is right when she observes in her book *Participation and Democratic Theory* that this theory does not merely describe.[8] The normative content of the theory reflects the view that Anglo-Saxon Westerners are living in the "ideal" democratic system. It is even implied that this system includes a set of standards or criteria by which a political system may be judged "democratic." In practice, the main emphasis in modern theory of democracy is on the stability of the political system, on its capacity for survival. According to most theoreticians, this stability is largely due to the fact that in western democracy participation is minimized and democracy amounts in fact to *polyarchy*, the rule of *multiple minorities* or even *competing élites*.[9]

The Classical Conception of Democracy

The representative system of Anglo-Saxon-type democracy, with its technocratic style and ineffective way of making policy, may easily undermine popular support for democracy, especially in Eastern Europe where several of the newly-developed democracies are in the process of carrying out a stringent program of social and economic reforms. In my view, a more participatory style of governing is required to maintain political support. In theory, there is always participation in democracy, but modern theoreticians are most reluctant to acknowledge this. They see participation mainly as a threat to stability.

In adopting this attitude, they react against what they call the "classical theory of democracy." Whereas to modern theory "participation" is merely participation in the choice of decision makers,[10] to classical theory maximum participation by all the people is central. The ideal of classical theory is to have all the decisions be made by "rational and active and informed democratic man" (Davis 1964: 29).

Among the wide range of names of classical theoreticians are those of famous philosophers such as Jean-Jacques Rousseau, Jeremy Bentham and the two Mills: James and John Stuart. What they have to say is, according to Pateman, not only misrepresented by Schumpeter, but in his effort to offer a new definition of democracy Schumpeter has also ignored that their writings include, in fact, two very different theories about democracy. The position of Bentham and James Mill is quite different from that of Rousseau and John Stuart Mill.

Pateman thinks it nonsense to speak of *one* "classical" theory of democracy.[11] Bentham (1843) and James Mill (1937) were almost entirely concerned with the national "institutional arrangements" of the political system, and to them the participation of the people has the very narrow, and purely protective function of it ensuring that the private interests of each citizen were protected.[12] In the theories of Rousseau (1953) and John Stuart Mill (1965), participation has far wider functions: It is central to the establishment and maintenance of a democratic polity, not only at the national level, but also at the "lower" levels.

Regrettably, Schumpeter's influence has obscured that the present-day theory of representative government is not the whole of democratic theory. He presents us with a false dilemma in which competing élites and "totalitarianism" are the only two alternatives. It may be true that the accepted theory of democracy is one in which the concept of participation has only the most minimal role and the emphasis is placed on the dangers inherent in participation, but by no means does this mean that the ideal of maximum participation must automatically be abandoned. Especially not since Schumpeter's main criticism of the central participatory role of the people in classical democratic theories rests on empirical arguments that do not do justice to the normative aims of these theories.

As Berelson and his co-authors put it in their book *Voting*, "certain requirements commonly assumed for the successful operation of democracy are not met by the behaviour of the 'average citizen'" (1954: 307). But precisely for this reason the classical theoreticians laid great emphasis on the need for better political and other education. According to Schumpeter in a critical analysis, in order that the participatory method may work, "everyone would have to know definitely what he wants to stand for [...], a clear *and prompt* conclusion as to particular issues would have to be derived according to the rules of logical inference [...]—all this the model citizen would have to perform for himself and independently of pressure groups and propaganda" (1950: 253-254). Leaving aside the gross exaggerations involved in this misrepresentation of the views of the classical theoreticians, I would say that these criticisms are in fact a good formulation of some normative requirements that adequate education in a democratic society should aim to fulfil.

Democracy as an Organisational System

In my opinion, for the survival of democracy in Eastern Europe, where tough economic and social measures have been, and will be, taken, participation is a prerequisite. But more participation will also be indispensable in solving some of the problems inherent in the democratic system institutionalised in the West. Perhaps it is even not unreasonable to consider a high degree of participation a necessary condition for any living democracy.

Of course, a more participatory democracy is to be preferred to a purely representative one only if it can be shown to work advantageously as an organisational system. I shall illustrate this point by following Bolman and Deal (1991) in making a distinction between various "dimensions" that are indispensable to any organisational system. In *Modern Approaches to Understanding and Managing Organizations*, they describe four different dimensions that have to be fulfilled in a well-balanced way in order for an organisational system to function well.

The first dimension, the so-called *rational* dimension, pertains to the formal or structural aspects of the system. Ideally, the organisational structure should be such that it best fits the purpose or rationale of the system. This structural level concerns the allocation of responsibilities in the organisation, and the hierarchies, rules, and policies created to coordinate the diverse activities. Problems arise when the organisational structure does not really fit the situation.

The second dimension is *social* and pertains to the human resources inhabiting the system and their engagement in its well-functioning. There must be a fit between people's needs, values, skills and limitations and the formal roles and relationships required to accomplish collective goals and purposes. The key to effectiveness is to find an organisational form that enables people to get the system going whilst feeling good about what they are doing. Problems arise when human needs are suppressed.

The third dimension is *political*; it pertains to the power aspect. How is practical authority negotiated and divided within the system? At the political level, the reality the organisational system has to deal with is seen as an arena where a constant struggle for power and influence is going on. Conflict is expected because of differences in perspectives, needs, and lifestyles. Solutions are developed through political skill and acumen—much as Machiavelli suggested. Coalitions form around specific interests: They may change as issues come and go. In this jungle the leaders need to manage power, coalitions, bargaining, and conflict.

The fourth dimension, the *symbolic* dimension, pertains to the ceremonial aspects of the system. In what ritualistic ways are the meaning and the image of the system built and maintained? At this level, the system is seen as a theatre that is held together more by shared values and culture than by goals and policies. The interest focuses on the way in which the system is propelled more by rituals, ceremonies, stories, heroes, and myths than by rules, policies, and managerial authority. Problems arise when actors play their parts badly, when symbols lose their meaning or when ceremonies and rituals lose their potency.[13]

It is only if all these four dimensions are given their proper due that the organisational system is likely to appreciate the full depth and complexities of real-life practice. Ideally, in a democratic organisation of society the four dimensions are blended into a clear and coherent meaningful whole. However, if a predominantly representative and a predominantly participatory democratic system are systematically compared along these four dimensions, some crucial differences come to light. For now I shall restrict myself to just a few observations. Along the same lines, more, and increasingly precise, observations can easily be made—and should be made, of course.

Let me start with the rational dimension. Although this is by no means beyond discussion, in principle, the representational democracy in the western countries seems reasonably well-adjusted to the organisational aims of governing. However, in systems of this type, there is a striking, and even disturbing, imbalance as to the relative weight that is attributed to each of the four dimensions: The rational, or structural, dimension outweighs the other dimensions by far. Even where the cause of problems is seen as personal, i.e. lies in the realm of human resources, there is a tendency to propose solutions amounting to restructuring.

In the social dimension of human resources participatory democracy has essentially a much better score than a merely representational democracy: If the system works, in a participatory democracy the personal commitment of all concerned is as it were by definition ensured.

What about the political dimension? In a representational-type democracy, by definition those that are represented do not play an active political role. They constitute the electorate and are at best engaged spectators to the political process—as long as they feel enough committed to read about political dealings in the papers, or to watch television or listen to the radio.

The strength of the symbolic dimension, whose importance is so often underestimated in a more technical conception of democracy, varies from country to country. Paradoxically, it is particularly important to countries that lack a democratic tradition, and, consequently, do not entertain any old ceremonies or rituals, let alone that they can refer to a stimulating historical background. In a purely representational democracy the problem might be that the citizens have become so far removed from the real exercise of power that the sense of the democratic rituals has been lost to them and the rationale of the democratic culture forgotten. In a participatory democracy this is less likely to happen.

There is no need to draw any far-reaching conclusions from this brief analysis, but the picture that arises from the comparison is clearly that, in principle, a more participatory democracy offers better prospects for an effective organisational system than a merely representational democracy. This will apply more so to cases such as the developing democracies in Eastern Europe where the organisational system is under heavy pressure from difficult economic and social problems without there being any possibility of relying on an established democratic tradition.

Participatory Democracy and Critical Discussion

It is, of course, nice to know that it is important to aim for a more participatory democracy. But what does this mean in practice?

Leaving aside matters of institutional organisation, important though they are, participation in democracy amounts first and foremost to an engagement of the members of the community, or the society at large, in a continual and public discourse about common interests, policies to be developed and decisions to be taken. Taking into account that preferences may change as a result of communication, Schumpeter rightly calls the will of the people "the product, not the motive power of the political process" (1950: 263). Nevertheless, in modern representative democracy the outcomes of the political process are predominantly a product of negotiations among political leaders rather than the result of a universal deliberative process.

It is probably no exaggeration that in western representative democracies, as others have said, limited participation and apathy are considered to have a positive function for the whole system by cushioning the shock of disagreement, adjustment and change. More often than not so-called political "discussions" are not more than a one-way traffic of leaders talking down to their voters. The leaders have the ideas, the voters just applaud them and follow. It is only when elections are close that the politicians adjust their campaign—sometimes embarrassingly opportunistically—to the avowed opinions of their voters, albeit that this adjustment is by no means the result of extensive discussion of potential issues.[14]

At this juncture, it is necessary to make a distinction between discussion as a regulated critical dialogue aimed at resolving a difference of opinion, and quasi-discussion that is in fact a monologue calculated to win the audience's consent to one's own views. In the latter case, the discourse is merely rhetorical in the narrowest sense. If discussion does not simply mean unidirectional persuading, but refers to a methodical argumentative exchange governed by the purpose of finding out together with one's opponent what is just or acceptable, allowing oneself also to be persuaded, then the discourse may be called *dialectical* in a critical-rationalist sense.

In my opinion—and in saying this I am only following greater minds such as Karl Popper's—democracy should always aim at such a critical discussion in the dialectical sense. This is the only way of making participation really contribute to the quality of the proceedings instead of being merely a token property of democracy. Whether the participation is channelled through proportional representation or otherwise, the institutional organisation should be such that it provides a procedural framework that enables critical discussion to come off the ground. Bachrach considers systematic rules of procedure to be necessary if the country's political method is to be called "democratic" (1967: 18-20).

In my opinion, dialectical rules for argumentative discourse are the crucial part of a discussion procedure that gives substance to the ideal of participatory democracy. Viewing argument dialectically means that argumentation is seen as occurring within a critical discussion. The argumentation is then regarded as part of a regimented procedure for testing a standpoint against the critical reactions of a rational judge. Following Crawshay-Williams's distinction between *methodological* and *conventional* validity (1957: 175), Barth and Krabbe have explained that a critical discussion procedure takes its reasonableness from a two-part criterion (1982: 21-22).

The methodological, or *problem-solving*, validity of the procedure (1) has—in my interpretation—to do with its efficacy for serving its purpose. If the purpose of critical discussion is thought to be resolution of disagreements, then the critical discussion model must be designed in such a way as to lead to efficient resolutions and to avoid obstacles to resolution or "false" resolutions.[15] The conventional, or *intersubjective*, validity of the procedure (2) has to do with the conformity between its various components and the values, standards, and objectives actual arguers find acceptable. One way to establish the intersubjective validity of a dialectical procedure is by showing that it is a specialized version of more general principles of cooperation.[16]

Such an emphasis on the functional aspects of argumentative discourse, and on its interactional context, allows us to both describe and evaluate argumentation in relation to its purposes. Argumentation arises in response to or in anticipation of disagreement, and particular lines of justification are fitted to meet the nature of that disagreement. The structure of argumentation, the requirements of justification, and the need for argumentation itself are all adapted to the context in which opposition, objections, doubts, and counterclaims arise. This functional and dialectical approach to argumentative discourse indicates how on a more specific procedural level justice can be done to our earlier claim that democracy is quintessentially institutionalised uncertainty.[17]

Higher Order Conditions for Critical Discussion

Let us think of the dialectical discussion procedure as a "code of conduct" for rational discussants. What sort of people could adopt such a code? In what situation would such a code be possible?

The code of conduct presumes, fundamentally, that both parties wish to resolve, and not merely to overcome or settle, the disagreement. With Barth and Krabbe (1982: 75), we can think of the assumed attitudes and intentions of the arguers as "second order" conditions that are preconditions to the "first order" rules of the code of conduct.[18] The second order conditions correspond, roughly, to the psychological make-up of the arguer and they are constraints on the way the discourse is conducted. Second order conditions concern the internal states of arguers: their motivations to engage in critical discussion and their dispositional characteristics as to their ability to engage in critical discussion.[19]

Second order conditions require that participants be able to reason validly, to take into account multiple lines of argument, to integrate coordinate sets of arguments, and to balance competing directions of argumentation. The dialectical model assumes skill and competence in the subject matter under discussion and on the issues raised. Sophistication, complexity, and subtlety of an argument should not be negative considerations against considering that argument.

But not only must participants be willing and able to enter into a certain attitude, they must be enabled to claim the rights and responsibilities associated with the argumentative roles defined by the dialectical model. To say that in dialectical discourse everyone should have the right to advance his view to the best of his ability is to presuppose a surrounding socio-political context of equality. This means that there are conditions of a still higher order to be fulfilled than second order conditions, "third order" conditions. Third order conditions involve ideals such as non-violence, freedom of speech, and intellectual pluralism. The dialectical model assumes the absence of practical constraints on matters of presumption in standpoints. The goal of resolution of differences "on the merits" is incompatible with situations in which one standpoint or another may enjoy a privileged position by virtue of representing the *status quo* or being associated with a particular person or group. Presumption is a matter to be decided in the discussion, not a matter to be imposed on a discussion.

No doubt, many of us will have realised that the conditions I am referring to are also among the necessary conditions for the operation of the democratic method summed up by some of the theoreticians of modern democracy.[20] Some of us will also have recognized this classification of higher order conditions as corresponding, roughly, to Heider's (1953) discussion of a naive theory of action as involving personal force and environmental force.[21] There are, of course, other ways to organize the factors influencing the success and failure of actions. Not a great deal hinges on this particular set of differentiations, but it is a useful expository tool.[22]

We have to take into account that actual human interaction is not "naturally" and automatically always resolution-orientated.[23] People involved in disagreement are often heavily vested in one outcome or another. They do not generally enter into discussion willing to subject all of their thinking to debate, but treat certain things as so fundamental as to be beyond challenge. They have deficiencies of skill. They argue within social conditions that virtually assure some degree of inequality in power and resources. And the same circumstances that often give rise to argument also place practical demands for settlement and practical constraints on the ability to truly resolve disagreement. Actual argumentative practices are shaped by these constraints, and institutions developed to control argumentation are built to overcome or compensate for these constraints.

So one might ask whether the dialectical approach is not a little bit Utopian. Maybe indeed a little bit—I hope. But not too much, I should say. I really wonder whether there is any other acceptable way of trying to cope with the overwhelming problems of change than by promoting a culture of critical discussion. And there are certainly realistic possibilities of doing something about the problems involved. The classical protagonists of a more participatory democracy were already aware of that. They pointed, for instance, at the need to get experience, experience in dealing with authority in other spheres of life, in non-governmental social relationships. "Social training," which they also thought to be important, can presumably help in developing argumentative attitudes that support the democratic norms. And, last but not least, there is always, of course, the major source of public good: education.

The Role of Argumentation in Democratic Change

Let me now, by way of conclusion, summarize what wisdom concerning the role of argument in democratic social change I have tried to convey to you. By the book, and this is confirmed by *Webster's* and *The Concise Oxford Dictionary*, "democracy" means "government by all the people," but it can be more profoundly characterised as "institutionalised uncertainty." Democracy, *per se*, is no guarantee that our social and economic problems will be solved, especially not if democracy, in the modern fashion, is interpreted as being exclusively representational. In my opinion, the problems of Eastern European and other young democracies can be confronted only with a more participatory democracy.

I have argued that, as an organisational system, because of its exploitation of human resources, a participatory democracy of the classical type is, in principle, superior to a merely representative democracy. Still, in practice, participation will only work if adequate procedures can be developed for public discourse. To my mind, such procedures need to be dialectical, allowing for a methodical critical discussion between protagonists and antagonists of the various—often conflicting—viewpoints. In this way, argument plays a crucial part in the managing of uncertainty that is inherent in the exercise of democracy.

For the purpose of achieving a more participatory democracy, a dialectical code of conduct for critical discussants can be instrumental. However, the possibility of resolving differences by means of argument does not only depend on the availability of an adequate set of rules for conducting a critical discussion, however problem-valid. It also depends on people's attitudes and competence, and on the realization of social and political principles. For one thing, this again illustrates the importance of the social dimension of human resources—of participation—to the maintenance of a vital, i.e. effective as well as inspiring, democracy.

NOTES

1. For an extensive overview of historical backgrounds of the study of argumentation and contemporary developments in the various approaches to argumentation theory, see van Eemeren et al. (1996).

2. What I have to say about the changes in Eastern Europe is largely (and sometimes even literally) taken from Przeworski's work.

3. Of course, these rules are not immutable: They can be changed.

4. According to some, the problem of compliance would not emerge if democracy were rational in the

sense of eigthteenth-century democratic theory. If social interests were harmonious, conflicts would be but disagreements about identifying the common good. They could be overcome by rational discussion. The role of the political process would be only epistemic, a search for the true general will.

5. There are competing views of compliance (and hence of the endurance of democracy). The justifications of democracy, and in particular of the coercion applied to force compliance, given in the philosophical literature vary from a reference to spontaneous self-enforcing outcomes (or equilibria), bargains or contracts, and a higher kind of moral norms.

6. Peter Houtlosser reminded me of an even more realistic example, i.e. the rejection of democracy in Algeria in 1992 after the fundamentalists were expected to win the elections.

7. It is on the competition between leaders for the votes of the people that "control" depends. The individual can switch his support. This competition is the specifically democratic element in the method. The value over other political methods is that it makes possible an extension of the number, size and diversity of the minorities that can bring their influence to bear on policy decisions, and on the whole political ethos of society (Dahl 1956a,b, 1971).

8. Modern theorists of democracy claim to be empirical and descriptive. Their work is grounded in the facts of present-day political attitudes and behaviour as revealed by sociological investigation. My philosophical observations concerning the theory of democracy are largely (and sometimes even literally) taken from Pateman (1990).

9. See Dahl (1956a,b) and Sartori (1962). All Sartori's arguments are coloured by the fear that the active participation of the people in the political process leads straight to totalitarianism. The people, Sartori says, must "react," they do not "act." As Eckstein expresses it: There must be a "healthy element of authoritarianism," and for a stable democratic system the structure of authority in national government cannot be really, or "purely," a democratic one.

10. The function of participation in the theory is solely a protective one: The protection of the individual from arbitrary decisions by elected leaders and the protection of these private interests. It is in its achievement of this aim that the justification for the democratic method lays.

11. Bentham and James Mill expected that electors would make each decision independently of "propaganda" and form their opinions "logically," but neither writer expected that opinions would be formed in a vacuum. Bentham laid in fact great emphasis on the role of public opinion. Mill stressed the importance of educating the electorate into socially responsible voting.

12. There is, in fact, nothing specifically democratic about this view of the function of participation. Similar views can be found in Locke's theory (and in the works of Hegel and Edmund Burke).

13. At this juncture, irrelevant to my argument as it may be, one cannot help thinking of the problems of identification with the system that have come to light in Los Angeles and other big cities in the United States in the last decade of the 20th Century.

14. The "coup de grace" against the theoretical view of democracy as rational deliberation seems to have been administered in 1923 by Carl Schmitt in his book The crisis of parliamentary democracy (1988). Schmitt argues that not all the political conflicts can be reconciled by discussion. At a certain point, issues are decided by voting. From this he concludes that conflicts can be resolved only by recourse to physical force. However, Habermas is certainly not the only one who thinks this a too hasty conclusion.

15. Our pragma-dialectical model of argumentation derives its problem-solving validity from the incorporation of preconditions and discourse mechanisms tailored to the cooperative search for resolution. See van Eemeren and Grootendorst (1992) and van Eemeren, Grootendorst, Jackson and Jacobs (1993).

16. A commitment to a dialectical approach to argumentation does not necessarily mean analyzing only those exceptional cases in which there is a one hundred percent rational and reasonable discussion. What it means instead is distinguishing between principles and practices, between rules and regularities.

17. Argument is very often described in structural terms. Although structural analyses of argument have much to recommend them, they tend to ignore the functional motivations and functional requirements that underlie the structural design of an argument. The functional view departs from a strictly structural view of argument by emphasizing the function of argument in managing the resolution of disagreements.

18. The first order conditions, if satisfied, provide certain guarantees against things that could go wrong in the search for a resolution to a disagreement. They assure, for example, that both parties to a dispute will have unlimited opportunity to cast doubt on standpoints and that both parties to a dispute will be obliged to respond to such doubts. See van Eemeren, Grootendorst, Jackson and Jacobs (1993).

19. Motivations and abilities are of course in complex ways interrelated: Defects in motivation may reflect various sorts of constraints on ability. For example, failure to maintain an impartial point of view may reflect difficulties in decentering from one's own concerns and taking the perspective of other parties. And heightened motivation can, to a certain extent, offset limited abilities to, say, follow complex arguments or to engage in impartial reflection on the issues. See van Eemeren, Grootendorst, Jackson and Jacobs (1993).

20. Among the necessary conditions for the operation of the democratic method mentioned in the literature are civil liberties, tolerance of others' opinions, a "national character and national habits of a certain type," unanimity in the allegiance to the "structural principles of existing society," limitation of the intensity of conflict, restraint of the rate of change, maintenance of social and economic stability, a pluralist social organisation and basic consensus, and consensus on norms, at least among leaders.

21. It might also be noted that, for the purposes of critical evaluation, many though not all of these higher order conditions have a moral or ethical dimension to them. Thus, we ordinarily hold people responsible for holding certain attitudes and values, and for having certain purposes and intentions. We require of people that they have the proper motivations in a way that we do not apply to deficits in ability. And likewise, we hold people responsible for "taking advantage of the situation" when it concerns a decision that is under their control. And we can hold institutions responsible for guaranteeing certain third-order conditions (e.g., political and social rights), but not necessarily others (e.g., constraints due to time or presumption). See van Eemeren, Grootendorst, Jackson and Jacobs (1993).

22. From a slightly altered framework, it might for example be useful to distinguish fourth order conditions relating to "normal input and output conditions" (as John Searle, 1969, calls them). They specify among other things that, for analytical purposes, the basic model of a critical discussion situation assumes that people have a normal communicative capacity and are in a physical situation that allows the transmission of interpretable signals. However, nonfulfillment of these conditions would affect communication in general, not just argumentation, and therefore these conditions can be left out here. See van Eemeren, Grootendorst, Jackson and Jacobs (1993).

23. Even if the interaction is resolution-orientated, there is still a tension in argumentative discourse between the participants' dialectical goal of dispute-resolution and their rhetorical aim of having things their own way. The need to overcome the tension between these two objectives gives rise to "strategic maneuvering." See van Eemeren and Houtlosser (2002).

REFERENCES

Bachrach, P. (1967). *The Theory of Democratic Elitism: A Critique*. Boston: Little and Brown.

Barth, E.M. and E.C.W. Krabbe (1982). *From Axiom to Dialogue. A Philosophical Study of Logics and Argumentation*. Berlin: Walter de Gruyter.

Bentham, J. (1843). *Works*. Edited by J. Bowring. Edinburgh: Tait.

Berelson, B.R., P.F. Lazarsfeld and W.N. McPhee (1954). *Voting*. Chicago: University of Chicago Press.

Bolman, L.G. and T.E. Deal (1991). *Modern Approaches to Understanding and Managing Organizations*. (1st ed. 1984). San Francisco: Jossey-Bass Publishers.

Coleman, J. (1989). Rationality and the justification of democracy. In: G. Brennan and L.E. Lomansky (Eds.), *Politics and Process*. Cambridge: Cambridge University Press.

Coser, L. (1959). *The Functions of Social Conflict*. New York: Free Press.

Crawshay-Williams, R. (1957). *Methods and Criteria of Reasoning. An Inquiry into the Structure of Controversy*. London: Routledge and Kegan Paul.

Dahl, R.A. (1956a). *Preface to Democratic Theory*. Chicago: University of Chicago Press.

———. (1956b). Hierarchy, democracy and bargaining in politics and economics. In: H. Eulau, S. Eldersveld and M. Janowitz (Eds.), *Political Behaviour*. Glencoe: Free Press.

———. (1971). *Polyarchy: Participation and Opposition*. New Haven, CT.: Yale University Press.

Davis, L. (1964). The cost of realism: Contemporary restatements of democracy. *Western Political Quarterly*, XVII, 37-46.

Eckstein, H. (1966). A theory of stable democracy. App. B. of *Division and Cohesion in Democracy*. Princeton, NJ: Princeton University Press.

Eemeren, F.H. van and R. Grootendorst (1992). *Argumentation, Communication, and Fallacies*. Hillsdale, NJ: Lawrence Erlbaum Associates.

Eemeren, F.H. van, R. Grootendorst, A.F. Snoeck Henkemans, J.A. Blair, R.H. Johnson, E.C.W. Krabbe, Ch. Plantin, D.N. Walton, Ch.A. Willard, J.Woods and D. Zarefsky (1996). *Fundamentals of Argumentation Theory. A Handbook of Historical Backgrounds and Contemporary Developments*. Mahwah, NJ: Lawrence Erlbaum Associates.

Eemeren, F.H. van, R. Grootendorst, S. Jackson and S. Jacobs (1993). *Reconstructing Argumentative Discourse*. Tuscaloosa/London: Alabama University Press.

Eemeren, F.H. van and P. Houtlosser (2002). Within the bound of reason: Strategic maneuvering in argumentative discourse. In: F.H. van Eemeren and P. Houtlosser (Eds.), *Dialectic and Rhetoric: The Warp and Woof of Argumetation Analysis*. Dordrecht etc.: Kluwer.

Habermas, J. (1975). *Legitimation Crises*. Boston: Beacon.

Heider, F. (1953). *The Psychology of Interpersonal Relations*. New York: John Wiley.

Lipset, S.M. (1960). *Political Man*. London: Heinemann/Garden City, NY.: Doubleday.

Linz, J. (1990). Transitions to democracy. *Washington Quarterly*, Summer, 143-164.

Mill, J. (1937). *An Essay on Government*. Cambridge: Cambridge University Press.

Mill, J.S. (1965). *Collected Works*. Ed. by J.M. Robson. Toronto: University of Toronto Press.

Pateman, C. (1990). *Participation and Democratic Theory*. (1st ed. 1975). Cambridge: Cambridge University Press.

Popper, K.R. (1971). *The Open Society and its Enemies*. 2 volumes. Princeton, NJ.: Princeton University Press.

Przeworski, A. (1991). *Democracy and the market. Political and economic reforms in Eastern Europe and Latin America*. Cambridge: Cambridge University Press.

Rousseau, J.J. (1953). *Political Writings*. Transl. by F. Watkins. London: Nelson.

Sartori, G. (1962). *Democratic Theory*. Detroit, MI: Wayne State University Press.

Schmitt, C. (1988). *The Crisis of Parliamentary Democracy*. 1st ed. 1923. Cambridge, MA: MIT.

Schumpeter, J.A. (1950). *Capitalism, Socialism and Democracy*. New York: Harper Bros.

Searle, J.R. (1969). *Speech Acts*. Cambridge: Cambridge University Press.

The Rhetorical *Phronimos*: Political Wisdom in Postmodernity

M. Lane Bruner

Abstract

To formulate a contemporary conception of political wisdom, this essay combines recent philosophical attacks on the rational subject with Aristotle's notion of phronesis, *or "practical" wisdom. Aristotle maintained that the phronimos is one who, through virtuous character, negotiates the uncertain political realm through the wise use of the rhetorical arts. Modern and postmodern theories, however, have profoundly complicated notions of meaning, identity and rationality, hence conceptions of knowledge and virtuous character. After a review of some of these theories, the essay concludes with a brief re-articulation of* phronesis *as political wisdom.*

Where is wisdom to be found in the political realm? Where is the wisdom to aid us in the never ending struggle to achieve the fullest human good within the uncertain, unpredictable, compelling, and oftentimes unjust realm of human action? Throughout history the answers have remained elusive. The incessant search for wisdom among his fellow citizens in ancient Athens led Socrates to a cup of poison for "corrupting the youth" and "denying the gods."[1] Across the ages, those who would dare to question political authority have been consistently imprisoned or publicly put to death, oftentimes with great fanfare. The history of what passes for statecraft has been a history of governments undermining the power of critical citizens and of wars waged between parties equally convinced of the virtuousness of their characters, the rightness of their causes, and the wisdom of their rulers. With its almost ceaseless violence and warfare, political history suggests that humans simply *lack* political wisdom.

And today, if we thought there might still be political wisdom somewhere, where would we go to look for it? Could we turn to our personal character, our religious faith, or our confidence in our way of life? Could we look for political wisdom in the ways our communities imagine themselves ethnically, culturally, and economically, or in the discourses that dominate the construction of those conceptions, or in the institutions that follow from those conceptions? If hard pressed to go out into the world and find political wisdom, where would we go and to whom could we turn? Surely we could not turn to our scientists with their "objective" forms of inquiry ("I only help design the computer technology that guides the bombs; I don't decide when to drop them."), or to technically proficient professionals who stay focused on the object of their particular professions rather than the human consequences of their techniques. Surely we could not turn to the managers of the self-interested organizations in which we work ("I am only responsible for the company's bottom line and the profitability of bomb making, not the social effects of our profit taking or of the bombs themselves."), where resources are always distributed according to prevailing discourses of power that seek to take more than they give, that constrain open deliberative processes, and where organizational goals "rationally" take precedence over social reason. And surely we could not turn to our self-interested governments in the explosive conditions of the "new world order," with its increasingly stark contrasts between the rich and the poor, its increasingly terrible military technologies, and its ethno-cultural and religious hatreds ("Let's use the bomb!").

Not only does the search for political wisdom in history prove relatively futile, previously influential notions of political wisdom such as Aristotle's concept of *phronesis* (roughly translated today as either prudence or practical wisdom) have been made increasingly suspect by centuries of philosophical debate over the possibility of human rationality.[2] The hallmark of Cartesian rationalism was the assumption that the same degree of certainty could be attained in the social sciences as well as the physical sciences.[3] Subsequently, political philosophers from Immanuel Kant to John Dewey to Jürgen Habermas have fought for the idea that every mature individual, given the right conditions, was capable of productively critiquing government (arguing that widespread political wisdom was both necessary and possible).[4] However, social and political philosophers over the last two centuries, like astronomers over the last millennium, have worked to "de-center" the rational subject, making the notion of political wisdom increasingly problematic. In astronomy, Ptolemy theorized that the earth was the center of the universe, just as Enlightenment philosophers theorized that humans could rationally and objectively govern the world. Copernicus next theorized that the earth revolved around the sun and was influenced by previously unrecognized forces, just as modernism ushered in an era of philosophy focused on how the "rational" subject was influenced by outside forces beyond their control (the psyche, the economy, the metaphorical nature of identity, etc.). Einstein then devised his theory of relativity, and postmodern philosophers left the fully rational, autonomous, and "centered" political individual for good, maintaining that humans, lost in violent fields of absence and difference, are compelled to maneuver through endless mazes of politically consequential language games, disciplinary practices, and patterns of subjection. The intellectual leaders of both modernism and postmodernism, in sum, have shown in a variety of ways that humans are irrational at their core, so what possible hope can there be for political wisdom and/or responsible statecraft?

Phronesis, therefore, although it is one of our few available conceptual resources for reconsidering the possibility of political wisdom in contemporary circumstances, is highly suspect. Not only does it predate the philosophical movement from modernity to modernism to postmodernism, it is a term centrally concerned with intentionality, virtuous character, and moral confidence (i.e. through wise deliberation, civic and personal virtue, and a keen sense of justice, individuals take intentional action in uncertain but compelling circumstances to maximize the virtue of citizens and states and to achieve the common good). It is a concept that appears to fly in the face of the contemporary philosophical conclusion that rational individuals, as political animals, simply do not exist. Despite this apparent conclusion, however, in this short essay I would like to revisit Aristotle's notion of *phronesis* as a thought experiment, carefully separating, as did Aristotle, the "rational" (theoretical wisdom) from the "reasonable" (practical wisdom). After briefly tracing some of the post-Cartesian attacks on the rational subject, reviewing Aristotle's notion of *phronesis*, and re-considering two contemporary debates in critical and political theory, perhaps it will be possible to overcome key objections and articulate a practical and theoretical conception of "postmodern" political wisdom.

"Rational" Citizens and Their Political Realms

In 17th and 18th century Europe and the United States, social and political philosophers such as John Locke, Jeremy Bentham, Immanuel Kant and Thomas Paine had a great deal of faith in the power of the rational public. Publics composed of autonomous individuals were thought to have the potential to check arbitrary state power through rational deliberation. Contemporary critics, however, could point out that many of the ideas prevalent in political theory at that time were "productive fictions" emerging with, and strengthened by, colonial-capitalism. Notions such as sovereignty, self-determination, free trade, the public, individuality and objectivity were related to notions of freedom ideologically ameliorating the painful disruptions in local (usually illiterate) community caused by urbanization and the expansion of market economies. In other words, there were ideological underpinnings behind Enlightenment political philosophy, oftentimes making it more "symptomatic" than "realistic."[5]

Subsequently, both modern and postmodern thinkers have reminded us of the numerous obstacles facing citizens who through their supposed rationality are to deliberate and rule wisely. Karl Marx, for example, undermined the notion of the fully free, objective, and rational individual by explaining how economic relations profoundly influence individual and social identities.[6] Sigmund Freud argued that unconscious impulses direct our patterns of daily actions and interactions and that society itself is based upon modes of repression.[7] Friedrich Nietzsche undermined the notions of rationality and objectivity by arguing that all of our language, and therefore our very apprehension of the world, is fundamentally metaphorical and that our poetic constructions, taken as concrete truths, directly impact our individual and social conditions.[8] Ferdinand de Saussure argued that identity itself was based on difference in his work on linguistics,[9] and continental philosophers such as Michel Foucault, Jacques Derrida, and Hans-Georg Gadamer extended these insights into various branches of critical theory. Foucault, for example, argued that identity/subjectivity unwittingly disciplines and necessarily establishes variously enabling constraints.[10] Derrida maintains that all attempts at moral closure and identity are doomed to shipwreck on the narrative absences and exclusions such closures and identities require.[11] And Gadamer has persuasively argued that meaning/subjectivity is always a "fusion of horizons" and that identity is not simply controlled by the interpreter but is always an encounter with an unexpected and ultimately unknowable Other.[12] Each thinker, in his own way, has pointed out how human beings are not as rational and objective as they might have once believed.

While such examples only scratch the surface of critiques that have been leveled against the rational individual, contemporary critics could rightfully maintain that to speak of "character" or "virtue" or "wisdom" today as a stable set of beliefs, characteristics, or deliberative practices designed to compel "right action" for the "common good" requires considerable qualification to remain philosophically informed. In light of these and other insights into human subjectivity, "strong positions" appear motivated by so many unintentional factors and irrational forces that moral certainty in the political realm is simply irresponsible, unless those "positions" are of a highly refined and reflexive type usually not found in the political realm.[13]

Not only are individuals generally incapable of being politically rational, they also experience "the political" on a variety of oftentimes mutually incompatible levels. The contemporary theorist of political wisdom, therefore, must both be philosophically informed about the wide range of constraints on rationality as well as with the range of political realms in which processes of identification (one of the main subjects of modern and postmodern political theory) take place.[14] Here, perhaps surprisingly, is where a review of Aristotle's notion of *phronesis* first proves useful, for he is generally believed to be the first to have systematically conceptualized four interactive "layers" to the political realm in which political wisdom was active: the realms of self-interest, family relations, legislation, and statesmanship.[15] In the "market democracies" of today, for example, there is a unique political terrain that involves self-interest (e.g. corporations as legal "individuals," economic liberalism/market ethics, radical individualism), family relations (the general breakdown of the extended family into a considerably weakened "nuclear" family under the ideological haze of "family values" discourse), legislation (a general dismantling of the New Deal in the United States and the "welfare state" worldwide, and a simultaneous trend toward unelected supra-national governance through trade and finance agreements), and deliberative and judicial procedures (the simultaneous expansion of the nation state system and the decline of the real political power of individual states, the decline of representative democracy, the rise of executive authority, and the rise of transnational court systems). Any contemporary characterization and enactment of *phronesis* would, at least according to Aristotle's conception, have to take such "layers" and their interactions into account.

But is a workable revision of *phronesis* even possible in our postmodern and post-essentialist age, where anyone absolutely certain (the True Believer) in the quasi-metaphorical realm of human affairs is viewed as philosophically naïve, if not downright dangerous? Socrates willingly drank the poison, because, guided as he was by the "voice" (of conscience?) that would come to him, he believed it was the practically wise thing to do, concerned as he was with educating the Athenian citizens to the virtue of incessant self-criticism.[16] But is Socrates' behavior, which was pre-Aristotelian, perhaps anti-democratic, and situated in a slave-holding and misogynist culture, or Aristotle's theory, obviously ignorant of the insights of modernism and contemporary identity theory, adequate models for political wisdom in postmodernity? In what follows, I respond to these questions and argue that it is indeed possible for a contemporary form of *phronesis* to exist in our post-rational age both in theory and practice. If Aristotle's definition of *phro-*

nesis as wise deliberation applied to virtuous character in action (where the ultimate form of practical wisdom is "statesmanship" in the realms of self-interest, family, legislation, and deliberative/judicial procedure) remains at all useful, then perhaps it will prove beneficial to review that definition and then to reconsider *phronesis* through the lens of contemporary philosophical and political debates.

Aristotle's Theory of Knowledge

To initiate a discussion on the possibility of a coherent contemporary conception of *phronesis*, it is helpful to understand Aristotle's own definition of the term and how it differs from his definitions of other forms of knowledge. Once *phronesis* is defined we can move on to an explanation of the role of rhetoric within Aristotle's epistemology, how identity philosophy relates to the rhetorical arts, and how recent debates in critical and political theory impact Aristotle's theory of political wisdom. At that point a rudimentary characterization of what postmodern political wisdom might look like can be offered.

In all, and as is relatively well known, Aristotle identified five "means of judgment": intelligence (*nous* and *dianoia*), scientific knowledge (*episteme*), art (*techne*), theoretical wisdom (*sophia*), and practical wisdom (*phronesis*).[17] Intelligence basically refers to the human capacity to apprehend the material world (sense perception and conceptualization), scientific knowledge concerns the relatively certain forms of knowledge associated with physical and mathematical laws, and art is concerned with the knowledge that comes from the mastery of a skill or profession. But the means of judgment of special interest here is not to be found in either the sciences or the professions, for the arts and sciences each have their own particular ends while *phronesis* is only concerned with what brings about the greatest human good. Furthermore, while the arts and sciences have relative certainty within the realm of their own disciplinary practices, negotiating among those practices requires another type of knowledge altogether: wisdom.

As noted, within Aristotle's epistemology, there are two distinct forms of wisdom: theoretical wisdom (*sophia*) and practical wisdom (*phronesis*). Theoretical wisdom deals with metaphysics, philosophy, theology and universal truths, and though "it is the highest form" of knowledge, according to Aristotle, practical wisdom has "greater authority" because of its concern with the concrete day to day affairs of human beings in action.[18] Practical wisdom deals with ethics (actions which result in a virtuous life) and politics (actions which result in a well-ordered state), and is principally concerned with wise deliberation, right action, and virtuous character.[19] It is, in Eugene Garver's words, "the ability to confront the permanent possibility of instability," for in the realm of practical wisdom there are no certainties, only probabilities. [20]

While the ancient Greek philosopher Heraclitus purportedly claimed that, "To be wise is one thing: to know the thought that directs all things through all things,"[21] he also noted that "the *Logos* proves incomprehensible, for although all things happen according to the *Logos*, many act as if they have no experience of it."[22] Following his distinction, there would need to be two forms of wisdom: one form that deals with transpolitical universal truths (*Logos*) and another that deals with the practical and imperfect realm of human affairs (a combination of *Logos, mythos, ethos, pathos,* and *praxis*). Generally speaking, philosophers tend to be more concerned with the former realm, while rhetoricians tend to be concerned with the latter realm: the public stage of human action where equally compelling if not equally influential or virtuous characterizations compete for allegiance in the formation of identity and community.

Phronesis and the Role of Rhetoric and Dialectic

Rhetoric, as a term, is oftentimes confusing because it can be conceptualized in a wide variety of ways: as a product (persuasive public speech), a process (the ongoing transformation of identities through discourse), and a critical practice (a critical analysis of identification practices and the systems of governance that result from those practices). Rhetoric can also be thought of as a tool (e.g. marketing), as a means of strengthening the values of a community (e.g. epideictic discourse), or as a menace to society (e.g. deceptive language used to obscure the truth or protect dishonorable interests). Defined narrowly, rhetoric is concerned with persuasive public discourse, while more widely it is concerned with all processes of identification and identity formation. Within both definitions, however, we are in the realm of rhetoric if I can change or reinforce your characterization of your self, your community, or your government, for then we are in the realm of language in use, in the realm of the political (for good and ill), in the realm of the probable rather than the certain, and therefore in the realm of practical/political wisdom.[23] Complicating the fact that rhetoric can be defined in a wide variety of ways and can refer to a wide range of objects, university English departments teach rhetoric as composition while Speech Communication departments teach rhetoric as public speaking to first year students. While those familiar with the history of rhetoric may not be surprised at this diversity, it nonetheless can bewilder those looking to nail down what "rhetoric" is all about, let alone the relationship between rhetoric and political wisdom.

Despite public confusion about "rhetoric" (it is all of these things and more), it is crucial for a coherent articulation of postmodern political wisdom to understand the significance of the term to philosophies of identity and contemporary political theories. However, it is useful to start by once again returning to Aristotle, his foundational definition of rhetoric, and how he understood the relationship between rhetoric and *phronesis*. In Aristotle's system of knowledge, rhetoric is an art (*techne*) that consists of observing the available means of persuasion, considering how they can be applied to achieve a civil state and virtuous citizens, then acting upon those considerations through *phronesis*.[24] *Phronesis* is neither an art nor a science because it cannot guarantee its object (human good) by logical deduction or rational method alone. Instead, *phronesis* is the virtue, if not the foundation of all virtues, of political actors attempting to take right action in the realm of the probable through good character.[25]

To properly position *phronesis* and rhetoric within Aristotle's theory of knowledge, it is also important to understand how his five "means of judgment" deal with different objects of knowledge. In a passage of great import for political scientists, Aristotle argues that "we must not look for the same degree of accuracy in all subjects; we must be content in each class of subjects with accuracy of such a kind as the subject matter allows, and to such an extent as is proper to the inquiry."[26] Knowledge, therefore, should properly be divided into two classes: the scientific (rational) and the deliberative (reasonable).[27] The former class deals with invariable principles and the relative certainties of math, the physical sciences, the productive arts, and theoretical wisdom, while the latter deals with variable principles and the relative uncertainties of political actions situated in time. Hence the unique role of rhetoric, for as the rhetorical theorist Barbara Warnick points out:

> Because *phronesis* can be applied only in the particular case and because human affairs are intrinsically changeable and contingent, the standards for right action must be relative and applied to the case at hand rather than invariant and universal. In determining such standards and the effects of action, rhetoric plays a vital role. It deals in probabilities and considers regu-

larities across situations. Since such regularities and the general convictions regarding them can be known, rhetoric possesses a kind of knowledge, but it is qualitatively different from that possessed by *episteme* or *sophia*.[28]

While we may ultimately discover that the standards for right action in the political realm have both universal (rational) and probable (reasonable) dimensions, it is nevertheless the kind of deliberative knowledge produced by rhetoric that is of special importance for the articulation of a postmodern understanding of *phronesis* as political wisdom.

Aristotle argued that there were two categories of persuasive arts related to practical wisdom: rhetoric and dialectic.[29] Both operate in the realm of the probable and are applied only to subjects that admit of more than one outcome. Dialectic, a counterpart of rhetoric, is interactive dialogue with (usually small) groups of interlocutors capable of following extended logical arguments where the purpose is to discern true and false reasoning.[30] Dialectic could be viewed as dialogue between experts within a technical field of expertise, but in a broader and arguably more important sense as open and critical dialogue on deliberative issues by experts in argumentation guided by mutual good will seeking a common good. However, such "ideal speech conditions" are hardly the norm.[31] Rhetoric, therefore, as opposed to dialectic, is the art of persuasion applied to (usually large) groups who are either incapable of following complex reasoning or who lack the motives, good will, skills, or shared premises required for dialectics. In this sense, rhetoric is "anti-dialogic" inasmuch as its application assumes a certain lack of deliberative skill and good will in the audience (but of course is dialogic in the broader sense of discourse entering into and circulating within an ideational economy).[32] With rhetoric, the persuader must understand and begin her work from the accepted opinions of audience members rather than claims already established through expert dialogue and wise deliberation. Assessing the prejudices, ideology, commonsense, etc., of the audience, therefore, is also of paramount importance to the practically, as opposed to the theoretically, wise.

Assuming that conflict rather than cooperation, misunderstanding rather than understanding, and self-interest rather than community interests are the norm in the vast majority of human relations, rhetoric at its best, coupled with dialectic when possible, produces a kind of knowledge in the service of *phronesis*: higher quality arguments and wiser deliberation in the service of virtuous character, right action, and a well-ordered state in the realm of the probable. But, as we now know, the criteria for "higher quality," "wise," "virtuous," "right," and "well-ordered" are incessantly subject to contestation, and "the good" in the political realm will be relative to the hegemonic characterizations that prevail at any given moment in time. Today, it is not so easy to assume, as Aristotle did, that rhetoric "is valuable because truth and justice are by nature more powerful than their opposites" and that "virtue" and "good character" can be easily determined. Social truth itself must be rhetorically negotiated in a way more radical than Aristotle may have supposed.

Practical Wisdom and Its Areas of Application

It follows that, at least according to Aristotle, we should think of practical wisdom (here conceived as political wisdom) as the wise use of the persuasive rhetorical arts to most probably construct virtuous character and good government. It is both a form of criticism (unmasking presumed certainty in the deliberative realm) and a form of praxis (contributing to wise/r deliberation for the sake of the common good).[33] Wisdom in the political realm is a practice of dealing not only with people usually incapable of extended dialogue on complex matters (both within and between disciplinary practices), but with people who are self-interested, who are constrained by various familial roles, who are employed by self-interested organizations, who are "represented" in various fashions, and who are "condemned to choose" from the possibilities provided by the broader material and ideational economies in which they find themselves.

As a result of the multi-layered form of the realm of political wisdom (personal identities, disciplinary identities, collective identities, state identities), it is arguable that political wisdom, to be effective in all of the political areas in which the persuasive arts prevail, needs to be *applied* to the realm of individual action within ideational/material economies (the art of the self), to the realms of disciplinary identity and collective identity construction (the arts of professional and public character), and to the realm of institutional design (the art of statecraft). In the realm of individual action, the individual is "separated" from his "natural" conditions through language and the consequences of language.[34] There are no promises whatsoever that reason, let alone rationality, will prevail. Maneuvering within the maze of assigned and achieved roles and the disciplinary practices in which those roles are embedded is one key area that must be incessantly tackled by the politically wise.

In addition to our personal ethics, and in light of the warnings about moral certainty in postmodernity, it is also important for the politically wise to recognize the importance of professional and public character. Familial roles, professional roles, "ethnic" roles, class roles, gender roles, citizen roles, each have a personal and a public dimension: personal in that individuals experience subjection to them and, sometimes, empowerment by them, and public in that they are negotiated through discourse and inter-subjectively enforced. In an age of competitive states that purport to represent the interests of "nations" and historically distinct "peoples," the persuasive arts are also central to the problem of state identity construction.[35] The eminent social historian Erich Kahler noted almost half a century ago that the history of the world, in many respects, is the history of the character of communities.[36] International relations theorists more recently are equally adamant in their insistence that transformations in discourse result in transformations in the nation-state system and vice versa.[37] Each of these areas applies to the realm of political wisdom in post-modernity.

In addition to being "subject" to personal and collective identities, individuals are also caught up in institutional structures that have ossified over the years because of certain kinds of agreements made by individuals in the past. Political wisdom, therefore, relates not only to concrete human action within matrices of disciplinary practices and the fabrication and political consequences of private and public character, it is also concerned with argumentation processes within and across disciplines and how different forms of consensus and identification lead to different kinds of institutions and governments. Therefore the final key areas of incessant concern to the politically wise would be public deliberative processes and statecraft.

These three dimensions of political wisdom (the rhetorical self, the rhetorical community, and the rhetorical state), would require the *phronimos*, at the very least, to understand from the outset that shared premises and good will are not to be expected in the political realm, that the deliberative arts of rhetoric and dialectic must be brought to bear on the particulars of the political moment, that any conception of the "common good" will necessarily lead to political exclusions with material consequences, and that it is crucial to have the capacity to distinguish "rational" arguments from reasonable arguments. Additionally, it is useful for the *phronimos* to have an understanding of the history of governments (i.e. the transformation of states from tribe to monarchy to nation-state to transnationalism), the evolution of constitutionalism, and consequent developments in civil society to understand the shifting relationships among collective identities and forms of state.

In sum, the political actor who claims to be politically wise realizes first and foremost the utter absence of certainty in the political realm; this is her wisdom. The *phronimos* does not expect "rationality" to prevail, does not expect dialogue (although institutional systems can be created that maximize the possibility that pseudo-certainties are maximally problematized), does not expect good will, does not expect shared premises, but does expect conflict, exclusion, faction, violence, self-interest, ethical shallowness and deceit. However, this is not a cynical but a practical wisdom based on the expectation that because identification happens as it does, the politically wise must interact with identification processes accordingly within the "systems of governmentality" that prevail. There is an obvious series of unavoidable paradoxes here. First, there is the paradox of agency. On the one hand, intentionality has been problematized by postmodern thought, forcing us to consider how we are "thrown" into identities and situations. On the other hand, it is arguable that postmodernism is actually an extension of the ongoing Enlightenment project of self-awareness and freedom from unrecognized authorities. Therefore, the postmodern rhetorical *phronimos* is simultaneously a willful agent and a constrained subject. Second, there is the paradox of forging common ground and establishing a common good. Clearly, the politically wise person, in her knowledge of the processes of identity formation, nonetheless must seek not only to act upon a notion of the common good and help to create a shared vision of the common good, but simultaneously must recognize that any attempt to do so entails exclusionary and marginalizing consequences. Therefore, part and parcel of the conception of the common good, the politically wise person must incorporate an incessant reflexive appreciation of limits and a willingness to allow transgressions to illuminate and modify those limits. Third, there is the paradox of action itself. Any decision is a limiting form of closure that does a necessary "violence" to alternative possibilities. However, since action in the political realm is unavoidable (actions must be taken to resolve issues characterized as needing attention given the constructed conception of the common good), this dimension of violence is unavoidable. The key, for the postmodern *phronimos*, is to so construct articulations of the common good and the personal, familial, professional, and collective institutions that support them, to minimize that violence. While enumerating the conditions for the possibility of such a state of affairs constitutes a certain idealism, the entire project is necessarily shot through with paradox (since any articulation of necessary conditions constitutes the "violent," even if temporary, imposition of ideational and institutional limits).

Such a characterization of contemporary political wisdom compares in interesting ways with current debates between philosophers and political theorists, particularly the debates between philosophical hermeneuts such as Gadamer, deconstructionists such as Derrida, and "rational" and "critical" political theorists. A review of these debates, I maintain, supports the characterization just provided of the politically wise person as a postmodern rhetorical *phronimos*.

Dialogue versus Deconstruction

Contemporary political theorists are centrally concerned today about how identification happens as it does, and they are generally well aware of recent developments in identity philosophy. It is not surprising, then, that many of their debates revolve around questions raised by the identity logics that follow from contemporary philosophies of identity formation. These debates should be of particular interest to those concerned about the role of dialogue in fostering more competent forms of political governance, particularly given the perspective of theorists who seek to multiply institutional and discursive sites of contestation, dissensus, and transgression rather than seek (or expect) unity, dialogue, and consensus. Given that "rational" certainty is conceptualized as the enemy of political reason, the debates are directly relevant.

To briefly outline the issues that inform these recent debates in political theory, the relatively recent philosophical debate between Gadamer and Derrida is particularly useful.[38] Some of the distinctions between these two thinkers provide the setting for the more recent debate in political theory between Habermas and Chantal Mouffe. The debate between Gadamer and Derrida can be summarized as two different identity logics: Gadamer's logic is based on philosophical hermeneutics and Derrida's is based on critical linguistics. Put simply, Gadamer believes that dialogue, based upon good will, is the paradigmatic instance of human communication. Derrida, conversely, maintains that all forms of consensus are based upon exclusions (all identity is based on absence and difference). According to Derrida, dialogue is not the paradigmatic instance of human communication because Gadamer's "good will" does not exist in the vast majority of communicative instances. Instead of seeking dialogue and consensus through good will, therefore, Derrida argues for a conception of justice as an incessant personal and institutional vigilance to the exclusions necessarily created by identification processes.[39]

There is little doubt that Gadamer has thoroughly explained how interpretation (hence meaning making) is an incessant process whereby the horizon of the Self fuses with the horizon of the Other (thus he definitely contributes to the general thrust of contemporary identity philosophy and the de-centering of the intentional subject). In his famous *Truth and Method,* he discusses in depth how meaning making and identification is a "fusion of horizons" when the image, characterization, or sign/symbol (with the meaning ostensibly offered by it) "fuses" with the individual's own apprehension of it through their unique ideational and experiential horizon. A child from a ghetto, for example, would likely interpret a pastoral scene of a child playing in an expansive field before a farmhouse in a much different way than would a child from a farm. The message is the same; the interpretation is different. However, Gadamer's further insistence on the primacy of "good will" as a prerequisite for communication and his belief that the paradigmatic instance of human communication is dialogue, at least in his philosophical debate with Derrida, drifts too far away from the teachings of continental philosophy of the Nietzschean-Saussurian-Foucauldian variety.[40] According to these latter thinkers, identity requires difference, freedom requires constraint, and disciplinary practices, language games, professions, collective identities, and institutional settings all impose certain capacity-generating limits. In the general clash of these discursive-material practices, we find ourselves situated in economies from which there is no escape and in which we find ourselves incessant transgressors. Since capacity-generating disciplinary systems (*technes*), each designed for a particular object, punish those who transgress their rules, and since rules change from system to system and "right action" in one is "wrong action" in another, instead of dialogue motivated by good will as the paradigmatic instance of human communication we actually have Hobbes' war of all against all.

Indeed, one would be hard pressed to seriously maintain that the history of the world has been a history of dialogue or that the normal communication situation in the political realm is not saturated with power, unless one were prepared to argue that violence, or at least transgression, is a form of dialogue (or at least communication). And one might not be equally hard pressed to say that violence certainly "sends a message."

Militaries have been used throughout history, as have their weapons, to send messages ("let's drop the bomb!"). Institutional constraints also send messages. If a college student enters a classroom late or turns in a late paper he may be punished with a lower grade. If a doctor fails to properly diagnose a condition she can be sued for malpractice. If a husband fails to adequately communicate with his spouse he may end up divorced. If a soldier refuses to obey an order and "defend his nation" he will either be imprisoned or executed. There are "familial" language games, gender games, professional games, citizenship games, legal games, etc., in which we all find ourselves variously embedded, and whenever we wittingly or unwittingly "break the rules" we immediately find out about those rules. Our transgressions reveal the limits, and since limits should be available for critical reflection, transgression and conflict arguably serve positive political purposes.[41]

So, at least according to Gadamer's critics, violence sends a message as do the constraints imposed by social institutions, and the general mode of social interaction is based on conflict, not dialogue. For the individual subject, life unfolds on an ultimately "undecidable" terrain. Freedom, therefore, is not some magical extraction from the fabric of these texts, but is the ability to recognize and react to the constraints imposed by characterizations, institutions, and communities, and that ability can only be nurtured through acts of transgression and subversion coupled with a mastery of the persuasive arts. Paradoxically, the more transgression there is the more freedom there is, under certain conditions, and those conditions are clarified when one examines the classical notion of practical wisdom in tandem with contemporary political theory of the Derridian variety.

The principal relevance of this debate to postmodern conceptions of political wisdom is that Gadamer appears to put the cart before the horse. Good will is not something to be presupposed in political communication; instead, it is the hoped for outcome. The problems revolve around the articulation and institutionalization of the "common good" in ways that encourage transgression and dissensus. Arguably, Derrida's notion of "deconstructive justice" and Judith Butler's discussion of the incessant problem of the relationship between the particular and the universal are good places to begin. Admitting the logical tension between any kind of willed action and postmodern attention to the constraining systems in which we are hopelessly enmeshed, Derrida's notion of deconstructive justice suggests a logic that seeks articulations of identity and the institutions that support them in ways that maximize self-critique. Judith Butler's philosophical position on the construction of concepts of the "common good" resonates with Derrida's.[42] Butler concurs that the problem with all universalizing discourses (such as those that might seek to articulate a "common" good) is that they necessarily marginalize; therefore, it is only reasonable to construct identification practices and institutions in ways that maximize the incessant realization of that fact. Only through such a procedure can the possibility for good will be maximized, and this, then, is the "ethical norm" suggested by postmodernism.

Critical Political Theory and the Rhetorical *Phronimos*

As already noted, debates among contemporary political theorists in many ways mirror the debate between Gadamer and Derrida. Should theory work to build a "rational" consensus based on deliberative norms and procedural practices that will mitigate against the problems associated with identity construction and maximize the possibility for wise deliberation and dialogue (e.g. Habermas), or should theory help to diversify sites of contestation and transgression given that consensus within the political realm tends toward tyranny (e.g. Mouffe)? Political theorists such as Mouffe and Ernesto Laclau, and identity theorists (broadly conceived) ranging from Nietzsche to Slavoj Žižek, maintain that subversion is at the heart of constitution, absence and difference are at the heart of identity, and that the abstract and complex processes of identification in which we participate have direct and profound impacts on our sense of self, the way others read us, and our forms of community.[43] This "identity logic" leads to the conclusion that any consensus does a certain violence, creates an Other. Whenever we have absolute closure in our characterizations a "not what it is" or "not who we are" is being created, and constraining sets of institutional limits are imposed. To reveal the limit, therefore, not to achieve consensus, at least according to these theorists, should be the watchwords of any contemporary understanding of political wisdom.

But here again a return to Aristotle's notion of *phronesis* is useful, for we discover that if Descartes had read his Aristotle more carefully, if he read Aristotle at all, he might have saved social philosophy over two centuries of grief. The central question among many political theorists today remains whether or not universal rules can be determined to maximize the human good, or, for others, to what degree theoretical wisdom and practical wisdom can intertwine. Aristotle made it clear that timing, appropriateness, and a lack of certainty were part of practical wisdom; therefore, the certainty of the arts and sciences was not possible in the political world. And yet here do we not already have theoretical principles applied to the world of particulars (i.e. that timing, appropriateness, and a lack of certainty are universal dimensions of practical wisdom)? Perhaps there are other dimensions of theoretical wisdom that apply to the rhetorical *phronimos*.

As we have seen, Aristotle noted that *phronesis* operates in four realms: the realm of self-interest, the family realm, the institutional realm, and the realm of government. Furthermore, through his discussions of government and his familiarity with the wide variety of constitutions and governments in his own time, he further embodied the qualities of a *phronimos* in ways that can be applied to our own age. For example, it is a curious thing that the contemporary world defends democracy at all, for if we read Aristotle's *Politics* carefully the best government possible when "the many" govern is not democracy but polity.[44] As is well known, Aristotle claimed that kingships, aristocracies, and polities are good regimes because in each the government was primarily concerned with the common advantage. When these healthy forms of government decay, they tend to fall into tyrannies, oligarchies, or democracies. Tyranny occurs when an individual uses government to their personal advantage at the expense of the people. An oligarchy is when "those with property" hold power at the expense of the people, and a democracy is when the poor use government to the disadvantage of the propertied classes or when there is a tyranny of the majority.

So how can we combine Aristotle's notion of *phronesis* and his theory of government with critical political theories seeking to multiply sites of political contestation and institutionalized transgression? How might the world today look to Aristotle? Initially, it seems likely, given his obvious concern for probable knowledge and the arts associated with persuasion, that he would not take issue with the renewed interest in symbolic persuasion as the basis for personal and collective identity construction. Given his belief that polities were potentially problematic because "where more are concerned it is difficult for them to be proficient with a view to virtue as a whole,"[45] and given his belief that "self-interest" was the norm, not the exception, in the political realm, it is also reasonable to assume that he might side with Derrida.

And how might today's hegemonic form of government and our general political conditions appear to Aristotle within his four realms of practical wisdom? Today, might he not likely note that we are under a global corporate oligarchy and far from global polity, although every state prefers to call themselves a democracy?[46] The dominant ideology (or the dominant unquestioned philosophy of political economy) he would likely note is market ethics combined with liberal democracy. Being an expert on comparative governments, he would undoubtedly recognize that the present neo-liberal world philosophy is based on the belief that when interests are set against interests (i.e. when markets are created) then political freedoms will naturally follow.[47] Representative of this point of view is F.A. Hayek, who claimed that "competition... is the only method by which our activities can be adjusted to each other without coercive or arbitrary intervention of authority. Indeed, one of the main arguments in favor of competition is that it dispenses with the need for 'conscious social control.'"[48]

Aristotle would undoubtedly lament such a conclusion, given that there is no such thing as government without social control. He would not be so naïve as to believe that unrestrained self-interest alone could provide a sufficient basis for practical wisdom (Kant certainly understood this as well). As Aristotle noted in his *Ethics*, "[T]he end of political science is the supreme good; and political science is concerned with nothing so much as with producing a certain character in the citizens or in other words with making them good, and capable of performing noble actions."[49] So practical wisdom must be centrally concerned with virtuous character, but can that character be confined to self-interest? No. According to Aristotle, "One species of knowledge then is the knowledge of one's own interests... yet it is perhaps impossible for a person to seek his own good successfully without domestic economy or statesmanship."[50] This is not to say that we can simply transplant Aristotle into our current context, but to suggest ways in which his theory of practical wisdom might be appropriately modified to become a more contemporary conception of political wisdom.

Identity Construction and Political Wisdom

Here is an initial attempt at outlining of a postmodern form of political wisdom. First, our notions of virtuous character must derive from our theoretical wisdom concerning identity construction and the political realm. The identity logic of Nietzsche, Foucault, and Derrida is persuasive, and it has now been effectively argued that identification processes necessarily constrain and only potentially enable. The *phronimos* must be practical and not expect rationality in the political realm, and the "art of the self" must be based on an eternal vigilance about the limits necessarily imposed by processes of identification. Second, in contemporary "market democracies" civic virtue is rarely a concern of institutional actors and oftentimes public deliberation occurs between corporate, government, and non-government actors representing competing interests and having different premises who compromise through a process of confrontation and transgression. Here we have a world of professions and sciences without *phronesis*. Within such a political milieu, whose ultimate logic is one of self-interest, the individual is subject to all of the constraints imposed by the available roles within those fundamentally dramatic and political situations (political in the sense that power is at work within the drama and the "wrong move," quite separate from any notions of "virtuous character," can have very concrete negative consequences—e.g. loss of job, excommunication, etc.). We have to be practical: in the human realm of political action any abstract notion of virtuous character and right action must be tempered by the constraints imposed by the particular discursive/institutional regime imposed on the actor at the time.

Third, the politically wise individual would also be concerned about any threats to political pluralism on both the local, national, and international levels. The rise of multinational corporations and multinational government organizations are at the forefront, for example, of a general trend that is transforming the landscape of government and replacing deliberative democracy with executive democracy. Organizations such as the World Trade Organization now have non-elected judges and unrepresentative internal court systems that adjudicate between competing states when conflicts arise.[51] When the WTO court renders a judgment against a particular country then that country must either change their policies or suffer economic and political consequences. To join the WTO, or to receive financial assistance from the World Bank, the International Monetary Fund, or international development banks, countries must oftentimes agree to "structural adjustments." These structural adjustments are guided by very clear meta-institutional characterizations guided by the market logic of corporate self-interest. New forms of supra-national governance are beginning to emerge, what some have variously referred to as global constitutionalism or cosmopolitan citizenship, and the characterizations that presently govern those forms of governance are not following the dictates of political wisdom, nor the warning of political theorists throughout the ages. Those in charge of these policies have clearly not read their Kant! If anything, we are moving away from managed antagonism and toward neo-liberal monologue, and the contemporary *phronimos* must be not only be concerned with such developments but act, within the logic of incessant identity critique, upon those concerns.

Arguably, then, there are profound connections between processes of identification, rhetorical praxis, and community building. Characterizations are provided through arguments and narratives that present the world in a particular way, and individuals act within and upon their world according to the particular way in which they experience and act upon those characterizations. The only way to intervene in such a world is through the persuasive arts. Clearly, different characterizations and different interpretations of characterizations are the stuff of the world of human meaning. Clearly, different material conditions compel individuals to focus on different characterizations that tend to best express the truth of their condition (whether consciously or not). Clearly, different kinds of political institutions and different sets of expectations by individuals within those institutions directly impact the material conditions in which people live. Characterizations, institutions, and communities are all intimately woven together to form the general economy of our world.

Our day-to-day interactions with people, with institutions, and with state systems are thoroughly rhetorical. We may try to "stay out of politics," but really that is hardly possible. Every characterization and every choice that we make follows from a rhetorical realism. At bottom, then, the politically wise person, like Socrates, must recognize that they are not wise, but are surrounded by people who think they are wise. Indeed, they may be technically wise, or artfully wise, but few are able to artfully and virtuously negotiate among the self-interested. And what, then, does it mean to negotiate virtuously? On the one hand it means not to impose an essentialist identity on the Other, but on the other hand to expect to be essentialized by others. It also means to attempt to create institutional infrastructures that recognize and respond to the universal principles inherent in the process of identification. The question of social intervention, then, becomes the degree to which one will tolerate that lack of wisdom in others, the failures of our current political institutions, and the price they are willing to pay for pointing it out.

In our contemporary world, with its various mass media sending out transversal messages in unprecedented volumes, the politically wise also have to consider the consequences of "nation building" and corporate "global constitutionalism" for this constitutes our present and our future. The politically wise will understand the political consequences of these fictions and will intervene, according to their bravery, to ensure those fictions are productive ones whose supporting institutions recognize the permanent dangers residing in the capacity/constraint dynamic with all identification processes.

Within such a framework good will, empathy, and openness to the Other are not considered the norm, but, as Mouffe has pointed out, "social relations and identities are always constructed through asymmetrical forms of power."[52] But perhaps, in the practically wise performance, Rhetoric and Dialectic, aware of certain blindnesses in the confidences of Governance, aid the fair *Phronesis* (whose virtuous character and wise deliberative process maximally guarantees peace and justice in the state and virtue among the citizens) in artfully persuading rash Governance (who never leaves the stage) to right action.

If the political is conceived as a realm in which self-interested individuals/groups "manage" ideational and material economies so as to maximize power for themselves or their group (and that group is not universal), then there is no hope for wise politics. If executive power is incessantly checked by representative power, if global economic and political power is maximally checked by local economic and political power, and if the political is conceived as a realm in which communication, law, economic policy, and military policy are coordinated to institutionalize principles of universal justice and maximally problematize assumed certainties, then there is hope.

NOTES

1. Xenophon, "Apology of Socrates to the Jury," Trans. Andrew Patch. *The Shorter Socratic Writings.* Ed. Robert C. Bartlett (Ithaca, NY: Cornell University Press, 1996), 9-17. Plato, *The Collected Dialogues of Plato.* Eds. Edith Hamilton and Huntington Cairns (Princeton, NJ: Princeton University Press, 1961), 3-26. Contemporary scholars disagree as to the political and philosophical import of Socrates, with accounts ranging from I.F. Stone's critical assessment in *The Trial of Socrates* (New York, NY: Doubleday, 1989) to Dana Villa's positive assessment in *Socratic Citizenship* (Princeton, NJ: Princeton University Press, 2001). Here, I lean more favorably to Villa's account, focusing more on Socrates' "negative dialectic" than on Plato's Socrates.

2. Here, the term "rational" refers to the classical liberal conviction that individuals are autonomous and capable of both social certainty and objective interpretations. See "The Rational and the Reasonable." *The New Rhetoric and the Humanities: Essays on Rhetoric and Its Applications.* Ed. Chaim Perelman (Boston: Reidel Publishing Company, 1979). The terms rational and reasonable should not be confused (although they usually are). Rationality refers to universal truth and theoretical wisdom (that which is always true), while reason refers to the probable truth (that which is usually true) and "practical" wisdom.

3. Rene Descartes argued that if two people disagreed then one must clearly be wrong and that the one who is right does not understand the truth sufficiently to correct the one who is wrong. See "Rules for the Direction of the Mind." *The Philosophical Works of Descartes*, Volume 1. Trans. E.S. Haldane and G.R.T Ross (Cambridge: Cambridge University Press, 1931), p. 3. This principle of "one rational truth" disregards the idea of *phronesis* altogether, since in the realm of rhetoric different people/groups can be

equally "correct" given their respective values and interests. As we shall see, Descartes' insistence on a universal rationality confuses Aristotle's distinction between theoretical and practical wisdom.

4. For Kant's criteria for wise government, see Immanuel Kant. *Political Writings*. Ed. Hans Reiss (New York, NY: Cambridge University Press, 1991). His essays "Idea for a University History with a Cosmopolitan Purpose" and "Perpetual Peace" are particularly to the point. For Dewey's position on wise government, see John Dewey. *The Public and its Problems*. (Athens, OH: Ohio University Press, 1954).

5. This is not meant as a condemnation. Arguably all political theory is symptomatic: a reaction to an "unjust" contagion and an attempt to "cure" the disease of the political (if conceived in the Hobbesian sense as the incessant war of self and group interest).

6. Marx, Karl. *The Economic and Philosophic Manuscripts of 1844*. Ed. Dirk J. Struik (New York: International Publishers, 1964).

7. Freud, Sigmund. *Civilization and Its Discontents*. Trans. Jams Strachey (New York: W.W. Norton, 1989).

8. Nietzsche, Friedrich. "On Truth and Lie in an Extra-Moral Sense." *Philosophy and Truth: Selections From Nietzsche's Notebooks of the Early 1870s*. Trans. and ed. Daniel Breazeale (Atlantic Highlands, NJ: Humanities Press, 1979); *On the Advantage and Disadvantage of History for Life* (Indianapolis: Hacket, 1980).

9. De Saussure, Ferdinand, *Course in General Linguistics* (New York: McGraw-Hill, 1966).

10. Foucault, Michel. *Birth of the Clinic*. Trans. A. Sheridan (New York: Vintage Books, 1973); *Discipline and Punish* (New York: Vintage Books, 1979); "The Subject and Power." *Michel Foucault: Beyond Structuralism and Hermeneutics*. 2nd Edition. Eds. Hubert L. Dreyfus and Paul Rabinow (Chicago: The University of Chicago Press, 1983): 208-226.

11. Derrida, Jacques. "Structure, Sign and Play in the Discourse of the Human Sciences." Reprinted in *Critical Theory Since 1965*. Eds. Hazard Adams and Leroy Searle (Tallahasee: University Press of Florida, 1986): 77-96.

12. Gadamer, Hans-Georg. *Truth and Method*. Trans. Joel Weinsheimer and Donald G. Marshall (New York: Continuum, 1993).

13. For articulations of what those conditions might be, see Mouffe, Chantal. "Democratic Politics and the Question of Identity." *The Identity in Question*. Ed. John Rajchman (New York: Routledge, 1995), 33-45; Laclau, Ernesto. "Universalism, Particularism, and the Question of Identity." *The Identity in Question*. Ed. John Rajchman (New York: Routledge, 1995), 93-108.

14. Processes of identification occur in communication, since "subjectivity" is co-constructed. Rhetoric and dialectic, therefore, is the beginning and end of politics.

15. Aristotle, *The Nichomachian Ethics*, trans. J.E.C. Welldon (Buffalo, New York: Prometheus Books, 1987), 197.

16. Villa, *Socratic Citizenship*, 53.

17. Aristotle, *Ethics*,189.

18. Aristotle, *Ethics*, 206.

19. Aristotle, *Ethics*, 199-208.

20. Garver, Eugene. *Machiavelli and the History of Prudence* (Madison: The University of Wisconsin Press, 1987), 8.

21. Geldard, Richard G. *Remembering Heraclitus* (Herndon, VA: Lindisfarne Books, 2000), 46.

22. Geldard, 32.

23. Perelman, Chaim. *The Realm of Rhetoric* (Notre Dame, IN: University of Notre Dame Press, 1982), 162.

24. Aristotle. *Rhetoric*. Trans. Lane Cooper (Englewood Cliffs, NJ: Prentice Hall), 1355b8; Kennedy, George. *The Art of Persuasion in Greece* (Princeton: Princeton University Press, 1963), 18-19; Warnick, Barbara. "Judgment, Probability, and Aristotle's *Rhetoric*." *Quarterly Journal of Speech* 75 (1989), 305.

25. Aristotle, *Ethics*, 210.

26. Aristotle, *Ethics, 25*.

27. Aristotle, *Ethics,* 186.

28. Warnick, 306.

29. Aristotle, *Rhetoric*, 1-7.

30. According to Aristotle, "it is the office of Dialectic to discern the true, and also the sham, syllogism" (*Rhetoric*, 7).

31. Jürgen Habermas has made a philosophical career out of identifying obstacles to wise deliberation and has worked to formulate an "ideal speech situation" where the effects of power within any deliberative forum are minimized. See, for example, *The Theory of Communicative Action*. Trans. T. McCarthy (Boston: Beacon Press, 1981); and *Toward a Rational Society*. Trans. J.J. Shapiro (London: Heinemann, 1971).

32. There are of course rhetorical dimensions related to all forms of knowledge, as testified to by the extensive work on the rhetoric of science.

33. Of course, for Aristotle the "common" good related only to the polis, whereas a postmodern form of political wisdom would understand the common good in global terms. However, it is the very difficulty of having "universals," let alone applying them to particular cases, that is at the heart of the project of postmodern political wisdom.

34. Kenneth Burke does a masterful job discussing how human life is a thoroughly rhetorical drama. See *A Grammar of Motives* (Los Angeles, CA: University of California Press, 1969); "A Dramatistic View of the Origins of Language," in *Language as Symbolic Action: Essays on Life, Literature, and Method* (Los Angeles: The University of California Press, 1966), 419-479.

35. For a useful introduction to collective identity construction as it applies to political community formation, see Anderson, Benedict. *Imagined Communities* (New York: Verso, 1991).

36. Kahler, Erich. *The Tower and the Abyss* (New Brunswick, NJ: Transaction Publishers, 1989), 7.

37. Hall, Rodney H. *National Collective Identity: Social Constructs and International Systems* (New York: Columbia University Press, 1999), 26-27.

38. This brief review is not intended as a full explication of the many complicated issues debated by these philosophers, but instead is designed merely to point out issues relevant to this essay. An extended analysis of their debate is provided in *Dialogue and Deconstruction: The Gadamer-Derrida Encounter*. Eds. Diane P. Michelfelder and Richard E. Palmer (Albany, NY: State University of New York Press, 1989).

39. Derrida's notion of deconstructive justice is discussed in detail, and defended by Derrida, in *Deconstruction and Pragmatism*. Ed. Chantal Mouffe (New York: Routledge, 1996).

40. For example, Gadamer asserts that "for a written conversation basically the same fundamental condition obtains as for an oral exchange. Both partners must have the good will to try to understand one another" (*Dialogue and Deconstruction*, 33).

41. Immanuel Kant understood the social value of managed antagonism and discussed its political import in his essays "Ideas for a Universal History with a Cosmopolitan Purpose" and "Perpetual Peace." Both essays can be found in Kant's *Political Writings*. Ed. Hans Reiss (Cambridge, UK: Cambridge University Press, 1970).

42. Butler, Judith. "Universality in Culture." *For Love of Country?* Ed. Martha C. Nussbaum (Boston, MA: Beacon Press, 1996).

43. Nietzsche, Friedrich. "On Truth and Lie"; Laclau, Ernesto, and Chantal Mouffe. *Hegemony and Socialist Strategy: Towards a Radical Democratic Politics* (New York: Verso, 1985); Connolly, William. *Identity/Difference: Democratic Negotiations of Political Paradox*. Ithaca: Cornell University Press, 1991); Haber, Honi Fern. *Beyond Postmodern Politics: Lyotard, Rorty, Foucault* (New York: Routledge, 1994); Simons, Jon. *Foucault and the Political*. New York: Routledge, 1995; Mouffe, Chantal. *The Democratic Paradox* (New York: Verso, 2000); Torfing, Jacob. *New Theories of Discourse: Laclau, Mouffe, and Žižek* (Malden, MA: Blackwell Publishers, 1999).

44. Aristotle. *Politics*. Trans. Carnes Lord (Chicago: The University of Chicago Press, 1984), 94-96.

45. Aristotle, *Politics*, 96.

46. Dunn, John, *Western Political Theory in the Face of the Future* (New York: Cambridge University Press, 1979), 12.

47. For a helpful discussion of the history of the idea of competitive capitalism, see Albert O. Hirschman. *The Passions and the Interests: Political Arguments for Capitalism before Its Triumph* (Princeton, NJ: Princeton University Press, 1977).

48. Hayek, F.A. *The Road to Serfdom*. Chicago: The University of Chicago Press, 1944), 41-42.

49. Aristotle, *Nichomachean Ethics*, 30.

50. Aristotle, *Ethics*, 197-198.

51. For an "insider" assessment of the development of global courts see Jackson, John H. "Designing and Implementing Effective Dispute Settlement Procedures: WTO Dispute Settlement, Appraisal and Prospects." *The WTO as an International Organization*. Anne Kreuger, ed. (Chicago: The University of Chicago Press, 1998). For a critical assessment see Wallach, Lori, and Michelle Sforze. *The WTO: Five Years of Reasons to Resist Corporate Globalization* (New York: Seven Stories Press, 1999).

52. Mouffe, *Democratic Politics*, 33.

Power and Force in Argumentation:
A Dialogic Response

*Christopher W. Tindale**

Abstract

This paper looks first at how power and force have been traditionally under-stood in argumentation, with the accompanying notions of 'arguer,' 'audi-ence,' and 'conflict'. It then turns attention to the development of a model of argumentation, drawn principally from some of Mikhail Bakhtin's theory of communication, in which such matters are considerably redefined. In par-ticular, the model of argumentation that emerges redistributes power within the argumentative situation in ways that promote cooperative interaction and aim at achieving agreement (rather than simple resolution). The paper builds its case around dual analyses (traditional and dialogical) of two texts, one drawn from one of Socrates' dialogues, and the other a 2001 speech of President Bush.

PART I: Power and Force in Argumentation

There are many reasons why we argue, but we do not always share a similar appreciation for the many ways in which we argue and the cor-responding differences in how arguing itself is conceived. Since the early work of scholars like Lakoff and Johnson (1980) drew attention to the aggressive nature of much argumentative language, others have come to see this as a consequence of the aggressive model of argument that dominated the tradition. That model is still there exerting its influ-ence, and its vestiges still appear in the language and strategies used by argumentation theorists, whether it be the protagonists and antagonists of critical discussions (van Eemeren & Grootendorst, 2004, p. 120); or the courtroom advocacy reflected in the challengers and defenders of the Toulmin model (Toulmin, 2003, p. 12). But we also have a range of more constructive accounts of argumentation that stress community and cooperation, and debates about the relative merits and values of these approaches. It is into this discussion that I wish to introduce a further alternative, cooperative model, one drawn from the work of Mikhail Bakhtin. This work is characterized by its central idea of dialogism.

What I intend to show is how that idea offers a model of argumentation richer and more dynamic than what we might otherwise associate with the dialogical. Central to this model of argumentation, and hence to this discussion, is its transformative power—of the argumentative situation, of the audience/participant, and, most importantly, of the arguer.

By way of entering the topic, I will examine ways in which power and authority are expressed and distributed in various models of argumentation, from the traditional to the modern. In the first half of the paper, I examine something of the traditional story and offer some examples that can be read as illustrating it. In the second half, I turn to the Bakhtinian material and then offer re-readings of the same examples to illustrate some of the points that have emerged.

1. The Appeal to Force

In May of 2002, as Israeli forces massed on the Israeli side of the border with Gaza in response to another Palestinian suicide attack inside Israel, Mohammed Dahlan, the head of the main Palestinian security force in the Gaza Strip, was reported as saying: "Everyone is prepared, and our people know how to confront the occupation…We said this before, and we mean it now: If the occupation forces carry out aggression, they will face aggression" (*Globe and Mail*, May 10, 2002, A12).

Israeli Prime Minister Ariel Sharon's earlier response to the same suicide bombing was reported as "He who rises up to kill us, we will pre-empt and kill him first" (*Globe and Mail*, May 8, 2002).

These are harsh words, and both sets of utterances can be construed as examples of argumentation. Both can be structured to show the scheme and intent of the traditional *argumentum ad baculum*, or the 'Appeal to Force'.

A clearer, and less volatile example, is that conveyed on buttons worn by students in Ontario recently: 'I support a tuition freeze. And I vote'. Implicit in the second statement is a threat; implicit in the first is a demand. The argument scheme 'Appeal to Force' occurs when force, or the threat of force, or a threat of some nature, is used in a confrontation. The name *argumentum ad baculum* alludes to the use of a stick, or club, to beat someone, and in the argument, the action threatened is the figurative club.

Most accounts treat instances of this argument as fallacious, since it adopts an illegitimate course of threats in place of legitimate rational persuasion. Fallacy theorists, however, debate whether all its instances should be judged fallacious. Its pervasiveness in our world, from the coercions of children to the maneuverings of nuclear deterrence, require that we take it seriously and suggest that it may, even if only in dilemmas, have acceptable instances. It is at least a phenomenon that has to be reckoned with and that exposes a kind of argumentative power.

Of course, beating someone with a stick is not exactly an argument (Woods, 1995) and, hence, some are loath to call it even a fallacy (insofar as fallacies are seen as flawed arguments). However, expressed in words, a threat can have the structure of an argument (with premises in support of a claim), and it remains only to be clear about the nature of the claims involved and the intent of the argument. (Arguments can serve for inquiry, for justification, for persuasion, among other uses). A threat or warning can change behaviour in ways that show recognition of the arguer's position and a belief that he or she means what has been said.

Take the less volatile of the examples: 'I support a tuition freeze. And I vote'. On one level the expresser (or wearer) of this point of view is simply stating two things about themselves.[1] Yet in the context (and this is always crucial) of a belief that a government is considering removing a freeze on university tuitions and allowing institutions to set their own fees, or simply allowing a set annual increase to continue, then this discourse can be seen to challenge such proposals with a claim and reason for that claim. The aim of the discourse is to influence the government's behavior (if not its belief pattern—if governments can have beliefs).

Claim—Do not allow tuitions to increase (freeze them).

Reason—A tuition freeze is supported by people who vote.

Implicit in the reason is the threat that if the government acts otherwise than is suggested, they risk their current position. Implicit also is the assertion that the arguer has power—that of the vote: 'You don't want to anger voters'. If government officials take the threat seriously (and that would depend on the number of voters involved, relative support for the proposal, current patterns of popularity, etc.), then they will see the reason as one relevant for holding the claim. Simply put, as this *ad baculum* is reasoned out contextually, it may well be seen as a legitimate instance of the argument scheme. On this level, the argument works as a particular kind of interaction predicated on the power relation involved (O'Keefe, 1982, p. 3-4). Still, it is difficult to shed a sense of impending violence from the use of this argumentative strategy, particularly as we see it in the first examples, and this influences the way we view the *ad baculum* generally. If we are to propose alternative ways of conceiving argument, we must also suggest alternative ways for dealing with argument schemes like this. I will return to this prospect at the end of the paper.

2. Argument as War: A Problematic Metaphor

Argumentation, then, can serve to express the particular types of social or relational power that individuals or groups hold. The argument scheme above is a vehicle specifically suited for conveying this. But more generally, argumentation *itself* as an activity can be seen to involve force and aggression, which may in turn be perceived as power over situations and those involved.

Recent critiques of argumentation have drawn attention to how it seems saturated by what is called the 'Argument as War' metaphor (Berrill, 1996; Palczewski, 1996; Cohen, 1995)[2]. This is illustrated both in the terminology by which arguing is described, and the aims that are professed for it. For example, positions are attacked and defended (and participants assume the appropriate postures); one's argument can be 'shot down', 'torn apart', 'destroyed' by an 'assault' of reason, and we could go on. Robin Smith, in the introduction to his recent translation of Aristotle's *Topics* (1997), while himself adopting the metaphor of sport ('This is obviously a kind of sport, a form of dialectic reduced to a competitive game'—Smith, 1997, p. xx), goes so far as to compare this form of dialectical argumentation with fencing and sword-fighting. Just as the sport of fencing prepares an individual for the real thing (in a society in which real sword-fighting takes place), so 'gymnastic' argumentation prepares a person for good dialectical practice (Smith, 1997, p. xx-xxi). It stands out, though, that the correlate of good dialectical practice in the analogy is 'real and deadly swordplay'. Of course, dialectical argumentation is but one variety, and Aristotle's model in the *Topics* but one variety of that. Still, the point stands that the very language in which argumentation has traditionally been conducted is a language of force and power. Insofar as much of our understanding of argument structure and process will derive from the metaphors by which it is communicated (Fulkerson, 1996), then this tradition is a serious impediment to more cooperative ways of thinking about argumentation.

Likewise, if we consider the aims: Setting aside argumentation that is directed at inquiry, most conceptions are connected to the notions of winning (and hence losing).[3] In such models, the arguer looks to impose an idea upon an audience or partner in dialogue, and that is seen by many to involve an imbalanced power relation. The beliefs of one are imposed upon another. More neutrally, a defender of the process might suggest that that other comes to see the merits of the argument. In fairness, though, this seems to ignore the agency of the arguer and the many devices or strategies that he or she has to bring about their desired outcome. The basic model of persuasion seems to suggest coercion. In many critiques, the adversarial model of argumentation becomes synonymous with the 'conquest/conversion model of interaction' (Gearhart, 1979, p. 202). Any attempt to persuade is judged an act of violence, and since argumentation is viewed as the means of persuasion, it in turn becomes a vehicle for violence.[4]

Beyond language and intent, Palczewski (1996) argues further that the metaphors used to describe arguments are built into the theoretical approaches by which argument is understood (p. 164). That is, not only is argumentation seen as aggressive in its language and effect but the ways we have developed of understanding it and developing theories about it are still framed within the constraints of that metaphor. Even a perspective as innovative as pragma-dialectics, for example, still sets a protagonist against an antagonist in the stages of a critical discussion (van Eemeren and Grootendorst, 1992, p. 35; 2004, p. 120). The metaphor, then, can pervade all aspects of our thinking about and working with argumentation.

3. The 'Arguer' as a Position of Power

In the account so far given, in this traditional understanding of how much argumentation works (particularly interactive argumentation), it is not difficult to see a specific conception of what an 'arguer' is, although we may rarely reflect upon this role.

The role of the arguer as so conceived fits a basic notion of intentionality wherein the author of a discourse knows what he or she wants to say, organizes that discourse and communicates it to another, whether a single partner in dialogue or a larger audience. We can even imagine this working for monological texts, constructed without an explicitly imagined dialogical partner. Here, then, the arguer is quite simply the source of the argument, and therefore has full control over what is said, why it is said, and how it is said (perhaps not where it is said, though). This is a source, then, of a kind of power: The power over meaning and interpretation, for example. If a term or phrase is unclear, we expect that the arguer is the one who can clarify that meaning; who, knowing her or his own mind, can express it. The audience passively receives and, on a basic level, accepts (perhaps not the conclusion, but the argument as given). If an objector raises a potentially damaging point, if the arguer risks losing some control, then that arguer can shift things by saying, 'No, that's not what I intended', and has the authority to do so. He or she thereby regains control over the discourse.

In this sense, the arguer has a close parallel in the 'expert', the one who has authoritative knowledge. When we accede to someone whose authoritative knowledge we recognize, we invoke what John Locke called an *argumentum ad veracundiam*. Nowadays, this appears as the argument from authority. In Locke's original sense, the appeal was to a person's own modesty (*veracundiam*) in the face of one who owns respect. But in the arguer's case the authority is a fiction and the respect (at least on this ground) unfounded. The idea of an all-knowing arguer completely in control over the meanings involved is a fiction, one that fails to grasp the way arguments emerge in the ebb and flow of contexts that far exceed the control of any of the participants.

4. Illustrations of Traditional Analysis

Two examples will help us to see this model at work. The first is dialogical, and by this I simply mean that we have a dialogue between two individuals (in contrast to the way I will develop this below); the second is monological, one voice speaking, and comes from one of George W. Bush's speeches. Neither example is overtly adversarial, but both reflect features and assumptions of the traditional model I have been considering.

4.1: Example #1: Socrates and Euthyphro

The first example comes from the dialogue Plato presents between Socrates and Euthyphro. It will be familiar to many, although the details of the dialogue (what they are talking, and at times arguing, about) is not important; we are interested in the moves made by the two participants as power shifts between them.

Socrates and Euthyphro both have an interest in how the idea of piety or holiness is to be understood (since Socrates is being prosecuted for this, and Euthyphro, an alleged expert on the idea and on matters of the gods generally, is prosecuting his own father and thereby risks himself acting impiously if he is wrong in his prosecution). It is fortuitous that Socrates should have found an interlocutor who claims to know what Socrates himself needs to know, and so he is happy to have Euthyphro tell him what piety is. It should be a simple matter: the expert who is the source of wisdom on this matter simply needs to say what he knows: 'I should be of no use to Socrates, and Euthyphro would be no different from other men, if I did not have exact knowledge about such things' (4e-5a).

Having agreed with Socrates that piety, or holiness, will always be the same in every action, Euthyphro proceeds to explain what it is: 'I say that holiness is doing what I am doing now, prosecuting the wrong-doer who commits murder or steals from the temples or does any such thing, whether he be your father or your mother or anyone else, and not prosecuting him is unholy' (6d-e). As a 'sure proof' for this claim, that is, as a reason in support of it, he offers the example of Zeus, who put his father in bonds because he devoured his children.

Socrates, in turn, doubts both the reason and the claim. However, he can accept the reason—from stories about the gods—if Euthyphro says such things are the case. Euthyphro is the expert, after all. (This illustrates both Locke's original sense and our modern idea of the *argumentum ad verecundiam*— Socrates feels modesty in acknowledging Euthyphro's authority as a reason for believing something.) What Socrates cannot accept is the conclusion, because it is not what was asked for: Euthyphro has presented examples of holiness, when what was requested was the standard, or definition, by which he can recognize such things as being holy (6d).

Now the dialogue has shifted to a different level. Euthyphro finds himself in a situation where he must defend his point of view, rather than simply dispensing wisdom. He is beginning to lose control over the direction of the discourse. He tries again: '[W]hat is dear to the gods is holy, and what is not dear to them is unholy' (6e-7a), and he agrees to show that what he says is true. Yet, this he cannot do, because they have agreed that the gods quarrel, and so what is dear to some may not be dear to others, particularly on an issue like this. When asked what proof he has that what he is doing is an act of which the gods will approve, he responds:

> Euthyphro: 'But perhaps this is no small task, Socrates; although I could show you quite clearly'.

Socrates: 'I understand; it is because you think I am slower than the judges; since it is plain that you will show them that such acts [like the killing of which he has accused his father] are wrong and that all the gods hate them'.

Euthyphro: 'Quite clearly, Socrates; that is, if they listen to me'. (9b).

Euthyphro has retained his confidence, but is soon to lose it. Socrates points out that what amounts to their revised definition (what all the gods love is holy) still does not give them what they want. He shows this by raising a pivotal question (it is pivotal because it is about to shift the discussion out of Euthyphro's domain of expertise and so quite beyond his control). Socrates asks, 'Is that which is holy loved by the gods because it is holy, or is it holy because it is loved by the gods?' (10a). To which Euthyphro naturally responds: 'I don't know what you mean, Socrates'. To which the latter retorts: 'Then I will try to speak more clearly...' Essentially, the power has shifted to Socrates at this point. Euthyphro's failure to defend his claims, to know his own mind, has led him to lose control over the dialogue.

Socrates' answer to the question just posed, put succinctly, is that the gods love the holy because it is holy and not that it is holy because they love it. That is, the gods are not the source of the holy, but they recognize it for what it is and love it. Thus, in this respect they are on par with humans, and Euthyphro's expertise (restricted to knowledge of the gods) has been surpassed. He has lost his status within the dialogue.

Socrates, we might imagine, is well aware of this. Still, he persists: 'But tell me frankly, what is holiness, and what is unholiness?' (11b). To which Euthyphro famously responds:

'But Socrates, I do not know how to say what I mean. For whatever statement we advance, somehow or other it moves about and won't stay where we put it.'

Nothing could more suggest that Euthyphro has lost control over this discourse: his statements have run away from him. This is emphasized in the exploration of a final attempted definition, ostensibly conducted by Euthyphro but now directed by Socrates who has assumed control of the discussion, where the investigation leads them back to the (failed) definition that they have just left. Lost in this labyrinth of words, Euthyphro has nowhere left to turn, except away from the discussion.

This interpretation of the dialectical exchange between Socrates and Euthyphro makes very traditional assumptions[5]: that the source of a position is the best person to know and explain that position; that one ought to be able to provide reasons for one's position; that there are, as it were, separate roles in a discourse of this type, quite distinct from each other; and that while the participants might change roles, they do so completely (moving from knowing to unknowing; from control to no control). While the dialogue presents a picture of two people cooperating on a venture, that cooperation is less than clear to both parties and, ostensibly, unsuccessful. They do not see themselves working together and the dialogue has more in common with the adversarial model.

4.2: Example #2: Bush Speaks to the Nation

My second example appears to be of the more monological type and involves a speech of President George W. Bush regarding military strikes against Afghanistan, and presented to the nation on Sunday October 7, 2001.[6] It follows the commencement of those strikes.

The opening paragraphs of the speech give a simple what, who, and why. He starts with a statement of power and authority by explaining that, on his orders, the United States military had begun strikes against Al Qaeda terrorist training camps and military installations of the Taliban regime in Afghanistan. The reason he gives for this action is to disrupt the use of Afghanistan as a terrorist base of operations and to attack the military capability of the Taliban regime.

The 'Who' consists of a number of 'friends', as cumulative support for the claim: 'We are supported by the collective will of the world'. And the 'Why' is effectively presented in the form of an 'Appeal to Force' that had failed to be effective: 'More than two weeks ago, I gave Taliban leaders a series of clear and specific demands: Close terrorist training camps. Hand over leaders of the Al Qaeda network. And return all foreign nationals, including American citizens, unjustly detained in their country. None of these demands was met. And now, the Taliban will pay a price'.

It seems a feature of such appeals that if the threat is not acknowledged and the required action is not taken, the arguer feels the obligation to follow through with the force. That is, the argument commits the arguer to certain actions. Another Appeal to Force is seen later, along with the argument scheme known as 'Guilt by Association': 'Every nation has a choice to make. In this conflict, there is no neutral ground. If any government sponsors the outlaws and killers of innocents, they have become outlaws and murderers themselves. And they will take that lonely path at their own peril'.

The charge that by sponsoring outlaws and killers one *becomes* such is a particularly forceful bit of construction. Descriptively, the claim would seem to be incorrect. So we must understand this as stipulative: they will become outlaws and killers in the eyes of the arguer, and will be dealt with accordingly.

This demonstrates a power to control meanings, to decide who will qualify under different categories. We see it elsewhere in the speech in the general determinations of who will count as 'friends', who as 'enemies'.

The remainder of the piece consists of various explanations and justifications, along with supporting information. He is aware of his audience, as we see through the rhetorical use of patriotic appeals and demonizing of the enemy, and the creation of himself as a figure of justice and peace (in contrast to those who oppose him). An emotional appeal is made near the end, when Bush relates a letter from a young girl with a father in the military. The fourth-grader's willingness to 'give him' to Bush adds to his overall case that the action is just and justified and supported.

Not only does his speech demonstrate control, but it is designed to do so manifestly: that is, he is seen in control of events. This, too, should reassure his audience.

Again, the argumentation appears to be cooperative: he is addressing people with whom he wishes to cooperate, or who he wishes to cooperate with him. Yet like those of Socrates and Euthyphro, these are, what we might call, 'isolated co-operations', they do not explicitly work together. To this end, Bush's argumentation is still recognizably the adversarial argumentation of winners and losers. It is a very forceful piece, well-organized and well-controlled, with the arguer clearly in control and arguing from a position of power.

Yet in both these pieces of text I think there is much more happening. At a deeper level, there are important types of cooperation taking place.[7] And I want to discuss these now by turning to what I call the 'dialogical' level.

PART II: A Dialogic Response

5. *The Dialogic*

Earlier in the paper I referred to the 'dialogic' simply as a synonym for the dialectical, for argumentation that involves a dialogue, either explicitly or implicitly. I now want to revise that meaning considerably.[8]

The term 'dialogic' is widely used in the literature to capture a variety of quite distinct ideas, from a way to rethink how we read (Hunt, 1996) to the dialogues that take place, or "dialogic student exchanges," in the classroom (Mitchell, 2000, p.142). In her empirical study of how well people use the skills of argument Deanna Kuhn describes her approach as dialogic, defining it as: '[A] dialogue between two people who hold opposing views. Each offers justification for his or her own view; in addition (at least in skilled argument), each rebuts the other's view by means of counterargument' (Kuhn, 1991, p. 12). This can certainly be taken as a minimal sense of the idea as it relates to argumentation, but it is still closer to a traditional model than what I wish to propose, and it fails to give us a clear way of dealing with the implicit dialogues of monological arguments (like Bush's). Likewise, although there has been a recent interest by argumentation theorists in aspects of 'dialogue' or 'dialectics', with attention paid to the two-sidedness or turn-taking nature of argumentation, this still leaves something to be desired. Douglas Walton's (1996, pp. 40-1) centralizing of 'dialogue' in his pragmatic account means that the dialogue provides the context that will determine the argument by virtue of telling us how the set of inferences or propositions at its core is being used. And Ralph Johnson (1996, p. 264) has focused on a dialectical tier that exists in relation to an underlying illative tier, which is the premise-conclusion part of the argument's structure. But still with these senses it is possible for dialogue-focused or dialectical argumentation to involve no more than an exchange of distanced, monological positions (perhaps through turn-taking, perhaps in whole), where each side presents its argument for acceptance or rejection (Shotter, 1997). If such were to become the standard understanding, the chance for a more genuinely interactive or 'involved' perspective might be lost. My concern here is aptly anticipated by Mikhail Bakhtin (1986) in his own judgment on dialectics: "Take a dialogue and remove the voices (the partitioning of voices), remove the intonations (emotional and individualizing ones), carve out abstract concepts of judgments from living words and responses, cram everything into one abstract consciousness—and that's how you get dialectics" (Bakhtin, 1986, p.147). The sense here is that the value of dialogue has been lost; it has been depersonalized, replaced with artificial and static concepts, and robbed of its essential sense of 'otherness'.

These insights are instructive, and I want to use many of what might be called Bakhtinian conceptions in reconsidering dialogical argumentation.[9] To this end, I will adopt several of the ideas that come through in Bakhtin's philosophy of language and theory of communication. In spite of having no explicit theory of argument, there is much in Bakhtin's work to contribute to an innovative model. I need first to prepare the ground by discussing some of the basic ideas that are relevant to this enterprise.

6: Bakhtin's Terminology

When we think of the argument as a product with premises and conclusion, we focus on the sentences or propositions involved. As we have seen earlier, the tradition that harbors this model conceives the logical proposition in the case of the well-formed sentence as the basic linguistic unit. For Bakhtin, however, these sentences are impersonal; they tell us nothing about the relations between speakers or arguers. As the tools of the logician, they communicate *their* own relations, the relations of statements themselves as they are set out on the page. In contrast to this Bakhtin advocates the utterance as the basic linguistic act, where spoken utterances acquire their meaning only in a dialogue.

Mention of 'utterance' evokes the familiar work of the philosopher Paul Grice (1989), whose investigations of utterances and implicatures have had an enormous influence on the development of pragmatics. Part of the richness of his writing has to do with the developed distinction between what is said in an utterance, and what is implicated by it. Thus, a speaker may 'intend' several, integrated things by an utterance, creating a layering of meanings, and the success of communication lies in the degree to which a hearer captures and correctly unpacks those layers. As influential as it has been, Grice's work has also received criticism for its reliance on suggestions rather than detailed analysis, and for the most part, his work on implicatures was left largely incomplete (Blakemore, 1992, pp. 57-8). Bakhtin's approach to the 'utterance' is essentially different.

For one thing, the utterance gives us the boundaries between different speakers. The sentence cannot do this: "The boundaries of the sentence as a unit of language are never determined by a change of speaking subjects." (Bakhtin, 1986, p.73). Secondly, the sentence is not "correlated directly or personally with the extraverbal context of reality (situation, setting, pre-history) or with the utterances of other speakers" (Ibid.), and is quite unlike the utterance in this respect. Thirdly, and importantly, the sentence "has no capacity to determine directly the responsive position of the *other* speaker, that is, it cannot evoke a response" (Bakhtin, 1986, p. 74). This last point captures a key feature of the utterance: it is marked by "its quality of being directed to someone, its *addressivity*" (Bakhtin, 1986, p. 95). Hence, it is directed toward a response, and accommodates it in its very structure. The arguer deliberates over what is said because he or she anticipates having to defend it. An utterance, then, has essentially both an author and an addressee; it cannot exist in isolation.

Moreover, the utterance arises within the context of a particular situation. Or, to put it in Bakhtinian terms, the situation is a constitutive element of the utterance. The extraverbal does not influence the utterance from the outside. "On the contrary, *the situation enters into the utterance as a necessary constitutive element* of its semantic structure" (Todorov, 1984, p. 41).

So understood, 'utterance' can help us to appreciate how Bakhtin employs the term 'dialogism' and its related sense of the 'word'. Michael Holquist (1990) indicates that normally 'dialogue' suggests two people in conversation (as with Kuhn's usage, above), "[b]ut what gives dialogue its central place in dialogism is precisely the kind of *relation* conversations manifest, the conditions that must be met if any exchange between different speakers is to occur" (Holquist, 1990, p. 40). Bakhtin himself marveled at the way that linguistics and the philosophy of discourse had valued an artificial, pre-conditioned notion of the word, which was lifted out of context and taken as the norm. By contrast, "[t]he word is born in a dialogue as a living rejoinder within it; the word is shaped in dialogic interaction with an alien word that is already in the object" (Bakhtin, 1981, p. 279). In this dynamic conception the word finds its meaning. Bakhtin continues:

> But this does not exhaust the internal dialogism of the word. It encounters an alien word not only in the object itself: every word is directed toward an answer and cannot escape the profound influence of the answering word that it anticipates.
>
> The word in living conversation is directly, blatantly, oriented toward a future answer-word: it provokes an answer, anticipates it and structures itself in the answer's direction...
>
> Responsive understanding is a fundamental force, one that participates in the formulation of discourse, and it is moreover

an active understanding, one that discourse senses as resistance or support enriching the discourse.

> Linguistics and the philosophy of language acknowledge only a passive understanding of discourse, and moreover this takes place by and large on the level of the common language, that is, it is an understanding of an utterance's neutral significa- tion and not its actual meaning. (Bakhtin, 1981, pp. 280-1)

This clarifies, or furthers, the essential notion of addressivity mentioned earlier. The word is directed towards a reply; it "anticipates it and structures itself in the answer's direction."

In contrast to this rich and vibrant model, Bakhtin places monologism. From the point of view of traditional rhetorical argument (Bakhtin, 1986, p. 150), we can appreciate this in the attempt to determine in advance an audi- ence's response by closing debate and ending further discussion. Bakhtin thus opposes victory (seen in monologic rhetoric) against mutual under- standing (dialogism). As described above, the traditional concept of argu- ment certainly fits the monological mold.

7: Dialogic Argument

The statements of the traditional model of argument are impersonal. As they are presented for evaluation in the typical logical analysis, arguments on this understanding might better be thought of as simply argument-*products*, rather than arguments. They appear here as residues of arguments, as visible remnants. Yet even this way of talking makes it sound as if the argument is finished, decided. From the point of view we are considering here, such an 'argument' appears torn from the flow of arguing itself, incomplete and inadequate for learning anything about the actual process involved.

A dialogic model of argument, as we are now starting to conceive of it, will not pull discourse from reality and treat it as a series of statements (premises and conclusions) disconnected from arguer and audience/respondent.

Furthermore, in this model the notion of the 'arguer' itself is reconceived. Instead, the arguer appears as co-agent and an essential component of the 'argument'. Traditionally, as we have seen, the arguer is distinct from the argument, able to distance her or himself from any integral involvement. This perspective "denies the existence outside itself of another conscious- ness with equal rights and equal responsibilities," and is one that is "deaf to the other's response, does not expect it and does not acknowledge in it any *decisive* force" (Bakhtin, 1984, pp. 292-3). This is consistent with that aim of persuasion that desires the "complete victory and destruction of the opponent" (Bakhtin, 1986, p. 150). But from a perspective that stresses the addressivity of dialogue, such separation is neither accurate nor possible. The arguer as the 'author' of a position in argument, or discourse, depends on the interlocutor for the direction and details of the utterances involved. In fact, the arguer as arguer exists only in relation to the other involved, and hence only in relation to the argument.

Beyond this, in the traditional model of argument that we have considered we find talk about the way the arguer/argument aims to persuade the audience. The movement of expected change is centrifugal (from arguer to audience). Where change does take place, it is in the audience. Overlooked is the way in which the act of engaging in argument can change the arguer herself or himself. One of the assumptions left behind with the monological model is that of the all-knowing author of a discourse, who fully forms ideas before they are communicated, and possesses authoritative control over their meanings. This, as I suggested earlier, is a fiction. No single participant has control over meanings and interpretations here, since the argument with its constituent features arises from a depth of background and context that extends beyond the control of the participants.

Instead, there is an opportunity for self-knowing. As an arguer, I must consider my audience in order to orient my speech towards them. This is a standard expectation that most of us have regarding argumentation. But when I consider my audience, I consider how 'I' appear to them. I look at myself through their eyes. I search for beliefs and attitudes that are implicated by the utterance between us, which is the product of our discourse, and of which we are a product. In turn, those beliefs and attitudes come to be understood and changed *in light of* the argumentative exchange. Argument is the occasion of change not just in the audience but also, and perhaps foremost, in the arguer. In articulating my position for my audience, I also articulate it for myself. Accordingly, we find suggested here a model of argument that eschews the metaphors of war discussed earlier, and adopts the virtues of understanding and agreement.

We should also consider the way in which the addressee (second party or audience) is a constituent of the utterance involved. In this sense, again recalling the essential 'addressivity' of the utterance, there seems no distinction between the audience and the 'counter-opinions' which a discourse must answer. Like the arguer, the addressee/audience is personalized in the argument and contributes specific actual and anticipated responses to a unique situation. Here there is more than the simple accommodation of a reply, the anticipation of objections to one's position (Johnson, 1996). Because, again, 'addressivity' captures the way an argument is always *addressed to* someone, and thus needs to include an understanding of that other (audience/respondent) in its structures or organization. Hence, the argument while having the arguer as a principal source can be said on this level to be co-authored by the addressee. For Bakhtin, we recall, "every word is directed toward an *answer* and cannot escape the profound influence of the answering word that it anticipates. The word in a living conversation is directly, blatantly, oriented toward a future answer-word: it provokes an answer, anticipates it, and structures itself in the answer's direction" (Bakhtin, 1981, p. 280). We can imagine here two people in a dialogue, anticipating and responding in a way that makes their argument a common discourse, and in a way that precludes the isolation of positions, speaking back and forth across a gulf. [10]

This turn in the discussion may give some of us pause as we wonder what consequences this has for our ideas of accountability in argument.[11] Who is responsible for the claims put forward if not the arguer? The proposal now is clearly that this is a shared responsibility. As co-authors of the claims advanced and agreed to in the ongoing argument, the participants share in a common venture and produce a common 'product'. This underlines, but in a more dramatic way, the very seriousness of much of the arguing in which we engage. For we are committed at a deep level to the statements we endorse and infuse with our meanings. We will see something of this urgency when we return to the discussion between Socrates and Euthyphro. Of course, as long as argumentation is conceived as an activity that can have only one successful participant, then traditional expectations like the concern expressed continue to be warranted.[12] But if we see it aiming for agreement, common resolution or shared understanding, then responsibility for what is said and decided must be redistributed.

This dialogic model would seem to be a model of argument that aims for such agreement, although on this point there is some debate among commentators that needs to be addressed here. According to Todorov (1998, p. 7), for Bakhtin "[t]he goal of a human community should be neither silent submission nor chaotic cacophony, but the striving for the infinitely more difficult state: 'agreement.'" The word used here means, at root, 'co-voicing', reminiscent of the 'double-voiced discourse' of which Bakhtin also writes (Bakhtin, 1981, p. 324). There is an intuitive appropriateness about this suggestion given the unifying nature of the utterance and the allowances that must be made by arguer and respondent. Yet, at the same time, not all commentators interpret Bakhtin this way. Some stress the sense of social struggle rather than agreement (Hirschkop, 1986, pp. 73-9). Others, like Shotter (1992), stress the way that speakers in a discourse always occupy different 'positions' and "can never completely understand each other; they remain only partially satisfied with each other's replies" (Shotter, 1992, p. 12). Again, we might insist, Bakhtin's central project is a rejection of the sameness of mind that affects monological discourse, and sameness is too clearly associated with agreement.

Of course, a close consideration of these points of view will indicate that they do not have to preclude each other, and while an agreement wrought from sameness of mind and outlook is antithetical to Bakhtin's project, the kind of agreement considered by Todorov is not. An agreement, where achieved through dialogical argumentation, does not mean an identity of two positions; it does not involve a winner and a loser, one of whom gives up her or his position. Nor is this necessarily agreement in the sense of shaking hands and following a common path. After all, Bush's audience will include components that will never be satisfied with his solutions to problems or ways of proceeding. But components of his audience can be drawn into an understanding of his position and his manner of holding it; just as he can develop similar appreciations. Rather than the holding of the same position, agreement here stresses such an understanding of the positions involved. As Todorov (1984, p. 22) recognizes, understanding is a type of reply, it is that to which both arguer and respondent move through the utterance. In this sense, understanding is dialogical, and serves as a goal of argumentation within the perspective being considered here.

To pull the foregoing considerations together, the essential ideas of dialogic argumentation, as I am using it here, are (i) involvement, (ii) anticipation, and (iii) response.

(i) Involvement stresses the interweaving of the participants' perspectives, or the growth of a shared view, rather than the traditional product of their encounter. Reading the argumentation from this view requires resisting the temptation to see the participants as separate and looking more for the commonalities of view that grows between them. This should hold for both the dialectical and monological arguments that were illustrated earlier.

(ii) Facilitating the process in (i) is the sense of anticipation at work in the model. At its deepest level, there is the 'addressivity' of which Bakhtin speaks. For our purposes, we would look at the ways in which the speech of participants anticipates the other's perspective in the very structure of its makeup and meaning of the words within the discourse that exists between them.

(iii) On the same terms, but worth keeping here as a separate thought, is the way a speech *already* responds to its objections. The ways in which the partici-pants think ahead of themselves, project themselves into the minds of the other and draw that counter position into the construction of their own.

8. A Balance of Power

Naturally, this has consequences for the ideas of power and force, and the associated idea of control. One principal change that we find in this model is that the author/arguer is no longer the source of the argumentation. Rec-ognized or not, it has become a joint venture. Through anticipation and response, the audience or 'other' of the dialogue has been as instrumental in deciding the structure of the argumentation as the one who initiates and organizes it. Hence, there is loss of control here, seen in one sense in that we no longer turn to the 'arguer' to determine meanings of what is said. We look as well to the audience with whom the argumentation is conducted—at their beliefs, interests and understandings.

Nor does the 'arguer' have full reign in deciding what to say or how to say it. He or she is constrained by the audience and must work with the ideas and meanings found there.

While we might not yet see an equality of roles (although we can imagine cases where this arises), there is a redistribution of power as much has shifted to the audience. In fact, the two roles 'arguer' and 'audience' have lost a lot of their previous distinctness.

They have also lost their stability. Dialogical argumentation as conceived here is interactive in such ways that we should expect change in the participants as the interaction proceeds. Participants reform their points and meanings, co-authoring them as they think together; they adopt and discard perspectives, shift allegiances, and generally become modified by the activity in which they are engaged. More traditional models of argumentation are ill-equipped to recognize this. The arguer there retains a stable position to which an audience passively responds and then later, somehow, miraculously, comes to believe what has been argued (that is, is modified after the fact).

To consider some of what is involved in this new perspective, we can turn back to our two working examples and review them as dialogical argumentation along the lines of what has just been elaborated. They are by no means perfect illustrations of all aspects of the model; but they serve to provide alternative readings that can highlight features of the new alongside the old.

9. Illustrations of Dialogical Analysis

9.1. Socrates and Euthyphro

Approached in this way, different aspects of the dialogue between Socrates and Euthyphro come to light. The goal first and foremost is no longer to seek a definition of piety or holiness but to reach an agreement of understanding—to reach a common point of insight into the nature of what they are investigating and the enterprise of that investigation itself. Yet the question of piety or holiness is still important because it frames the context or situation out of which the utterances arise. As the model suggests, the context is a constitutive element of the utterance. The meaning of piety is crucial to the very self-understanding Socrates and Euthyphro each has of himself. It haunts their discourse at every turn. Each exchange is textured by the urgency of knowing what they seek: Socrates will die for lack of this; and Euthyphro's father may die. This context cannot be shed from their utterances.

Still, the example I have chosen here does not fit my interests in every sense, because it is clear that differences of inequality exist between the two participants. Now, however, those differences are not simply as they appeared in the other reading. They are differences that force Socrates to work at the dialogical level I have suggested.

At the start, he and not Euthyphro is in control, insofar as it is Socrates and not Euthyphro who sets the conditions for the agreement that will govern their inquiry:

> Socrates: '[T]ell me what you just now asserted that you knew so well. What do you say is the nature of piety and impiety, both in relation to murder and to other things? Is not

holiness always the same with itself in every action, and, on the other hand, is not unholiness the opposite of all holiness, always the same with itself and whatever is to be unholy possessing some one characteristic quality?'

Euthyphro: 'Certainly, Socrates' (5d).

This is a point on which Euthyphro will quickly founder, since his attempts at definitions do not reveal the standard that they agree they need. Euthyphro will be reminded of this agreement as the dialogue proceeds. It is a commitment that he may have cause to regret, but within the parameters of which he agrees to stay.

Beyond this, as the dialogue proceeds, the two participants become as one. Or rather, Socrates, who has established control over the discussion, loses himself in Euthyphro. Because what they argue about are Euthyphro's statements: his beliefs expressed in words. If power is source, then Euthyphro, who is the source of each definition, never gives it up completely. Instead, he shares it in a common venture, since for most of the discussion Socrates has no words of his own, but works with those of Euthyphro.[13] Socrates becomes Euthyphro in this sense: he thinks his thoughts with him, and lives his statements to see where they will lead them. And he does this well, often thinking ahead, anticipating what will come next and adjusting to accommodate it, while allowing Euthyphro still to 'lead' the dialogue through to its terminal points, from which it needs to restart.

Most explicitly, this comes after that earlier point of perplexity in Euthyphro (11d) where they have picked up a further definition, which leads them back to their previous (inadequate) point, that holiness is what all the gods love:

Socrates: '[Y]ou remember, I suppose, that awhile ago we found that holiness and what is dear to the gods were not the same, but different from each other; or do you not remember?'

Euthyphro: 'Yes, I remember'.

Socrates: 'Then don't you see that now you say that what is precious to the gods is holy? And is this not what is dear to the gods?'

Euthyphro: 'Certainly'.

Socrates: 'Then either our agreement a while ago was wrong,

or if that was right, we are wrong now'.

Euthyphro: 'So it seems'. (15c).

Euthyphro has come to see what Socrates had already grasped through his understanding of Euthyphro's statements, but as earlier, it is an insight they must share before they can move on. They think together, through the terms that they will use, through their understanding of the gods and the kinds of things they would dispute about among themselves, and arrive in each case at a common way of seeing that allows them to advance further.

After this last failed definition, the dialogue breaks up. Socrates proposes that they start again, but Euthyphro confesses to being in a hurry and rushes off. The dialogue is identified by commentators as one that ends in *aporia*. That is, it is unsuccessful, since it fails to discover what it sets out to discover—a definition of piety.

Yet much else has happened: the participants have been transformed. Socrates has become Euthyphro, has lived through his words and experienced the failure of those words to deliver the knowledge claimed. Euthyphro, who claimed he knew, has discovered himself to be the one who does not know—the position Socrates always claimed for himself. He has become Socrates. This is not a simple shift of power from one to the other. Rather, it is the reaching of a commonality between them. They both come to understand what it is they do not know, and thus need still to learn. One likes to believe that this is a successful dialogue, that such an agreement of understanding has been achieved through this dialogical exchange, and that when Euthyphro rushes off at the end, it is to withdraw the charges he had laid against his father.

In these general ways the dialogue expresses features of the dialogical model. We see the flow of the conversation towards understanding. Each utterance expects a response and, as we have seen, anticipates that response and is so framed to express that anticipation:

Socrates: 'For surely, my friend, no one, either of gods or men, has the face to say that he who does wrong ought not to pay the penalty'.

Euthyphro: 'Yes, you are right about this, Socrates, in the main' (8e).

Each statement is forward looking, moving the discussion along, as they think together through language, developing common understandings. As this flow proceeds, the participants change their views and perspectives. Or, at least, Euthyphro does, but in this dialogue his is the only perspective that is revealed—the one being investigated. He shifts, revises, recants and repeats. And at the end he is not the same as the discussant who began. He has, at the least, understood something important about himself.[14] On the earlier model, Socrates knew what he believed and manipulated his interlocutor along the same path. This is indeed one way in which he can be understood. But viewing the exchanges as we just have reveals a more positive, constructive and cooperative Socrates, one genuinely interested in his interlocutor's ideas and willing to invest in a joint venture of argumentative inquiry.

9.2. Bush Speaks to the Nation

The speech of President Bush reveals still more of the dialogical encounter. Here we have, of course, a monological text. But this is only superficially so. The model we have been developing invites us to think about ways in which such texts work as dialogues in the deeper senses discussed. One key to this lies in what Bakhtin calls 'hidden dialogicality':

> Imagine a dialogue of two persons in which the statements of the second speaker are omitted, but in such a way that the general sense is not at all violated. The second speaker is present invisibly, his words are not there, but deep traces left by these words have a determining influence on all the present and visible words of the first speaker. We sense that this is a conversation, although only one person is speaking, and it is a conversation of the most intense kind, for each present, uttered word responds and reacts with its every fiber to the invisible speaker, points to something outside of itself, beyond its own limits, to the unspoken words of another person. (Bakhtin, 1984, p. 197)

This is profoundly suggestive because it implicates the way we read what we might have taken to be non-dialogical texts: argumentative texts produced by one author that do not contain the explicit responses of an audience. The suggestion is that these responses are there, but hidden. This is how we in fact read an argumentative text when we read it from a dialogical perspective—looking for the presence of the audience, for the way it is recognized, accommodated, and anticipated by what the arguer says.

Bush has another participant with whom he is reasoning, a real and very important one—the American people. Read dialogically, his speech is a response to the points contributed by that participant, the concerns and fears that the people share. His text is filled with anticipation and response. Those he is addressing are as much authors of the speech as he is. Some examples will illustrate this.

After providing the What, Who and Why of our earlier analysis, obvious points that the audience will require be first addressed, Bush goes on in the following three paragraphs:

> By destroying camps and disrupting communications, we will make it more difficult for the terror network to train new recruits and coordinate their evil plans.

> Initially the terrorists may burrow deeper into caves and other entrenched hiding places. Our military action is also designed to clear the way for sustained, comprehensive and relentless operations to drive them out and bring them to justice.

> At the same time, the oppressed people of Afghanistan will know the generosity of America and our allies. As we strike military targets, we will also drop food, medicine and supplies to the starving and suffering men and women and children of Afghanistan.

From the first to the second paragraph here there is a shift, a hesitation, even. What the second does is address the effectiveness of the operation, allowing that it will not be straightforward. In this Bush anticipates a response from his participant, who would want to know the prospects for quick success. Again, we can imagine the question: Will this be a war on the people of Afghanistan? A question that the third paragraph promptly answers.

The speech proceeds like this in subsequent paragraphs, taking up the question of whether this is a war on Islam, and responding in the negative; taking up the question of whether war was necessary and the US the aggressor, and responding 'We're a peaceful nation'. And, importantly, taking up the question of whether there will be reprisals with points about security and the measures he has enacted.

These are matters he has to address; to ignore the concern about reprisals would be to fail in his dialogical obligations. The participant in dialogue requires that he address these points. In this sense they are not his alone; he shares them with this co-contributors who through their expectations and known values influence the construction of what has been said. As Socrates becomes Euthyphro, so Bush, to be effective, must become the American people, as he understands such a complex audience,[15] and think through them. The power and control that we saw in our earlier reading is thoroughly diluted here because we have a different picture of the intentionality involved. The value here is that it points the way forward; it gives an alternative reading from which to derive, and on which to build, understandings.

This audience is also instrumental in the way things are said. He responds to their emotions and character. He assesses them to be angry and indignant, and responds with harsh words and indignation that the US has been attacked and forced into this position. He senses their fear and answers with reassurances tempered with realism. He judges them compassionate in character and speaks early on to the ways in which the people of Afghanistan will receive aid. He judges them peaceful and responds accordingly. He knows them to be deliberative and logical, and so does not simply speak to incite emotions (this also comes through in his tone of delivery, absent from the transcript), but answers the need for deliberation with remarks on risks and costs. He understands their own sense of their role in the world and brings that out in his remarks on freedom and Americans' responsibility to protect it at home and abroad. These are beliefs already held by his audience. He is recalling them and focusing them so as to reach a common understanding on what is happening, what is at stake and why it must be done.

10. Conclusions

One of the values of argumentation is that it brings people to see the dialectical obligations that they assume by interacting with others in this way. In order to fully understand one's own position, one needs to have thought carefully about the alternatives to it. To understand how strong a case we have for a position we hold, we need to be able to conceive what would count as evidence against our position. That leads us to enter a dialogical sphere of thought, where we imagine what our position looks like to others, particularly those who do not hold it. What objections will they raise? What clarifications will they require? The ability to imagine counterarguments is synonymous with the ability to evaluate one's own arguments.

All the better, if the dialogical encounter is real (as in the case of actual dialogues) and not simply monological.

Through such exercises, participants can come to discover their beliefs and preferences. Even where we are aware of our responses to certain issues in a general way, it is through the specific challenges of dialogical argumentation that those responses become fully realized beliefs with accompanying reasons, and the choices and decisions made become identified preferences that may be applied to other contexts. Arguers come to discover themselves through the exercise of arguing, and develop themselves through what builds power of thinking and character. And obviously, through such argumentation we come to discover the thought patterns of others and appreciate the positions they hold and their reasons for holding them.

This, then, can allow for the kind of agreement of understanding that I have discussed here. While there are still other positive features of the process in general, the achievement of such shared understanding (or in the monological cases, the prospect of it) must count as an important measure of success of any such argumentation. That agreement will be seen through how people respond, what choices they make in light of argumentation. This is, arguably, a better measure than the correctness of arguments gauged through the instruments of validity and soundness, and a constructive complement to such tools.

It might be objected that this is simply persuasion delivered under a different guise: the arguer never completely loses sight of her or his desire to convince the audience of some position or claim, and immersing themselves in this dialogical process just allows them to achieve it more efficiently and, perhaps, ethically. The empirical measure of adherence to an idea seems the same in either case.

This loses sight, however, of the transformative powers of argumentation with respect to both (or all) participants. The process allows for the modifications of all perspectives, including the arguer's, and this makes possible reaching a result not first anticipated by the arguer, but agreeable to all parties. Besides, persuasion on the traditional model is marred by the passive role of an audience subject to the aggression of the arguer. In what we have considered here, the audience is an active participant, and if conclusions are persuasive it will be because the parties involved come to persuade themselves of their merits. And this will result if the arguer has appropriately accommodated the audience by anticipating and responding to its contributions so as to achieve a joint understanding.[16]

What, finally, do we say to the *ad baculum*? Can we discard it as an archaic form of argumentation thoroughly non-conducive to constructive outcomes? Such a response will not, of course, make it go away. While people may have been trained to think and argue in such ways, it too, like the traditional model we considered earlier, might be a candidate for transformation. If it fails to persuade and appears fallacious this is because it represents, even encapsulates, a position of isolation. As such it seems antithetical to dialogical thinking. But if we see it not as a finished argument, but the first move in an exchange, then it can open the door for that exchange to develop further. Looked at closer, it anticipates a response that does not have to be a matched threat. 'I support a tuition freeze. And I vote' speaks directly to the other participant's interests. The position of a voter is important to those who rely on votes for their success. As such, it can be seen as an invitation designed to address the other on a level that they care about and engender discussion. The measure of its success will be the degree to which that discussion follows and its results. What the arguers must first be prepared to give up is their alleged position of power, which is after all, quite illusory.

NOTES

* This paper was first delivered to a colloquium of the research group on 'Procedural Approaches to Conflict Resolution', Centre for Interdisciplinary Research, Bielefeld, Germany, in June of 2002. I am grateful to Matthias Raith, Christoph Fehige, Olaf Gaus and Andreas Wenzel for their comments. I have also benefited from the insights and objections of several anonymous referees for this journal. While none of them will be persuaded by everything I have to say; their contributions have led to a number of improvements.

1 This simple utterance expresses an argument in the argument$_1$ sense (O'Keefe, 1982).

2 These more recent analyses supplement the seminal account given by Lakoff and Johnson (1980).

3 As with Aristotle's dialectical argumentation: 'The contests Aristotle has in view were highly competitive, and the contestants were eager to win' (Smith, 1997, p. xxi).

4 Several more recent alternatives to this way of conceiving argument have been proposed, like argumentation as invitational (Foss and Griffin, 1995), as cooperative (Makau, 1992; Makau and Marty, 2001), or as a cooperative partnership (Fulkerson, 1996). There is no space to develop any of these important proposals on this occasion (See Tindale (2004, p. 50ff.)), but I believe the account drawn from Bakhtin's work below takes some of the essential insights of these perspectives to a deeper level.

5 And it is to further illustrate those assumptions that I am using it, rather than to suggest it is an example of the more aggressive argumentation in which these assumptions are often rooted.

6 The transcript of this speech is available at: http://www.cnn.com/2001/US/10/07/ret.bush.transcript/

7 This is to suggest that while the discourses we have considered in this preliminary way appear to lack anything of the important senses of deliberative community (Makau and Marty, 2001) or cooperative

partnership (Fulkerson, 1996, p.212) they can still be read in a positive cooperative manner.

8 J. Anthony Blair (1998) laments a proliferation of terms that appear to be used without discrimination or distinction: 'dialogue', 'dialogical', 'dialectic', 'dialectics', and 'dialectical'. While he doubts it will occur, Blair proposes that 'dialectical' be reserved for 'the properties of all arguments related to their involving doubts or disagreements with at least two sides, and the term 'dialogical'…for those belonging exclusively to turn-taking verbal exchanges'. What Blair observes is a trend toward a certain type of thinking and terminology, but his proposal will not be adhered to, at least not in this paper.

9 For recent attempts to apply Bakhtin's idea of dialogism to argumentation see Mendelson (2002), Rühl (2002) and Tindale (1999). None of these gives the kind of developed account that I attempt here.

10 Bakhtin (1986) adds to the speaker and respondent (first and second parties) a third consideration: 'Each dialogue takes place as if against the background of the responsive understanding of an invisibly present third party who stands above all the participants in the dialogue (partners)' (Bakhtin, 1986, p.126). This third party has a special dialogic position (because, of course, there can be an unlimited number of participants in a dialogue, so this is not simply a third member). As Bakhtin further explains this role:

> in addition to this addressee (the second party), the author of the utterance, with a greater or lesser awareness, presupposes a higher *superaddressee* (third), whose absolutely just responsive understanding is presumed, either in some metaphysical distance or in distant historical time (the loophole addressee). In various ages and with various understandings of the world, this superaddressee and his ideally true responsive understanding assume various ideological expressions (God, absolute truth, the court of dispassionate human conscience, the people, the court of history, science, and so forth) (Bakhtin, 1986, p.126).

These 'just' or 'true' responses suggest that we have here an objective standard; it is an active participant and conceived with various degrees of awareness by the author of the utterance. Like the first and second parties (and other features discussed earlier) the third party is a constitutive aspect of the utterance. As presupposed by the author, this party must be understood in some essential relation to the second party who is being addressed and who is, as we have seen, co-authoring the utterance itself.

11 I am grateful to an anonymous referee for bringing this concern to my attention.

12 And, of course, what is being presented here is one alternative understanding to the model of aggression among other valuable alternatives, many which have been mentioned earlier.

13 Even when he makes contributions, after the point seen earlier at which Euthyphro becomes completely perplexed, he does so only insofar as he can solicit the agreement of Euthyphro. They work together in this way throughout.

14 It must be conceded that the lessons here are limited because the dialogue is artificial. It has one author—Plato, and is not a piece of live discourse between two participants, speaking naturally and without forethought.

15 One reviewer for this journal stresses the concern we should have here that Bush is simply defining his audience and controlling meanings on this level. This is a real concern and one that I would attach to any reading of a monological text such as this where an arguer has to be interacting with a complex audience that is not present as in the case of a strict dialogue. Even here, though, I would insist that such an interaction compels the arguer to make allowances for the expected responses; that once others' ideas have been brought into one's language and thinking, there is the prospect for that language and thinking to be modified over time.

16 Clearly, there is more to be said about the transformative power of dialogical argumentation, particularly as this involves the arguer. This is something I see developing in future research.

REFERENCES

Bakhtin, Mikhail (1986). *Speech Genres & Other Later Essays.* V. W. McGee (Ed.), C. Emerson and M. Holquist (Trans.). Austin: University of Texas Press.

Bakhtin, Mikhail (1984). *Problems of Dostoevsky's Poetics.* C. Emerson (Ed. and Trans.). Minneapolis: University of Minnesota Press.

Bakhtin, Mikhail (1981). *The Dialogic Imagination: Four Essays.* Michael Holquist (Ed.), C. Emerson & M. Holquist (Trans.) Austin: University of Austin Press.

Blair, J. Anthony (1998). "The Limits of the Dialogue Model of Argument," *Argumentation* 12, 325-339.

Blair, J. Anthony and Ralph H. Johnson (1987). "Argumentation as Dialectical," *Argumentation* 1, 41-56.

Blakemore, Diane (1992). *Understanding Utterances: An Introduction to Pragmatics.* Oxford: Blackwell.

Berrill, Deborah P. (1996). "Reframing Argument from the Metaphor of War," In: D.P. Berrill (Ed.) *Perspective on Written Argument* (pp. 171-187, Ch. 8), Cresskill, New Jersey: Hampton Press.

Cohen, Daniel H. (1995). "Argument is War...and War is Hell: Philosophy, Education, and Metaphors for Argumentation," *Informal Logic* 17, 177-188.

Eemeren, Frans van and Rob Grootendorst (1992). *Argumentation, Communication, and Fallacies: A Pragma-Dialectical Perspective.* Hillsdale, N.J.: Lawrence Erlbaum Associates.

Eemeren, Frans van and Rob Grootendorst (2004). *A Systematic Theory of Argumentation: The Pragma-Dialectical Approach.* Cambridge: Cambridge University Press.

Fulkerson, Richard (1996). "Transcending Our Conception of Argument in Light of Feminist Critiques," *Argumentation and Advocacy.* 32:199-217.

Gearhart, Sally Miller. (1979). "The Womanization of Rhetoric," *Women's Studies International Quarterly.* 2:195-201.

Grice, Paul (1989). *Studies in the Way of Words.* Cambridge, MA.: Harvard University Press.

Hirschkop, Keith (1986). "A Response to the Forum on Mikhail Bakhtin," in G.S. Morson (Ed), *Bakhtin: Essays and Dialogues on His Work* (pp. 73-79), Chicago: University of Chicago Press.

Holquist, Michael (1990). *Dialogism: Bakhtin and His World.* London: Routledge.

Hunt, Russell A. (1996). "Literacy as Dialogic Involvement: Methodological Implications for the Empirical Study of Literary Reading," *Empirical Approaches to Literature and Aesthetics. Advances in Discourse Processes.* Roger J. Kreuz and Mary Sue McNealy (Eds.). Norwood, N.J.: Ablex. 52:479-494.

Johnson, Ralph H. (1996). *The Rise of Informal Logic.* Newport News, Virginia: Vale Press.

Kuhn, Deanna (1991). *The Skills of Argument.* Cambridge: Cambridge University Press.

Lakoff, George and Mark Johnson (1980) *Metaphors We Live By.* Chicago: University of Chicago Press.

Makau, Josina (1992). "Revisioning the Argumentation Course," *Women's Studies in Communication.* 15:79-91.

Makau, Josina M. and Debian L. Marty (2001). *Cooperative Argumentation: A Model of Deliberative Community.* Prospect Heights, Ill.: Waveland Press, Inc.

Mendelson, Michael (2002). *Many Sides: A Protagorean Approach to the Theory, Practice, and Pedagogy of Argument.* Dordrecht, Holland: Kluwer Academic Publishers.

Mitchell, Gordon (2000). "Simulated Public Argument as a Pedagogical Play on Worlds," *Argumentation and Advocacy.* 36:134-150.

O'Keefe, D. (1982). "The Concepts of Argument and Arguing," *Adavances in Argumentation Theory and Research.* J. Robert Cox and Charles Arthur Willard (Eds.). Carbondale: Southern Illinois University Press:3-23.

Palczewski, Catherine H. (1996). "Argumentation and Feminisms: An Introduction," *Argumentation and Advocacy.* 32:161-169.

Plato. (1966). "Euthyphro," *Plato in Twelve Volumes*, Vol. 1 translated by Harold North Fowler; Introduction by W.R.M. Lamb. Cambridge, MA, Harvard University Press.

Rühl, Marco (2002). *Arguing and Communicative Asymmetry: The Analysis of the Interactive Process of Arguing in Non-ideal Situations.* Frankfurt am Main: Peter Lang.

Shotter, John (1992). "Bakhtin and Billig: Monological Versus Dialogical Practices," *American Behavioral Scientist* 36, 8-21.

Shotter, John (1997). "On a Different Ground: From Contests Between Monologues to Dialogical Contest," *Argumentation* 11, 95-112.

Smith, Robin. (1997). "Introduction," *Aristotle:* Topics, *Books I and VIII.* Oxford: Clarendon Press.

Tindale, Christopher W. (1999). "Arguing for Bakhtin," in Frans van Eemeren *et. al.* (Eds.) *Proceedings of the Fourth International Conference of the International Society for the Study of Argumentation.* Amsterdam: Sic Sat.

Tindale, Christopher W. (2004). *Rhetorical Argumentation: Principles of Theory and Practice.* Thousand Oaks, CA: Sage Publications.

Todorov, Tsvetan (1984). *Mikhail Bakhtin: The Dialogical Principle.* Minneapolis: University of Minnesota Press.

Todorov, Tsvetan (1998). "I, Thou, Russia," *Times Literary Supplement* No. 4954, March 13, 7-8.

Toulmin, Stephen E. (2003). *The Uses of Argument* (Updated Edition). Cambridge: Cambridge University Press.

Walton, Douglas (1996). *Argument Structure: A Pragmatic Theory.* Toronto: University of Toronto Press.

Woods, John (1995). "Appeal to Force," in *Fallacies: Classical and Contemporary Readings,* edited by Hans V. Hansen and Robert C. Pinto, Penn State Press.: pp. 240-250.

Navigating Dangerous Deliberative Waters: Shallow Argument Pools, Group Polarization and Public Debate Pedagogy in Southeast Europe[*]

Gordon R. Mitchell, Damien Pfister, Georgeta Bradatan, Dejan Colev, Tsvetelina Manolova, Gligor Mitkovski, Ivanichka Nestorova, Milena Ristic and Gentiana Sheshi

Abstract

Can student-driven public debate depolarize fragmented societies by cultivating democratic ethos and promoting political accountability? Post-communist transitions in Southeast Europe are rich sites to study the political impact of student-driven public deliberation. Public debate pedagogy conducted under the auspices of the Southeast European Youth Leadership Institute (SEEYLI) presents a useful case study to explore this issue. From 2001-2005, SEEYLI taught hundreds of young people about debate and civil society. SEEYLI participants, in conjunction with local social movements, then fueled public debate projects as vehicles of political transformation in Albania, Bulgaria, Kosovo, Macedonia, Montenegro, Serbia and Romania. By recounting these unique deployments of public debate in broader spheres of public deliberation, this essay considers the possibilities and limits of applied public debate praxis as a driver of democratic change and response to the social phenomenon of "balkanization."

Dodging questions in public debates has become stock-in-trade for American politicians. Perhaps this is not surprising given that influential public debate coaches such as Washington, D.C. lawyer Robert Barnett have taught a generation of presidential aspirants (including Bill Clinton, Michael Dukakis and Walter Mondale) that one sure-fire key to debate success is the 'peas and carrots' strategy: "When all you have is peas and they want carrots, give them peas and tell them they are getting carrots" (qtd. in Mitchell, 2002, 87). This evasive approach has proven rhetorically effective in public spheres where citizens are unwilling or unable to hold their political leaders' feet to the proverbial fire of robust dialectical exchange (see Farah, 2004).

However, as Artan Haxhi discovered in a public forum convened in Shkodra, Albania, the peas and carrots strategy can misfire. In a November 2004 forum, citizens of Shkodra were fed up with the fact that Haxhi, the chief municipal official of the city, had not delivered on his 2003 election campaign promises to address electricity shortages, problems with the water supply, unemployment, and other pressing social issues. He deflected questions on these topics with the refrain: "Ah, this is not Municipality's responsibility" (qtd. in IRSH, 2004). Audience members were not satisfied with the response; they peppered Haxhi with follow-up queries, such as: "Why have you undertaken impossible responsibilities?" (qtd. in IRSH, 2004).

These probing citizen questions, building on a record generated from a previous public debate involving Haxhi, are signs that a political awakening is underway—the Albanian citizenry is emerging from decades of apathetic slumber under stultifying communist rule. As one debate organizer observes, "In Albania, where the culture of debating has not existed for a long time, public debates are breaking the silence" (Mazniku, 2004). This phenomenon may pique the interest of argumentation scholars, since Albanian student debaters have been among those making the most sophisticated wake-up calls.

The Shkodra forum was convened by an Albanian social movement called Mjaft!, which has forged ties of solidarity with other prominent student movements such as Otpor (former Yugoslavia) and Kmara (Georgia) (Musavat, 2005). Translated into English, 'Mjaft' means 'enough'—enough corruption, enough poverty, enough apathy.[1] Mjaft!'s goal is to empower civil society and inspire positive change in Albania, by increasing active citizenship, strengthening the sense of community, promoting responsible government, and improving Albania's world image. Since its founding in 2003, Mjaft! has organized many peaceful protests, and Mjaft! activists have initiated debates on television about topics such as environmental pollution, casino gambling, and genetically modified foods. The organization has contributed directly to the life skills of several thousand young people, most of them young women. Mjaft! now has a tangible presence in 17 cities in Albania and has links to 36 public high schools and all of Albania's eight universities. In 2004, the United Nations recognized Mjaft!'s efforts by honoring the organization with its Civil Society Award. During the 2005 presidential election cycle, Mjaft! worked with Gallup International to produce Albania's first series of public opinion polls (see Boustany, 2005; Wood, 2005). Notably, a significant part of Mjaft!'s leadership and rank-and-file membership is made up of academic debaters, particularly those associated with the Albanian National Debate Association (ANDA). Regarding the relationship between ANDA and Mjaft!, policy director Arbjan Mazniku explains:

> [T]hey are very closely connected. You cannot do one with-out the other. That's why this link of the two organizations has worked very well. ANDA is more academically focused, train-ing people in debate ability, while Mjaft! has tried to use this pool of people for actual, real change in the community. They have a symbiotic relationship. (Mazniku, 2004)

Mjaft! serves as a synecdoche for wider trends unfolding in Southeast Europe, where student-driven public deliberation is enlivening the politi-cal landscape not only in Albania, but also in Bulgaria, Kosovo, Macedo-nia, Montenegro, Serbia, and Romania. What do these initiatives suggest about the political dynamics of linkages formed between academic debating groups and civil society organizations? Can public debate democratically energize Southeast European citizenries? What general insight does this case study reveal about argumentation as applied critical practice? This paper explores these questions by drawing from collaborative research conducted by the authors under the auspices of the Southeast European Youth Lead-ership Institute, a summer workshop for Balkan high school students and community leaders, hosted by Towson University and Wake Forest Uni-versity and co-sponsored by the U.S. Department of State and the Open Society Institute.

'Balkanization' and Group Polarization

Nietzsche compared 'dead' metaphors to coins that lose value when their markings wear off from overuse. If the metaphor of 'balkanization' is not yet dead, it is at least very tired—through widespread usage, the meaning of the term has been stretched to denote the generic phenomenon of separatism, in areas ranging from automobile parking (Casey, 2001), to port security (Edmonson, 2005) and gasoline prices (Scherer, 2001). Largely forgotten is the original context in which the term balkanization emerged. In the end of the nineteenth and the beginning of the twentieth century, Balkan nations had just managed to reestablish their statehood after the fall of the Ottoman Empire. In this transition period, a series of localized conflicts threw the region into a period of instability and ultimately contributed to the outburst of World War I. Therefore, in 20th century European history the Balkans are frequently characterized as the powder keg of Europe.

Legal scholar Cass Sunstein (2003) deploys balkanization as a metaphor to elucidate what he calls the 'law of group polarization.' According to Sunstein (2001), "If certain people are deliberating with many like-minded others, views will not be reinforced, but instead will be shifted to more extreme points." When groups engage in 'enclave deliberation'—communicating exclusively with like-minded interlocutors—the polarization effect is heightened. Enclave deliberation creates a paradox; as members of society communicate more, they grow further apart and become less capable of coming to terms with unfamiliar viewpoints:

> The phenomenon of group polarization has conspicuous importance to the communications market, where groups with distinctive identities increasingly engage in within-group discussion. Effects of the kind just described should be expected with the Unorganized Militia and racial hate groups as well as with less extreme organizations of all sorts. If the public is *balkanized* and if different groups are designing their own preferred communications packages, the consequence will be not merely the same but still more *balkanization*, as group members move one another toward more extreme points in line with their initial tendencies. At the same time, different deliberating groups, each consisting of like-minded people, will be driven increasingly far apart simply because most of their discussions are with one another. (Sunstein, 2001, 66, emphasis added)

This finding has serious implications for public argument scholarship, since it challenges the shopworn idea among some First Amendment scholars that when it comes to dealing with noxious ideas, "more speech is always better" (Chemerinsky, 1998). Group polarization theory turns this axiom on its head: "With respect to the Internet and new communications technologies, the implication is that groups of likeminded people, engaged in discussion with one another, will end up thinking the same thing that they did before—but in more extreme form" (Sunstein, 2001, 65). Argumentation plays a key role here, since according to Sunstein (2001, 68), "the central factor behind group polarization is the existence of a limited argument pool."

Sunstein's balkanization metaphor is evocative, as group polarization theory suggests novel explanations for the causes of ethnic strife in the former Yugoslavia. The received view holds that such strife is the result of long suppressed ethnic hatreds that were released when the lid of the Cold War pressure cooker flew off. However, the limits of this explanation are apparent when one considers anomalies, such as the fact that instead of keeping a 'tight lid' on Yugoslav society during his rule from 1943-1980, Marshal Tito supported the interaction of diverse ethnic groups and provided a wide berth for the airing of different opinions among six different republics. He resisted efforts by external actors (e.g. the U.S. and U.S.S.R.) and internal actors (e.g. Franjo Tudjman) to polarize public life, and the result was a relatively peaceful era in the region. Building on this empirical fact, and challenging the 'Cold War pressure cooker' hypothesis, Timur Kuran (1998) argues that ethnic conflict in the Balkans is better understood as the inadvertent product of recent efforts by 'polarization entrepreneurs' to consolidate political power through propaganda campaigns designed to promote enclave deliberation and group polarization in Balkan society (see also Somer, 2001).

A recent swing in Bulgarian political life offers an example that illustrates this point. The results of the 2005 Bulgarian elections caught both the government and the greater society off guard, when a nationalist party of the extreme right called Ataca or 'Attack' appeared for the first time on the political scene and won seats in parliament (BTA, 2005). This unprecedented political phenomenon can be analyzed from the perspective of Sunstein's (2003) 'law of group polarization.' First, Attack's sudden appearance just a month before the parliamentary election can be regarded as a premeditated move toward 'enclave deliberation' which deprived potential opponents of the opportunity to challenge the party's nationalist and minority views. Second, this one-sided propaganda campaign led to group polarization, which even further limited the 'argument pool' and radicalized Attack's extreme ideas.

Public Debate and Group Depolarization

While 'enclave deliberation' has a tendency to shrink the 'argument pool' and foster 'group polarization', Sunstein (2001, 26) notes that this process is reversible: "As a corrective, we might build on the understandings that lie behind the notion that a free society creates a set of public forums, providing speakers' access to a diverse people, and ensuring in the process that each of us hears a wide range of speakers, spanning many topics and opinions" (see also Mitchell & Suzuki, 2004). Exposure to assorted ideas and interlocutors, on this logic, moderates the tendency of deliberative enclaves to be echo chambers that incubate extremism: "[G]roup polarization is diminished, and depolarization may result, if members have a degree of flexibility in their views and groups consist of an equal number of people with opposing views" (Sunstein, 2000, 118).[2]

An ideal context to explore Sunstein's theory is Southeast Europe, where a nascent public debating culture is currently emerging. A host of debate-oriented organizations, such as Mjaft!, have spun off from the Southeast Europe Youth Leadership Initiative (SEEYLI), a U.S.-based civic exchange program designed to promote student-driven public deliberation in the region (see IDEA, 2005; Mitchell, 2002). Since its inception in 2001, SEEYLI has brought over 500 high school students and community leaders to Baltimore, Maryland and Winston-Salem, North Carolina, for intensive study of argumentation theory, research on specific content areas, practice in debating techniques, and exploration of how public debates can help develop enlightened citizenries by spurring democratic deliberation on pressing issues (the teaching method is laid out in Broda-Bahm, Kempf & Driscoll, 2004).

Mjaft! leaders Erion Veliaj and Arbjan Mazniku played key roles in the early stages of SEEYLI, and later program alums have used SEEYLI as a rallying point to implement public debate projects. For example, Romanian students participating in the 2005 SEEYLI program have developed a follow-on project designed to raise awareness of major public ideas and promote deliberation through student training in critical thinking, advocacy skills and research. Students will begin in their own towns, then move on to other locales in need of training. The design concept evinces the idea of an octopus, with efforts beginning in a core area and then branching out.

This loose network takes various institutional forms. For example, the Romanian Association of Debates, Oratory and Rhetoric (ARDOR) encourages a more robust civic spirit amongst Romanian youth, promoting communication and argumentation as centerpieces of a new democratic society. ARDOR's mission is "to educate youngsters in Romania, through the debate program, by providing them with the necessary tools in order to effectively involve in the progress of a more and more democratic and tolerant society."[3]

Other elements of overlap between the SEEYLI curriculum and Romanian public debate efforts illustrate how public debate pedagogy yields civic engagement. While studying at Wake Forest, student debaters Radu Cotarcea and Danijela Djokic appeared on *The Mike Finley Show* broadcast from Winston-Salem, North Carolina, on WSJS radio (600AM). During their appearance, the students promoted SEEYLI public debates and discussed topics such as the U.S. Supreme Court and the transition to democracy in post-Communist Europe. A culminating event at SEEYLI has been the 'Public Debate Festival,' in which a series of public debates on various issues are organized by the students. This festival concept has been replicated in Romanian cities like Constanta, which has hosted 'DebateFest' in 2004 and 2005. Romanian students participating in such public debates have subsequently utilized their skills on the widely viewed, national state television station. There, a program called 'Generatia Contra' (Generation Against) regularly hosts debates on salient political issues and draws from the pool of local debate talent to amplify public deliberation.

While the Albanian and Romanian initiatives show great promise, ongoing efforts to promote public debate in Southeast Europe are likely to face obstacles. Members of the older generation in Southeast Europe may very well dismiss such initiatives as child's play or challenge them as unjustified ways of expressing modern points of view. For example, Serbia and Macedonia have always been old-fashioned countries, a quality perhaps connected to the Turkish occupation that lasted 500 years. That experience instilled a strong sense of deference based on age and status, with younger people expected to listen to older people, children to defer to parents, students to obey teachers, workers to follow bosses, and so on. In this culture, there is a strong presumption in favor of the way things are. Thus it is very hard for young people to press for change because the older generation controls the status quo. However, there is room for hope. The student group Otpor succeeded in challenging Slobodan Milosevic's fraudulent election victory in 2000, even in the face of humiliating tactics deployed by Serbian police forces (Agovino, 2000). "We created a possible parallel universe," explains Veran Matic, founder of the independent B-92 radio network (qtd. in Ford, 2003). The fact that new communication technology facilitated such an achievement redoubles optimism that similar dramatic projects may be possible in other contexts (Tunnard, 2003). In our final section, a comparison between Otpor and Mjaft! sets up concluding commentary regarding the prospects for public debate pedagogy to shape Southeast European political terrain in positive ways.

Closed Fist or Open Palm?

Originally, the main political goal of Otpor was to overthrow Milosevic by organizing actors in Serbia into pro- and anti- Milosevic camps. To achieve this, Otpor relied partially on politically charged street theater in the early years of the movement. In August 1999, Otpor hosted a mock celebration of Milosevic's birthday in which a participant played the aloof president (smoking a Cuban cigar in a plush chair) while citizens brought him gifts— including a ticket to the Hague, a straitjacket, and handcuffs (Jestrovic, 2000; on the role of performance as a means of political protest in Southeast Europe, see Clemons 2005). Street performances highlighted the authoritarian nature of Milosevic's government and the arrests that followed brought even more negative attention to the regime. Otpor paired the publicity it received from these carnivalesque performances with a campaign to activate the citizenry through politically-themed rock concerts, poster campaigns, and grassroots organizing (Bieber, 2003; Krnjevic-Miskovic, 2001).

The groundwork laid by Otpor paved the way for direct mobilization of Serbian citizens during the 2000 election. The group's 2000 election motto was: "There are more of us," amplifying that 'us' meant Milosevic opponents. Coordinating with other civil society organizations, Otpor led a march on Belgrade that marshalled nearly ten percent of the Serbian population. The mass mobilization of Serbs overwhelmed the token resistance provided by the faltering state apparatus (McFaul, 2005). By the end of the day, the opposition had occupied the central nodes of state power, paving the way for Milosevic's resignation.

However, when the job was done, many Otpor activists fell prey to what Robert Michels' (1915/1959, 388-92) calls the 'Iron Law of Oligarchy'— the tendency of social movement activists to moderate their oppositional stances after assuming positions of power in the establishment. After defeating Milosevic, Otpor retired its trademark red fist symbol (Grubanovic, 2003) and many activists took up posts in the state apparatus.[4] From these positions, they were less effective in energizing civil society, some argue to the detriment of ex-Yugoslavian society (see e.g. Ramet & Lyon, 2002).

The contrast between Otpor and Mjaft!'s signature symbols illustrates some key differences between the two movements. Otpor's closed fist (Figure 1) signals the group's defiant commitment to oust a strongman from power. Mjaft!'s open palm (Figure 2) symbolizes a more nuanced program of political struggle, with activists focusing on the arena of civil society, steering clear of the power matrix of party politics. Notably, Mjaft!'s approach bears its own set of risks. Widespread cynicism about the value of dissent was a serious impediment to the movement's success. Erion Veliaj succinctly captured the prevailing attitude by asking: "How do you rehabilitate protest if people see it only as an attempt to overthrow government that ends with beatings and burning of cars?" (quoted in Boulton, 2004). Rather than the clenched fist of Otpor, designed to smash the current state apparatus, the open palm of Mjaft!'s symbol invites the participation of Albanians in a national dialogue.

Figure 1: Otpor movement symbol   **Figure 2:** Mjaft! movement symbol

Mjaft! has primarily relied on public debates to activate citizen agency and draw attention to issues of national concern. For example, in March of 2003, the Albanian National Debate Association and 60 partner organizations joined together in a loose coalition to raise Albanians' civic consciousness. After a summer youth leadership workshop, Mjaft! emerged with a cadre of energized and skilled students ready to organize public debates. These public debates were part of a countrywide campaign called 'Ketu Vendos Une!' (As for Here, I Decide!). Public debates were designed to spark and then sustain higher levels of citizen activism, as well as ensure that citizen tax dollars were being spent wisely (Mazniku, quoted in 'Citizens take action', 2005).

The Shkodra forum discussed in the opening pages of this article was a follow-up event building on a previous Mjaft! barnstorming 'caravan' that featured debates, music concerts and political performances at many towns in Albania where 2003 municipal elections were being held. During the 2003 caravan debates, Mjaft! activists recorded candidates' promises carefully on a laptop computer, then printed out the list of such promises as a 'citizen contract.' After speeches but before audiences would disperse, Mjaft! representatives presented such contracts to the candidates and asked them to sign their names, alongside the signature of a 'co-signing' citizen representative. The signed contracts were then subsequently used as evidence to structure audience questions in post-election public debates such as the November 2004 forum featuring Artan Haxhi in Shkodra. As Mazniku (2004) explains, "we were looking for something that can be a link to hold politicians accountable. That's how the citizen contract came up." The Shkodra forum was part of a 12-city public debate tour, reminding local officials of the promises they had made to respond to Albanian citizen concerns.

Mjaft! coupled public debates, which raised the civic energies of Albanians, with 'Rock the Vote' style music and theatre tours, as well as media spots on television and radio. As Mjaft! has matured, the organization has adopted traditional social movement tactics like protest and petition. A 20,000 signature petition played a part in pressuring the Greek government to improve conditions for Albanian immigrants abroad in Greece. Mjaft! also organized pressure on the Albanian government to raise the Education Budget in December of 2003—a move widely heralded as the first time that the Albanian Parliament responded to direct pressure from civil society actors. Mjaft! continues to host youth leadership events, sponsor public debates, organize protests, and participate in international human rights campaigns.

Mjaft!'s success, like the success of Otpor in Serbia, created opportunities for activists to acquire more prominent political positions. For example, in 2004, Sali Berisha's Democratic Party approached Mjaft! to forge a political alliance. Mjaft! leaders turned down the offer: "They [the Democrats] are surfing on the wave that the civic protest created," said Mazniku. "They want to get power, which is okay for a party, but a civic movement demands better governance, and that is where we differ" (qtd. in Raxhimi, 2004). In this respect, Mjaft!'s strategy bears a similarity to new social movements that make "revitalizing and enlarging civil society" a permanent project, one that seeks "to generate subcultural counterpublics and institutions" (Habermas, 1992/1996, 370).

Jean Cohen and Andrew Arato (1992, 199-204) suggest that by focusing on civil society as a key arena of action, new social movements gain unique purchase on the so-called Michelsian dilemma posed by Michels' 'Iron Law of Oligarchy.' In this vein, the new social movements' commitment to civic society activism provides inoculation against the bureaucratizing tendencies of institutional politics. Here, citizen communication generates political power that shifts the center of civic gravity, without obligating activists to take up posts in the administrative state apparatus (see Habermas, 1977; Olivo, 2001; Todd, 2004). Perhaps one fertile area of follow-on research would track the progress of Mjaft! and Otpor through time, observing how the two movements navigate the Michelsian dilemma, with particular attention given to whether Mjaft!'s public debate *telos* provides helpful resources for this task. Such study might elucidate the political benefits and drawbacks of both approaches, producing knowledge that could inform future activist projects and deepen understanding of social movement protest.

An additional area of research suggested by the foregoing analysis relates to the generational dimension of public debate as a tool of political transformation in Southeast Europe. As we noted previously, the older citizens of Albania, Serbia, Macedonia and Romania developed political consciousness in a time when public opinion and citizen activism were largely alien concepts. Public debate projects spinning out of SEEYLI could be examined as instances of what Thomas Goodnight (1987) terms 'generational argument'—discourse formations with unique patterns that can be analyzed comparatively. Can the 'critical spirit' (Siegel 1997) exhibited by young debate activists inspire citizens from previous generations to embrace participatory democracy? The answer to this question may hinge on the outcome of a generational argument, one that crosses boundaries marked by political traditions and cultural sensibilities. Since this seems to be precisely the sort of heterogeneous, public forum interaction that Sunstein prescribes to counteract the corrosive effects of balkanization, it will be particularly illuminating to observe whether cross-generational public argument in Southeast Europe produces the type of group depolarization anticipated by Sunstein.

As public debate initiatives stir controversy, they are bound to yield another form of discourse called 'oppositional arguments'—forms of deliberation that perform the double function of contesting issues and shaping precedents that govern subsequent discourse (see e.g. Olson & Goodnight, 1994; Doxtader, 2000). Consider a possible analogy between American anti-fur protest activity and Mjaft!'s public debate performances. In Olson and Goodnight's account, anti-fur protests exhibit two-tiered performativity. On one level, activists contest substantive issues regarding cruel treatment of animals. On another level, the communicative style through which this specific message is conveyed presents an independent challenge to the prevailing order, by clearing space for new forms of argument revealed in provocative displays such as public nudity. Perhaps Mjaft!'s mode of political action can be elucidated using a similar model of two-tiered performativity. This theoretical perspective would focus attention on the double aspect of Mjaft!'s debating activity; such initiatives raise concrete issues for public discussion and simultaneously set precedents for future episodes of political decision. By isolating these precedents and interrogating their political implications, future scholarship could contribute much to our understanding of argumentative *praxis*.

Finally, our case study raises fresh questions about debate activism that pick up on Douglas Ehninger and Wayne Brockriede's (1969, 306-307) discussion about the value of 'total' debate programs that mix together synergistically academic tournament debating and public debating activities. Albanian debate activists have already outdone their American counterparts in developing a model of this sort that bridges the safe pedagogical space of contest round advocacy to the more turbulent waters of public deliberation. Their efforts create a raft of issues that deserve scholarly reflection. For example, while Ehninger and Brockriede believe that each and every student should pursue both academic debating and public debating, the Albanian model positions the academic debate organization more as an entry point that eventually feeds a select few (advanced) debaters into the more political world of Mjaft! politics: "We start with academic debating, and after students get excited about it, we say, 'see, this can also be done publicly.' I believe only a small group of the academic debaters will move to be public debaters, because it takes extra skills and extra interest in public issues" (Mazniku, 2004). For Albanian debaters, this transition often entails a shift in roles: "Most of our core of people are academic debaters. In the academy, they are used to debating amongst themselves. But in public debate, they are usually faced with either public officials or they just moderate or promote the debate" (Mazniku, 2004). The switching-station that connects competitive and public debate contexts is a fertile site for argumentation research. One might study, for example, how the ingenious Albanian concept of the 'citizen contract' and other similar innovations represent possible solutions to what William Rehg (2002, 25) calls the 'transfer' challenge—how to enable students of argumentation to transfer what they have learned in the classroom to the world beyond (see also McPeck, 1990; Talaska, 1992). Similarly, it is possible to envision experiments in argumentation praxis that would test proposals to link contest round practices with wider public spheres of deliberation, such as Damien Pfister and Jane Munksgaard's (2005) blueprint for 'switch-side public debating.' While switch-sides debating is the norm for competitive debate, public debate often entails an expectation that one defends only their convictions (for a representative rehearsal of this argument, see Weiss, 1995). A commitment to the *process* of democratic deliberation can be underscored, however, by the willingness of debaters to argue against their opinions. Such performances require the understanding of opposing arguments well enough that one can advance them in a debate. This process provides an opportunity for the individual debater to develop more sophisticated personal opinions through research and argument and, more importantly, for an audience to witness the complex negotiations characteristic of democratic public life. Such uptake may be a crucial prerequisite for the sort of 'dynamic updating' that Christopher Karpowitz and Jane Mansbridge (2005) argue is needed for deliberation to unfold as an "open-minded, ongoing discovery of each party's values and interests."

Public debate performances that demonstrate debaters' democratic commitments can model effective deliberation techniques for audience members. Public arguers engage in what Ehninger (1970) describes as the person-risking enterprise: they open their opinions to revision through research and dialectical exchange. Participants in public debates in Southeast Europe have set a deliberative tone capable of expanding the political imagination of an otherwise cynical and skeptical public to see the possibilities of change. As the political gains directly linked to public debates continue to accrue, civil society groups that sponsor public debates become gradually ratified in their approach. Such groups can then move on to subsequent political engagements with enhanced symbolic capital. The initial process of engaging in public debates has energized a whole swath of civil society in Southeast Europe—the actions of a relatively few active citizens have resulted in a rippling outward of deliberative vigor. Further study on this 'demonstration effect' could provide a powerful research agenda for public debate pedagogy, especially in Southeast Europe and other similarly situated countries. Since the process of debate inherently involves the airing of differing viewpoints in a constructive manner, the homogeneous communication that Sunstein critiques is less likely to take root. As public debates that harness critical publicity continue to proliferate in Southeast Europe, the propaganda entrepreneurs responsible for so much bloodshed in past years might find it more difficult to find audiences willing to embrace their divisive messages.

Unfortunately, it will be impossible to pursue such research questions under the auspices of SEEYLI, the program in civic leadership funded jointly by the US Department of State and the Open Society Institute—the State Department opted recently not to renew funding for a sixth year of the SEEYLI program. Some suggest that this decision was a politically motivated jab by the US government at Open Society Institute founder George Soros, who campaigned vigorously against President George W. Bush's re-election in 2004. If this is the case, the Bush administration may be cutting off its nose to spite its face, since the SEEYLI program's five-year track record establishes it as one of the United States' most effective public diplomacy and democracy promotion initiatives.

NOTES

* Portions of this paper were prepared during the Southeast European Youth Leadership Institute, sponsored by the U.S. Department of State and the Open Society Institute, held at Wake Forest University in Winston-Salem, NC, during July 2005. A draft of the paper was presented at the 14th Alta Conference on Argumentation in Alta, Utah, August 4-7, 2005.

1. The meme of "enough" has also been adopted by the organization Khopits in Belarus. Khopits means "enough" in Belarussian. Like Mjaft!, Khopits does not support particular opposition candidates but instead focuses on habituating Belarussians into civil society practices (Myers, 2006; for more on Khopits, see their website at http://www.xopic.info/).

2. A significant caveat to Sunstein's thesis is his stipulation that in certain circumstances, enclave deliberation performs an important social function: "A special advantage of 'enclave deliberation' is that it promotes the development of positions that would otherwise be invisible, silenced, or squelched in general debate. In numerous contexts, this is a great advantage; many social movements have been made possible through this route (as possible examples, consider feminism, the civil-rights movement, religious conservatism, environmentalism, and the movement for gay and lesbian rights)" (Sunstein, 2000, 111; see also Asen & Brouwer, 2001; Griffin, 1996; and Mitchell, 2004). Here, enclave deliberation provides those speakers who may feel excluded or intimidated in mass public spheres with opportunities to develop their public voices and to share their views with like-minded interlocutors. Yet, there is an important catch—while such activity has potential to enrich a society's overall argument pool, "enclave deliberation is unlikely to produce change unless the members of different enclaves are eventually brought into contact with others. In democratic societies, the best response is to ensure that any such enclaves are not walled off from competing views, and that at certain points, there is an exchange of views between enclave members and those who disagree with them" (Sunstein, 2000, 113).

3. "ARDOR at a Glance," fact sheet provided to the second author by Radu Cotarcea.

4. It should also be noted that some Otpor activists went on to play a significant role in Ukraine's "Orange revolution," training Ukranian activists in methods of non-violent resistance starting in 2003 (see Ackerman & Duvall, 2005).

REFERENCES

Ackerman, P. & Duvall, J. (2005). People power primed: Civilian resistance and democratization. *Harvard International Review*, 27, 42-47.

Agovino, T. (2000, 4 August). In Yugoslavia, a campus-born resistance movement fights for freedom. *Chronicle of Higher Education*, p. A44.

Asen, R. & Brouwer, D.C. (Eds.). 2001. *Counterpublics and the state*. New York: SUNY Press.

Bieber, F. (2003). The Serbian opposition and civil society: roots of the delayed transition in Serbia. *International Journal of Politics, Culture and Society*, 17, 73-90.

Boulton, L. (2004, May 18). Young generation decides that enough is enough! *Financial Times*, p. 11.

Boustany, N. (2005, June 13). Albanian advocacy group facing a fight it didn't anticipate. *Washington Post*, p. A16.

Broda-Bahm, K., Kempf, D. & Driscoll, W. (2004). *Argument and audience: Presenting debates in public settings*. New York: International Debate Education Association.

BTA (2005, 26 June). Bulgarian nationalists reject cooperation with other parties. Lexis-Nexis Academic database, online at <http://www.lexis-nexis.com>.

Casey, R. (2001, March 9). Politics of parking shows balkanization of the courthouse. *San Antonio Express-News*, p. 3A.

Chemerinsky, E. (1998). More speech is better. *UCLA Law Review*, 45, 1635-1651.

Citizens take action in Albania. (2005, Spring). *UN Office on Drugs and Crime Newsletter.* Online at <http://www.unodc.org/newsletter/en/200502/page007.html>.

Clemons, L. (2005). The winds of change: Alternative theatre practice and political transformation in the former FRY (Federal Republic of Yugoslavia). *Theatre History Studies*, 25, 107-124.

Cohen, J. & Arato, A. (1992). *Civil society and political theory.* Cambridge, Mass.: MIT Press.

Doxtader, E. (2000). Characters in the middle of public life: Consensus, dissent and ethos. *Philosophy and Rhetoric*, 33, 336-369.

Edmonson, R.G. (2005, 11 July). Tired of waiting; With no TWIC, ports are developing their own identification cards. *Journal of Commerce*, p. 18.

Ehninger, D. (1970). Argument as method: its nature, its limitations, and its uses. *Speech Monographs*, 37, 101-110.

Ehninger, D. & Brockriede, W. (1969). *Decision by debate.* New York: Dodd, Mead & Co.

Farah, G. (2004). *No debate: How the Republican and Democratic parties secretly control the presidential debates.* New York: Seven Stories Press.

Ford, P. (2003, 27 January). How the Balkan strongman was toppled. *Christian Science Monitor.* Academic Search Premier database, online at <http://www.ebscohost.com>.

Goodnight, G.T. (1987). Generational argument. In F.H. van Eemeren, et al. (Eds.), *Argumentation across the lines of disciplines: Proceedings of the 1986 ISSA conference on argumentation*, 129-144. Providence: Foris Press.

Griffin, C. (1996). The essentialist roots of the public sphere: A feminist critique. *Western Journal of Communication*, 60, 21-39.

Grubanovic, S. (2003, 18 August). Raising the fist of resistance—again. *Transitions Online.* Online at <http://www.tol.cz>.

Habermas, J. (1996). *Between facts and norms.* Trans. W. Rehg. Cambridge, Mass.: MIT Press. (Original work published 1992).

Habermas, J. (1977). Hannah Arendt's communications concept of power. *Social Research*, 44, 3-23.

Intelektualet e Rinj Shprese (IRSH) (2004, 24 November). IRSH and MJAFT organized in Shkoder the first citizens' forum on local governance. Southeast European Portal. Online at <http://see.oneworld.net/article/view/99286/1/3195>.

Jestrovic, Silvija. (2000). Theatricalizing Politics/Politicizing Theatre. *Canadian Theatre Review*, 103. Online at <http://www.utpjournals.com/product/ctr/103/103_Jestrovic.html>.

Karpowitz, C.F. and J. Mansbridge. (2005). Disagreement and consensus: The importance of dynamic updating in public deliberation. In J. Gastil and P. Levine (Eds.), *The deliberative democracy handbook: Strategies for effective civic engagement in the 21st century,* 237-253. San Francisco, CA: Jossey-Bass.

Krnjevic-Miskovic, D. Serbia's prudent revolution. *Journal of Democracy,* 12, 96-110.

Kuran, T. (1998). Ethnic norms and their transformation through reputational cascades. *Journal of Legal Studies,* 27, 623-649.

Mazniku, A. (2004). Interview with Gordon Mitchell. 19 July. Winston-Salem, NC. Recording and partial transcript on file with the lead author.

McFaul, M. (2005). Transitions from postcommunism. *Journal of Democracy,* 16, 5-19.

McPeck, J.E. (1990). *Teaching critical thinking: Dialogue and Dialectic.* New York: Routledge.

Michels, R. (1959). *Political parties: A sociological study of the oligarchical tendencies of modern democracy.* Trans. C. Paul. New York: Dover. (Original work published 1915).

Mitchell, G.R. (2002). The blooming of Balkan public debate. *Controversia: An International Journal of Debate and Democratic Renewal,* 1, 86-90.

_____ . (2004). Public argument action research and the learning curve of new social movements. *Argumentation and Advocacy,* 40, 209-225.

Mitchell, G.R. & Suzuki, T. (2004). Beyond the Daily Me: Argumentation in an age of enclave deliberation. In T. Suzuki, Y. Yano & T. Kato (Eds.), *Argumentation and social cognition: Proceedings of the 2nd Tokyo conference on argumentation,* 160-66. Tokyo: Japan Debate Association.

Munksgaard, J. & Pfister, D. (2005). The public debater's role in advancing deliberation: Towards switch-sides public debate. In C. Willard (Ed.), *Critical problems in argumentation: Proceedings of the thirteenth NCA/AFA conference on argumentation,* 503-09. Washington, D.C.: National Communication Association.

Musavat, Y. (2005, 7 June). Azeri youth movement signs international pact of support. *BBC Monitoring International Reports.* Lexis-Nexis Academic database Online at <http://www.lexis-nexis.com>.

Myers, S. (2006, 26 February). Bringing down Europe's last ex-Soviet dictator. *New York Times Magazine,* pp. 48-53.

Olivo, C. (2001). *Creating a democratic civil society in Eastern Germany.* New York: Palgrave.

Olson, K.M. & Goodnight, G.T. (1994). Entanglements of consumption, cruelty, privacy and fashion: The social controversy over fur. *Quarterly Journal of Speech,* 80, 249-277.

Open Society Institute. (2005). Southeast Europe Youth Leadership Institute program description. Online at <http://www.idebate.org/seeyli/>.

Ramet, S.P. & Lyon, P.W. (2002). Discord, denial, dysfunction: The Serbian-Montenegrin-Kosovar triangle. *Problems of Post-Communism,* 49, 3-19.

Raxhimi, A. (2004, 8 March). Albanian opposition holds biggest rally since 1997. *Transitions*

Online. Academic Search Premier database. Online at <http://www.ebscohost. com>.

Rehg, W. (2002). The argumentative theorist in deliberative democracy. *Controversia*, 1, 18-42.

Scherer, R. (2001, May 4). 50 reasons gasoline isn't cheaper. *Christian Science Monitor*, p. 1.

Siegel, H. (1997). *Rationality redeemed? Further dialogues on an educational ideal.* New York: Routledge.

Sunstein, C.R. (2000). Deliberative trouble? Why groups go to extremes. *Yale Law Journal*, 110, 71-119.

_____ . (2001). *Republic.com.* Princeton: Princeton University Press.

_____ . (2003). The law of group polarization. In J.S. Fishkin & P. Laslett (Eds.), *Debating deliberative democracy*, 80-101. London: Blackwell.

Somer, M. (2001). Cascades of ethnic polarization: Lessons from Yugoslavia. *Annals of the American Academy of Political and Social Science*, 573, 127-146.

Talaska, R.A., ed. (1992). *Critical reasoning in contemporary culture.* Albany, NY: SUNY Press.

Todd, A.M. (2004). Global justice movement networks: New technology and the mobilization of civil society. *Controversia*, 2, 17-38.

Tunnard, C.R. (2003). From state-controlled media to the 'anarchy' of the Internet: The changing influence of communications and information in Serbia in the 1990s. *Southeast European and Black Sea Studies*, 3, 97-120.

Weiss, R. (1995). *Public argument.* Lanham, MD: University Press of America.

Wood, N. (2005, 3 July). Albania prepares to vote amid accusations of fraud and intimidation. *New York Times*, p. 6.

PART TWO: Public Argument, Public Policy, and Democratization

Manifest Destiny on a Global Scale: The U.S. War on Terrorism

Carol Winkler

Abstract

The war on terrorism becomes an international site of controversy when America's European allies raise concern over the U.S. military's treatment of al-Qaida and Taliban detainees at Guantanamo Bay. Grounded in Kathryn Olsen's and Thomas Goodnight's perspective that "controversy" serves as a lens for identifying argumentative rules and presumptions, this essay examines the Bush administration's rhetoric as a renegotiation of the discussion parameters for governments engaged in asymmetrical conflicts. It argues that the administration's approach transposes the doctrine of manifest destiny into the global arena. Paralleling the early experience of the U.S. with Native Americans, the U.S. government develops an argumentation strategy that denies individual, national, and religious identity to those who impede the progress of civilization.

The horror of the September 11th attacks on the World Trade Center and the Pentagon prompt unprecedented international unity in support for the war on terrorism. George W. Bush enjoys domestic approval ratings that exceed those of any other modern U.S. president.[1] Countries abroad comply with U.S. requests for diplomatic, legal, intelligence, and military assistance. A parade of world leaders visits the White House offering public support for the war effort. Some heads of state lobby other nations on America's behalf to take more active steps to stamp out terrorism. The international community comes together as never before to fight against the threat of terrorism.

The emergent consensus of world opinion, however, breaks down on the issue of the treatment of captured al-Qaida and Taliban forces held at Guantanamo Bay. Many members of the international press pan the U.S. failure to resolve issues of legal standing for the detainees, as well as U.S. treatment of the suspected terrorists. Britain's conservative *Evening Standard* opines, "By its treatment of the prisoners in Cuba, it [the United States] risks finding itself isolated from the rest of us, whether it chooses or not."[2] Britain's centrist *Independent* is more blunt: "America is acting like a schoolyard bully. Instead of a high-profile demonstration of superior moral values of the coalition against terror, we are presented with the depressing spectacle of behavior that demeans America—and her allies. It is an immoral as well as a dangerous situation...."[3] Defense Secretary Donald Rumsfeld counters the growing controversy with his own assessment that the Guantanamo detainees receive treatment consistent with standards of the Geneva Conventions, despite the fact they do not qualify for such protections under international treaty provisions.

Kathryn Olsen and Thomas Goodnight define "controversy" to be "an extended rhetorical engagement that critiques, resituates, and develops communication practices bridging the public and personal spheres."[4] Viewed from such a perspective, the international debate over the treatment of the Guantanamo Bay detainees becomes a lens for understanding "rules and presumptions of who gets to talk, what counts as proof, whose language is authoritative, what reasons are recognized, which grounds are determinative, along what lines context is invoked, and whether penalties should be attached to making objections."[5] The social controversy between members of the international community and the United States related to al-Qaida and the Taliban emerges as a critical, extended engagement for understanding the Bush administration's perspective on globalization and the role of the United States within it.

A cursory glance at the Bush administration's terrorism war rhetoric reveals the intention to critique and reconstitute public thinking about the appropriate role of government in asymmetrical conflicts. This enemy is new, according to the Bush camp, because it hides, it lacks high value targets, it uses different type of weapons, it resides in a wide range of host countries, it exceeds previous standards of barbarity, and it attacks the United States at home and abroad simultaneously. Within such a context, the administration insists that conventional response options will inevitably fail. Spokesperson after spokesperson reiterates that both domestic and foreign audiences must accept one principle maxim: security depends on a multiple front, sustained effort that reconfigures the traditional roles of those responding to the new, more dangerous threats.[6]

While the nature of the enemy and the U.S. response may be new, the public communication strategy the administration uses to justify the war on terrorism is not. As the following will demonstrate, Bush officials borrow heavily from the rhetorical history of the United States' experience with American Indians to construct the public rationale for the government's response to al-Qaida and the Taliban. The approach establishes the argumentative parameters for public discussions about terrorism, as well as providing a context for evaluating the appropriateness of various U.S. response options.

Interpreted from such a perspective, international controversy in response to U.S. treatment of captured members of al-Qaida and the Taliban becomes a debate over the rules and presumptions of a transposed doctrine of manifest destiny into the global arena. The manifest destiny doctrine develops out of the need for the framers, on behalf of Americans more generally, to morally justify the takeover of hundreds of thousands acres of land formally occupied by Indian nations and tribes. The doctrine imbues mainstream American society with the responsibility for advancing civilization, while denying status, if necessary, to those who might impede progress.

The Bush administration explicitly rejects any notion that it harbors any intention of imposing a manifest destiny doctrine in Afghanistan. Officials are emphatic that the government's motives are not imperialistic. Rumsfeld insists, "The United States covets no-one else's land—certainly not Afghanistan. We're there to do a job. We're there to root out the terrorists and the terrorist networks and to see that the Taliban government who invited them in and has been harboring terrorists is gone. And that is our interest, period."[7] A desire to end terrorist repression, not economic self-interest, drives U.S. policy.

Such a stance is not unlike the framers' initial position in response to the nation's indigenous populations as America transitions into a new republic. President George Washington confides in a letter to James Duane:

> As the Country, is large enough to contain us all; and as we are disposed to be kind to them and to partake of their Trade, we will ... establish a boundary line between them and us beyond which we will *endeavor* to restrain our People from Hunting or Settling, and within which they shall not come, but for the purposes of Trading, Treating, or other business unexceptionable in its nature. In establishing the line, in the first instance, care should be taken neither to yield nor to grasp at too much. But to endeavor to impress the Indians with an idea of the generosity of our disposition to accommodate them... ."[8]

Following Washington's suggestion, the Continental Congress issues a proclamation that forbids any person from settling or purchasing lands inhabited or claimed by Indians without the consent of the U.S. government.[9] The initial public posture of the new republic is unequivocal: the United States does not covet the land of the nation's indigenous populations. And yet, more than eighty percent of all land inside the continental United States now belongs to non-Indian American citizens.

In the current war on terrorism, it is too soon to tell whether the leadership of the United States will stop at its stated goal of ending terrorism or begin capitalizing on Afghani lands for economic gain. Nevertheless, the Bush administration uses the U.S. conflict with al-Qaida and the Taliban to establish a rhetorical justification for denying basic freedoms to international terrorists and those that support them. Borrowing from the experience of the United States with American Indians, the Bush administration denies individual, national and religious identity to terrorists and their supporters. Stripped of their fundamental identities, terrorists become unworthy to possess individual, national or sacred rights. The approach privileges an argumentative framework that justifies U.S. encroachment on the global stage.

Revoking Individual Identity

The experience of Native Americans provides a prototypical case for how a nation founded on principles of freedom and liberty can deny individual identity to those within its midst. Thomas Jefferson's original draft of the Declaration of Independence distinguishes clearly between two groups inhabiting U.S. soil: American patriots who recognize the need to resist the tyranny of the British crown and stand up for their "separate and equal station to which the Laws of Nature and of Nature's God entitle them" and Indians who at the behest of King George engage in "an undistinguished destruction of all ages, sexes and conditions."[10] By the final draft of the declaration, the phrase, "merciless Indian Savages," refers to all Native Americans regardless of demonstrated proclivity to commit acts of violence. The approach strips individual Indians of their own identity, while simultaneously creating a homogenous group defined by the barbarism of a few. [11] Conversely, violent acts committed at the hands of white male colonialists receive forgiveness, permitting them to acquire the fundamental freedoms and liberties associated with civilized society.[12]

Jefferson's rationale for excluding the nation's indigenous populations springs from his belief that all Indians are savages, not prepared to assume the responsibilities of civilized society.[13] Historical anthropologist Anthony Wallace traces the origins of Jefferson's savage-to-civilization continuum to two sources: Scottish philosophy which maintains morality stems from environmental factors such as differing standards of moral refinement and the Enlightenment conviction of universal, progressive stages toward modern civilized society.[14] President John Adams apparently agrees with Jefferson, announcing that Indians "cannot bear democracy any more than Bonaparte and Talleyrand. ..."[15] Initially denied the opportunity to demonstrate their capacity to assume the responsibilities of citizenship, individual Native Americans find themselves designated inferior subjects on society's evolutionary scale.

Proof that the nation's indigenous populations are not prepared to handle fundamental American freedoms comes from criticism related to their brutal treatment of female members. Somewhat ironically, it is Jefferson, author of the phrase, "all men are created equal," who argues the Indian's cultural assumption of male supremacy perverts the foundation of a just social order.[16] The use of male force against women, as well as the repetitive, onerous chores tribes assign to women, illustrate the Indians' basic lack of respect for human dignity, according to Jefferson. He insists in his *Notes on the State of Virginia* that, "It is civilization alone which places women in the enjoyment of their natural equality."[17] Unwilling to respect the rights of the physically weaker sex, Indians demonstrate their unfitness for the responsibilities of civilized life.[18]

Additional proof for the incapacity for citizenship includes the unwillingness of Native Americans to conform to the colonialists' preferred use of their land resources. The framers find many Indians' dependence on hunting for the tribes' sustenance troubling; instead, agriculture is the preferred method of livelihood. Jefferson considers the need to develop an enduring relationship with the land an essential requirement for the nation's continued survival.[19] The preference of many tribes to rely on the land's natural provisions to sustain their continued existence thwarts Jefferson's vision for the future of the republic. He warns that should Indians fail to adopt more civilized methods of livelihood, they will "disappear from the earth."[20] Survival, as well as access to the privileges of a free society, depends on strict adherence to the colonial approach of cultivation.

Over the course of time, methods of further reinforcing the lack of individual identity of Native Americans become more pronounced. Boarding schools operating during the late nineteenth and early twentieth centuries require Indian children both on and off reservations to cut their hair, abandon their tribal clothing for standard uniforms, and even change their names to ease the pronunciation burdens on the teachers![21] In 1887 the U.S. Congress passes a legal standard for who qualifies as an Indian based on the ability to document that half or more of one's bloodline comes from Indian parents.[22] Seeking to assimilate as many Native Americans into the dominant culture as possible, the institutional systems of the United States seek to deny many individuals their self-identity as Indians.

Stripped of individual identity, Native Americans in the new republic do not warrant fundamental liberties. The government's handling of Geronimo and other Apache prisoners of war at the end of the nineteenth and early twentieth century demonstrates the willingness of the United States to subordinate the individual rights of Native Americans to further the nation's interests. The U.S. government orders General Nelson A. Miles to capture Geronimo and his tribe in the early 1880s when it becomes frustrated by the nomadic lifestyle and evasive tactics of the Apache. Unable to seize Geronimo through traditional military means, Miles determines to persuade the Indian leader to surrender by isolating him from his fellow tribes. The plan, which ultimately succeeds, involves creating false rumors of an Apache raid to justify the capture and relocation of the tribe to the eastern United States. Ignoring a direct order by President Grover Cleveland not to negotiate, Miles achieves Geronimo's surrender by offering him "protection, reunion with his family, and a large well-stocked reservation."[23] The U.S. government does not fulfill the agreement's conditions for decades.

The U.S. government severely restricts the individual rights of the more than three hundred Apache it holds in captivity. Initially, the U.S. government confines the Apache prisoners of war for six weeks while debating their fate. Suspicion of having committed a crime is sufficient to warrant continued imprisonment. Eventual relocation across the span of the United States occurs in the name of preventing further atrocities. The government ignores demands by many in Arizona to return Geronimo and the rest of the Apaches to their home territory to stand trial for their crimes. Despite an insistence that they do not understand the charges against them, some Apaches receive death sentences from all white juries who admit to "bias and prejudice" in their cases.[24] Not provided the due process protections afforded U.S. citizens, some of the Apaches prisoners of war remain incarcerated for more than thirty years.

This experience and others like it provide a framework for understanding the Bush administration's treatment of suspected members of al-Qaida and Taliban. Initially, the administration's public communication strategy denies the members of such groups their individual identity by treating the entire collective as a homogenous entity. The implementation of the strategy begins even before the administration can identify the individual or groups responsible for the September 11th attacks. Just eight days after the attacks, Bush maintains that all terrorists, regardless of their national, ethnic, religious, cultural, or individual identity, have the same motivation for conducting political acts of violence. He pronounces that terrorists "have a common ideology... they hate freedom and they hate freedom-loving people. And they particularly hate America at this moment."[25] The approach denies those responsible the possibility of independent thought, thereby diverting attention away from any subsequent claims they might proffer for U.S. culpability for the tragedy.

Going a step further, Bush creates an indistinguishable collective by grouping terrorists with those who harbor them into a single entity. He insists that his administration will "make no distinction between the terrorists who committed these acts and those who harbor them."[26] As the public campaign develops, the administration broadens the parameter of the homogenous group to include those who harbor, house, support, facilitate, finance, tolerate, provide haven, and provide succor to terrorists. Individuals, entities, organizations, and states all qualify for inclusion.[27] Bush offers the Taliban and al-Qaida as his representative example: "That regime and the terrorists who support it are now virtually indistinguishable."[28] Stripped of individual identity, all those who associate with terrorists assume an oppositional stance toward freedom and liberty in the leadership's public campaign against terrorism.

Antithetical to fundamental freedoms, terrorists possess a barbaric savagery reminiscent of Jefferson's portrayal of Native Americans. Bush encourages all members of the international community to understand that the perpetrators of the September 11th attacks hold a low position on the evolutionary scale. He sets up the dichotomous relationship between the terrorists' savagery and a higher order civilization. Terrorists are no better than alligators that live in a swamp, while civilized society represents a superior, moral form of life.[29] Terrorists are "an enemy of all law, all liberty, all morality, all religion."[30] By contrast, the U.S. and the rest of civilized society must fight for "all who believe in progress and pluralism, tolerance and freedom."[31] Like the Indians before them, the terrorists' lack of understanding and respect for the nation's cherished values threatens the entire body politic at home and abroad.

As before, proof that terrorists are not prepared to assume the responsibilities of free citizenship focuses on poor treatment of women. Bush openly criticizes the Taliban's history of "subjecting women to fierce brutality."[32] He offers vivid examples of the Taliban's reign of terror on the Afghan people. He notes, "Women are executed in Kabul's soccer stadium. They can be beaten for wearing socks that are too thin."[33] Rumsfeld adds, "... in Afghanistan, women have been persecuted, denied education, [and] confined to home."[34] The administration insists that the Taliban's treatment of women is an affront to basic human rights and the norms of civilized behavior.

Further proof that terrorist regimes are unfit for benefits of civilized society includes their inattention to the proper prioritization of their own resources. The Bush administration maintains the Taliban makes poor choices that result in the suffering of the Afghani people. Rumsfeld provides a list: "... while the Afghani people live in poverty the terrorist oppressors spend millions of dollars training people and sending them all over the globe to kill people. They traffic in opium, worsening the conditions of Muslims throughout the world. At a time when millions of Afghans are starving, in search of food and water, they have disrupted the distribution of international aid, seized warehouses of food intended for the poor, and created catastrophic starvation."[35] Like the Native Americans (at least as depicted by the early colonialists), the Taliban's inattention to the long-term survival needs of people disqualifies them for fundamental individual rights.

> While the long-term U.S. policies toward the Taliban and al-Qaida are still unfolding, parallels already exist to the late 1800's and early 1900's strategy of reinforcing the loss of individual identity. The U.S. military shaves the beards of those it captures and issues them standard orange uniforms. A photograph, released by the Department of Defense of the Guantanamo Bay detainees, shows each bound and positioned on their knees. Each also wears a uniform facial mask. The purpose of the mask, according to administration spokespersons, is to guard against the spread of tuberculosis, but the covering serves a dual function of obscuring the identity of the detainees. The Secretary of Defense refuses to release the names of the Guantanamo Bay detainees or state their country of origin. Undifferentiated as to whether they are members of the Taliban, al-Qaida, or something else altogether, the photographed detainees have graphically illustrated homogeneity.

Denied their individual identity by the Bush administration's approach, the Guantanamo Bay detainees are no more entitled to the basic individual liberties than Geronimo and the other Apache prisoners of war. Like the Apache, the detainees spend weeks in captivity while the U.S. government determines their fate. Suspicion is sufficient to hold them prisoner. The government relocates over vast distances in the name of preventing future acts of terrorism. When members of the international community request extradition of certain detainees whose national origin is public, the administration claims to be open to the possibility, but is cautious in its response. Each detainee faces the prospect of facing a military tribunal made up of American military personnel that has the power to impose the death penalty. What due process rights the tribunals will afford detainees remains an open question.

The denial of individual identity, and, by extension, the denial of individual rights dehumanizes the enemy. Based in generalized assumptions about group character, the approach does not permit considerations of independent thought or action. The crimes of a few transpose to the collective, requiring radical steps against the group in its entirety to purify the society. Grounded in the moral justifications and rationalizations of the early republic, the Bush administration's denial of individual dignities to the Guantanamo detainees becomes a reconstituted enactment of America's memory with its own indigenous populations.

Revoking National Identity

The early republic's leadership compounds the loss of individual identity for Native Americans by denying them national identity. The underlying rationale for denying status as independent nations with attendant rights of self-governance results from the need to secure the survival of the new republic. The need to create a stable, unified government with authority over the thirteen colonies guides the reasons offered for denying the legitimacy of Indians' sovereignty.

One primary threat is the ability of the new states to secede from the union. Native Americans magnify the problem as a source of concern because of their multiple affiliations. Rather than identify themselves as members of a single nation-state, many Indians have a wide network of tribal and familial ties that produce fluid communities and a complex net of complementary group identities. The Algonquians, who encounter Europeans on America's east coast, serve as an example given their extended relationships with various tribes, bands and villages. Historian David Wilson describes the interconnected attachments of the Algonquians:

> If you did not like where you were living, you could leave and join relatives somewhere else; whole communities might break away and form their own tribe, or attach themselves to another leader. By the same token, a successful *sachem* [leader in New England] or *werowance* [leader in Virginia] could extend his (or occasionally, her) influence by attracting or conquering a number of smaller groups and forging them into a larger alliance capable of concerted action.[36]

The framers conclude that the fragile union can ill afford to tolerate such a lack of allegiance to the nation state.

Besides the fear of secession, the framers have concerns about the ease with which European capitals can corrupt the Native American tribes against the colonialists. Thomas Jefferson refers to Indian tribes as "shadow nations" deeply dependent on foreign funds.[37] He argues without financial support of various European nations, Indian violence would dissipate. The weakened tribes would have to retreat from the lands they occupy. The Indians would then face, in the words of Jefferson's first inaugural address, "the strongest government on earth … where every man, at the call of the law, would fly to the standard of the law, and would meet invasions of the public order as his own personal concern."[38] Jefferson's approach places the blame for the new republic's problems with the Indians on the nations that support them.

Regardless of who is responsible, acts of Indian violence against the colonialists serve as the primary justification for the denial of Native American sovereignty. Jefferson is unambiguous about his commitment to deny nationhood to any Indians who commit atrocities. He writes in a letter to William Henry Harrison in February of 1803: "Should any tribe be foolhardy enough to take up the hatchet at any time, the seizing of the whole country of that tribe, and driving them across the Mississippi, as the only condition of peace, would be an example to others, and a furtherance of our final consolidation. …"[39] By the turn of the next century, President Theodore Roosevelt no longer considers evidence of a tribal offensive necessary to warrant denial of national identity. He believes that American Indians are savages who "infest" lands legally belonging to the United States.[40] He unabashedly proclaims, "The simple truth is that Indians never had any real ownership of it [the land they occupied] at all."[41] In

Roosevelt's view Indians need not attack the nation; the United States has justification to act from an offensive or defensive posture.

Convinced of the illegitimacy of Indian occupancy of lands in the New World, the nation's leadership employs a number of approaches to deny Native Americans national identity. An early strategy involves isolation. The Committee of Indian Affairs recommends to the Continental Congress that the republic outlaw inter-tribal trading and land purchasing without prior agreement of the federal government.[42] The General Allotment Act of 1887 prohibits communal land holding by Indians (with at least one-half blood line). U.S. courts refuse to recognize treaty obligations and identify Indian nations as "quasi-foreign states."[43] With neither claims to domestic nor foreign sovereignty, Native Americans lack national standing.

Removal is a second approach that the leaders of the new republic employ to deny Native Americans a recognized sense of national identity. The United States relocates the Winnebago tribe five times.[44] The forcible removal of the Cherokee along the trail of tears results in the deaths of between twenty and forty percent of the tribe.[45] The government moves more than three hundred members of the Apache tribe from Arizona and New Mexico to Kansas, Texas, and Florida. The requirements of the General Allotment Act result in Indian nations moving off of ninety million acres of their land holdings.[46] The diminishment of space occupied by the nation's indigenous populations is so commonplace that it leads to the popular American narrative of the vanishing Indian.[47]

When removal fails to accomplish the denial of Indian national identity, the U.S. government chooses extermination as its final recourse. As the U.S. Secretary of the Interior would argue in 1851, "The policy of removal ... must necessarily be abandoned, and the only alternatives left are, to civilize or exterminate them."[48] The massacre at Wounded Knee is perhaps the best example of the policy's implementation, but other approaches, like the intentional spread of smallpox to defeat the Pontiac's Algonkian Confederacy, also qualify.[49] Once Captain Ecuyer of the Royal Americans introduces the smallpox virus into the indigenous population's environment, upwards of one hundred thousand Indians die in Ohio River nations from the disease over the next few months.[50]

The Bush administration's public justification for its war on terrorism reflects the argumentative choices of the nation's framers. Each of the rationales that the new republic's leadership uses to deny national identity reappears in the modern context. Like Native Americans, terrorists lack a basic respect for or a commitment to primary national identity. Terrorists "have no borders"[51] and they "have no geography."[52] U.S. spokespersons reiterate that al-Qaida forces move frequently through more than sixty countries worldwide. Loosely organized into cells of variable duration, al-Qaida shifts across national borders and lacks any stable homeland. Even in Afghanistan, where members of al-Qaida offer the appearance of residency, administration officials announce that they come "for one single purpose; to invade that country, be a foreign presence, a hostile presence in Afghanistan so they could conduct terrorist activities around the world."[53] Bin Laden's predicament is prototypical; having lost his Saudi Arabian citizenship, he remains foreign to all nations. Unwilling to allow the secession of the poor and disaffected from the world community, the Bush administration approach denies national standing to those who would side with terrorists.

Further reflecting the concerns of the nation's founders, the Bush administration demonstrates concern for those who would finance terrorist activities around the globe. Bush maintains that individuals and organizations in many nations provide the funding for terrorists to establish Internet service, secure telecommunications service, and other means of communication. He stresses the transnational character of these financial transactions, insisting that under the guise of legitimate business, these organizations "enable the proceeds of crime in one country to be transferred to pay for terrorist acts in another."[54] Director of Homeland Security Tom Ridge even recalls the specific language of Jefferson, labeling the terrorists "shadow warriors" or "shadow enemies."[55] Perhaps cognizant of the Jefferson's first inaugural, Bush sounds the same note of optimism: "For money is the oxygen of terrorism. Without the means to raise and move money around the world, terrorists cannot function."[56] Bush provides a public vision of a secure world freed from the scourge of financed killers.

Like the founders, the administration is unequivocal that support for terrorists who attack American citizens or property warrants a denial of national standing to the host government. Rumsfeld considers the Taliban, who harbors al-Qaida within its borders, to be "an illegitimate, unelected group of terrorists."[57] The administration uses metaphors of cancer and parasites to reflect the predatory nature of the Taliban government on the Afghani people. Rumsfeld promises that America "will help the people of [Afghanistan] get rid of the foreign invaders who have come in and taken over a major chunk of your country."[58] Rendered illegitimate by their support for or participation in terrorism, such governments must yield the lands they occupy to others willing to assimilate into civilized community.

The administration uses the priority of security to justify the shift from a defensive to an offensive posture in the war effort. Again reminiscent of the leadership of the early republic, Bush administration officials maintain that they cannot wait until they are attacked before engaging the enemy in battle. Rumsfeld explains the shift in perspective: "The reality is that a terrorist can attack at any time in any place using any technique, and it is physically impossible for a free people to defend in every place at every time against every technique. Now what does that mean? It means...that we have to take this battle, this war to the terrorists, where they are. And the best defense is an effective offense in this case, and that means they have to be rooted out."[59] With the new standard, the administration need not provide evidence that a group has previously attacked U.S. citizens or property; the nation becomes justified in going on the assault to prevent what such individuals or groups might do in the future.

The administration's means for accomplishing the usurpation of national identity mirrors the blueprint of the founders. Initially, the administration moves to isolate terrorists and those who support them. Colin Powell warns of a bleak future for those nations unwilling to stop supporting terrorism: "We have designated those [who harbor and aid terrorism] as sponsors of terrorism ... it is not in their interest to continue acting in this way, because they will risk further isolation and increasing pressure if they participate in such activities. And hopefully the message will get through and they'll start to change past patterns of behavior."[60] The strategy of isolation, when implemented, takes many forms. The U.S. pressures Saudi Arabia, Pakistan and the United Arab Emirates to withdraw their diplomatic recognition of the Taliban government. Bush signs an executive order forbidding the U.S. government or U.S. businesses from engaging in commerce with those who support terrorists. The administration encourages the media not to offer a public forum for the leaders of al-Qaida and the Taliban and the U.S. military targets Afghanistan's communications systems early in the air campaign. The approach disqualifies nations, organizations, or individuals that participate in or support terrorism from having voice in the controversy.

For those who fail to respond to isolation, the option of removal awaits them. The task of the United States, as Rumsfeld defines it, is "to root out the global terrorist networks—not just in Afghanistan but wherever they are—and to ensure that they cannot threaten the American people or our way of life."[61] Administration officials rely on a number of metaphors to demonstrate their commitment to removing the terrorists. Among the oft-repeated phrases that recall the history of the early republic's response to Native Americans are "rooting them out," "draining the swamp," "smoke them out," and "get them running." America promises not to leave Afghanistan until the forces of the Northern Alliance completely remove the former Taliban government.

As before in the history of the United States, removal alone does not qualify as a sufficient strategy for the defeat of terrorism. Perhaps cognizant of the criticism that his own father receives for allowing Saddam Hussein to continue in power after he withdrew from Kuwait, Bush and other senior leaders of his administration rely on the rhetoric of extermination when discussing the war on terrorism. When asked by a reporter "Do you want bin Laden dead," Bush's recalls an old poster from the American west: "Wanted, Dead or Alive."[62] The administration revokes the previous presidential directives forbidding U.S. sponsored assassination. Rumsfeld insists we will have a "long and sustained campaign to liquidate terrorist networks... ."[63] Bush's states his belief that, "the only way to defeat terrorism as a threat to our way of life is to stop it, eliminate it and destroy it where it grows."[64] U.S. allies in the region, most notably the Afghani Minister for Frontier and Tribal Affairs, announce that Eastern Afghanistan will undergo an "Al-Qaida cleansing" campaign.[65] Even Bush's antithesis that the United States will "bring justice to the terrorists or bring the terrorists to justice,"[66] suggests a form of vigilantism that threatens the continued existence of the American nemesis.

The denial of national identity, and by extension national sovereignty rights, pervades the Bush administration's public communication strategy for its war on terrorism. Without any claim to land to call their own, terrorists and the regimes that support them, like Native Americans before them, lose control of their own rights of self-determination. The laws of more civilized others will govern the behaviors of those who would be terrorists, as well as minimize the risks to those who would participate in the new global order. Rendered "quasi-foreign," terrorists become outsiders in any homeland under the Bush strategy.

Revoking Religious Identity

Having denied individual and national identity to the nation's indigenous population, the leaders of the new republic work to undermine the remaining distinctiveness of Native Americans by renouncing their religious identity. As with their other forms of identification, Indian religious affiliations threaten the security and values of the new republic. Sexual promiscuity and other "heathen" practices of many of the tribes constitute an affront, if not temptation, to the puritan morality of the nation's Christian settlers.[67] The colonialists consider many of the indigenous populations' religious practices to be primitive and uncivilized.[68] As Peter Nabakov, anthropologist and Indian studies scholar, reports:

> When white men first witnessed Indians impersonating animal spirits in costume and dance, and worshipping rocks and rainbows, they failed to see this as a deep form of religious expression. To their Christian minds, these were deplorable pagan rites. Worship of more than one deity, and sacrificial offerings directed at the natural world, stamped Indians as a misguided lesser form of mankind. Here were the Christless heathens crying to be rescued from eternal damnation.[69]

Many tribes' respect for sacred places, tolerance for diversity in religious practice and belief, and preference for communal ritual draw even more contrasts with the principles and practices of the Christian faith.[70] John Smith expresses the conclusion of many of the early colonialists to these unfamiliar practices: Indians are "all Savage... . Their chiefe God they worship is the Divell."[71] Portrayed as evil by nature and bent on corrupting the faithful, American Indians pose a threat to fundamental American values.

Convinced of need to civilize the savages that occupy the New World, colonialists in the early republic consider it their responsibility to "Christianize" their heathen brethren.[72] As Christopher Columbus writes on his first day in the New World, "I believe they [the Indians] would easily be made Christians because it seemed that they had no religion."[73] Inspired by a divine calling, the colonists attempt to persuade Native Americans to cast aside their reliance on false prophets. One example of the misguided, as defined from the colonialists' perspective, is the Delaware shaman Neolin, who calls on Indians to abandon alcohol, Christianity and other European influences for the purposes of defeating the white invader.[74] Fighting for their own survival and the enlightenment of the nation's indigenous populations, the early colonialists view the spread of Christianity a necessary precursor to the protection and expansion of civilized society.

To accomplish the usurpation of religious identity from the Native American, the new republic adopts multiple strategies. Primary among these involves the removal and reduction of influence of the Indian nations' religious leaders. After the defeat of the eastern Sioux in the late 1800s, thirty-eight leaders are executed by hanging, while others get distributed across a variety of reservations located from Nebraska to Canada. In Thomas Mail's biography of Dakota Sioux holy man, Fools Crow, he relates:

> Considering the success of the spiritual leaders in leading the Teton warriors against the armies of the United States, one can easily understand why the government and civilians alike would make them prime targets in the subjugation of the Sioux. Once they were confined within the reservations, every possible pressure was brought to bear upon the healers and their followers in an effort to root out and destroy their influence. And it is not surprising that they withdrew to the remotest areas to carry on until now their traditional ways.[75]

Focus on undermining the religious leaders from the perspective of the early republic denies many tribes their future, given that these individuals purportedly had prophetic, visionary perspective.[76]

With the power of the leadership diminished, the new republic moves to curb religious practices that function to establish cultural identity for Native Americans. In 1881, the U.S. government bans the religious ceremony, the Sun Dance, on Sioux reservations. In 1892 and 1904, federal regulations ban tribal religions altogether. Punishments handed out for failure to abide by the bans include imprisonment and the denial of food rations.[77] As late as 1973, the U.S. 10th Circuit Court rules that a public school hair length regulation does not violate the religious rights of Pawnee Indian school children.[78] These examples, reflective of a much larger group of cases denying Indian religious practices, demonstrate how the government uses the denial of religious rites and rituals to assimilate Native Americans into the dominant culture.

Essential to the abrogation of religious identity is the strategy of denying tribal access to sacred lands. Early on, Native Americans are moved off of sacred lands through armed engagement and legal constriction of their territory. Contemporary Native Americans experience ongoing attempts to continue restricting their access to sacred lands. In 1977, the Supreme Court, for example, rules against Navajo plaintiffs who argue that the creation of the Glen Canyon Dam in Colorado violates their religious freedom. The creation of the dam floods Navajo prayer grounds and areas where members of the tribe believe some of their gods reside. Assessing the outcome of the case, law associate Martin Loesch notes, "Economic development for the benefits of the majority outweighed the fundamental religious rights of the minority."[79] Governmental removal policy, coupled with a prioritization of other interests over the right to access sacred lands, diminishes the ability of the nation's indigenous populations to practice their religious beliefs.

As in the case of individual and national identity, the experience of Native Americans with regard to their religious identity has obvious parallels in the current war on terrorism. The Bush camp depicts bin Laden and his Islamic fundamentalist followers as antithetical to any religious faith. Resurrecting John Smith's claim that Indians worship the devil, Donald Rumsfeld argues the terrorists are believers "not in the theology of God, but the theology of the self and in the whispered words of temptation, 'ye shall be as gods.'"[80] Colin Powell adds that, by nature, the actions of al-Qaida are antithetical to religious faith. He surmises that, "It is terrorism that is directed against people. It represents no faith, no religion. It is evil. It is murderous... and that's why the word terrorist is the right noun to apply to people like Osama bin Laden."[81] To gain credibility on the issue, the administration points to the statement by fifty-six Islamic nations denouncing the September 11th attacks and declaring that such attacks violate the principles of Islam.[82] From U.S. perspective, Osama bin Laden and his followers are the antithesis of fundamental tenets of all religious faiths.

The administration offers various examples for how Islamic fundamentalists, represented by bin Laden and the Taliban, distort the teachings of religion. Bush decries the lack of religious freedom in Afghanistan, maintaining, "They destroy great monuments of human culture and religious faith. They execute people who convert to other religions. They steal food from starving people."[83] Rumsfeld stresses the Taliban's basic lack of humanitarian values by reminding his audiences they killed hundreds of Afghanis when they took over the country initially, they were cruel to the Afghanis during their reign, and now they are executing Afghani citizens who are trying to leave the country.[84] The Taliban becomes the Bush administration's example of the results the world can expect should they accept the words of false prophets claiming Muslim fundamentalists act in the name of Allah.

Throughout public discourse for its war on terrorism, the Bush administration limits its denial of religious identity to those who participate in Islamic fundamentalism as practiced by al-Qaida and the Taliban. Recalling "the American tradition of tolerance and religious liberty,"[85] Bush is emphatic the United States is not attacking the Muslim faith or the Afghani people.

Offering a story he claims demonstrates the "true nature of America,"[86] Bush tells of Christian and Jewish women going shopping with Muslim women afraid to go outside alone. Administration officials recall prior conflicts, such as Bosnia or the 1979 Soviet invasion of Afghanistan, to demonstrate the historical willingness of the United States to come to the aid of its more moderate Muslim neighbors. From the personal to the policy level, Bush insists the United States will uphold the religious freedoms of moderate, deserving members of the Muslim faith.

Soon after the attacks of September 11th, government officials establish the goals of the U.S. war on terrorism to include the removal of Islamic fundamentalist leaders in Afghanistan. One goal of administration policy, according to Donald Rumsfeld, is "to go after the Taliban and see that that government is thrown out of office."[87] Mullah Omar, the leader of the Taliban, remains a primary target, as do other high-ranking religious figures in the former government. Maintaining removal of false prophets to be sanctioned by the divine, Bush refers to his goals in the war on terrorism alternatively as a "mission," "calling," or "crusade." While in the latter case, the administration later apologizes for the unintended reference, Bush's repeated call to stamp out the "evildoers" echoes the word choice of Protestant radical Thomas Muntzer at the inception of the reformation: "Don't let them live any longer, the evil-doers who turn us away from God ... For a godless man [he was referring to Catholics] has no right to live if he hinders the godly."[88] Targeting the religious leadership of the Taliban, the Bush administration begins the process of dismantling Islamic fundamentalism around the globe.

The administration continues the path of the early republic by denying Islamic terrorists certain religious practices that define their culture. The leadership of the U.S. military vows to continue its "Enduring Freedom" air campaign through the Islamic holy month of Ramadan. Having cast both the Taliban and al-Qaida as antithetical to religion, the Bush administration insists that they do not merit normal consideration of their religious identity as Muslims. Further, in a move that draws international criticism, the shaving of the Guantanomo Bay detainees' beards (a required sign of religious affiliation previously dictated by the Taliban) recalls memories of the treatment of Indian children when U.S. boarding schools require them to cut their hair (with hair length a sign of religious belief in many Indian tribes).

While the Bush administration takes incremental steps toward abrogating religious practices of captured al-Qaida and Taliban forces, the approach remains cautious. Unwilling to risk alienating the broader Muslim world, the administration still permits some religious affiliation by its captives, such as the issuance of prayer blankets and the posting of a sign pointing to Mecca at Camp Xray. The administration's approach to a gradual reduction in religious identity once again parallels the incremental approach of the framers who wait many years before legally banning the rights of religious practice to Native Americans.

The Bush administration's denial of sacred place augments the removal of religious leaders and the restriction on religious practices. On August 23, 1996, bin Laden frames the conflict between al-Qaida and the United States as a battle for sacred space. He issues "The Declaration of Jihad on the Americans Occupying the Country of the Two Sacred Places," a reference to the continuing U.S. military presence in Saudi Arabia. After the September 11th attacks, he makes reference to the establishment of Israel on Muslim holy lands by the Allied Forces at the end of World War II.[89] Continued occupation by U.S. forces and allies on the sacred spaces of Islam demonstrates the administration's belief that violent, Islamic fundamentalists undermine their own case for religious identity.

The Bush administration public communication strategy treats terrorists and those who support them as evil and unworthy of divine providence. As the antithesis of the sacred, such individuals and groups risk the faithful and falsely proselytize to the vulnerable. Having undermined their religious identity, the United States incrementally moves to disqualify the Taliban and al-Qaida from receiving protections to ensure the free exercise of their religious faith.

The Doctrine of Global Manifest Destiny

Taken together the rhetorical strategies of the Bush administration in relation to the Taliban and al-Qaida evoke the rules and presumptions associated with the doctrine of manifest destiny. As before, the United States claims it is obliged to preserve and promote the advancement of civilization, only this time the responsibility extends into the global arena. By denying individual, national, or religious identity to resistant forces, the leadership's strategy attempts to diffuse group identities that might compete with the fulfillment of its mission.

As the doctrine of manifest destiny moves into the global arena, the object of conquest appears to shift from the physical frontier of the land to the economic frontier of global markets. Members of the Bush administration insist they do not want to hold Afghani land, but they do nonetheless possess motivations of economic self-interest within the region. Curbing violence in the Middle East and South Asia maximizes the ability of U.S. businesses to locate in the area. Access to local markets previously not open to U.S. products enhances the region's economic benefits for American commerce. A friendly Afghani government, willing to enter into joint ventures with the United States or its businesses, expands the economic incentives for increased globalization.

A primary example involves the energy resources in the region. From 1992 through 1995, discoveries of valuable oil and gas reserves occur in Kazakhstan and Turkmenistan. Afghanistan emerges as the least-expensive, most politically viable route for retrieving the region's oil resources. In 1995, a U.S. company, Unocal, begins negotiating with the Taliban to construct oil and gas pipelines from Turkmenistan, through Afghanistan, to Pakistani ports.[90] Former oil executive and current Vice President Cheney tells a large group of oil-industry executives in 1998 that, "I can't think of a time when we've had a region emerge as suddenly to become as strategically significant as the Caspian."[91] Removal of the Taliban and the terrorists it harbors opens up possibilities for increased expansion into a lucrative, oil-rich region of the world.

Viewed from such a context, the comment of General Tommy Franks, commander of U.S. forces in Afghanistan is far from innocuous: "Yes, we are interested in Mazar-e Sharif. We're interested in it because it would provide a land bridge, as has been said, up to Uzbekistan, which provides us, *among other things*, a humanitarian pathway for us to move supplies out of Central Asia and down into Afghanistan."[92] [emphasis mine] Uzbekistan, located on the northern border of Turkmenistan, provides a useful pathway for beginning a realized, global doctrine of U.S. manifest destiny.

Using argumentative strategies already familiar to its domestic audiences, the Bush administration evokes certain rules and presumptions from American history as foundational principles for understanding its war on terrorism. Without a similar historical context, the broader international community lacks preparation for a U.S. approach that justifies denying individual, national, and religious identity. As the controversy continues, it will provide a public forum for negotiating the argumentative standards of the new global environment.

NOTES

1. George W. Bush, "Bush's Approval Ratings Tops Father's; But President, Supporters Acknowledge Popularity Surge Will Not Last," Milwaukee Journal Sentinel, 11/25/01, p. 1A, Lexis-Nexis, 11/27/01.

2. As quoted in "Issue Focus: Critics Charge America Seeking 'Vengeance' not Justice at Guantanamo," Foreign Media Reaction, U.S. Department of State, Office of Research, 1/25/02. http://208.37.97.178/scripts/cqcgi.exe/@pdqtest1.env?CQ_SESSIONS_KEY=siocjpiephx...2/7/2002.

3. Ibid.

4. Kathryn M. Olson and G. Thomas Goodnight, "Entanglements of Consumption, Cruelty, Privacy and Fashion: The Social Controversy Over Fur," Quarterly Journal of Speech, 80.3 (1994): 249.

5. G. Thomas Goodnight, "Controversy," in Argument in Controversy: Proceedings of the Seventh SCA/AFA Conference on Argumentation, ed. Donn Parsons (Annandale, VA: Speech Communication Association, 1991), 6.

6. I derive this summary of the Bush administration stance from all of the public speeches of George W. Bush, Dick Cheney, Donald Rumsfeld, Colin Powell, Tom Ridge, and John Ashcroft from September 11, 2001 through December 31, 2001.

7. Donald Rumsfeld, "Department of Defense News Conference with Secretary of Defense Donald Rumsfeld and General Tommy R. Franks, Commander In Chief, CENTCOM," 11/27/01. Federal News Service, 2001. Lexis-Nexis, 11/27/01.

8. "George Washington to James Duane," September 7, 1783, in Writings of George Washington, ed. John C. Fitzpatrick, 27:133-40, as cited in Documents of United States Indian Policy, ed. Francis Paul Prucha (Lincoln, NB: University of Nebraska Press, 1990), 1.

9. See "Proclamation of the Continental Congress," September 22, 1783, in Journals of the Continental Congress, 25: 602, as cited in Documents of United States Indian Policy, 3.

10. Thomas Jefferson's "Original Rough draft" of the Declaration of Independence, in The Papers of Thomas Jefferson, eds. Julian Boyd et. al., Vol. 1 (Princeton, NJ, 1950——), 427, as cited in Peter S. Onuf, Jefferson's Empire: The Language of American Nationhood (Charlottesville, VA: University Press of Virginia, 2000), 26.

11. For a more extensive discussion of the homogenization of American Indians, see Mary E. Stuckey and John M. Murphy, "By Any Other Name: Rhetorical Colonialism in North America," American Indian Culture and Research Journal 25 (4), 2001 (In press) and David E. Wilkins, American Indian Sovereignty and the U.S. Supreme Court (Austin, Tx: University of Texas Press, 1997).

12. Acts of violence perpetrated by the white settlers are well-documented. For example, more than 50,000 natives die at the hands of Christopher Columbus' soldiers. See David E. Stannard, American Holocaust: The Conquest of the New World (New York: Oxford Press, 1992).

13. James Wilson, The Earth Shall Weep: A History of Native America (New York: Atlantic Monthly Press, 1998) and Richard Drinnon, Facing West: The Metaphysics of Indian-Hating and Empire-Building (Norman, OK: University of Oklahoma Press, 1990).

14. Wallace, 1999.

15. As quoted in Drinnon, 1990, 75.

16. Onuf, 2000.

17. Thomas Jefferson, *Notes on the State of Virginia* ed. William Peden (Chapel Hill, NC: Chapel Hill, 1954) as cited in Onuf, 2000.

18. Contemporary scholars who study the role of women in Native American culture argue that, unlike Jefferson's conclusion, women in Indian tribal societies occupy complementary, rather than unequal, positions with their male counterparts. See Daniel Maltz and JoAllyn Archambault, "Gender and Power in Native North America: Concluding Remarks," in *Women and Power in Native North America,* eds. Laura F. Klein and Lillian A. Ackerman (Norman, OK: University of Oklahoma Press, 1995), 230-250.

19. Onuf, 2000.

20. Thomas Jefferson to the Chiefs of the Ottawas, Chippewas, Powtowatamies, Wyandots, and Senecas of Sandusky, April 22, 1808, as cited in Onuf, 2000, 49. In actuality, Jefferson's prophecy turns out to be true for many Native Americans, but not for the reasons he outlines. Gretches, et. al. argue that, "Deprived of a land base large enough to supply a subsistence, [Indians] become dependent on federal rations promised in treaties." See David, H. Getches, Charles F. Wilkinson, and Robert A. Williams, Jr. *Cases and Materials on Federal Indian Law,* 3rd ed. (St. Paul, MN: West Publishing Co., 1993), 168.

21. David Wallace Adams, *Education for Extinction: American Indians and the Boarding School Experience 1875-1928* (Lawrence, KS: University of Kansas, 1995).

22. M. Annette Jaimes, "Federal Indian Identification Policy: A Usurpation of Indigenous Sovereignty in North America," in *The State of Native America; Genocide, Colonization, and Resistence* (Boston, MA: South End Press, 1992), 123-138.

23. Donald E. Worcester, *The Apaches: Eagles of the Southwest* (Norman, OK: University of Oklahoma Press, 1979), 308.

24. Worcester, 1979.

25. George W. Bush, "George W. Bush Meets with Indonesian President Megawati Soekarnoputri," 9/19/01. Federal Document Clearing House Political Transcripts, 2001. Lexis-Nexis, 11/27/01.

26. George W. Bush, "George W. Bush Addresses the Nation," 9/11/01. Federal Document Clearing House Political Transcripts, 2001. Lexis-Nexis, 11/27/01.

27. Again, I take this summary from the statements of Bush, Cheney, Rumsfeld, Ashcroft, Ridge and Powell from September 11th through December 31, 2001.

28. George Bush, "President George W. Bush's Weekly Radio Address, 11/10/01. Federal News Service, 2001. Lexis-Nexis, 11/27/01.

29. See, for example, Donald Rumsfeld, "Special Defense Department Briefing with Secretary of Defense Donald Rumsfeld," 9/18/01. Federal News Service, 2001.

30. George W. Bush, "George W. Bush delivers Keynote Address at Memorial Service for Victims of the September 11th Attacks on the Pentagon," 10/11/01. Federal Document Clearing House Political Transcripts, 2001.

31. George W. Bush, "George W. Bush Addresses a Joint Session of Congress," 9/20/01. Federal Document Clearing House Political Transcripts, 2001.

32. George W. Bush, "George W. Bush Delivers Keynote Address at Memorial Service for Victims of the September 11th Attacks on the Pentagon," 10/11/01. Federal Document Clearing House Political Transcripts, 2001. Lexis-Nexis, 11/27/01.

33. George W. Bush, "George W. Bush's Weekly Radio Address," 10/10/01. Federal News Service, 2001.

34. Donald Rumsfeld, "Defense Department Regular Briefing," 11/13/01. Federal News Service, 2001. Lexis-Nexis, 11/27/01.

35. Ibid.

36. Wilson, 1998, 52.

37. Onuf, 2000, 45

38. Thomas Jefferson, "First Inaugural Address," March 4, 1801, in *Jefferson Writings,* ed. Merrill D. Peterson (New York, 1984), 493.

39. Thomas Jefferson to William Henry Harrison, February 27, 1803, in Documents of United States Indian Policy, 23.

40. Mario Gonzalez and Elizabeth Cook-Lynn, *The Politics of Hallowed Ground: Wounded Knee and the Struggle for Indian Sovereignty* (Chicago, IL: University of Illinois Press, 1999), 146.

41. Theodore Roosevelt, "Hunting Trips of a Ranchman," in *Works*, vol. I., 19, as cited in Gonzalez and Cook-Lynn, 1999, 146.

42. See "Report of Committee on Indian Affairs," October 15, 1783, as cited in Documents of United States Indian Policy, 1975.

43. Wallace, 1999, 18.

44. Fikes, 1996.

45. Wilson, 1999.

46. Jaimes, 1992.

47. Mary Stuckey, "Americans in Light and Shadow: Presidential Articulations of National Identity," unpublished Mss, under review, University of Kansas Press.

48. Letter, President Jefferson to William Henry Harrison, February 27, 1803, as cited in Documents of United States Indian Policy, 23.

49. Ward Churchill, Indians are Us? Culture and Genocide in Native North America (Monroe, MA: Common Courage Press, 1994).

50. Lazarus, 1991.

51. George W. Bush, "President George W. Bush Holds News Media Availability," 9/17/01. Federal Document Clearing House Political Transcripts, 2001. Lexis-Nexis, 11/27/01.

52. Colin Powell, "Secretary of State Colin Powell Holds Media Availability with Turkish Foreign Minister Ismail Cem," 9/27/01. Federal Document Clearing House Political Transcripts, 2001. Lexis-Nexis, 11/27/01.

53. Colin Powell, "Colin Powell Delivers Remarks to Business Leaders (as released by the State Department)," 10/18/01. Federal Document Clearing House Political Transcripts, 2001. Lexis-Nexis, 11/27/01.

54. George W. Bush, "George W. Bush Delivers Remarks at the Treasury Department's Financial Crimes Enforcement Network," 11/7/01. Federal Document Clearing House Political Transcripts, 2001. Lexis-Nexis, 11/27/01.

55. Tom Ridge, "Special White House Briefing by Tom Ridge, Director of the Office of Homeland Security," 10/30/01. Federal News Service 2001. Lexis-Nexis, 11/27/01.

56. Ibid.

57. Donald Rumsfeld, "Special Defense Department Briefing with Secretary of Defense Donald Rumsfeld and Joint Chiefs of Staff Chairman General Richard B. Myers," 10/29/01. Federal News Service, 2001. Lexis-Nexis, 11/27/01.

58. Donald Rumsfeld,, "Defense Department Special Briefing," 10/12/01. Federal News Service, 2001. Lexis-Nexis, 11/27/01.

59. Donald Rumsfeld, "Donald Rumsfeld Holds Department of Defense News Briefing," 9/16/01. Federal Document Clearing House Political Transcripts, 2001. Lexis-Nexis, 12/7/01.

60. Colin Powell, "Media Availability with Secretary of State Colin Powell and Chinese Foreign Secretary Tang Jiaxuan Following Their Meetings," 9/21/01. Federal News Service, 2001. Lexis-Nexis, 12/6/01.

61. Donald Rumsfeld, "Defense Department Operational Update Briefing," 11/1/01. Federal News Service, 2001. Lexis-Nexis, 12/7/01.

62. George W. Bush, "President George W. Bush Holds News Media Availability," 11/17/01. Federal Document Clearing House Political Transcripts, 2001. Lexis-Nexis, 12/6/01.

63. Donald Rumsfeld, "Special Defense Department Briefing Re: Operational Update on Afghanistan," 10/18/01. Federal News Service, 2001. Lexis-Nexis, 12/7/01.

64. George W. Bush, "George W. Bush Addresses a Joint Session," 9/20/01. Federal Document Clearing House Political Transcripts, 2001. Lexis-Nexis, 2001, 12/6/01.

65. As reported in Philip Smucker, "Hunt for Al-Qaida Intensifies," Christian Science Monitor, January 18, 2002, p. l, col. 2.

66. George W. Bush, "George W. Bush Addresses a Joint Session of Congress," 9/20/01. Federal Document Clearing House Political Transcripts, 2001. Lexis-Nexis, 2001, 12/6/01.

67. Stannard, 1992.

68. Martin C. Loesch, "The First Americans and the 'Free' Exercise of Religion,'" in Native American Cultural and Religious Freedoms, ed. John R. Wunder (New York: Garland Publishing, 1999), 19-84.

69. Peter Nabakov, Native American Testimony: A Chronicle of Indian-White Relations From Prophecy to the Present, ed. Peter Nabakov (New York: Penguin Books, 1991), 50-51.

70. Ibid.

71. John Smith, as quoted in Travels and Works of Captain John Smith, President of Virginia and Admiral of New England, 1580-1631, vol. I (Edinburgh: John Grant, 1910), 75.

72. Fikes, 1996.

73. As quoted in Daniel K. Inouye, "Discrimination and Native American Religious Rights," Native American Cultural and Religious Freedoms, ed. John R. Wunder (New York: Garland Publishers, 1999), 10.

74. Wilson, 1996.

75. Thomas E. Mails (Assisted by Dallas Chief Eagle), Fools Crow (Lincoln, NE: University of Nebraska Press, 1979), 17.

76. Mails, 1979.

77. Loesch, 1999.

78. Getches, et. al, 1993.

79. Loesch, 1999, 346.

80. Donald Rumsfeld, "George W. Bush Delivers Keynote Address at Memorial Service for Victims of the September 11th Attacks on the Pentagon," 10/11/01. Federal Document Clearing House Political Transcripts, 2001, Lexis-Nexis, 12/7/01.

81. Colin Powell, "Colin Powell Delivers Remarks to the National Foreign Policy Conference," 10/26/01. Federal Document Clearing House Political Transcripts, 2001. Lexis-Nexis, 12/6/01.

82. George W. Bush, "George W. Bush Holds News Conference," 10/11/01. Federal Document Clearing House Political Transcripts, 2001. Lexis-Nexis, 12/6/01.

83. George W. Bush, "Remarks by President George W. Bush at Signing of Proclamation For 'National Employer Support of the Guard and Reserve Week,'" 11/9/01. Federal News Service, 2001. Lexisnexis, 12/6/01.

84. See, for example, Donald Rumsfeld, "Defense Department Regular Briefing," 11/13/01. Federal News Service, 2001. Lexis-Nexis, 12/7/01; Donald Rumsfeld, "Defense Department Operational Briefing," 11/19/01. Federal News Service, 2001. Lexis-Nexis, 12/7/01; and Donald Rumsfeld, "Media Availability with Secretary of Defense Donald Rumsfeld on Airplane en Route to Fort Bragg, North Carolina," 11/12/01, Federal News Service, 2001. Lexis-Nexis, 12/7/01.

85. George W. Bush, "George W. Bush Delivers Weekly Radio Address," 11/24/01. Federal Document Clearing House Political Transcripts, 2001. Lexis-Nexis, 12/6/01.

86. George W. Bush, "George W. Bush Holds News Conference," 10/11/01. Federal Document Clearing House Political Transcripts, 2001. Lexis-Nexis, 12/6/01.

87. Donald Rumsfeld, "Defense Department Operational Update," 1/22/01. Federal News Service, 2001.

88. As quoted in Stannard, 1992, 190.

89. Associated Press, "Text of Osama bin Laden's Statement," ABCNEWS.com. 10/7/01, 5:20 ET.

90. George Monbiot, "Comments & Analysis: America's Pipe Dream: A Pro-Western Regime in Kabul Should Give the US an Afghan Route for Caspian Oil," *The Guardian*, October 23, 2001, Sec. Guaradian Leader Pages, p. 19.

91. "The Great Gas Game," *Christian Science Monitor*, October 25, 2001, p. 8.

92. General Tommy Franks, "Defense Department Regular Briefing," 11/8/01. Federal News Service, 2001. Lexis-Nexis, 12/7/01.

Hypocrisy and Hatred

Robert P. Newman

Abstract

From the time of the Pilgrims, many Americans have believed they were anointed by God to lead a sinful world into righteousness. After the Herculean effort of World War II in banishing fascist evil, we were plunged into the nastiness of the Cold War. The communist threat was magnified by ignorant chauvinists to justify clandestine dirty tricks to match the tactics of the Soviet Union. This was quite at odds with our self-image, and with our proclaimed lawfulness and kindliness. In the last half of the 20th Century the United States conducted, organized, directed, financed, and was otherwise responsible for terrible death and destruction, of which Vietnam was the major tragedy and the only instance in which our hypocrisy and duplicity were fully displayed. The world is not fooled; it now sees us as a rogue state with terrifying destructive power, to be brought low by any means available.

> *What makes it so plausible to assume that hypocrisy is the vice of vices is that integrity can indeed exist under cover of all other vices except this one. Only crime and the criminal, it is true, confront us with the perplexity of radical evil; but only the hypocrite is really rotten to the core.*
>
> Hannah Arendt, *On Revolution*

On March 24, 1955, a secret ceremony was held in Dwight Eisenhower's White House. It was attended by the President, Director of Central Intelligence Allen Dulles, Secretary of State John Foster Dulles, and the American Ambassador to Iran, Loy Henderson. The ceremony was to honor Kermit (Kim) Roosevelt, grandson of Theodore Roosevelt and cousin of Franklin. The honoree, his wife, and two children entered the White House through a side door; if the press had seen a Roosevelt entering this Republican White House, embarrassing questions would have been asked.[1]

Kermit Roosevelt was being given the National Security Medal; he was only the fourth person to receive it. The medal itself was secret, awarded entirely at the discretion of the president, hence unlike the Medal of Honor for military achievement, which has to be approved by Congress. The

National Security Medals are kept in CIA vaults. No awards are announced until the recipient has left government service and the agency decides its action will not have undesirable consequences.

The ceremony was not on the records, and it was timed to take place ten minutes before a scheduled meeting of the National Security Council so that the top officials could attend without attracting notice. Kermit Roosevelt was being rewarded for successfully directing the first clandestine overthrow of a pro-Soviet or neutral (John Foster Dulles hated neutrality) government in the intensifying Cold War. This was regime change with a vengeance. Despite American adherence to all the progressive doctrines of various Geneva, Hague, and United Nations conventions covering the use of force in international relations, and the prohibitions on interfering in the affairs of sovereign nations, the United States had just carried out the first of what was to be a long series of overturning democratically-elected governments. The country was Iran; the government overturned was that of Mohammed Mossadegh, an aristocratic nationalist with good anti-Communist credentials but who had the gall to nationalize the Anglo-Iranian Oil Company; the regime installed by Kermit Roosevelt was that of Muhammad Reza Shah Pahlevi; the Shah's regime ruled Iran by torture and repression, using primarily American arms, for 26 years; and when he was swept away in the revolution of 1978, every Iranian knew who was to blame for the long reign of terror—The Great Satan, America.[2]

Every Iranian knew, as did the rest of the Muslim world; but few Americans did, and by 1978, most of them had forgotten. Only a handful of insiders had been aware that early on July 19, 1953, with a major slush fund to hire thugs and demonstrators, and with a twenty-two-page plan outlining how Mossadegh was to be overthrown, Kermit Roosevelt entered Iran from Baghdad. The plan had been approved on June 25 by the American high command.

By the 21st century, scholars were generally agreed that the regime change in Iran had been stupid and counterproductive, as were most of the interventions carried out by clandestine American forces in the post-World War II period. I do not argue the substantive case against these interventions; others have done that well. The thrust of this account is that Arendt's condemnation of hypocrisy is squarely on target, and that the swelling anti-Americanism throughout the world is due largely to the fact that we pose as righteous moralists while condemning our opponents—first in the Soviet world, now in the Third World—as terrorists, barbarians, inhabitants of a subhuman, 'evil' world.

We ourselves are guilty in spades, for at least half a century, of the evil against which we say we are now fighting. We, these United States, have conducted, organized, financed, trained, and condoned terrorists in our client states to the extent of millions of victims. This terror was not just occasional incidents carried out by rogue agents, nor was it "collateral damage" in a legitimate war. It was officially sanctioned, codified, enshrined in documents such as NSC-68 (National Security Council document no. 68), often called the blueprint for the Cold War. This document bore the imprimatur of the National Security Council and the president of the United States. It authorized whatever it takes to defeat what was falsely labeled a Stalinist program to conquer the whole world. This authorization of terror was not based on a realistic evaluation of the Soviet challenge; it was a panicky judgment by ignorant jingoists.[3]

How could it happen that the United States, a country whose self-image is so righteous, so squeaky clean, so committed to benevolence, humanitarianism, democracy, the rule of law—so *Christian*—would adopt an operational code justifying terrorism? And why is the electorate so invincibly ignorant of any such code, allowing the president to rail about the degeneracy of the September 2001 hijackers and completely foreclose the possibility of anyone saying, "Well, this is what happens when you have been corrupted by fifty years of a Cold War"?

The first question is easy to answer. Our sublime righteousness made it impossible to acknowledge that we had made the same commitment to dirty tricks that our Soviet opponents had made. Consequently NSC-68 had a Q classification, higher than top secret, and the document was not declassified until 1975. By then, Watergate, Vietnam, and the Nixon resignation overshadowed a 25-year-old document that no one had heard of. The paper trail showing how NSC-68 was constructed was not completely available until 1999.

NSC-68 was constructed and ultimately approved during 1950, the year that marked the point of no return in the Cold War. Before that, there had been disagreements and minor conflicts with the Soviet Union, but it was not until the fall of 1949 that really traumatic events shattered the nation. In 1949, China went Communist, and the Soviet Union exploded an atomic bomb.

The impact of China's defection from "our side" has disappeared from foreign policy discourse; we have become accustomed to the fact that China is Communist, and have forgotten what trauma that defection entailed and how it contributed to the legitimation of an "anything goes" code of covert activities. Here one must begin with the religious foundations of our national policy. Many of the early colonists came to this continent for religious reasons.[4] They took the Abrahamic code seriously, but the Jews had rejected God's messenger-son, the Christians were now the Chosen People, fated to establish a City on a Hill, and be a Light unto the Nations. Hence, the manifest destiny that drove the American missionary enterprise.

China was the largest single theater of American Protestant missionary enterprise. In 1936, there were 6,059 missionaries in China, and each of them had a built-in constituency back home to which they regularly reported. Sherwood Eddy, prominent chronicler of China missions, noted of his youth, "China was the goal, the lodestar, the great magnet that drew us all in those days."[5] It was not just Eddy for whom China was the lodestar: Henry Luce, born in China of missionary parents, developed a lifelong devotion to the cause served by his father, and to Chiang Kai-shek, the great Christian leader of that country. In the Luce theology, which all of his publishing empire promulgated until his death, missions and righteousness, Republican politics, Chiang and Americanism were all bound together and inseparable.

But the atheists defeated the Christians in 1949, and drove them out of China. The Communists (of course controlled by the Soviet Union) won the *theological* battle, the battle for men's souls. Now there was a unified Communist behemoth from Germany to the Pacific, furnishing fodder for the wickedest demagogue of the century, Joseph McCarthy. McCarthy's crusade to root out subversion from the Democratic government had as its first victims the China Foreign Service officers. China could only have rejected American hegemony because there were traitors in the State Department. In McCarthy's lexicon, anything at all was justified to reverse this horrible calamity.

The same autumn that saw the declaration of the People's Republic of China saw an even more startling and fateful development: earlier than most physicists expected, the Soviet Union exploded its first atom bomb. Truman made the announcement on September 22, 1949. Exclusive control of the Ultimate Weapon had been the greatest defensive asset the United States possessed. Soviet ground armies could overrun our European allies almost at will, or so many thought, and the hope was that before the Soviets had their bomb, we would have built up NATO defenses to a more powerful level. The early Soviet bomb also stimulated talk of treason; our physicists knew Soviet science could produce a bomb, but the jittery politicians were sure this was the work of spies. When the patrician Alger Hiss was convicted of lying about whether he had passed state secrets to a former Communist agent, Whittaker Chambers, McCarthy appeared to be vindicated, and the American Inquisition took off.[6]

American atomic bomb production had languished since World War II; now Truman knew he had to confront the problem of maintaining American superiority in arms. Physicist Edward Teller and his supporters were pressing for the construction of the Super, or hydrogen bomb, which could be 1,000 times more powerful than the fission bombs; but the Joint Chiefs of Staff, in 1947, held that the United States could use no more than 150 Nagasaki-type bombs.[7] By 1950 they had changed their minds.

Shortly after the Soviet bomb was announced, the scientists on the Atomic Energy Commission's Advisory Committee convened. They were agreed that the Super was not needed. Enrico Fermi and I.I. Rabi wrote a section of their report that condemned the project out of hand: "Necessarily such a weapon goes far beyond any military objective and enters the range of very great natural catastrophes. By its very nature it cannot be confined to a military objective but becomes a weapon which in practical effect is almost one of genocide. It is clear that such a weapon cannot be justified on any ethical ground... It is necessarily an evil thing considered in any light."[8] James B. Conant, a member of the committee, was particularly firm. At one meeting he allegedly said that the bomb would be built "over my dead body."

Here were some of America's finest brains, confronting a moral challenge of great moment. That they lost their battle indicates the growth of the hysteria and jingoism that enabled a code endorsing terror as an official government policy. The Atomic Energy Commission was divided, two for the new weapon and three against. In the Department of State, Secretary Acheson requested both George Kennan and Paul Nitze to study the matter. Nitze, arguably the arch hawk of all time, had no trouble deciding that there should be no limit to American striking power: build everything.

Kennan studied the matter for two months, interviewed some physicists, and wrote a 79-page analysis that he later considered to have been "one of the most important, if not the most important, of all the documents I ever wrote in government." He was absolutely against the Super: "It is entirely possible that war will be waged against us again... by these weapons. If so, we shall doubtless have to respond in kind, for that may be the price of survival. I still think it vital to what it is that we are about that we not fall into the error of initiating or planning to initiate, the employment of these weapons or concepts, thus hypnotizing ourselves into the belief that they may ultimately serve some positive national purpose."[9] After the decision went against him, Kennan fought hard for a "no first use" declaration; he lost that battle too.

Acheson, pilloried by the Republican rightwing as soft on Communism, was instead already a member of the "sky-is-falling" Cold Warriors. He did not even show Kennan's paper to Truman. He sided with the military, an AEC subcommittee appointed by Truman, and Nitze. Truman ordered a crash program to build H-bombs on January 31, 1950. We will never know whether, as some of the doves thought, a public declaration of refusal to build H-bombs would have deterred the Soviet from doing so. But in the 21st century, one has to perceive the frantic race to overkill capacity on both sides as pathological. Our warhead stockpile crested in 1967 at 32,500 deliverable bombs.[10] The H-bomb decision, not the use of two fission bombs to shock Japan into surrendering, was the tragic decision of the century. No hawk could then, nor can a chauvinist today, contend that we accomplished anything necessary. Did some super patriot think we needed to destroy Moscow 300 times over? Perhaps, in the 21st century, our support of repressive regimes, our provision of helicopter gunships to oppose Palestinian rockthrowers, our use of "smart" bombs to flush terrorists out of Afghan caves (and incinerate an occasional wedding party) are more generative of anti-American feeling than was mid-century nuclear proliferation. Attentive publics around the world, however, have not forgotten that madness.

Even though he approved the Super, Truman realized there was uncertainty about military policy. He therefore wrote his two prime advisors at the end of January 1950, "I hereby direct the Secretary of State and the Secretary of Defense to undertake a re-examination of our objectives in peace and war and of the effect of these objectives on our strategic plans, in light of the probable fission bomb capability and the possible thermonuclear capability of the Soviet Union."[11] This was the mandate for the production of NSC-68.

Acheson was given the lead in supervising this inquiry; the vehicle came to be known as the State-Defense Policy Review Group. Defense contributed members to the group, but Secretary Louis Johnson thought it unnecessary—didn't we need every weapon we could build to hold off the Asian hordes?—and paid little attention until toward the end, when he tried to derail it. So the State Department dominated. The chairman was Paul Nitze, a hawkish slavophobe who had gained Acheson's attention as a member of State's Policy Planning Staff. Kennan, now the leading dove in government, was replaced as head of PPS by Nitze.

The choice of Nitze determined the outcome of the inquiry. He may have been the most intense Cold Warrior in the country, and the least principled. In 1946, well in advance of most American officials, he consigned the Soviet to perdition; he thought Stalin's election-eve speech of that year, clearly designed to produce a 99.9% vote for the party list, was a thinly-veiled declaration of war against the United States.[12] When Nitze reported to Eisenhower some years later on a scenario for fighting and winning a nuclear war, Ike said, "We can't have that war. There aren't enough bulldozers to scrape the bodies off the streets."[13] In 1950, Nitze wrote in NSC-68 that the Soviet Union might have the capability, and would have the incentive, for a first nuclear strike against the United States in 1954.

The pressure point in deliberations of Nitze's Policy Review Group was deciding precisely what Soviet objectives were. All the commentaries on NSC-68 with which I am familiar assume that the fever was upon them, that a worst-case scenario was overwhelming, that Nitze was but reflecting his environment. A study of the paper trail yields a different conclusion. There was a furious argument over Soviet intentions, and over the extent to which the Soviet was committed to a plan of world conquest similar to Hitler's. Nitze of course privileged the super-hawks; *but buried in the archives is abundant evidence that more of the experts consulted by the committee sided with Kennan than with Nitze.* Of course, they believed the Soviet was aggressive, and would expand into any vacuum where it was safe to do so, but that it would not commit open aggression. The doves in this argument absolutely endorsed Kennan's contention that the United States should contain Soviet expansion by primarily political and economic means.

Tellingly, the three officials best qualified to assess the true aims of the Soviet Union, George Kennan, Charles "Chip" Bohlen, and Llewellyn Thompson, insisted that Stalin's two main objectives were preserving his total control of the USSR, and creating a cordon of buffer states to prevent a third invasion of Russia from the West. By every evidence available in the 21st century, these three were correct. The alarmism of NSC-68, the "whatever it takes" morality, the tripling of defense expenditures in 1950, the endless hemorrhage of American treasure authorized by this pernicious document was unnecessary and largely avoidable.

But Nitze was quite capable of internalizing what is a common American delusion: proclaiming high moral standards while ignoring them when "necessary." On page 31 of this seminal document, we find a lengthy discussion of "Means." It begins with "The free society is limited in its choice of means to achieve its ends.... The Kremlin is able to select whatever means are expedient in seeking to carry out its fundamental design.... The differences between our fundamental purpose and the Kremlin design, therefore, are reflected in our respective attitudes toward and use of military force."[14] Fair enough.

But then comes Nitze's disclaimer, not to be made public: "Our free society, confronted by a threat to its basic values, naturally will take such action, including the use of military force, as may be required to protect those values. The integrity of our system will not be jeopardized by any measures, covert or overt, violent or non-violent, which serve the purposes of frustrating the Kremlin design, nor does the necessity for conducting ourselves so as to affirm our values in actions as well as words forbid such measures, provided only they are appropriately calculated to that end and are not so excessive or misdirected as to make us enemies of the people instead of the evil men who have enslaved them." Anything goes, so long as it is not counterproductive. Do we have moral standards? Certainly, if it is convenient.

Cold-hearted realism? Not quite. This document was infused with religiosity, redolent of Chosen People ideology, laced with apocalypticism: any further extension of Kremlin-dominated areas may be impossible to overcome, and "It is in this context that this Republic and its citizens in the ascendancy of their strength stand in their deepest peril. The issues that face us are momentous, involving the fulfillment or destruction not only of this Republic but also of civilization itself. They are issues which will not await our deliberations." We need to conduct this struggle, in the words of the Declaration of Independence, "with a firm reliance on the protection of Divine Providence, we mutually pledge to each other our lives, our Fortunes, and our sacred Honor."[15]

American scholars had no access to this document until 1975. By then, the operational code it endorsed had been thoroughly absorbed in the routines of soldiers and diplomats alike. But through it all, our presidents, secretaries of state, and purveyors of propaganda maintained the farce that we played by Marquis of Queensbury rules. Collateral damage, and the occasional atrocity that came to light, were unplanned, unwilled. Such was the public story.

By 1950, a popularly elected Iranian government was pressuring the Anglo-Iranian Oil Company, which controlled oil throughout Iran, to negotiate better terms. Mohammed Mossadegh was elected head of government in 1951. He was an aristocrat and nationalist; the Truman administration thought him the most likely politician to resist Soviet attempts to get control of Iranian oil, and to resist domestic communists.[16]

Mossadegh believed that the British stranglehold on Iranian oil woefully shortchanged Iran; he introduced a bill in the Majlis to nationalize the oil fields. There followed bitter negotiations with the British. American mediators were called in; neither side would budge. The British Secret Intelligence Services, closely involved in such matters, presented a plan to the U.S. Central Intelligence Agency for a joint operation for what is now called a "regime change." Together they would get rid of Mossadegh, restore the lucrative oil business, and frustrate the Soviet. The Truman administration was not buying.

After the 1952 U.S. elections, with Eisenhower in the White House and the Dulles brothers running State and CIA, the British again called for intervention. Despite opposition from the American ambassador in Tehran, the plan was approved. Kim Roosevelt, a swashbuckling CIA agent, was put in charge as noted earlier.

Mossadegh resisted and mustered impressive crowds supporting him; the shah weakened and fled the country. At this stage the coup appeared to have failed. But Roosevelt spread some money around, and called on the contacts of General H. Norman Schwartzkopf, who had trained thousands of Iranian police from 1942 to 1948. With 6,000 hired demonstrators, Mossadegh was isolated and neutralized. The shah was brought back from Italy in August 1953. As John Prados puts it, "So ended Operation AJAX, the first apparent United States paramilitary victory. . .. The big winners were the shah and his men, who gained absolute power, which they held for 26 years, until themselves swept away by a religious conservatism even more potent than the populism of Mossadegh."[17]

The American public knows little or nothing about why the label "The Great Satan" was first attached to the United States by Iranians. The answer is simple: we saddled that once great and still proud (despite the ayatollahs) civilization with twenty-six years of terror. We do not know details of dirty tricks the CIA pulled during the intervention; agents are sworn to secrecy, and most of them observe it. We do know that Schwartzkopf and his successors trained SAVAK (the shah's secret police) in torture, terror, and intimidation. For a long time, the U.S.-Iranian PR effort shielded the world from knowledge of even the most egregious repression.

Amnesty International's 1974-75 report says, "The shah of Iran retains his benevolent image despite the highest rate of death penalties in the world, no valid system of civilian courts and a history of torture which is beyond belief."[18] Barry Rubin, in *Paved With Good Intentions*, notes "western estimates suggest that the shah's regime killed around 10,000 people...about half of them during the 1978 revolution." In explaining the intensity of anti-shah (and hence anti-American) hatred after his removal, Rubin writes, "SAVAK'S victims were not merely a small group of active dissidents or a politically-conscious minority. The existing system meant that the entire population was subjected to a constant, all-pervasive terror." This terror was organized and financed by the United States.

The American public was outraged when Iranian students seized the American embassy in 1979, holding some hostages for 444 days. Two decades later, in March 2000, the American secretary of state, Madeleine Albright, took the unprecedented step of approaching an apology for what had gone before: "The Eisenhower administration believed its actions were justified for strategic reasons, but the coup was clearly a setback for Iran's political development. And it is easy to see how many Iranians continue to resent this intervention by America in their internal affairs."[19] Dangerous business, admitting error, but not to worry. Within two years the American tune had changed. Iran is now part of an "axis of evil." A reformist Iranian premier has been in Kabul voicing support for a new American-sponsored Afghan regime, and pointing out how Iran is cooperating in the 'war' against terror, with a few remarkably mild words for the arrogance, unilateralism, and scurrilous insults coming from the White House.

Despite its precedent-setting status, the Iranian caper was a modest start for the long U.S. career in foreign interventions. Only about 10,000 people were killed by our man in Tehran. As for terrorism and torture, weren't the Iranians already used to that? But things picked up with the next big operation.

Guatemala was not long in coming. The most long-lasting obscenity in the U.S. terror enterprise was the forty-year tragedy resulting from the overthrow of the democratically elected Jacob Arbenz of Guatemala.[20] Arbenz was elected as a reformer in March 1951. State Department and CIA officers portrayed him as leaning toward the Soviet Union, though it is hard to see the basis for this: he certainly voted with the United States in the United

Nations. But he did attempt a land reform, and anything that disturbed the equanimity of United Fruit was automatically suspect. My belief is that the banana growers were not quite as important as the growing hysteria of the Cold War, which previewed the current dictum that if you're not clearly with us, you're against us. John Foster Dulles was the grandfather of this doctrine.

The original drama was much like that in Iran. The CIA produced a plan to topple Arbenz in the closing months of the Truman administration; Truman was at first sympathetic but changed his mind and canceled. When Eisenhower took the reins in 1953, with the Dulles brothers working for him, the plan was resurrected and put into action. It did not succeed; popular support for Arbenz was too strong. The CIA looked for weaknesses in the plan, obtained increased resources, and got ready to try again in 1954.

Meanwhile, Eisenhower felt a need for improved efficiency in the general area of dirty tricks. Perhaps the doctrine in NSC-68 was not clear enough. Ike appointed a committee headed by Lt. Gen. James Doolittle, he of the famed Tokyo raid, who began work in July 1954, consulted the CIA, the Department of State, the Department of Defense, and the FBI. On September 30, 1954, the "Report of the Special Study Group on Covert Activities" went to the president. How could the U.S. defeat the Communists? "As long as it remains national policy, another important requirement is an aggressive covert psychological, political and paramilitary organization more effective, more unique {really, he wrote that} and, if necessary, more ruthless than that employed by the enemy. . . there are no rules in such a game. Hitherto acceptable norms of human conduct do not apply."[21] Presumably *this* was clear to Eisenhower.

Certainly it was clear to the CIA agents in charge of the revived putsch in Guatemala. The offensive began in June, with the planes dropping leaflets demanding that Arbenz resign and lift the communist threat to the country. Then CIA bombed and strafed ports, fuel tanks, barracks, the airport, and schools. Radio announcements warned of an army coming from Honduras to liberate Guatemala. Francis Cardinal Spellman of New York arranged to have a message read in every Catholic pulpit in the country calling for opposition to "this enemy of God and country." There was much threat and bluster, the sinking of a British ship supposedly carrying Soviet arms to Guatemala that turned out to hold only coffee and cotton, and black propaganda coming from Washington D.C. by the ton. On June 30, 1954, Arbenz left the country, and the long nightmare began.

For the rest of the century, Guatemala was a killing field. If casualties from the shah were modest, those from the succession of U.S.-blessed thugs ruling Guatemala mounted into six figures. This time much leaked into the press and academic channels.

A whole shelf of books documents the carnage. In February 1999, when a Historical Clarification Commission appointed by the United Nations issued a report, CIA involvement was identified and the deaths from this long "campaign of terror" were estimated to be more than 200,000. This terrible scourge caught the attention of President Clinton, who told a meeting of Guatemalan leaders on March 10, 1999, that U.S. "support for military forces and intelligence units which engaged in violence and widespread repression was wrong, and the United States must not repeat that mistake."[22]

The Guatemala narrative is still vibrant in the 21st century. An American lawyer and peace activist, Jennifer Harbury, who in 1991 married a rebel leader sought by the Guatemalan military, appealed to the U.S. Supreme Court on March 19, 2002. Her husband had been arrested and had disappeared—presumably killed by a CIA asset; the U.S. government had refused to inform her of his arrest, preventing her from taking action to get him counsel. She demanded the right to sue the then secretary of state Warren Christopher and subordinates. The Supreme Court, to no one's surprise, refused her writ of certiorari.

Clifford Krauss of *The New York Times*, in a major story March 7 1999, identifies only one whistle blower, an insider who went public with his horror at the tactics of CIA in Guatemala. This was Viron Vaky, who was number 2 in the U.S. embassy in Guatemala in the 1960s. Vaky wrote a long memo of protest: the indiscriminate violence of U.S.-sponsored tactics presented "a serious problem for the U.S. in terms of our image in Latin America and the credibility of what we stand for." Poor fellow: he did not understand what we stood for—nothing except to oppose communism. And Johns Hopkins professor Piero Gleijeses said of our operators there, "it was the Kennedy and Johnson administrations that gave them muscle to create a murderous machine…That's when the Frankenstein was created."

The Eisenhower administration tried other anticommunist adventures during its eight years. Most of them were comparatively minor, most of them failed. The momentum of the Iran and Guatemala successes, however, led the Dulles brothers to try covert armed intervention again, this time in the nation with the world's largest Islamic population: Indonesia.[23]

For John Foster Dulles, nonalignment in the Cold War was a crime. Dulles was possibly the most gullible ideologue to serve as secretary of state in the 20th century; certainly he was the most hypocritical. His attempt to align the Asian nations with the United States was frustrated by a clique of neutrals: U Nu of Burma, Nasser of Egypt, Nehru of India, and Sukarno of Indonesia. Sukarno committed the unforgivable sin of tolerating a legal communist party, which had at least a million members. At Bandung in 1955, Sukarno hosted a conference of unaligned nations. Chou En-lai attended the conference with great glee and much publicity. In 1957, Soviet president Kliment Voroshilov was a welcome guest in Indonesia for two months.

Sukarno had internal opposition from many Indonesian Army officers, most of them trained by the United States. In 1956, this group began a revolt in the outer islands that threatened to spread to Java. Allen Dulles approved a plan similar to that used in Guatemala, with a "stalling period" during which there would be psychological pressures on Sukarno, and military supplies would be dropped to the rebels. All through 1957 the paramilitary machine geared up. Tens of thousands of rebels were armed and trained by the U.S. Army. Navy submarines put over-the-beach parties ashore on strategic islands. The U.S. Air Force dropped thousands of weapons deep in Indonesian territory. A fleet of B-29 bombers was sanitized so as to be deniable. Rebellion began to break out on island after island in early 1958.

Unfortunately for the Eisenhower administration, cover did not hold. There was a foretaste of the embarrassing U-2 incident of 1960, where Ike was caught in a glaring falsehood by denying that American spy planes were overflying the Soviet Union, only to have Khrushchev produce the downed Francis Gary Powers. In Indonesia, the Dulles brothers made strenuous efforts to keep the American role in the rebellion secret; even the *New York Times* was fooled. On April 30, 1958, Eisenhower himself commented publicly for the first time: "Our policy is one of careful neutrality and proper deportment all the way through so as not to be taking sides where it is none of our business. Now on the other hand, every rebellion that I have ever heard of has its soldiers of fortune."[24]

Then on May 18, 1958, a B-26 bomber with no identifying marks raided Ambon, bombing a village crowd on their way to church. The plane was hit and damaged, the crew bailed out and was captured by the Indonesian army. The pilot was an American, Allen Lawrence Pope. John Foster Dulles knew of Pope's capture the next day, but CIA had "a lot of confidence in the man."[25] They believed he could stand up to torture, and his plane too had been carefully sanitized. Pope had undergone a strip search to ensure no incriminating evidence in case of capture. Dulles faced the press on the 20th: the Indonesian rebellion was none of his concern; it should be resolved without foreign intervention.

Pope had fooled them. He concealed papers aboard the plane: U.S. Air Force and Civil Air Transport ID cards, his contract for the operation, and a post exchange card for Clark Air Force Base. All this was displayed for the world press May 27 in Djakarta. End of intervention, end of revolt. American hypocrisy was searingly displayed, along with the unforgivable bombing of innocents, but the U.S. Government learned no lasting lesson.

Casualties from this misguided effort were barely into the thousands, but such as they were, the U.S. was clearly to blame. The significant carnage came a decade later, when a new crew occupied Washington. Sukarno was still in power, but many officers continued to object to his tolerance of the communists, and his inept rule. By the mid-1960s, according to Roger Hilsman, "one-third of the Indonesian general staff had had some training from Americans and almost half of the officer corps...Bonds of personal respect and even affection existed."[26] CIA, according to the *New York Times,* was said "to have been so successful at infiltrating the top of the Indonesian government and army that the United States was reluctant to disrupt CIA covert operations" despite Sukarno's increasing insults and provocations.[27] But the cover held: no dangerous overflights, no leaked memos.

Then on October 1, 1965, a dissident General Suharto seized on (or engineered, no one knows for sure) a minor rebellion to justify a coup. Only years later were American officials willing to discuss the Suharto coup. CIA files remain closed, but a CIA-authored version of events denies any involvement—the takeover "was a purge of the Army leadership," nothing more.[28]

It was a dreadful purge. The press described torture and murder everywhere. *Time* magazine, *The New York Times,* academic observers such as George McT. Kahin of Cornell and Neville Maxwell of Oxford agree that Suharto decimated the communist party. Amnesty International estimated that deaths ranged from 500,000 to 1,000,000. This was on Lyndon Johnson's watch. Why would he tolerate or even encourage such a bloodbath? Because he remembered clearly what happened to Harry Truman for the "loss" of China. As Daniel Ellsberg analyzed Johnson's catastrophic thrust into Southeast Asia, "This is not a good year for the administration to lose Vietnam to Communism." The same applied to Indonesia.

The documents describing precisely who gave what orders when are not available, and may never be, but the inference that the United States was instrumental in bringing Suharto to power is hard to avoid. Former U.S. Ambassador Marshall Green in 1973 said, "In 1965 I remember, Indonesia was poised at the razor's edge. I remember people arguing from here [he was speaking in Australia] that Indonesia wouldn't go communist. But when Sukarno announced in his August 17 speech that Indonesia would have a communist government within a year then I was almost certain.... What we did we had to do, and you'd better be glad we did it because if we hadn't Asia would be a different place today."[29]

Twenty-five years later, U.S. diplomats revealed that they had compiled vast lists of "communists" and turned over as many as 5,000 names to Suharto's military, who hunted them down and killed them. Robert Martens, U.S. political officer in the embassy then, said in 1990: "It really was a big help to the army. They probably killed a lot of people, and I probably have a lot of blood on my hands, but that's not all bad. There's a time when you have to strike hard at a decisive moment."[30]

Jump to the next decade. In 1975, Indonesia invaded the former Portuguese East Timor, which claimed independence after World War II. There was a long, bitter, atrocity-studded struggle. Amnesty International estimated that Indonesian troops killed at least 200,000 people, and this estimate is not challenged. Jack Anderson, a columnist with good sources, described on November 1979 how this came about. Intelligence dispatches in late 1975 had reported that when the Indonesian government decided to launch an open offensive, "it was essential to neutralize the United States. For the Indonesian army relied heavily on U.S. arms, which, under our laws, could not be used for aggression."[31] President Ford was on his way to Indonesia for a state visit. He knew that Suharto would bring up the Timor issue, and would solicit a sympathetic attitude. Anderson writes, "That he succeeded is confirmed by Ford himself. The United States had suffered a devastating setback in Vietnam, leaving Indonesia as the most important American ally in the area. The U.S. national interest, Ford concluded, 'had to be on the side of Indonesia.' Ford gave his tacit approval on December 6, 1975. Five days after the invasion, the United Nations voted to condemn the attack as an arrant act of international aggression. The United States abstained."

In 2002, the National Security Archive at George Washington University got a Freedom of Information Act release revealing when President Ford and Secretary Kissinger gave Suharto the green light for the East Timor operation.[32] There is no smoking gun placing American personnel with the invading army, but there is considerable Timorese testimony that we had people on the ground in other capacities. In this case, we only know that we trained and supplied terrorists, even though Americans may not have fired a shot.

This brief survey of three terroristic interventions all of which began in one administration does not include the horror in Vietnam. How many souls perished, or were maimed or stunted, in that long, painful and entirely unproductive war? This was a war in which the greater part of the slaughter was committed not by surrogates with the U.S. egging them on or financing them; it was committed by Americans. More than the bomb tonnage dropped in all of World War II fell on that small, brave, and at the time of our attack, largely inoffensive people. Whatever of Christian charity still clung to the American policy cried out in undisguised anguish. On September 11, 2001, the United States sustained a terrorist attack with around 3,000 deaths; how many thousand times greater was the terror we inflicted on the Vietnamese for reasons the *Pentagon Papers* expose as corrupt?

But there is one big difference, apologists for that war tell us. The enemy committed atrocities all the time, with malice and no qualms. Our atrocities were sporadic, and when they came to light, we apologized and prosecuted the evil doers. I read the account of Lt. Calley's trial for the massacre at My Lai of 397 civilians. He was indeed convicted, and spent all of three years under house arrest. General W. R. Peers, whose fearless and thorough investigation of My Lai might be held up as a model, found his report to be his swan song, and he was quietly eased out. The forms of justice were obeyed, the substance was ignored. There were two million Vietnamese killed in that war, and 50,000 Americans. We remember the latter, but have almost forgotten the former, and the American terror that destroyed them.[33]

The handling of the My Lai massacre was the perfect exemplar of the hypocritical pretension of this country to be fighting a moral war while the enemy were evil terrorists. In fact, our operational code, that articulated by Paul Nitze and James Doolittle, was one approving whatever served to defeat the enemy. Now comes a straight-arrow Lt. Gen. William R. Peers, who is assigned the task of investigating one atrocity that penetrated the wall of silence protecting our moral self-image. Peers digs into this for four months, and on March 14, 1970, issues a three-part report finding that 28 officers and 2 enlisted men suppressed information about criminal activity in their possession.

The Secretary of the Army, Howard H. Calloway, felt compelled to release part of this report *four and a half years later*, on November 13, 1974. How does he spin this report of the murder of 397 civilians, and the cream-puff punishment of one lieutenant for three years? He says the following: "The release of this report concludes a dark chapter in the Army's history. It is an incident from which the Army has learned a great deal. The lessons have been acted upon. Army training has been revised to emphasize the personal responsibility of each soldier and officer to obey the laws of land warfare and the provisions of the Geneva and Hague Conventions."

Army training has been revised. Does this mean that the whatever-it-takes doctrine is cancelled, or does it mean, "We mustn't get caught like this again"? The code has never changed, even with the demise of the Soviet Union. "Terrorists" (mostly Islamic now) have simply replaced communists as enemies whose methods we have to match in order to win. But we rehabilitated our tarnished self-image.

Equally subject to condemnation, though it produced fewer casualties, was the U.S.-sponsored, financed, and advised campaign against the moderate Marxist reformer Salvador Allende in Chile. The CIA was involved in this intervention also, and it was signed off on by Richard Nixon and Henry Kissinger.[34] Allende, whose offenses included nationalizing mines owned by U.S. companies, giving free milk to undernourished Chilean children, and winning a free election despite some two million American dollars spent to elect his opponent, was ultimately assassinated, as was the pro-democracy General Rene Schneider.

The Chilean tragedy is still alive in American foreign policy discourse, but the press is as ahistorical as the culture in general, and, as Elliott Negin counts them, at the time of Pinochet's arrest in Britain (1998), only eight of 150 stories about this in eleven prominent newspapers mentioned that the United States had put Pinochet in power twenty-five years earlier.[35] Costa-Gavras' film *Missing* did something to promote awareness of U.S. skullduggery and lying, but the film was 16 years old by then.[36] It accurately conveys the random violence, all-pervasive fear, constant disappearance of Allende supporters, and the sheer terror of living under Augusto Pinochet's dictatorship. Later, Allende's defense minister, Orlando Letelier, a refugee in Washington D.C. after the assassination of his leader, was killed by a car bomb. The vast publicity from this created an outcry that government spin doctors valiantly countered, but despite the publicity, the government stonewalled an investigation. No one has been indicted for this murder.

When Pinochet lost power due to economic difficulties in 1989, a non-partisan commission to investigate the terror was appointed, with prominent lawyer Paul Rettig as chairman. Rettig reported in 1991 that at least 3,197 people had been slain for political reasons or had vanished forever.[37] This report began a steady erosion of Pinochet's dogged right wing following, and in 1998, while Pinochet was residing in England for medical treatment, a Spanish magistrate, Balthasar Garzon, asked the British to extradite the general to Spain to stand trial for the murder of Spanish subjects by Pinochet's government. The British at first arrested Pinochet, then waffled, and finally denied the Spanish request, allowing Pinochet to return to Chile. Chilean courts found him too fragile to stand trial.

To my mind, Christopher Hitchens captures the essence of the episode in a review of a book about Pinochet: "Even before Allende had taken the oath of office in 1970, death squads paid for by Henry Kissinger had embarked on a campaign of murder and destabilization and had shot down the chief of the Chilean General Staff, Rene Schneider, in the street, for nothing more than his legalistic opposition to a coup."[38] The United States of America, which has partially acknowledged its complicity in the Chilean coup, is as responsible for those three thousand dead, and the 200,000 tortured, as the Taliban is for 9/11.

The messy war in Angola began in 1975; it occurred because the United States was unwilling to see a Soviet-backed regime take power. We trained, financed, and advised one of the warring factions there, and a minimum of 300,000 lives were lost, the carnage still going on into the 21st century.[39] Nicaragua? A totally destructive clientele Reagan chose to call the Contras was enabled to challenge a democratically elected government, with enough hypocrisy (the ruling Sandinistas were terrorists, the Contras freedom fighters) and fraud (arms were sold to Iran illegally, the proceeds used secretly to arm the contras) to produce several felony convictions. When it was over, and the Sandinistas were voted out of office with major American aid, at least 10,000 people had been killed.[40]

About Afghanistan, perhaps little need be said, other than that our intervention on the side of the forces that eventually became the Taliban was hypocritical from beginning to end. We pretended to be working in the interests of the Afghanis, but we were not. We were interested only in giving the Soviets a black eye. The speed with which we disengaged when the Soviets withdrew is remembered clearly by those we are now courting to support our war on terror. That we overlook the human rights violations of potential allies (Egypt, Saudi Arabia, and Pakistan) only intensifies the widespread perception that we are hypocrites.

Here tribute must be paid to the valiant and humane Roy Bourgeois, of the Maryknoll Order, for standing up to the immense pressure the U.S. Army exerted to keep secret the activities of its School of The Americas (SOA). This is an operation incorporating the spirit of Nitze's "whatever it takes." The curriculum included specific instructions in terror, torture, intimidation, and concealment. Thousands of Latin American military and police officers learned how to suppress insurgencies unapproved by the United States.[41]

Where did these graduates practice their trade? Argentina, Chile, Nicaragua, El Salvador, Guatemala, Honduras, Mexico, Colombia, and probably every other Latin American nation. When a training manual leaked, the Army changed the name of the school but not the curriculum. Father Bourgeois organizes a protest at Benning every fall; more than a thousand Americans come to show their opposition, and, if they trespass on Benning soil more than once, do hard time.

There are at least twelve other interventions since our "anything goes" code of conduct was officially articulated in 1950. Taking only a conservative count of deaths attributable to our actions in the seven major operations discussed above, the U.S. has a moral burden of at least 2,000,000 killed. With the exceptions of Guatemala and Vietnam, we have managed to sweep them under the rug. Much of our terror having been committed by proxy, which to some seems more legitimate than that carried out by American citizens, we strain to recover our moral self-image. This is no mitigation. If we contract for the deed, pay the surrogate, and put him in place, it is our deed. We can, and do, pretend our motives were pure, but those pesky memos, buried in archives, never supposed to see the light of day, do sometimes leak out. This is less likely to happen now. The Bush administration has issued orders authorizing rejection of Freedom of Information Act requests if any official deems it desirable for any reason. The God of Justice needs to intervene here.

One of the most naïve reactions to 9/11 is believing this kind of terrorism to be something new under the sun. Of course the scope of the damage done exceeded previous attempts by a non-state actor to terrorize a giant, but the difference is quantitative. Islamic countries, for which the Christian crusades of the tenth and eleventh centuries are still live memories, have powerful modern evidence of western ill will. American-caused carnage in Iran and Indonesia has been described above; yet another sad stupidity came under the leadership of the most xenophobic of American presidents, Ronald Reagan.

It happened in Lebanon, a country with both Christian and Islamic citizens. In April 1983, seventeen people were killed in a bomb attack on the U.S. embassy in Beirut. Reagan sent the battleship USS New Jersey to batter Lebanon's hills with behemoth shells, each hit leaving "a crater as big as a tennis court." The Shiite area sustained thousands of such hits. There can be no pretense of this bombing being targeted on military installations; hence it was in no way compatible with any legitimate rules of engagement. The Lebanese Muslims were outraged; they responded with bombing U.S. Marine barracks at the Beirut airport, killing 243. As Michael McClintock describes the situation, "The Reagan administration was appalled and disconcerted by the rage unleashed against the United States in Lebanon. It had come into office hooting derision at Carter's inability to deal with the Iranian hostages—and pledged tough programs and policies to combat terrorism."[42]

Reagan the blusterer had no adequate response. The United States was under attack. The best his strategists could come up with was the invasion of tiny Grenada, which came on October 25, 1983. Nothing about this farce even began to compensate for Beirut, but the PR machine went into overdrive, and the attentive public had at least the satisfaction of seeing 6,000 American troops defeat 3,000 Grenadians and a few Cuban civilians.[43] Stray Americans are still puzzled by Hezbollah curses in Lebanon directed toward "New Jersey"; it is only our ahistoricity that makes this puzzlement possible.

As the U.S. came to support ever more closely the aggressive tactics of the Israelis, the hypocrisy of our holier-than-thou attitude toward Middle Easterners increased. If we sustain massive hatred because of our own hypocrisy, it is magnified by unquestioning support of what Ian Buruma reports is "the world's most hated nation."[44]

Go back to the Holy Scriptures. Consider God's instructions to Joshua for the conquest of Canaan. They called for terror from start to finish. When Joshua attacked Amalek under Moses' direction, he defeated the Amalekites and put them all to the sword; Moses had the Lord's order "to blot out all memory of Amalek from under heaven." Joshua's entire campaign for the Holy Land was brutal and terrifying. When he got to Jericho, a prize for the Israelites and a charming city to this day, he sent two spies to learn of its defenses. They lodged in the house of Rahab the harlot, who kept them hidden from the King of Jericho. She told them:

> ...I know the Lord hath given you the land, and that your terror is fallen upon us, and that all the inhabitants of the land faint because of you.... For we have heard how the Lord dried up the waters of the Red Sea for you. . . And what ye did unto the two kings of the Amorites... whom ye utterly destroyed. And as soon as we had heard these things, our hearts did melt, neither did there remain any courage in any men... .

When the priests blew the trumpets, the walls fell down, and the Israelites "utterly destroyed all that was in the city, both man and woman, young and old, and ox, and sheep, and ass, with the edge of the sword." The rest of the campaign in Canaan was similar; in the King James terminology *everything was "utterly destroyed"* and the cities were burnt and made "a heap forever."[45]

While the ancient Israelites were quite candid about what they did following Jehovah's orders in the original conquest of Canaan, the Israel of today exhibits a degree of hypocrisy defying belief. The State of Israel came about only by use of the crudest of terror to drive the British out of their Palestine Mandate.

Rejecting the pacific advice of Chaim Weizmann, the brilliant chemist who engineered the Balfour Declaration, early political leaders of the Zionist organization adopted instead the terrorist techniques of the Palestinian Arabs and the British Army, neither of which was squeamish. All sides were terroristic in 1940s Palestine. One need not claim that the Zionists were the worst, but it is hard to top the assassination of Lord Moyne in 1944, the spectacular simultaneous destruction of all eleven bridges over the Jordan River in June 1946, the bombing of the King David Hotel with the loss of ninety-one lives in July 1946, and the assassination of Count Folke Bernadotte in September 1948.

It was the Moyne assassination that as much as any other shock planted a seed of suspicion about how Zionists would go about governing; it still reverberates in scholarly discourse about Israel. On November 6, 1944, Lord Moyne, the British minister resident in Cairo, was shot dead by Irgun terrorists. This affected Churchill personally. He told Commons, "If our dreams for Zionism are to end in the smoke of assassin's pistols and our labours for its future to produce only a new set of gangsters worthy of Nazi Germany, many like myself will have to reconsider the position we have maintained in the past."[46]

The day after Moyne's murder, Weizmann wrote Churchill:

> I can hardly find words adequate to express the deep moral indignation and horror which I feel at the murder of Lord Moyne. I know that these feelings are shared by Jewry throughout the world. Whether or not the criminals prove to be Palestinian Jews, their act illumines the abyss to which terrorism leads. ... I can assure you that Palestine Jewry will, as its representative bodies have declared, go to the utmost limit of its power to cut out, root and branch, this evil from our midst.[47]

Bad prediction. More Zionists seem to have rejoiced at the killing of Lord Moyne than regretted it. Weizmann had already lost his battle. The Holocaust, the failure of the Allies to rapidly resettle remaining Jewish refugees, Britain's waffling about setting up the Zionist state, caused Walter Laqueur to observe, "The liberal element in Zionism, the faith in humanity, suffered a blow from which it did not fully recover...They had learned their lesson: no one could be trusted, it was everyone for himself."[48]

Any date for the beginning of the still raging terror-counter terror is arbitrary. Each side had its zealots, committed to pushing the other out of Palestine, and if the Israeli terror was more effective—across the years Israelis have killed three or four times more Palestinians simply because they were allowed by the British to build up a stronger military force—we hear less about it because of the vastly superior propaganda skills of the Israelis. Taking the situation as of May 1947, when wartime conditions prevailed, Benny Morris writes that:

> Israeli reprisal raids tended to be disproportionate to the original Arab offense. This strategy tended to spread the conflagration to areas that had so far been untroubled by the hostilities. From the first [Irgun and Stern], to a lesser degree the Haganah, used terror attacks against civilian and militia centers. The Arabs responded by planting large bombs in Jewish civilian centers, especially in Jerusalem.[49]

On July 12, 1947, Irgun abducted two British sergeants, hanged them, booby-trapped their bodies; a British captain was injured when they were cut down. For some reason, the staid (London) *Times* wrote about this incident, "The bestialities practiced by the Nazis themselves could go no further."[50] The British replied with atrocities of their own. But they were wearying of the mandate. In August 1947, there was an all-party consensus to get out of Palestine quickly. Even Churchill agreed. Morris tells us, "The judgment of historians familiar with the British state archives is that Irgun's draconian methods, morally reprehensible as they were, were decisive in transforming the evacuation option of February 1947 into a determined resolve to give up the burdens of the mandate."[51] What happened to Weizmann's promise that after the Moyne assassination Jewry would cut out this evil root and branch? Three of the four credentialled 1940s terrorists were subsequently elected prime minister of the Israeli government.

Israel was established by terror, consolidated its control by terror, and as of this writing is governed by a terrorist government. Only Zionist zealots attempt to claim that the "draconian measures" which brought Israel into being are really legitimate freedom fighting methods, while the Palestinians, who believe (probably mistakenly) that terror is their only weapon against jet fighters, helicopter gunships, tanks, and bulldozers, are illegitimate. A hypocrisy greater than Israel's refusal to negotiate a settlement until terror ceases is difficult to imagine. An old proverb puts it well: sauce for the goose is sauce for the gander.

I find it necessary to return to Weizmann to restore some sense of humanity to the latter-day odyssey of this tortured people. At the Zionist Congress in Basel December 9, 1946, he fought perhaps his most bitter battle for humaneness and righteousness. The situation as Laqueur describes it: "Speaking in Yiddish at the seventeenth session, he again condemned in the sharpest terms the terror, that 'cancer in the body politic of the (Jewish people),' which would destroy it if it were not stamped out."[52] American Zionists were his main targets now. Too many fancy speeches were made in Washington and New York by people whose lives were not on the line. An American, Emanuel Neumann, interrupted him by shouting "Demagogue" whereupon Weizmann, "deeply offended, gave vent to his fury." Laqueur's translation:

> I—a demagogue! I who have borne all the ills and travails of this movement. The person who flung this word in my face should know that in every house and every stable in Nahalal, in

every workshop in Tel Aviv or Haifa, there is a drop of my blood. You know that I am telling the truth. Some people don't like to hear it—but you will hear me. I warn you against bogus palliatives, against short-cuts, against false prophets, against facile generalizations... If you think of bringing redemption nearer by unJewish methods, if you lose faith in hard work and better days, then you commit idolatry and endanger what we have built. Would I had a tongue of flame, the strength of prophets, to warn you against the paths of Babylon and Egypt. Zion shall be redeemed in Judgment—and not by any other means.[53]

The rhetorical victory was Weizmann's; he got great applause, but the vote went against him. The Congress would not attend talks on resolving the fighting to be held in London, and Weizmann was not re-elected as president.

Britain got out of Palestine; Israelis fought Palestinians and surrounding Arab states; Israel won; and terror continues. Yitzhak Rabin and Anwar Sadat tried hard to quell it; Americans (especially Rabbi Meir Kahane), Jewish zealots, and Palestinians who refuse to accept the existence of Israel have until time of writing frustrated many thousands of hours of negotiations.

While the evils of American interventions, and the terrorism of fanatic Zionists, may not exceed similar practices by other powers, the worldwide perception that these two allied miscreants pretend to a moral standard that they constantly violate sullies both of them. From one point of view, the United States suffers most: the major colonial repression presently attracting world attention is that of the Palestinians by Israel, which clearly is underwritten by money from a Zionist-controlled congress. The Bush administration occasionally pays lip service to the need for allies to defeat Al Qaeda, but more often, administrative rhetoric demonstrates super-power determination to go it alone—meaning with only Israeli support. Hence the long string of UN votes on matters concerning the Middle East: 100+ to 2, with 2 being the U.S. and Israel.

Evangelists of American manifest destiny belittle this problem; the vulgar slogan of Vietnam days, "Get'em by the balls, and their hearts and minds will follow" still seems to attract chauvinists. But power is not all that matters. In a perverse sense, Nixon was right when at one stage he was considering a bellicose offensive in Southeast Asia, and complained that the U.S. was a "pitiful, helpless giant."

The limitations of sheer power expose themselves in the bankruptcy of Israeli policy. The overwhelming power of the Israeli military can occupy any Palestinian area at will, but it cannot create security for its people. This truth has been obvious for decades, but it goes unacknowledged. In 1983, Abba Eban, a former Labor foreign minister, wrote an article entitled "Politics of Failure," complaining that under the Begin/Sharon government, "The nation's business is being conducted by the most unsuccessful government in the modern history of the democratic world. The failure is demonstrated by hundreds of soldier's graves, by hundreds more maimed and shocked… by deadlock in the peace process… and by a blatant absence of any gains remotely commensurate with the sacrifice and loss."[54]

The Israeli Defense Forces have, up to now, been willing to kill about four Palestinians for every Israeli killed, thereby intensifying the rage that guarantees continued suicide bombing, rather than obtaining safety.[55]

There is another factor vitiating whatever benefits the U.S. gains from its alliance with "the only democracy in the Middle East." This is the belief that this "pitiful helpless giant" is scandalously manipulated by the diminutive, bellicose associate. This theme crops up in fugitive sources, but Americans who go abroad with open ears cannot avoid it. It was first brought home to this writer by a mild-mannered Palestinian taxi driver on the Tel Aviv to Jerusalem highway in April 2002. We had had a low-key, touristy conversation until the subject of Israeli-American relations came up. This brought forth a torrent of invective against the supineness of the U.S. for bowing to every Israeli wish. The tail was wagging the dog. Israel was calling the shots, why did we let them push us around so publicly, and so on. I soon discovered this is now a common theme: Brits, Germans, and Scandinavians all subscribe to it. We may be the only superpower, but when it comes to the power of the Israel lobby, we are craven.

This raises the issue of how the lobby can get away with it. The short answer is, because of the effective politicization of the Holocaust by American Jewry. There is not room here to even begin to explain how this was achieved. One can understand the use of the Holocaust as a bludgeon in American politics by reading either of two thoroughly researched books: Peter Novick, *The Holocaust in American Life,* or Norman G. Finkelstein, *The Holocaust Industry.*[56] There is a direct correlation between U.S. Government support for Israeli state terrorism and colonial expansion, and opposition to

American policy throughout the world. This is now acknowledged widely in scholarly circles, even if ignored by government. I refer in particular to two analyses, each well before 9/11: Richard Betts of the Council on Foreign Relations, and Ivan Eland of CATO Institute.

Betts is Director of National Security Studies at the Council. In the January-February 1998 *Foreign Affairs*, his essay "The New Threat of Mass Destruction" concludes that Middle East radicals would not likely be "hatching schemes like the destruction of the World Trade Center if the United States had not been identified for so long as the mainstay of Israel, the shah of Iran, and conservative Arab regimes and the source of a cultural assault on Islam."[57]

Eland is director of defense policy studies at CATO, a Libertarian think tank that is generally anti-government, but pro-military. His 1998 study, *Protecting the Homeland: The Best Defense is to Give No Offense* reviews various studies of security problems, concluding that we have given unnecessary offense, and should stop it:

> ...For example, U.S. military and economic aid to certain nations-such as Israel and Egypt-may cause nations unfriendly to those countries to covertly sponsor terrorism using WMD in the U.S.... The first World Trade Center bombing was perpetrated by an Egyptian fundamentalist group unhappy with U.S. support for the governments of Israel and Egypt.[58]

To bring the matter up to date, Rohan Gunaratna of the Centre for the Study of Terrorism at the Scottish University of St. Andrew's, who is arguably the most accomplished scholar of Al Qaeda, takes aim at many stupidities of American policy in Afghanistan, Pakistan, and elsewhere. Throughout his 2002 book *Inside Al Qaeda,* however, he identifies American support of Israeli state terrorism as a crucial energizer for Islamists. He does not deny the lure of 72 virgins ("beautiful ones of paradise") for potential suicide bombers, but the basic force is religio/political: "the world Islamic Front for the Jihad against Jews and Crusaders."[59] And one must account not just for the perversions of Islamic doctrine; the wide support Islamism "enjoys today is driven by the strong belief among Muslims that the West has persistently wronged them. It is international neglect of the Muslim interest in the Palestine and Kashmir conflicts, the presence of U.S. troops on Saudi soil and the frequent double standards of the big players that have legitimized the use of violence."[60]

Which big players? He avoids excessive finger-pointing at the United States, but notes that the failure of Malaysian Prime Minister bin Mohamad to secure passage of a resolution condemning suicide terrorism at the Organization of Islamic States meeting in April 2002 was due to "failure of the West adequately to condemn incursions by the Israel Defence Forces into Palestinian territory."[61] If we expect to win against Al Qaeda, we have got to put our own house in order.

The United States government buys the absurdity that there is no moral equivalence between the killing of civilians by Palestinian suicide bombers and the "accidental" and "collateral" killing of civilians by the Israeli Army, which claims not to target civilians, only terrorists. Soldiers who fought in a war, and most of the rest of the world, know that adequate military rules of engagement properly enforced will not produce the excessive civilian casualties Israel causes. B'Tselem, Amnesty International, and dozens of correspondents have seen Israeli troops fire point blank at rock throwers and other civilians just walking down the street. Rules of engagement that produce a killing a day in an area as small as the West Bank and Gaza are not designed to avoid casualties; they are designed with malice aforethought.

Iain John Hook, senior United Nations aid official in Jenin, was killed by a shot in the back as he stood in a UN compound on November 22, 2002. The Israeli Army claimed its men were defending themselves from attack by militants in the refugee camp, a ludicrous explanation for killing someone with a shot in the back. Sixty-two UN workers wrote a scathing letter to the Israeli Government saying the IDF had refused to let an ambulance remove Mr. Hook, and denying there had been any firing at all from the UN compound.[62]

Suzanne Goldenberg, for two and a half years the *Guardian Weekly*'s Jerusalem correspondent, wrote a validictory on that tour of duty that exposed Israeli hypocrisy:

> Despite two years of atrocity and siege, and growing criticism in Europe and even in the United States of Sharon's pursuit of a military solution, Israelis continue to see themselves as part of an ideal. Many believe that their country operates on a higher ethical standard than most. Phone-in callers to radio chat shows regularly congratulate themselves-with no apparent irony-on living in the best country in the world before going on to bewail the mess the Palestinians-not their own leaders-

have got them into. Israeli politicians and generals are fond of describing their army as the most 'moral' force in the world, and its citizens generally believe them.[63]

The United States is complicit in this hypocrisy. Israel could not conduct the same scale of murder and mayhem without American weapons and financial support. Every Muslim knows that.

Little has been said so far about the ideological divide, which is not the Muslim world against the West as Samuel Huntington would have it, but is the moderate, progressive forces against zealous fundamentalists within each of the Abrahamic religions.[64] The wisdom of Solomon would not be sufficient to guide the world to peace when every polity is confronted with powerful groups who insist that only they have the true word of God, the true interpretation of their holy scriptures. The sage who can tell us how to deprogram the American true believer from his conviction that the second coming of Christ can be hastened by getting the Muslims off the Temple Mount, building the Third Temple, thus bringing on the millennium (and getting us all killed)—where is he?[65]

Or the genius who can reason effectively with the screaming young Jewish settler confronting the Women in Black (Jewish peaceniks who demonstrate every Friday in Jerusalem). The settler has Torah in hand, proclaiming that God gave the Jews *all* of the Holy Land for them alone forever—and what are the Palestinians complaining about? Don't we let them live here? And to the author of this article on April 12, 2002, one of them yelled, "You're a Christian. Don't you believe what is in your Bible? It says right here. ..."

Or the peacemaker who can neutralize the powerful poison of the Islamist who denies there ever was a Jewish Temple on Temple Mount, who believes the Jews use human blood to make certain ceremonial foods, that Israel carried out the 9/11 outrages, that the Protocols of the Elders of Zion is a legitimate document, and that Allah commands them to kill nonbelievers whenever they have opportunity? No rectifying of American hypocrisy, no dampening of American arrogance and hegemony, no promise of democracy and prosperity will remove these ideological barriers to peace completely.

Of course there are moderates in all the Abrahamic faiths. I empathize especially with the Jewish followers of Weizmann, Rabin, and Michael Lerner.[66] They are suffering hugely from the hijacking of Jewish integrity by Gush Emunim, the Kahanists, and Gamla (an organization with strong support in the Likud coalition that intends to force Palestinians completely out of Biblical Palestine).[67]

The moderates cannot win without substantial policy changes and greater candor on the part of the United States. President Bush's "with us or against us, bin Laden dead or alive" rhetoric only intensifies the world-wide perception that we are a cowboy nation run amok with a monopoly on sophisticated weapons, and determination to play only by rules we approve, and only when those rules are convenient. Every time Bush goes on television to assert American purity and the depravity of various "axis of evil" opponents he creates a thousand new recruits for Al Qaeda. State terrorism, and terrorism of the repressed, have always been part of the human condition. If there is one thing that can be said about 9/11, it is that we should not have been surprised. The America of the Marshall Plan, the benevolent treatment of the nations we defeated in World War II, the grudging amounts we contribute to world hunger and other causes, conceal from us, but not from a skeptical world, that under the veneer we are as terroristic as we want to be.

In 1950, at the crucial impact point of the Cold War, one can understand, though not condone, the hypocritical adoption of a clandestine "anything goes" operational code, which turned American trained and financed goons loose all over the world. Such a double standard is clearly counterproductive in the 21st century.

NOTES

1. This account of the awards ceremony depends on John Prados, *President's Secret Wars*. Chicago: Ivan R. Dee, 1996, 91-92.

2. In addition to Prados, see Richard Cottam, *Nationalism in Iran*. Pittsburgh: University of Pittsburgh Press, 1979; William Blum, *Killing Hope*. Monroe, ME: Common Courage Press, 1995; Barry Rubin, *Paved with Good Intentions*. New York: Oxford University Press, 1980; Zachary Karabell, *Architects of Intervention*. Baton Rouge: Louisiana State University Press, 1999; Kermit Roosevelt, *Countercoup*. New York: McGraw-Hill, 1979.

3. See Robert P. Newman, "NSC (National Insecurity) 68: Nitze's Second Hallucination," in Martin J. Medhurst and H.W. Brands, editors, *Critical Reflections on the Cold War*. College Station: Texas A & M Press, 2000, 55-94.

4. There are more than a dozen good accounts of the religious foundations of the American colonies. I depend especially on Loren Baritz, *City on a Hill*; Conrad Cherry, *God's New Israel*; Martin Marty, *Righteous Empire*; Russel B. Nye, *This Almost Chosen People*; and Ernest Lee Tuveson, *Redeemer Nation*.

5. For the quote from Eddy, and this account of the "loss" of China, see Robert P. Newman, "Lethal Rhetoric: The Selling of the China Myths," *Quarterly Journal of Speech* 61 (April 1975): 113-28.

6. See Stanley I. Kutler, *The American Inquisition*. New York: Hill and Wang, 1982; and Robert P. Newman, "Clandestine Chinese Nationalist Efforts to Punish Their American Detractors," *Diplomatic History* 7 (Summer 1983): 205-22.

7. Richard Rhodes, *Dark Sun*. New York: Simon and Schuster Touchstone, 1996, 298.

8. Rhodes, 401-02.

9. Kennan as quoted in Newman, "NSC 68," 61-65.

10. This figure is from Stansfield Turner, *Caging the Nuclear Genie*. Boulder CO: Westview, 1997, 9.

11. The President to the Secretary of State, January 31, 1950. FRUS, 1950, 1:141-42.

12. Strobe Talbott, *The Master of the Game*. New York: Knopf, 1988, 43.

13. Gregg Herken, *Counsels of War*, expanded edition. New York: Oxford University Press, 1987, 116.

14. I use the text in Ernest R. May, *American Cold War Strategy*. Boston: Bedford Books, 1993, 32.

15. Ibid., 26.

16. See note 2, and Elaine Sciolino, "A Country Making History is Too Busy to Read It," *New York Times* (April 23, 2000). Sciolino puts the overthrow of Mossadegh "at the top of Iran's list of grievances against the United States."

17. Prados, 97.

18. Rubin, 176-77.

19. David E. Sanger, "U.S. Ending a Few of the Sanctions Imposed on Iran," *New York Times* (March 18, 2000).

20. For this account of the Guatemalan intervention, I depend on Francesco Goldman, "Victory in Guatemala," *New York Review* XLIX (May 23, 2002), 77-83; Clifford Krauss, "The Spies Who Never Came in From the Cold War," *New York Times* (March 7, 1999); David Gonzalez, "An American Death Bares Guatemalan Blunders," *New York Times* (June 28, 2002); Stephen Kinzer, "U.S. and Central America: Too Close for Comfort?" *New York Times* (July 28, 2002); John Prados, *President's Secret Wars*, 98-106; Stephen Schlesinger and Stephen Kinzer, *Bitter Fruit*. Garden City: Anchor/Doubleday, 1983; and Richard H. Immerman, *The CIA in Guatemala*. Austin: University of Texas Press, 1982.

21. Prados, 110.

22. John M. Broder, "Clinton Apologizes for U.S. Support of Guatemalan Rightists," *New York Times* (March 22, 1999).

23. For this account of the Indonesian intervention, I depend on Kenneth Conboy and James Morrison, *Feet to the Fire: CIA Covert Action in Indonesia*. Annapolis: Naval Institute Press, 1999; Audrey R. Kahin and George McT. Kahin, *Subversion as Foreign Policy*. New York; New Press, 1995; Department of State, Indonesia, 1964-1968, volume in FRUS series printed by GPO then suppressed, with one copy reaching the National Security Archive, George Washington University, and posted at http://www.edu.nsarchiv; Joseph Burkholder Smith, *Portrait of a Cold Warrior*. New York: G. P. Putnam's Sons, 1976; and David Wise and Thomas Ross, *The Invisible Government*. New York: Vintage, 1973.

24. Wise and Ross, 145.

25. Prados, 143.

26. Roger Hilsman, *To Move A Nation*. Garden City NY: Doubleday, 1967, 377.

27. *New York Times*, (April 27, 1966).

28. As cited in Blum, 410.

29. Peter Britton, "Indonesia's Neo-Colonial Armed Forces," *Bulletin of Concerned Asian Scholars*, July-Sept. 1975.

30. Cited by Blum, 194; original in article by Kathy Kadane, *San Francisco Chronicle* (May 20, 1990).

31. Jack Anderson column, various papers including *San Francisco Chronicle* (November 9, 1979).

32. Ruth Rosen, "The Day Ashcroft Foiled FOIA," *San Francisco Chronicle* (January 7, 2002).

33. For this account of the Vietnam War, I depend on Seymour M. Hersh, *My Lai 4: A Report on the Massacre and Its Aftermath.* New York: Random House Vintage, 1970; Loren Baritz, *Backfire.* New York: Ballantine, 1985; *Report of the Department of the Army Review of the Preliminary Investigations Into the My Lai Incident,* Volume I. Washington, D.C.: GPO, 1970; and Michael Belknap, *The Vietnam War on Trial.* Lawrence: University Press of Kansas, 2002.

34. Larry Rohter, "As Door Opens for Legal Actions in Chilean Coup, Kissinger is Numbered Among the Hunted," *New York Times* (March 28, 2002); Thomas S. Blanton to Friends of the Archive, December 18, 2000, Documents of the Month-Subject: Operation Condor, July-August 1976, National Security Archive, George Washington University, Washington, D.C.; and Elizabeth Becker, "On World Court, U.S. Focus Shifts to Shielding Officials," *New York Times* (September 7, 2002).

35. Elliott Negin, "Pardoning Pinochet's Pals," *Progressive* 63 (February 1999), 30.

36. Saul Landau and John Dinges, "The Truth Behind Missing," *Inquiry* (April 12, 1982), 10.

37. Philip Shenon, "U.S. Releases Files on Abuses in Pinochet Era," *New York Times* (May 4, 2000).

38. Christopher Hitchens, "11 September 1973," *London Review of Books* 24 (July 11, 2002), 3.

39. Blum, 257.

40. Statistics from Patrick Brogan, *World Conflicts.* Lanham MD: Scarecrow Press, 1998, 647. The landmark history of the Nicaraguan war is Theodore Draper, *A Very Thin Line.* New York: Hill and Wang, 1991.

41. The major source on SOA is Jack Nelson Pallmeyer, *School of Assassins.* Maryknoll NY: Orbis Books, 2001.

42. Michael McClintock, *Instruments of Statecraft.* New York: Pantheon, 1992, 362-69.

43. McClintock, 366-69.

44. Ian Buruma, "On the West Bank," *New York Review* (December 5, 2002), 69.

45. Deuteronomy 25; Joshua 2 and 6.

46. Benny Morris, *Righteous Victims.* New York: Knopf, 1999, 171.

47. Chaim Weizmann, *Trial and Error, two volumes.* Philadelphia: Jewish Publication Society of America, 1949, 437-38.

48. Walter Laqueur, *A History of Zionism.* New York: MJF Books, 1972, 558.

49. Morris, 197.

50. Morris, 181.

51. Morris, 182.

52. Laqueur, 575.

53. Laqueur, 575-76.

54. Abba Eban, "Politics of failure—Israel under Begin," originally in *Jerusalem Post,* carried also in *Pittsburgh Post-Gazette,* January 6, 1983. The extent to which the United States suffers from its close relationship with Israel is examined in many places. One of the best is Rosemary Radford Ruether and Herman J. Ruether, *The Wrath of Jonah.* Minneapolis: Fortress Press, 2002. The Ruethers include an exposition of the beliefs about Israel held by such fundamentalist Christians as Jerry Falwell: "Indeed, in Falwell's mind the two nations are like Siamese twins, linked together not only by common self-interest of a pragmatic kind, but because they are identical in values" (177).

55. Ze'ev Sternhell, "Zionism or Colonialism?" *Ha'aretz* (June 20, 2002).

56. Peter Novick, *The Holocaust in American Life.* Boston: Houghton Mifflin, 1999; Norman G. Finkelstein, *The Holocaust Industry.* London: Verso, 2001. Other useful analyses are Chalmers Johnson,

Blowback. New York: Henry Holt, 2000; and Zbigniew Brzezinski, "Confronting Anti-American Grievances," *New York Times* (September 1, 2002).

57. Richard Betts, "A New Threat of Mass Destruction," *Foreign Affairs* 77 (January-February 1998), 41.

58. Ivan Eland, *Protecting the Homeland: The Best Defense is to Give No Offense*. Washington, D.C.: CATO Institute, 1998, 39.

59. Rohan Gunaratna, *Inside Al Qaeda*. New York: Columbia University Press, 2002, 236.

60. Ibid.

61. Ibid, 241.

62. Michael Wines, "Four Palestinians Die in Clashes with Israelis," *New York Times* (December 3, 2002).

63. Suzanne Goldenberg, "It's gone beyond hostility," *Guardian Weekly* (August 22-28, 2002).

64. Samuel P. Huntington, *The Clash of Civilizations and the Remaking of World Order*. New York: Simon and Schuster, 1996.

65. One cannot understand the grip of apocalypticism without reading those seductive and malignant best sellers, Hal Lindsey's 1970 *The Late Great Planet Earth*, and *The 1980's: Countdown to Armageddon*. Scholarly accounts of end-of-time theory include Gershom Gorenberg, *The End of Days*. New York: Free Press, 2000; Stephen D. O'Leary, *Arguing the Apocalypse*. New York: Oxford University Press, 1994; Karen Armstrong, *The Battle for God*. New York: Knopf, 2000.

66. *Tikkun Magazine*, and Michael Lerner's *Jewish Renewal*. New York: Grosset/Putnam, 1994, along with *Ha'aretz*, *Washington Report on Middle East Affairs*, and the various church-based periodicals help understand the terrible reality of Palestine/Israel. While I do not cite him in this argument, no one concerned about the Middle East is innocent of the great work of Edward Said.

67. On Gamla, see Ali Abunimah, on the Electronic Intifada, at http://electronicIntifada.net/features/articles/020828ali.shtml.

Between the Arab Street and the Arab Basement: Dimensions of Civility & Civil Society in American Public Diplomacy

Gordon Stables*

Abstract

This essay examines the manner in which conceptions of civil society inform representations of Islamic audiences in the post 9/11 era. Beginning with the Bush administration's communication strategies, often developed by the State Department's Public Diplomacy program, the project considers how lively debates over the potential of democratic development or the future of global cosmopolitan society are now increasingly recognized as important components of policy formulation. This essay argues that the polarized scholarly debates about the nature of civil society in the Middle East need to be contextualized against contemporary articulations of American foreign policy. Finally, these perspectives are applied as a means to interrogate the recent campaigns of American public diplomacy, that is, the specific national efforts to communicate to Islamic audiences. The conclusions drawn from this comparison provide a cautionary tale for the prospects of similar public diplomacy campaigns to foster democracy, at least until the contours Islamic publics are more fully considered and better understood.

September 11th 2001 was a day of sudden and massive violence in the United States of America. After the shock of the terrorist attacks began to slowly subside, the realization emerged that a new era of American foreign policy was dawning. Decades worth of international relations and policy decisions were suddenly outdated and irrelevant; the United States urgently needed to develop and define a foreign policy that could protect American security and interests against this new genre of threat. This essay examines the attention devoted to nations with large Islamic populations, especially those nations located in the Middle East, as central actors in this new foreign policy epoch.

The fluid, non-state centered nature of the Al-Qaeda threat required an American response that could identify potential adversaries around the world.[1] Understanding who would become American allies and adversaries required a renewed attention to Islamic peoples, and specifically demanded some means to identify potential threats. It is within this highly volatile environment that the scholarship of civil society needs to be explored. The difficulty in employing a single geographic or national referent to Islamic publics underscores the importance of theories like civil society that attempt to explain the trajectories of diverse communities in an era of globalization.

Civil society emerges as a central element in the Bush administration's communication strategies, often developed by the State Department's Public Diplomacy program, precisely because of the fragile conceptions of specific audiences. Faced with unfamiliar political parties, media outlets, and religious organizations, lively debates over the potential of democratic development or the future of global cosmopolitan society are now increasingly recognized as important components of policy formulation. If, for example, policymakers determine that the practice of Islam necessarily negates the possibility of a functioning democratic polity, then the entire premise of persuading ambivalent audiences to join the American coalition against terrorism appears faulty. Alternately, if it is determined that a certain nascent element of civil life is emerging in these nations then communication strategies should be tailored to enhance the development of potential allies.

This essay argues that the polarized scholarly debates about the nature of civil society in the Middle East need to be contextualized against contemporary articulations of American foreign policy. The challenges of American communication with the Islamic world are revealed in our integration of several different bodies of research. First, the essay explores the central role that the particular conceptions of Islamic publics play in the development of American foreign policy. Second, the essay turns to the background in which these audiences are understood. From the perspective of both the debate over global cosmopolitan ethics to prominent conceptions of civil society, the context of these communicative exchanges is explored. Finally, the essay applies these perspectives as a means to interrogate the recent campaigns of American public diplomacy, specifically the national efforts to communicate to Islamic audiences. The conclusions drawn from this comparison provide a cautionary tale for the prospects of similar public diplomacy campaigns to foster democracy, at least until the contours of Islamic publics are more fully considered and better understood.

Islamic Publics as the Object of American Foreign Policy

Stephen M. Walt argued that the 9/11 terrorist attacks against the United States "triggered the most rapid and dramatic change in the history of U.S. foreign policy" (2002, p. 56). The changes are unmistakably visible and evidenced in the state of permanent crisis explained by the new Department of Homeland Security's color-coded threat alert system. The danger level rises and falls as the Bush administration's doctrine of pre-emptive warfare moves from confrontations in Afghanistan, Iraq and beyond. These policies define the objects of American foreign policy, answering the decade-long question of what comes "post" the Cold War.

Since the events of 9/11 the U.S. government has focused on finding those who planned and executed these attacks and on preventing others from launching similar attacks. These efforts have required an examination of what motivated Osama bin Laden and his followers. Just as scholars and national leaders alike once turned their attention to the Soviet Union, hoping to glean insights from enhanced knowledge of language, politics, religion, economics, and culture, a new attention is focused on those who practice Islam. The prominent question of "Why do they hate us?" has been clarified and woefully oversimplified so the "they" is now understood as those of the Islamic faith. Attention now turns to efforts to reduce or contain this powerful hatred.

It would be irresponsible to contend that Islamic publics were not prominent audiences of American foreign policy before September 11, 2001. Several decades' worth of historical events helped to develop a popular view of "Islamic fundamentalism" that was primarily defined by a relationship to terrorism, hostage taking, and radical anti-Americanism. While Islamic audiences once captivated American attention during the Iranian Hostage Crisis, the new international dynamic has once again catapulted the Islamic world to the forefront of international policy, this time without any visible means of resolution. These confrontations have developed alongside a vibrant scholarly effort to more fully understand the Islamic world. This debate, however, has hardened into a chasm, with some claiming that democracy and Islam are fundamentally incompatible. This next section summarizes this debate before turning to consideration of how specific discussions of civil society inform the effort to communicate with global publics.

Although their opinions are by no means universally shared, those who argue that Islam is a religious doctrine that is fundamentally anti-western, anti-modern, and inherently violent are increasing in number. Two of the most prominent, and perhaps the most controversial, foreign policy theories of the past decade seem to support this cynical view. Samuel Huntington (1993) and Francis Fukuyama (2002) develop explanatory principles that seek to explain the rise of terrorist violence and its relationship to Islam.

Samuel Huntington's (1993) "cultural clash" theory contended that cultural differences and not political or ideological conflict would be the primary cause of international tension over the next several years. This view has assumed a dominant place in many discussions of the Islamic world because it helps to explain terrorist violence as a consequence of disputed cultural interactions. This theory explains that the traditional expectations of Islamic societies may be threatened by the constant encroachment of western-led models of global capital. Islamic groups will, in this system, feel compelled to confront the West as the face of this particular strand of modernity. In this future, "A West at the peak of its power confronts non-West that increasingly have the desire, the will and the resources to shape the world in non-Western ways" (Huntington, 1993, p. 25). The will to shape the world emerges as a temptation for the "re-Islamization" of the Middle East that can better insulate it against Western norms.

The desire to fight modernity is also seen in the work of Francis Fukuyama. Fukuyama's (2002) contention that societies had arrived at "the end of history" has been clarified to explain that modern liberal democracies are the most sophisticated form of governance and that, "The September 11 attacks represent a desperate backlash against the modern world, which appears to be a speeding freight train to those unwilling to get onboard" (2002, p. 3). For both Huntington and Fukuyama, the premise that the tensions produced by contrasting modes of social organization will produce violent outcomes casts a long shadow over the prospect of the development of common global citizenry.

Communication scholars David M. Cheshier and Cori E. Dauber (1998/1999) have noted that these theories, particularly Huntington's work, have touched "raw nerves" (p. 36) in the effort to understand the formation of national identity. Perhaps the only agreement about their work is that it must be confronted by any scholar seeking to explain the current dynamics of international relations. Even when these central tenets are rejected as fundamentally misguided, these views often form the contrasting opinion to more hopeful perspectives of international relations. Thus, although Huntington and Fukuyama's perspectives may be disparaged, they are difficult to ignore. These pessimistic and even fatalistic views of Islam have also been reflected in other recent scholarship about the Middle East.

A survey of the works of Bernard Lewis (2001; 1990), Daniel Pipes (2002), and Martin Kramer (2002) reveals the prominence of notions regarding the emergence of a cultural clash in the assessments of how Islam functions as a system of governance and ideology. The prevailing logic of these views argues that before the West can communicate with, or even understand Islam, it must first recognize that Huntington's fault lines may be more precisely found within Islam. Bernard Lewis, eleven years before the attacks on the New York and Washington, detected the same rejection of western norms in "a surge of hatred that distresses, alarms, and above all baffles Americans" (Lewis, 1990, p. 60). The significance of this observation is that it supports the civilizational clash hypothesis by describing the Islamic anger as far deeper and more dangerous than any single American policy could produce.

This deep-seated hostility can be understood by the common metaphor that Islam is at war with itself. Fukuyama, for example, notes, "The Islamic world is at the juncture today where Christian Europe stood during the Thirty Years War in the 17th century" (2002, p. 7). Pipes similarly predicts that, "The battle for the soul of Islam will undoubtedly last many years and take many lives, and is likely to be the greatest ideological battle of the post-cold-war era" (2002, p. 7). The determinations of how far the virulent anger will spread may, ultimately, "... have to come from inside Islam itself. The Muslim community will have to decide whether to make its peace with modernity, and in particular with the key principle of a secular state and religious tolerance" (Fukuyama, 2002, p. 7). The separation of factions within Islam clarifies the distinctions between those who espouse the anti-modernity perspective and those reformist elements who seek some form of accommodation with the West. It is in this division between publics that the emerging diversity of Islamic audiences in American foreign policy can be understood.

Cheshier and Dauber (1998/1999) provide an important critique of both Huntington and his critics, contending that many theories of identity formation potentially overdetermine the role of history and memory in the formation of national culture. They counsel that instead of either blindly accepting or dismissing these factors, scholars should instead analyze the manner in which these people, events, and prominent themes become invested and extended through public argument. One of the most prominent argumentative topoi employed to differentiate and explain Islamic public opinion is the notion of the Arab Street. The phrase has become understood as shorthand for dissenting, and often hostile, public opinion. This allows a bifurcation between the perspectives of governments traditionally supportive of American interests and a far more divergent perspective from the mass public.

The post 9/11 campaigns to understand Islamic public opinion have involved a re-working of the metaphor of the Arab Street as a crucial audience. In traditional accounts of Islamic audiences, it is not uncommon to see a division between states and their citizenry. This view may involve the concern that pro-American policies would incite the "street" to rise up in revolt. A new concern is found in those who espouse anti-American ideologies, but who fail to be represented by the larger public. In an attempt to further isolate the support for violence from the broader public opinions, the notion of the Arab "basement" has emerged in western discourse. Thomas L. Friedman of *The New York Times* explains the distinction:

> The "Arab street" is the broad mass of public opinion, which is largely passive and nonviolent. The "Arab basement" is where small groups of hard-core ideologues, such as Osama bin Laden and his gang, have retreated and where they are mixing fertilizer, C-4 plastic explosives and gasoline to make the bombs that have killed Westerners all over the world (2002, October 23, p. A23).

Jordanian columnist Rami Khouri, who first coined the notion of an Arab basement, contends:

> The centre of gravity of populist Middle Eastern reaction to the US and Israel has shifted from the street to young bomb makers in the basements of buildings in Nablus and Nairobi, and in garages in New Jersey, Hamburg, Manila and Brooklyn ... To seek the pulse of the Arabs primarily in the street is to look in the wrong place (2002).

This view argues that the Arab basement is more dangerous than the Arab street, because despite the successes of Arab governments in "coping with" the Arab street, the sheer anger of those in the basement offers no peaceful resolution. Quoting Friedman again, "no diplomacy can defuse the Arab basement" and only some form of "shock therapy to this whole region" like that of overthrowing Saddam Hussein by military force to install a democratic government can "stop the drift of young Arabs from the street to the basement" (2002, October 23, p. A23).

The nuances of this shifting metaphor help to bring the different Islamic audiences into clearer focus. If communication was once targeted at either the state or the mass public, it still implicitly recognized the relevance of political authority. The means of interacting with these collectives retained similar forms, either as partners in economic assistance or as potential dissidents who need to be satisfied. The presence of this third dimension, geographically disparate from any single state and capable of comprehending only a language of violence, provides for a fundamentally new dynamic. Having established the violent tendencies of the Arab basement, American policymakers must determine how to interact with this seemingly hidden, but powerful, audience.

Determining the size of the basement remains one of the most important tasks. Perhaps the most explicit effort to trace the dimensions of this threat are found in the work of Richard Pipes (2002) who develops a typology of the concentric rings of militant Islam which categorizes individuals by their shared beliefs and actions. This framework alleges that 100 to 150 million people who, although not physically involved with Al-Qaeda, are supportive of anti-American efforts and another 500 million, who although they reject violence, share a broad anti-American ideology. This perspective suggests that there is a significant population around the world who at least sympathize with the Arab basement. Even as the violent core of this population is identified and recognized, these larger accounts function to explain where the support from the basement originates. Despite the seemingly narrow scope, this line of analysis explains Friedman's call for "shock therapy to this *whole region*." Pipes warns that the basement has a great deal of support, noting, "A radicalized Islam has taken hold, possibly over a wider swath than at any other time in the fourteen centuries of Muslim history, and it has driven out or silenced every serious rival" (Pipes, 2002, p. 25). The challenge of communicating with the Islamic world then, according to this perspective, must take heed of this violent perspective that cannot be determined by analyzing states or publics. These views are embedded in an ideology that Fukuyama describes as "Islamo-fascism" (2002, p.6), and that Pipes refers to as the "only truly vital totalitarian movement in the world today" (2002, p. 21).

The implications of accepting or rejecting this view of Islam are increasingly the subject of foreign policy scholarship and policy propositions. The perspective that one takes on understanding the relationship between the Arab Street and the Arab basement, and the need to win the cooperation if not the sympathies of the Islamic states, clearly influences the desirability of targeting certain segments of publics as the critical actors for specific foreign policies. Just as Friedman calls for a shock to the entire region in order to root out the violence, Mark Lynch (2003) argues for a vibrant dialogue with elite and middle class Arabs to influence their public opinion. Lee Harris explores the possibility that the terrorist attacks are best understood as a "fantasy" ideology of radical Islam (2002, p. 22). Depending on which communicative perspective is embraced, policy responses can vary dramatically. In Harris' view, for example, the attacks should not be understood as means of intimidating the American public, but instead function as a purifying act; proof that radical Islam can produce a new political order.

This repositioning of the motivations of radical Islamic factions necessarily de-emphasizes the role played by the United States and other outside actors. If violence is primarily intended to produce an imaginary vitality in the violent tenets of Islam, then:

> ... it is absurd for us to look for the so-called "root" causes of terrorism ... Such factors play no role in the creation of a fantasy ideology ... Equally absurd ... is the notion that we must review our policies toward the Arab world ... There is no political policy we could take that would change the attitude of our enemies—short, perhaps, of a massive nationwide conversion to fundamentalist Islam (Harris, 2002, p. 34).

This interpretation of Islam argues that nonviolent policies cannot prevent future violence against American interests. Those who adhere to this perspective maintain that militant Islam must be met with force. Martin Kramer, whose work aggressively challenges mainstream Middle Eastern studies in the United States, worries about, "the American scholars who have picked and chosen their way through the Qur-an and Islamic legal theory, in a deliberate effort to demilitarize both, or even to turn Islam into a pacifist faith—a kind of oriental Quakerism" (2002, p. 91).

Liberal scholars, whose agendas have provoked Harris and Kramer, provide a differing opinion about Islam. Mustapha Tlili, the Director of the UN Project for the World Policy Institute, worries that discussions of the democratic capabilities of Islam all too often degenerate into "pointless polemic[s]" (2001, p. 47). This perspective offers concern that visions of Islam predetermine the necessity of military force as the only means to neutralize the Arab basement. Edward Said, whose examination of the normalization inherent in representations of the non-Western "Orient," also worries that the current historical moment may over-determine the results of quests to decipher the nature of Islam because this context, "is too inflamed, too urgent, too locked up in questions of defense, war, the clash of civilizations" (2002, p. 70).

It is the controversy between these views of Islam that lies at the heart of so much of contemporary public policy. The debate between these schools of thought is not confined to the pages of academic journals; the recent controversy over Daniel Pipes' nomination to the board of the United States Institute of Peace (ISIP) typifies the consistently public character of the debate about the image of Islam in America (Cooperman, 2003). Groups opposed to Pipes' nomination worry that his beliefs are too dangerous to allow into the policy formulation of the USIP. The struggle to explain the views of Islamic publics is one of the most visible ideological contests in American public discourse. Opinions regarding how Americans should view Islam are fiercely contested, even as there is widespread acknowledgment that how the world views America is also in dispute.

In recognition of the importance of public opinion, Patrick Tyler of *The New York Times* declared the current era may not be a moment of unipolar dominance. Tyler observed, "…there may still be two superpowers on the planet: the United States and world public opinion" (2003, p. A1). The Bush administration's emphasis on reshaping the political landscape of the Middle East ensures the prominence of the conflict between these superpowers. How America imagines the world and how the world imagines America will animate foreign policy debates for the foreseeable future. The struggle between these 21st century superpowers therefore is often explained as fundamentally a communicative contest, with "Ideas as the major battleground in this war" (Tomlinson, 2003, p. 3). As the administration seeks to foster new democratic states, the next phases in the War on Terrorism will keep alive questions of winning the "hearts and minds" of Islamic publics.

Reclaiming Civility from within Civil Society

Civil society exists as a widely used and contested conceptual term that broadly describes the location of personal activity not synonymous with state regulation. Michael Walzer (1991), for example, emphasizes the set of relational networks that provide for a space of uncoerced human association. Amyn Sajoo, a visiting fellow at the Institute of Ismaili Studies in London, clarifies the common elements of that space, arguing that modern civil society generally features "the rule of law, equal citizenship, and participatory politics with accountability to the civic sphere" (2001, p. 13). Within the uncoerced space, civil society is understood to recognize shared social identities, linked to a political entity (Norton, 1995, p. 11). This sense and place of fluid identity is captured in David Held's (2002b) examination of the processes of globalization. Held contends that globalization can be understood through the tensions associated with governance becoming a complex, layered process, even as identity remains rooted in expressions of local communities (2002b, pp. 5-6).

Explaining models of citizen engagement within these participatory practices remains tumultuous, and often provides culturally specific means of explaining how individuals conduct and organize themselves. The production of citizenship can therefore be explored through the cultural narratives that normatively unify the place of the individual within a milieu of cultural and historical factors (Thomas, 2001). This dimension of civil society emphasizes the neutrality inherent in seemingly stable visions of individuals seeking affinity through social networks. As Thomas explains, "The self reaches outward to the grand narratives of the national project and inward to the biographies of interests, desires, needs, and moral character" (Thomas, 2001, p. 518). It is in this outward movement that Held (2002a; 1997) locates cosmopolitanism or those commonalities that transcend the local. It is through cosmopolitanism that citizens may enjoy multiple citizenships and thus move from purely local identities to more global commonalities (Held, 1997, p. 310).

Moving from these broad concepts to the specificity of regional studies often produces tensions similar to those found in the works of Huntington, Lewis, and Said. The western ancestry of civil society is well noted, and often serves to stagnate analysis amidst questions of Islam's capability to function as one of those meta-narratives that constitute civic identities. A concern from this line of research is what Sajoo identifies as the "normalization of Islam" (2001, p. 17), that is the reduction of the complexities of over one billion people to an inherently Islamic character that may inhibit other, typically secular and modernist, narratives from expressing individual identity in social contexts. Civil society is then often understood as a litmus test for the democratic capabilities of a particular people. If a nation possesses a vibrant civil life, it can support the volatile exercise of democracy. Robert Hefner bemoans the manner in which civil society has, all too often, become understood as a most crucial social indicator.

... civil society has been attributed the power to create

countervailing forces, eliminate anomie, unleash business enterprise, strengthen the family, radicalize democracy, reduce teenage pregnancy, and inculcate republican virtue ...

rarely has so heavy an analytic cargo been strapped on the back of so slender a conceptual beast (1998, p. 17).

Perhaps then a useful means of analyzing civil society is to reduce its scope, and ask it to examine a more narrow set of criteria. To extricate the utility of civil society from this debate about the character of Islam, it may be necessary to narrow conceptions of civility.

Farhard Kazemi (2002) astutely notices that the debate surrounding Islam and civil society often overlooks Augustus Norton's (1995) analysis of the essential nature of civility as an attitude toward both dissenting political or social perspectives as well as toward the social institutions (p. 39-40). Norton is careful to acknowledge and attempt to move beyond the practical concerns with civil society as a historical reflection of western social systems, contending that the utility of civil society analysis may lie in the ability to envision "an outline image of Middle East society" (1995, p. 11). This shift is consistent with the work of Michael Dawahare (2000) and Roberto Alejandro (1993) that seeks to move beyond traditional definitions of civil society that emphasize group membership in secular communities or institutions and toward constructs that inform indigenous conceptions of identity.

An important element of this civility includes what Norton refers to as a quality that values tolerance and acknowledges the legitimacy of multiple perspectives. For Norton, "Civil society is also a cast of mind, a willingness to live and let live" (1995, p. 11-12). Locating this value system in public behavior allows critics to evaluate the manner in which respect is demonstrated toward others, especially in those circumstances where personal self-interest would dictate a repudiation of alternate views. This demanding interpretation of civility, explained by Nicole Billante and Peter Sanders (2002), provides a means of narrowing the scope of civil society into a useful and discrete means of analyzing social systems.

Exploring civil society as a demeanor, instead of as a structural component, may offer a useful lens to examine how publics compare to each other and how willing they are to engage one another. Civility offers a target for social systems to strive toward, even as it allows for the complexities of local identities and belief systems. Despite the prominent historical examples where this willingness has failed to effectively guide societies toward greater tolerance of minority populations, Hefner (1998) underscores the importance of the struggles to ensure this ideal. Civility may function as much as an ideal, or target, of social activity, as it does as a gauge of democratic capability. How the Bush administration articulates this democratic indicator can provide critics with a means to understand the future of Islamic civil society.

Engaging Islamic Publics: American Public Diplomacy

Beginning in the days immediately after September 11th, President George Bush began to explain the administration's view of Islam, a perspective sufficient to substantiate the administration's foreign policies. In his national address on September 20, 2001 he explained:

> The terrorists are traitors to their own faith, trying, in effect, to hijack Islam itself. The enemy of America is not our many Muslim friends; it is not our many Arab friends. Our enemy is a radical network of terrorists, and every government that supports them (2001, September 20).

This radical network was thus engaged in a dual struggle, to conquer Islam and the West. Despite occasional gaffes, such as Bush's description of the military campaign as a "crusade" (2001, September 16), the administration's public commentary carefully defined both a moderate Islam that emphasized peaceful conduct as well as a radical element that embraced violence to reject modernity. The administration's foreign policies, most clearly enunciated through the State Department's public diplomacy campaigns, can therefore be understood as an effort to communicate with those "Muslim friends" as they struggle to recapture the soul of Islam. Senator Richard Lugar explains the importance of public diplomacy to this task:

> Successful public diplomacy … is about clearly and honestly explaining the views of the United States, displaying the humanity and generosity of our people, underscoring issues of commonality, and expanding opportunities for interaction between Americans and foreign peoples (2003, p. 2).

The magnitude of this persuasive mission is confirmed by a steady stream of polling data that confirms the tremendous disjunction between how

Americans view themselves and how those in a number of regions under-stood as the Islamic world, do the same. Recent studies by the Pew Research Center, the Brookings Institution, and Boston University all confirm the presence of a giant chasm in world public opinion, even before the recent hostilities in Iraq.[2] The scale of the problem can be appreciated through findings such as the one that claims that only 4% of those surveyed in the American ally of Saudi Arabia have a favorable opinion of the US (Telhami, 2003, p. 2). The Pew Research Center's Andrew Kohut contends, "The most serious problem facing the U.S. abroad is its very poor public image in the Muslim world" (2003, p. 1).

This image problem is far from a cosmetic concern. Failure to provide a more "accurate" interpretation of America is understood to ensure more violence. Charlotte Beers, who served as the Bush administration's first Undersecretary of State for Public Diplomacy, provided insight into how the communication of negative images of America was central to the produc-tion of violence: "We are talking about millions of ordinary people, a huge number of whom have gravely distorted, but carefully cultivated images of us—images so negative, so weird, so hostile that I can assure you a young generation of terrorists is being created" (2003, February 27, 2-3).

This perspective clearly emphasizes the importance of communication in the development of violent Islam. Significantly, and perhaps representing a concession to globalization trends, the central audience for the administra-tion's narrative is understood to be non-state actors. Communicating with a mass public audience that has been brought together by the twin forces of demographics and ideology to rehabilitate America's international reputa-tion is one of the primary goals in this campaign.

Miscommunication—The Distortion of Civility

Two primary elements of civility are apparent in this popular narrative of Islam. First, the administration presumes that American notions of what constitutes civility, or lack thereof, should be a primary concern for Islamic publics. Displays of American civility are expected to communicate certain universal truths about the character of Americans. The failure to commu-nicate this social expectation is located as one of the United States' primary problems. The second dimension of civility is the assumption that only certain segments of Islamic publics are capable of engaging in democratic discourse. The differentiation of these populations provides evidence of how generational divisions are understood as important demarcations in the struggle to define political Islam. Taken together, these dimensions of civility provide a great deal of explanation about how American foreign policy attempts to engage the potential democratic character in Islamic civil society.

The need to demonstrate the sense of unselfish cooperation may offer a verdict on the importance of Bush's emphasis of Islam's peaceful character. Bush took great effort to declare that "Islam is Peace" as he did in a visit to the Islamic Center of Washington, D.C. days after the attack. The peaceful nature, he declared, could be seen in American Muslims: "America counts millions of Muslims amongst our citizens, and Muslims make an incredibly valuable contribution to our country ... And they need to be treated with respect. In our anger and emotion, our fellow Americans must treat each other with respect" (2001, September 17).

The mutual respect that Bush asks Americans to display to each other exemplifies Norton's (1995) sense of groups providing the space for others to live and flourish. The ability to exhibit such behavior differentiates America's allies from its enemies. When the war entered new phases, such as when the campaign in Afghanistan began in October of 2001, Bush pledged friendship to the Afghan people and "almost a billion worldwide who practice the Islamic faith." In the same speech he described Al Qaeda as "barbaric criminals who profane a great religion by committing murder in its name" (2001, October 7).[3] The space between these populations is apparent in those who show respect for Islam and by extension other peoples. The mutuality of civility can be understood as an expectation, even as a normative standard for behavior, in the discourse of American foreign policy.

If this tolerance is expressed as an international norm, it should not be surprising that its absence can signify a larger crisis. This crisis arises when international audiences fail to "effectively" comprehend American intentions. Mamoun Fandy (2001, B2), a Professor at National Defense University, repeats a frequent refrain when, in *The Washington Post*, he explains that the Bush administration needs a new means of communicating its message much more than a new message. For Fandy and others, the Bush administration has failed to embrace new broadcasting mediums and channels, leaving Islamic audiences to be served by media with an anti-American bias. Charlotte Beers agrees with the weakness of the US position because "in the volatile information revolution, the U.S. has a smaller and smaller voice" and the world, and especially the Middle East, is full of conflicting ideas, biases boldly told, rumors that harden into "truth" overnight, and curiously, a real lack of relevant information (2002, May 7). The fear is that rumors, like the one that claims that Jewish-Americans were told to leave the World Trade Center before the attacks occurred on 9/11, become accepted truth in regions exposed to anti-American media. This emphasis on misinformation helps to explain the tension between America's self-image and international perceptions. Barraged by conspiracy theories, many people around the world cannot avoid developing a poor image of the United States.

Citing the weapons of "hate radio and television" Norm Pattiz (*We Hate You But,* 2002, p. 7), the chairman of Westwood One radio and a leading figure behind American radio efforts in the Middle East, argues that the presence of hostile media forms constitutes "a media war." This war metaphor enhances the urgency of these communicative challenges and legitimates those solutions that can overcome such entrenched media forms. Board of Broadcasting Governor Kenneth Tomlinson has argued that persuading Islamic audiences will ultimately be the measure of American success in this war. Americans must overcome efforts to "grotesquely misrepresent who we are" if we are to win "the hearts and minds of a tremendous audience" (2003, p. 3).

Beers' (2003, February 27, p. 3) conclusion that there is a large divide "between who we are and how we wish to be seen" can be understood as the rallying cry for American efforts in this war for Islamic public opinion. To close the gap is to overcome what Thomas Friedman coins the "iron curtain of mistrust and misunderstanding" (2002, January 23), which may be "even more insurmountable than the old one that divided Europe" (Tomlinson, 2003, p. 9). Kenton Keith, a Senior Vice President for the Meridian International Center provides the final instrumental logic for engaging this audience: "To ultimately defeat terrorism, we must also engage the Muslim world in the realm of ideas, values, and beliefs. No previous foreign affairs crisis has been so deeply rooted in cultural misunderstanding, and we must address this gulf of misunderstanding if we are to succeed" (2003, p. 1). Public diplomacy campaigns thus become essential efforts to bridge gaps in international perception. Even acknowledging the limited manner in which these campaigns can alter important tenets of American foreign policy, public diplomacy becomes the crucial tool by which others may come to support these policies.

The public diplomacy campaigns produced under Secretary Beers have been assailed for what they failed to accomplish, namely having any real impact on Islamic public opinion, but little attention has been devoted to what they attempted.[4] A significant component of the administration's programs focused on the production of materials that would amplify Bush's message that Islam remains compatible with the American political system. The campaign that ended in January 2003 included "a series of mini-documentaries of Muslim Americans describing their freedom here, their ability to practice their faith, and their integration into the life of America" (Beers, 2003, February 27, p. 6), including the booklet titled *Muslim Life in America*. These materials were ultimately exposed to 288 million people and Beers argued that the preliminary efforts to follow up this campaign in Indonesia found high enough rates of information recall and retention to describe the booklet as "one of the most successful pieces we've produced" (Beers, 2003, February 27, p. 7).

The decision to emphasize shared values can be traced to the apparent disconnect between perceptions of American lifestyles and the corresponding political space for the practice of Islam. Before the National Press Club, Beers explained:

> In these key countries, people believe, very strongly that there is so much decadence and faithlessness in the United States that there is no way that the practice of Islam could survive here ... Every single time we have been on the road in these countries, the question we are always asked is: "How badly are the Muslims being treated in your country?" And they're not kidding (2003, February 11).

This campaign thus accesses a dimension of civility by proceeding from the assumption that American civility, or lack thereof, is a primary concern for Islamic publics. The misperceptions that Beers, Tomlinson and others identify can be understood as the "mistaken" belief that American civil society lacks a fundamental willingness to exercise tolerance towards others. The fifty-five-page booklet explores a variety of contexts where Islam could be understood to be incompatible with traditional American life, including education, banking, and rap music. The pictures and stories describe "average" Muslim-Americans who are, according to one section, "Living in Two Cultures," as expressed by the comments of Dr. Laila al-Marayati, "I don't view myself through separate identities. The yardstick I measure by is my faith; everything else falls into place. My identity is an American Palestinian who is a Muslim" (*Muslim Life in America*, p. 9). This type of success of synthesizing American and Islamic identities is prominent throughout the accounts.

The Tagouri family, who appear as the cover story and lead article, describe how they not only possess the legal freedom to live as they wish, but also feel supported by their communities, both Islamic and non-Islamic. The description of how they can be both devout Muslims and fully integrated into American society, through schools, professions, and communities, explains how it is that American society has come to possess a vibrant sense of civility. The willingness to incorporate the beliefs of individual Muslims is described alongside the broader mosaic of American diversity; a nation strong enough to foster the inclusion of new communities. The presence of a national map that features the respective number of mosques in each state is included alongside a narrative of ever-expanding social inclusion. Not only is American society capable of providing sufficient space for the expression of Islamic identities in day-to-day issues like attending schools and practicing their faith, Muslim Americans are themselves engaged in the process of strengthening the social fabric of the United States by becoming prominent members of society.

> American Muslims appear to be moving into another stage of identity in which these kinds of issues are being confronted and resolved in new ways. The result may well be that a truly American Islam, woven from the fabric of many national, racial, and ethnic identities, is in the process of emerging (Muslim Life in America, p. 19).

Bush's post 9/11 narrative arrives at its logical conclusion: an American vision of Islam that can undergo the cultural assimilation that has long been celebrated as a hallmark of the immigrant experience in the United States. Unlike the secular rule in nations such as Turkey that prohibit displays of Islamic faith, this perspective appears to embrace Held's cosmopolitan goal of multiple, reinforcing political identities. The emphasis placed on miscommunication thus becomes the artificial barrier that separates these two cultures.

Moderates and Messengers: Separating Islamic publics

The depiction of ideologically moderate Muslims is not solely a means of erasing differences between the cultures. The presence of a moderate force within Islam confirms the battle-within-cultures hypothesis and requires a category of messengers capable of communicating with other Islamic publics. Taken alone the first dimension appears to explain that Islamic audiences, much to the dismay of Pipes and Lewis, are inherently peaceful. The second dimension of civility, differentiating the ability of only some audiences to posses this trait, reverses this perspective and affirms the conclusion that there are limits to how "better" communication can resolve international grievances. Drawing upon the inner circles of Pipes' theories, this perspective argues that only certain segments of Islamic publics are capable of engaging the West, so the moderate forces must act as messengers.

In order to reach these more extreme audiences, traditional American (i.e., non-Muslim) messengers cannot be trusted to provide the evidence of American tolerance. Although some of the administration's earlier efforts featured the use of prominent American representatives on media available in the Muslim world, including Al-Jazeera, both *Muslim Life in America* and the Council on American-Islamic Relation's *Islam in America* campaigns heavily emphasize first-person testimonials as a means to demonstrate America's true civil character. Richard Pipes chastised the early efforts, including the decision to have American officials appear on Al-Jazeera, because "The U.S. government lacks any religious authority to speak about Islam, though it does not realize this" (2002, p. 26). His solution predicts much of the logic of the *Muslim Life in America* campaign:

> Someone other than Madison Avenue types, and other than Americans, will be needed to conceptualize and deliver the anti-bin Laden message, someone with the necessary Islamic credentials and deep understanding of the culture. That someone is the moderate Muslim, the Muslim who hates the prospect of living under the reign of militant Islam and can envisage something better (2002, p.27).

Pipes' identification of the moderate Muslim is the necessary corollary to the efforts to separate the Islamic extremist from those peaceful adherents of Islam. If there is a battle being waged inside of Islam, then the US must identify and communicate with those who have reconciled a role for modernity and their faith. This does not remove the need for military action against those who practice violence in the Arab basement, but it does provide an agenda to de-link those few from the millions who currently sympathize with their views.

Beginning with this framework for Islamic audiences helps to explain the enthusiasm for consumer models of public diplomacy. Identifying a target audience allows the use of spokespeople to engage in new media campaigns. The launch of Radio Sawa, for example, provides a sophisticated media format to expose American interests to these Islamic audiences largely through surrogate voices. The mixture of popular music and news is designed to "reach" those audiences who would not otherwise be interested in an American perspective. Norm Pattiz defends the decision to blend news into a music-dominated format, "If you lead with policy, you'll get one-share. Nobody wants to hear our policy because our policies are unpopular" (*We Hate You But,* 2002, p. 32). Surrogates, both Islamic moderates themselves and popular music, provide the means of communicating with these otherwise hostile audiences.

The successes of these campaigns are then logically expressed in terms of exposure. Tomlinson cites survey data that shows Sawa "is already the most popular station in many Arab capitals" (2003, p. 2). Pattiz concurs, noting that Sawa now has moved far beyond the one-share as it reaches 80 percent of the target audience (*We Hate You But,* 2002, p. 8). Buoyed by these indicators of success, the administration now develops new campaigns that build upon these familiar models of communication. Charlotte Beers supported "Brave and bold plans" for new television initiatives toward the Middle East including a version of *Sesame Street* for teens and an Arabic-language television channel (2003, February 27, p. 4). The proposed Arabic-language television station has been hailed as a major advance in moving the region "away from extremism and violence and toward democracy and freedom" (Beers, 2003, February 27, p. 7). If surrogates can continue to be found and involved in media campaigns, then the process of demonstrating civility can be extended to even the most extreme audiences.

Conclusions

Historians may one day look back on the early 21st century as the period where the United States awoke from its relative isolation of the early post-Cold War period and was forced to confront the presence of Islam as a complex system of political and religious identities. The early efforts to communicate with Islamic publics are most clearly on display in the work of the public diplomacy campaigns because they are both overt and intentional. These campaigns reveal a great deal about how Islam is categorized and explained by American policy-makers; they also provide crucial insights into how America desires to be seen around the world.

Charlotte Beers acknowledged her task as "the most sophisticated brand assignment I have ever had ... It is almost as though we have to redefine what America is" (Powers, 2001). This sense of redefining what it means to be American is at the heart of communicating with such an unfamiliar other as Islamic publics. The insistence on displaying dimensions of civility can be understood as the tenets of social order that are valued inside the United States and, by extension, as the indicators of democratic development that are valued internationally. Civility can be appreciated as the lowest common denominator for expressions of democratic social orders. After banishing the believers of violence to the basement of civic life, an emphasis on civility for the remaining audiences necessarily defines away any concerns not already congruent with American perspectives.

Between Huntington's and Said's perspectives, proponents of civility attempt to utilize the willingness to respect other perspectives as the measure as to whether or not further democratization of Islamic nations will be possible. Compared against the vitriolic debate about the democratic capabilities of states, this perspective may offer one potentially useful perspective. The significance of an emphasis of civility is, unfortunately, not solely as a test of civil society. Civility alone appears to more prominently reflect Craig Calhoun's (2001, p. 17-18) concern for shallow cosmopolitanism that espouses traits of multiple global citizenships, but in effect, provides only a recognition of the binary of western and non-western cultures, without an examination of how lived experiences may promote shared worldviews.

The incredible complexity associated with understanding the myriad of individuals who can, through some of level of association, fall under the rubric of "Islam" appears to require some level of categorization, but the terms of this process may be the foundation for the American interpretation of Islam as a political force in the 21st century. As important decisions for new American media forms and formats are being developed with an eye toward Islamic audiences, it is imperative that scholars examine which audiences are deemed appropriate members of the dialogue.

If, however, American public diplomacy campaigns position civility as a fundamental American political value in a world of increasing miscommunication and hostility, the mooring of a receptive Islamic public appears extremely unsteady. Michael Calvin McGee's (1998) perspective on the substantial differences between the construction of publics and people explains the dangers embedded in the division of un-civil audiences. McGee argues that notions of publics underwrite all political systems, but that in political discourse orderly behavior is understood as the domain of the "public" and dangerous irrationality is associated with the "people" (1998, pp. 125-126).

Both of the strategies to present civility ultimately provide legitimacy to both Islamic publics and Islamic peoples. The metaphoric struggle to define the future of Islam is an acknowledgement that while civility is a means for moderate elements to communicate, these boundaries simultaneously act to identify some people as incapable of communicating with the appropriate language of democratic norms. As both critics and supporters of new public diplomacy campaigns demand new strategies of communication, critics must look beyond the "public relations" or "traditional diplomacy" models to more closely review the types of publics imagined by these efforts. If the 21st century is to be understood as a time of cultural clash, either between or within cultures, the early steps in defining the participants may resonate much longer and much further than the messages given life in any specific campaign.

NOTES

* The author would like to thank Thomas Hollihan and two anonymous reviewers for their helpful comments.

1. This essay attempts to analyze the categorical perspectives associated with Islam and, as such, describes Islam in generally categorical terms. This essay does not purport that there is any single "Islam" that can be homogenized to overwrite differences in sect and national origin.

2. The studies are "A View from the Arab World: A Survey in Five Countries." Shibley Telhami, Brookings Institution, March 13, 2003; "What the World Thinks in 2002: How Global Publics View: Their Lives, Their Countries, The World, America." Pew Research Center, December 4, 2002; and "The Next Generation's Image of Americans. Attitudes and Beliefs Held by Teen-Agers in Twelve Countries. A Preliminary Research Report," Margaret H. DeFleur and Melvin L. DeFleur, October 17, 2002.

3. Bush used a similar template for Iraq, contending that, "We come to Iraq with respect for its citizens, for their great civilization and for the religious faiths they practice" (Bush, 2003, March 19). In this interpretation, Hussein seeks to promulgate a false view of Islam, even as religious freedoms are denied to the Iraqi people. The White House's Office of Global Communications publication, Apparatus of Lies: Saddam's Disinformation and Propaganda 1990-2003, explains Saddam's role in manipulating the tenets of Islam, "Saddam Hussein tries to harness feelings of solidarity among Muslims to his advantage. By portraying himself as a devout believer and invoking the name of Allah in his struggles with the international community, he seeks to frame his conflicts as an Islamic struggle and fashion himself as standard-bearer for Muslims" (White House, 2003).

4. This criticism is typified by the congressional testimony of R.S. Zaharna, who located the problems of the current efforts in that they contained a culturally-specific effort to "speak straight" and that they ignored long-term relationship building (2003, p. 1).

WORKS CITED

Alejandro, R. (1993). *Hermeneutics, citizenship, and the public sphere*. Albany, NY: SUNY Press.

Apparatus of lies: Saddam's disinformation and propaganda 1990-2003. (2003) The White House Office of Global Communications. Washington, DC. {Online} Available: http://www.whitehouse.gov/ogc/apparatus/index.html (2003, March 21).

Beers, C. (2003, February 27). *Hearing on American Public Diplomacy and Islam*. Testimony before the Committee on Foreign Relations, United States Senate.108th Congress, 1st Session{Online} Available: http://foreign.senate.gov/testimony/2003/BeersTestimony030227.pdf (2003, March 12).

———. (2003, February 11). Remarks to the Advisory Committee for Voluntary Foreign Aid. *National Press Club*. {Online} Available: http://www.state.gov/r/us/18260.htm (2003, March 2).

———. (2002, May 7, 2002). Remarks at the Washington Institute for Near East Policy. {Online} Available: http://www.state.gov/r/us/10424.htm (2003, February 5).

Billante, N. & Saunders, P. (2002, Spring). Why civility matters. Policy: A review of public policy and ideas. {Online} Available: http://www.cis.org.au/Policy/Spring02/polspring02-6.htm (2003, February 11).

Bush, G.W. (2003, March 19). President Bush addresses the nation. {Online} Available: http://www.whitehouse.gov/news/releases/2003/03/iraq/20030319-17.html (2003, March 27).

———. (October 7, 2001). Presidential address to the nation. {Online} Available: http://www.whitehouse.gov/news/releases/2001/10/20011007-8.html (2003, March 3).

———. (2001, September 20). Address to a Joint Session of Congress and the American People. {Online} Available: http://www.whitehouse.gov/news/releases/2001/09/20010920-8.html (2003, May 3).

———. (2001, September 17). "Islam is peace" Says President. Remarks by the President at Islamic Center of Washington, D.C. {Online} Available: http://www.whitehouse.gov/news/releases/2001/09/20010917-11.html (2003, March 3).

———. (2001, September 16). Remarks by the President upon arrival. {Online} Available: http://www.whitehouse.gov/news/releases/2001/09/20010916-2.html (2003, March 3).

Calhoun, C. (2001, March 2-3). Cosmopolitanism Is Not Enough: Local Democracy in a Global Context, Presented at the University of North Carolina. {Online} Available: http://www.unc.edu/depts/anthro/talks/calhoun.pdf.

Cheshier, D.M. & Dauber, C.E. (1998/1999, Winter/Spring). The place and power of civic space: Reading globalization and social geography through the lens of civilizational conflict. *Security Studies*, 8 (2/3), 35-70.

Cooperman, A. (2003, April 7). Muslims protest Bush nominee: Groups say Peace Institute choice sends 'Wrong message.' *The Washington Post*, A13. {Online} Available: http://www.washingtonpost.com/wp-dyn/articles/A42881-2003Apr6.html (2003, April 9).

Dawahare, M.D. (2000). *Civil society and Lebanon: Toward a hermeneutic theory of the public sphere in comparative studies*. Parkland, FL: Brown Walker Press.

DeFleur D.H. & M.L. DeFleur. (2002, October 17). "The Next Generation's Image of Americans. Attitudes and Beliefs Held By Teen-Agers in Twelve Countries. A Preliminary Research Report. {Online} Available: http://www.bu.edu/news/releases/2002/defleur/report.pdf (2003, July 13).

Fandy, M. (2001, December 2). To Reach Arabs, Try Changing The Channel. *The Washington Post*, B2.

Friedman, T.L. (2002, October 23). Under the Arab Street. *The New York Times*, A23.

————. (2002, January 23). Run, Osama, Run. *The New York Times*, A19.

Fukuyama, F. (2002, Winter). Has History Started Again? Policy: A review of public policy and ideas, 2 (1), 3-7{Online} Available: http://www.cis.org.au/Policy/winter02/polwin02-1.htm (2003, February 10).

Harris, L. (2002, August-September). Al Qaeda's fantasy ideology. *Policy Review*, 114, 19-36. {Online} Available: http://www.policyreview.org/AUG02.harris.html (2003, March 4).

Hefner, R.W. (1998, Mach-April). Civil society: Cultural possibility of a modern ideal. *Society*, 35 (3), 16-27.

Held, D. (2002, Summer)a. *Globalization and Cosmopolitanism*. Logos, 1 (3), 1-17.

————. (2002)b. Globalization After September 11th. {Online} Available: http://www.polity.co.uk/global/pdf/After%209.pdf (2003, May 4).

————. (1997, September). Globalization and Cosmopolitan Democracy. *Peace Review*, 9 (3), 309-315.

Huntington, S. P. (1993, Summer). The Clash of Civilizations? *Foreign Affairs*. 72 (3), 22-28.

Kazemi, J. (2002). Civil society and government in Islam. In J. Miles, *Islamic political ethics: Civil society, pluralism, and conflict*, 3-37. Princeton, NJ: Princeton University Press.

Keith, K. (2003, February 27). Hearing on American Public Diplomacy and Islam. Testimony Before the Committee on Foreign Relations, United States Senate.108th Congress, 1st Session{Online} Available: http://foreign.senate.gov/hearings/KeithTestimony030227.pdf (2003, March 12).

Khouri, R.G. (2002, October 24). From the Arab street to the basement bomb factory. *Jordan Times*. {Online} Available: http://www.aljazeerah.info/Opinion%20editorials/2002%20Opinion%20editorials/Oct%202002%20op%20eds/Oct%2024,%202002%20op%20eds.htm (2003, February 10).

Kohut, A. (2003, February 27). Hearing on American Public Diplomacy and Islam. Testimony Before the Committee on Foreign Relations, United States Senate.108th Congress, 1st Session{Online} Available: http://foreign.senate.gov/hearings/KohutTestimony030227.pdf (2003, March 12).

Kramer, M. (2002, Summer). Jihad 101. *Middle East Forum*, IX (2), p. 87-95. {Online} Available: http://www.meforum.org/article/208 (2003, February 10).

Lewis, B. (2001, September 27). Jihad vs. crusade: A historian's guide to the new war. *The Wall Street Journal*. {Online} Available: http://opinionjournal.com/extra/?id=95001224 (2003, February 10).

————. (1990, September). The roots of Muslim rage. *The Atlantic Monthly*. 60-62 {Online} Available: http://www.theatlantic.com/issues/90sep/rage.htm (2003, February 10).

Lugar, R. (2003, February 27). Hearing on American Public Diplomacy and Islam. Opening Statement Before the Committee on Foreign Relations, United States Senate.108th Congress, 1st Session{Online} Available: http://foreign.senate.gov/hearings/LugarStatement030227.pdf (2003, March 12).

Lynch, (2003, September/October). Taking Arabs Seriously. *Foreign Affairs*, 81 (Online) Available: http://www.foreignaffairs.org/20030901faessay82506/marc-lynch/taking-arabs-seriously.html (2003, September 5).

McGee, M. (1998). *Rhetoric in Postmodern America: Conversations with Michael Calvin McGee*. (Ed.) Corbin, C. New York: The Guilford Press.

Muslim Life in America. (2002). U.S. Department of State's Office of International Information Programs. Washington, DC.

Norton, A. R. (1995). Introduction. In A.R. Norton, *Civil society in the Middle East*. Volume 1, 1-26. New York: E.J. Brill.

Pew Research Center. (2002, December 4). "What the World Thinks in 2002: How Global Publics View: Their Lives, Their Countries, The World, America." {Online} Available: http://people-press.org/reports/files/report165.pdf (2003, May 9).

Pipes, D. (2002, January). Who Is the Enemy? *Commentary*. 113 (1), 21-27. {Online} Available: http://www.danielpipes.org/article/103 (2003, January 18).

Powers, W. (2001, November 16). State Department works to create brand of the free. *GovExec.com*. {Online} Available: http://www.govexec.com/dailyfed/1101/111601nj2.htm (2003, March 2).

Said, E. (2002, July). Impossible Histories: Why the Many Islams Cannot be Simplified. *Harper's Magazine*, 305 (1826), 69-74. {Online} Available: http://www.harpers.org/online/impossible_histories/?pg=1 (2003, January 18).

Sajoo, A.B. (2001). The ethics of the public square: A preliminary Muslim critique. polylog. Forum for Intercultural Philosophizing, 2, 1-35. {Online} Available: http://www.polylog.org/them/2/asp4-en.htm (2003, February 7).

Telhami, S. (2003, March 13). A View from the Arab World: A Survey in Five Countries. *The Brookings Institution*, {Online} Available: http://www.brookings.org/fp/saban/survey20030313.pdf (2003, March 15).

Thomas, G. M. (2001, Winter). Religions in global civil society. *Sociology of Religion*, 62 (4), 515-553.

Tlili, M. (2001, Fall). Arab democracy: A possible dream? *World Policy Journal*, 28 (3), 47-48.

Tomlinson, K. (2003, February 27). Hearing on American Public Diplomacy and Islam. Testimony Before the Committee on Foreign Relations, United States Senate. 108th Congress, 1st Session{Online} Available: http://foreign.senate.gov/testimony/2003/TomlinsonTestimony030227.pdf (2003, March 12).

Tyler, P. E. (2003, February 17). A new power in the streets. *The New York Times*, A1.

Walt, S. M. (2001/2002, Winter). Beyond bin laden: Reshaping U.S. foreign policy. *International Security*, 26 (2), 56-78.

Walzer, M. (1991, Spring). The Idea of Civil Society: A Path to Social Reconstruction. *Dissent*, 38 (1), 293-304.

We Hate You (But Keep Sending Us Baywatch) The Impact of America's Entertainment on the World. (2002, December 5). Panel discussion hosted by the Public Affairs Committee of the Writers Guild of America. Los Angeles: CA. Moderated by M. Kaplan. {Online} Available: http://www.wga.org/craft/wehateyou/WeHateYou.pdf (2003, February 12).

Zaharna, R.S. (2003, February 27). Hearing on American Public Diplomacy and Islam. Testimony Before the Committee on Foreign Relations, United States Senate. 108th Congress, 1st Session{Online} Available: http://foreign.senate.gov/testimony/2003/ZaharnaTestimony030227.pdf (2003, March 12).

We'll Guarantee Freedom When We Can Afford It: The Free Market, the Russian Constitution, and the Rhetoric of Boris Yeltsin

*James A. Janack**

Abstract

This essay highlights the discrepancies between the Constitution that Russian President Boris Yeltsin proposed in a speech in June 1993 and the actual Constitution that Yeltsin's team drafted and the Russian electorate adopted six months later. The apparent inconsistencies between the speech and the constitution are explained through an analysis of Yeltsin's speeches in 1993 and 1996. Drawing on Kenneth Burke's dramatistic pentad, the essay argues that Yeltsin's discourse emphasized scenic aspects in the form of economic conditions. The analysis of Yeltsin's rhetoric at important points in Russia's democratic development, the Constitutional drafting process, and the 1996 presidential campaign, suggests that the Russian president's discourse conceptualized a democracy in which democratic acts were enabled by a prosperous market economy rather than constitutional guarantees.

With his resignation on December 31, 1999, Boris Yeltsin left a confused and contradictory legacy. Yeltsin unquestionably dominated Russia's political transition from a Soviet republic to an independent state, yet, as the new millennium begins, Russia finds itself in a complicated situation with a multitude of serious problems to face, at least in part due to Yeltsin's policies. Certainly Russia has become more democratic than it was fifteen years ago, but it is hardly what many Americans would consider a free and just society. Contested political elections are now the norm in Russia. However, the government control of the media raises concerns about the fairness of these elections (Ellis; Mickiewicz; Tyler; Wines). Economically, Russia has started the transformation to a free market, yet only the select few (mostly former Communist Party bosses) benefit, and much of the population remains mired in poverty. Although the infrastructure of open political debate and discussion has been slowly developing, Yeltsin was often more comfortable ruling by decree and attempting to resolve conflicts with violence.

Despite this mixed record, Yeltsin may eventually come to be known as the father of Russian democracy. In 1991, then President George Bush declared Yeltsin "a courageous individual, duly elected by the people, standing firmly and courageously for democracy and freedom" (McManus & Shogren, A1). Two years later, President Clinton stated that he had "no reason to doubt the personal commitment that Boris Yeltsin made to let the Russian people decide their own future [and] to secure a new constitution with democratic values and democratic processes…" (Elsner). Indeed, the constitution that Yeltsin and his advisors drafted and that the Russian people adopted in a referendum in December 1993 may turn out to be Yeltsin's most significant, though thorniest, contribution to Russian democratic culture. While certainly an improvement over the Soviet era constitution, several Western scholars have expressed serious concerns about the authoritarian nature of the constitution and its inadequate guarantees of basic democratic principles (Ahdieh; Hoffmann; Sharlet "New Russian"). As Stephen Holmes explains, the constitution establishes a system of "super-presidentialism," where the separation of powers and guarantees of basic rights are compromised by swollen presidential powers (123-124). Holmes contends that Yeltsin's constitution may not protect individual rights any better than did Brezhnev's (123).

Such a mixed record may leave Yeltsin's credentials as a democrat in question, particularly for a Western audience. Some may question what kind of democrat he was, or whether he was a democrat in any sense of the word. Official discourse in the West anointed him the protector of the nascent Russian democracy; however, the constitution produced largely through his influence establishes a democracy with potentially serious flaws, at least from a common Western perspective. One possible explanation is that Yeltsin and his team of advisors understood democracy qualitatively differently from the prevailing Western conception. Kenneth Burke's dramatistic pentad, as a means for determining "motivations of 'democracy'" (Grammar 17), offers insight into the vision of democracy created through the Russian President's rhetoric, how that democracy functions, and how it is sustained. Pentadic analyses of Yeltsin's discourse during key periods in Russia's transition toward free market democracy, namely the constitutional drafting process and the 1996 Russian presidential election, shed light on an understanding of democracy articulated in his addresses. Specifically, a close reading of two of Yeltsin's speeches delivered in March 1993 and June 1993, and of his campaign discourse during the 1996 Russian presidential race, suggests that Yeltsin's rhetoric emphasized scenic aspects, particularly economic conditions, which in turn influence the nature of the acts that can occur within that scene. Put simply,

Yeltsin's discourse suggested that a free market economy (scene) would ensure democratic acts. By prioritizing economic reforms over political, some may consider his democratic reforms, in particular the constitution, inadequate. However, closer analysis of the Russian President's rhetoric suggests that economic reform was meant to lead to stable democracy. This perspective on the relationship between economics and government influenced the type of constitution that President Yeltsin supported. As a dramatistic analysis of Yeltsin's speeches reveals, the constitution was probably not meant to guarantee democracy solely through legal processes, but instead was meant to establish an economic scene that would enable and encourage democratic acts.

I. Burke's Pentadic System

Burke suggests that his dramatistic pentad can be productive in illuminating a rhetor's understanding of how democracy is established and maintained (Grammar 17-18). Burke's "five key terms of dramatism" (act, scene, agent, agency, and purpose) offer a systematic process for understanding human motivation through analysis of linguistic activity, including "political works" such as speeches and constitutions (Grammar xv). The act names what took place; the scene describes the situation in which the act occurred; the agent performed the act; the agency describes the means used by the agent; the purpose names the agent's reason for performing the act. A rhetorical critic can discern motive by studying the interrelationships among the terms, either within one particular artifact or in a broader rhetorical situation (Birdsell; Ling; Tonn et al).

Though anyone describing a situation would likely incorporate all five pentadic terms, a rhetor often favors one or two terms of the pentad over the others. By studying the ratios of the various terms within a rhetorical act, a critic can identify featured terms and can then detect a sense of propriety and requirement within a discursive world articulated in the text. An examination of the featured terms within any given text or group of texts provides a method for discovering the type of world that the text invites the audience to imagine and also provides clues for understanding humans' responses to various situations (Burke, Philosophy 1; Kenny 387; Ling 222). For example, the scene-act ratio is most obvious when one explains human behavior in terms of the environment. The dominance of the ratio suggests that implicit in the quality of the scene is the quality of the action that is likely to take place within it (Grammar 6-7).

One can also enlist the pentad in order to analyze the symbolic actions of crisis management when a government, like Russia's, tries to negotiate the transition to democracy and the establishment of democratic institutions. Burke ruminates on an understanding of democracy based on the scene-act ratio: "if one employed... the scene-act ratio, one might hold that there are certain "democratic situations" and certain "situations favorable to dictatorship, or requiring dictatorship. ..." By the scene-act ratio, if the "situation" itself is no longer a "democratic" one, even an "essentially democratic" people will abandon democratic ways (Grammar 17-18). In other words, by applying Burke's pentad, a rhetorical critic can achieve a sense of whether a rhetor understands democracy to reside in the scene, in the agent, or elsewhere.

Burke has also noted that the scene-act ratio can shed light on how a rhetor understands the foundations and development of socio-political systems. In particular, Burke cites Marx and Lenin in explaining dialectical materialism's preference for the scene-act ratio. Both Marx and Lenin suggested that justice is a property of the material situation, specifically the economic conditions, or the scene in which justice is to be enacted (Grammar 13). As Marx and Lenin claimed that justice followed a socialist economy, a pentadic analysis of Yeltsin's discourse reveals an emphasis on the scene-act ratio, suggesting that justice, in the form of democracy, would follow from a prosperous market economy. Within such a materialist worldview, the potential for non-democratic abuses of power would not be restricted by a constitution's guarantee of a balance of powers, but instead a market economy would ensure democratic acts and disallow unjust acts. Despite the faith that Yeltsin's administration, many political elites, and the Russian electorate may have had in the power of economic determinism (at least in part due to seventy years of Marxist-Leninist ideological dominance), virtually all political actors in Russia in the early 1990s recognized that a new Russian constitution was necessary to replace the Brezhnev-era document that Russia inherited from its days as a Soviet republic.

II. Viable Constitutionalism

A constitution is vital to any state, especially one seeking to re-invent itself as was Russia. Erik P. Hoffmann notes that constitutions can foster civil or totalitarian societies and civic or repressive cultures. They can encourage presidential or legislative predominance (a key issue in Russia's constitutional debates), economic progress or retardation, and the protection or violation of human rights (22).

Hoffmann contends that transitional democracies ought to strive for viable constitutionalism. Viable constitutionalism is the concept upon which many Americans base their understandings of the role and nature of a proper constitution. At a minimum, it fosters "negative freedom" (freedom from), and, at best, it fosters "positive freedom" (freedom to). A viable constitutional government has "limited powers vis-à-vis all citizens, and government bodies in all branches and arenas have limited powers vis-à-vis one another. Authority is derived from the people and the national constitution, and even the highest political leaders are constrained by the electorate and the law" (21). Furthermore, a viable constitution clarifies the obligations of different branches and levels of government and safeguards their rights. It encourages compromise and collaboration among the branches of government, deters political leaders from violating citizens' rights, fosters respect for the law, strengthens democratic pluralism, stimulates economic performance and safeguards nonmaterial needs such as religious freedom, education, health care, and cultural diversity (23). Perhaps most important for the development of democracy, viable constitutionalism requires a system of checks and balances among governmental institutions (53). Much of the cause of Russia's political upheavals from 1991-1993 can be traced to the need for a new constitution that clearly resolved the issues that Hoffmann notes.

III. The Road to the Russian Constitution

From the time of the Soviet Union's collapse to the elections in December 1993, Russia's political scene was dominated by the conflict between the executive branch and the legislative branch. This conflict, in turn, could be traced to the constitution that Russia had inherited from its Soviet period. That constitution had been subject to so many contradictory amendments that both the legislature and the executive branches had legitimate claims to act as the head of the Russian government. As a result, President Yeltsin and the Russian Parliament (the Supreme Soviet and the Congress of People's Deputies), led by Ruslan Khasbulatov, engaged in a power struggle to determine which branch of government would set Russia's political and economic agenda. By spring 1993, both Yeltsin and Khasbulatov were growing increasingly impatient.

A. Yeltsin's March 1993 Speech

On March 20, 1993, Yeltsin delivered a nationally televised address in response to the 8th Congress of People's Deputies, which had met on March 10-13. During that session, Congress had stripped Yeltsin of many of his powers. Yeltsin's decrees would no longer carry equal weight with parliamentary laws. Furthermore, he would no longer be allowed to appoint heads of administration or government ministers without Parliament's approval (Sakwa 125).

In the address, Yeltsin condemned the Congress and the Supreme Soviet, declaring that they sought to re-establish the Soviet system of government, in effect to stage a "second October revolution" (2). He also announced a presidential decree establishing special presidential rule until the "crisis of power" was overcome (2). The decree would not have suspended the Congress and the Supreme Soviet. However, it declared that any decisions that Parliament made in an effort to cancel or suspend "decrees and instructions from the President" would not be valid (2). Yeltsin also set an April 25, 1993 deadline for a national vote of confidence in the President and the Vice President and expressed his hope to put a new constitution before the people. The new constitution would establish a new Russian Parliament to replace the Congress. A revised referendum was held in April of that year in which 58.7% of the voters expressed confidence in Yeltsin and 67.2% expressed a desire for early parliamentary elections (Sakwa 391). However, the Congress blocked early elections and the governmental crisis worsened.

After announcing the decree, the speech quickly evolved into a commentary on Russia's painful transition away from communism and toward democracy. According to Yeltsin, much of the blame for the lack of progress belonged to the Parliament. Not only did the Congress seek to obstruct the adoption of a new constitution, but it also "buried the referendum on citizens' ownership of land" (2). In his indictment of the Congress and Supreme Soviet, Yeltsin criticized their "absolute power over the banks and extra-budgetary funds" (2). Furthermore, if such power was not limited, "the financial crisis will continue to deteriorate, the chaos surrounding the payment of wages, recalculation of pensions, and exorbitant taxes will persist" (2). Importantly, most of Yeltsin's examples were economic in nature, emphasizing the scene of the drama: banking, land ownership, wages, and taxes.

Indeed, as Yeltsin moved into the body of the speech, he suggested that the conflict between the branches of government revolved around economic considerations at least as much as people's rights of expression and the limits on government. Yeltsin recalled the Soviet past: "for centuries, the country lived in debt, mercilessly exhausting its natural resources at the expense of future generations.... The main vice of this system was its desire to control everything and everybody, to block any initiative and independence, whether it concerns the right of man to work the land, to undertake free enterprise, or to express one's own point of view. This is where they [Congress of People's Deputies] are calling us, this is where they want to drive us again" (2). The body of Yeltsin's speech makes explicit the connection between the scene and the acts that occur within that scene. Living in debt (economic conditions) provides the scene that enables undemocratic acts: the control of the Russian people's activities and expression.

In addition to announcing his decree and assigning blame to the Parliament, Yeltsin also listed the measures he had instructed his Prime Minister, Viktor Chernomyrdin, to undertake. The measures that Yeltsin stated were designed to: establish private land ownership, speed up privatization, improve support for small businesses, address unemployment, and combat inflation. Though condensed here for reasons of practicality, discussion of these and other economic measures comprised the bulk of the address. Much of the body of the speech was devoted to the discussion of the scene: the economic situation in the country. Specifically, Yeltsin outlined how he hoped to establish a prosperous market economy in Russia. Only in the peroration did Yeltsin return to what many Westerners would deem important considerations of democracy: freedom of choice and rule at the consent of the governed. "What I suggest is a civilized way out of the crisis, based on fundamental constitutional principles. ... You are to make all the main decisions, citizens of Russia, through your voting. It will be your choice. The choice of the people" (2). One expects a speaker to summarize briefly and accurately her/his speech in the conclusion. However, Yeltsin summarized his speech as if he had spent the whole time talking about democracy, when in fact he had spent most of the speech discussing the material conditions (scene) necessary for democratic acts.

In the end, Yeltsin's address did little to alleviate the governmental crisis. However, the April referendum offered clear evidence of the electorate's support of the President and dissatisfaction with the Parliament. This allowed Yeltsin to press his advantage and more aggressively lobby for a new constitution (Nichols 72-73). In his next move, Yeltsin called for a Constitutional Conference to be held in June of that year.

B. Yeltsin's June 1993 Speech

Once the Conference opened on June 5, 1993, Yeltsin attempted to clear the way for passage of his preferred constitutional draft with a speech designed to justify limiting discussion to his so-called "presidential draft," to articulate his vision of a democratic Russia and to distinguish the new Russia from the Soviet system. On the surface, Yeltsin's opening speech stressed the importance of a constitution that would guarantee individual rights and freedoms and establish a division of powers among three branches of government. Indeed, a superficial reading of Yeltsin's June speech suggests a clear understanding and advocacy of viable constitutionalism. Yeltsin stressed the importance of guaranteeing individual rights and freedoms (17), the importance of a balance among "all branches of power," where "no one institution of the state will have the opportunity to monopolize power" and the necessity of "a strong and truly independent judiciary" (19).

However, a closer reading of the speech reveals a more nuanced description of the preconditions of democracy. In particular, the speech features a heavy reliance on the scene-act ratio. Shortly into the speech, Yeltsin declared that "life itself proves to us that a true democracy will not be established in a country of poor people, in a country where people have no chance to provide appropriate standards of living, initiative, and enterprise, and no chance to create the most favorable conditions for economic activity" (13). In fact, his very first proviso for any proposed constitutional draft was that it must provide the basis for economic reform.

In the speech, discussing his own preferred draft constitution, Yeltsin stressed the fact that the individual's rights and liberties are paramount. To illustrate this aspect of his constitutional draft, he restricted himself to one example. Importantly, Yeltsin illustrated his point with the clause that states that "the right to private property is a natural human right. Citizens have the right to hold land as private property. Property is inviolable" (17). As his one example, Yeltsin chose an economic right, one that establishes the material conditions in the country. Similarly, as Yeltsin elaborated on the role of the constitution in maintaining the territorial integrity of the Russian Federation, he noted that of utmost importance was the maintenance of "economic uniformity throughout the Russian Federation" (17). The President then discussed at length the economic mechanisms necessary to ensure the integrity of the federation. Throughout the speech, the text offered significant emphasis on economic measures included in the presidential draft of the constitution, suggesting that the economic scene was vital to Russia's democratic progress. Over the following two weeks, the Conference managed to hammer out a draft that was eventually rejected later by the federal legislature as well as many local legislatures and executives. In the meantime, the conflict between the executive and legislative branches of government worsened.

III. Yeltsin's "Democratic Coup"

Throughout the summer of 1993, the relationship between the President and Parliament continued to deteriorate. Eventually, Yeltsin became convinced that the breakthrough to constitutional change and to the realization of his vision of democracy was being blocked by the paralyzing conflict with the Parliament, and in early August he threatened to dissolve the legislature if they failed to work with him (Rigby 220). In response, on September 18, Ruslan Khasbulatov argued that Yeltsin should be removed from office because he was nothing more than a "common drunkard" attempting to impose a "dictatorial plutocratic regime" (Brudny 94). Additionally, he warned Yeltsin that any attempt to dissolve the Parliament would immediately lead to his impeachment (Sakwa 127). Perhaps most critical of all, the Supreme Soviet had drawn up a package of amendments to the existing constitution that would have rendered the president a figurehead, and planned to vote on those amendments in November (Ahdieh 65). Khasbulatov continued to insist that only the Parliament was empowered by the existing constitution to adopt a new constitution, and that accepting the Conference's draft would be nothing less than an abrogation of responsibility (Moore 54).

On September 21, in a nationally televised address, Yeltsin declared that Russia was "experiencing a profound crisis of its state structure" and issued Decree no. 1400, "On the Step-by-Step Constitutional Reform of the Russian Federation" (Ahdieh 66; Yeltsin, "Text of President"). The decree dissolved Parliament, announced new parliamentary elections and a referendum to adopt a new constitution for December 1993, and asked the Constitutional Court to refrain from meeting. Yeltsin next banned the publication of several opposition newspapers. Not heeding the President's request, the Russian Constitutional Court met to declare that Yeltsin had exceeded his authority. In response, Yeltsin issued another decree suspending the operation of the Constitutional Court (Tucker 22). Upon issuance of Decree 1400, many members of the legislature remained in the parliament building (White House) in defiance. Security forces loyal to the President sealed the

White House, and after several increasingly tense days some supporters of the Parliamentarians attacked the police lines, stormed the Moscow mayor's office and briefly seized Ostankino, a national TV broadcasting center. The military eventually sided with the President and defeated the deputies and their supporters ("Constitution Watch" 17-18; Huskey 33-34; Remnick 37-83; Sakwa 127-130; Schwartz 141), and the Parliamentarians were removed and jailed, thus completing Yeltsin's "democratic coup" (Lapidus & Walker 99).

During this crisis President Clinton expressed his support for Yeltsin as the best hope for Russian democracy. White House Press Secretary Dee Dee Myers claimed that Clinton trusted Yeltsin when the Russian President claimed that "obstacles to democracy and reform had been removed" (Kaplan 1). Strobe Talbott, ambassador-at-large for Russia, noted that Americans were "not in the habit of applauding the suspension of parliaments or con- stitutions," but suggested that the circumstances in Russia at the time were "exceptional" ("Yeltsin's Victory").

At this point, little seemed to stand in the way of Yeltsin implementing a constitution that would serve as a solid basis for a democratic Russia, just as he had articulated in his speech to open the Constitutional Conference. His opposition had been removed and the executive branch was the only branch of government left until the promised elections in December. Cer- tainly Yeltsin's advisors, the recent crisis, and Russia's own legal traditions influenced the final draft of the constitution (Sharlet, "Russian" 328). Like- wise, the President's drafters were influenced by and borrowed from other Western constitutions, namely the American, German, and French, as well as Soviet constitutions and preceding drafts of the new Russian constitution (McFaul; Monticone; Moore; Nichols). I do not wish to imply that the constitution was a pure reflection of Yeltsin's worldview. However, Yeltsin's vehement support of the constitution suggests that, at the very least, the President did not disagree with the type of democracy it would establish. Stephen Holmes describes Yeltsin's approach to its ratification as "take-it-or- leave-it," because it was composed in secret and the Yeltsin team created no forum for its discussion (126). Indeed, the Yeltsin-appointed head of the central election committee forbade parties to criticize the draft leading up to the vote, and Yeltsin himself declared "don't touch the Constitution!" a few weeks before the referendum (Urban 135). Clearly, Yeltsin and his team had immense latitude during the final drafting process (McFaul 210). As Gennadii Burbulis, former advisor to Yeltsin, explained to journalist David

Remnick, "the paradox of Russia in the 1990s is that the constitution of 1993 was written essentially without any alternatives; it was written in the personal interests of Yeltsin and like him, it contains both democratic and authoritarian tendencies" (Remnick 83). Similarly, Oleg Rumyantsev, once appointed by Yeltsin as Secretary of the Constitutional Commission before siding with Khasbulatov, claimed that the sole purpose of the new constitution was to "legalise the authoritarian regime that has come to power and to preserve the vision of the state and society held by the radical liberals. Boris Yeltsin has lost his self-control. His personal ambition has been exposed" (qtd. in Lester 75).

A. Yeltsin's Constitution

While the West viewed Yeltsin's "democratic coup" as a victory for democracy, a comparison of Yeltsin's June speech with the constitution ultimately adopted reveals several glaring disparities, particularly in light of Hoffmann's suggestions for viable constitutionalism. In particular, the articles of the constitution that relate most directly to Yeltsin's main democratic criteria from his June speech, protection of human rights and a system of checks and balances, seem to suggest that the new Basic Law may not live up to the standards articulated in that speech. In his address to the Conference in June, Yeltsin took pains to emphasize that "in the center of everything is the individual, his rights and liberties, and the guarantee that they will be implemented" ("O Rossiiskoi gosudarstvennosti" 17), and that the legal system created by the constitution would be the "guarantor of the rights of the individual" (13). Indeed, Article 2 of the constitution states: "The individual and his rights and freedoms are the supreme value. Recognition, observance, and protection of human and civil rights and freedoms is the obligation of the state," and the entire second chapter of the constitution is devoted to human and civil rights and freedoms. Among the rights and freedoms listed are: the right to life (Art. 20.1), the right to freedom and inviolability of the person (Art. 22.1), the right to privacy (Art. 23.1), freedom of religion (Art. 28), freedom of thought and speech (Art. 29.1), the right to private ownership (Art. 35.1), and the right to education (Art. 43.1). Such guarantees suggest the promise of a viable constitutional order. However, despite the long list of guarantees, Article 55.3 states that "human and civil rights and freedoms can be curtailed by federal law only to the extent to which it may be necessary for the purpose of protecting the foundations of the constitutional system, morality and health, rights and legitimate interests of other individuals, or of ensuring the country's defense and the state's security." In other words, under the auspices of protecting "the interests of other individuals" and other such vague pretenses, one's right to privacy, speech or life can be revoked. Article 56.1 states that "individual restrictions of rights and freedoms can be introduced, with an indication of their extent and duration, in a state of emergency in order to ensure the safety of citizens and the protection of the constitutional system in accordance with federal constitutional law." Such ambiguous terms as "morality," "interests," and "state security" paired with the president's power to declare a state of emergency (Art. 88) and rule by executive decree (Art. 90) allow for open-ended compromise of many civil and human rights at the president's discretion (Ahdieh 166). In the end, it has turned out that the individual's rights and freedoms are not supreme, but rather are subjugated to the state's, and particularly the president's, interest.

The status of the judicial branch of the Russian federal government, so vital to Yeltsin's description of democracy before the Conference, further threatens a viable constitutional order. Though allowances for abridging civil rights may exist in the constitutions of more smoothly functioning democracies, such as our own, those allowances are mitigated by a strong, independent judiciary. In the Russian constitution, the judicial branch is independent of neither the executive nor the legislative branch. However, one would not have predicted such a weak judiciary based on Yeltsin's speech to the Constitutional Conference. In his June speech, Yeltsin stressed the importance of a balance "between all branches of power" and " a strong and truly independent judiciary" ("O Rossiiskoi gosudarstvennosti" 19). In contrast, when looking at the constitution one sees that the judiciary is not independent at all. Though the constitution states that "judges are independent and subordinate only to the constitution of the Russian Federation and to federal law" (Art. 120.1) and that judges may not be removed or subjected to criminal proceedings "except in accordance with the procedure defined by federal law" (Art. 121.2; 122.2), federal law includes any presidential decrees (Art. 90) or legislation passed by either house of parliament. In other words, the judiciary is not insulated from either the executive or legislative branches.

Further undermining the balance and separation of powers is the fact that the legislature and cabinet are also potentially at the whim of the president. The president may dismiss the cabinet without the consent of either house of parliament (Art. 117; Art. 83c). The president can also dismiss the State Duma (the lower house of parliament) and call for new elections if the lower house expresses no confidence in the government twice within three months (Art. 117.3), or if it rejects the president's nominee for prime minister three times (Art.111.4). In effect, the legislature has very little say in the make up of the cabinet. As Holmes argues, the constitution's framers "decided to punish the new Parliament... for the sins of the old Parliament (124). The lack of an effective system of checks and balances, combined with the president's immense powers to rule by decree contained in the constitution, has guaranteed that Yeltsin's own vision that "no one institution of the state will have the opportunity to monopolize power" will not be realized in the foreseeable future ("O Rossiiskoi gosudarstvennosti" 19).

Consistent with an economically determined understanding of democracy, the constitution emphasizes the establishment of the economic scene. This is to be expected, perhaps, as Burke writes that "a Constitution is scenic" because it lays down the "environment" for future acts (Grammar 362). In chapter 2 of the constitution, devoted to human and civil rights and freedoms, no fewer than eight articles are related to economic issues. Included in them are: "Each person has the right to make free use of his abilities and property for purposes of entrepreneurial activity and other economic activity not prohibited by law" (Art. 34.1), "The right of private ownership is protected by law" (Art. 35.1), "Labour is free. Each person has the right freely to dispose of his abilities for labour and to choose a type of activity and occupation" (Art. 37.1), and "Housing is provided free or at affordable cost to low-income and other citizens indicated in the law who require housing from state, municipal and other housing stocks in accordance with the norms prescribed by law (Art. 40.3). All of these economic considerations are quite admirable and none seem obvious threats to democratic principles. Still, considering the constitution's allowances for the suspension of civil rights and the violation of the separation of powers, the Russian Federation's fundamental law is less a guarantee of democratic behavior on the part of those in government, than an attempt to establish and preserve a scene that Yeltsin's administration considered conducive to democratic acts. Nevertheless, the constitution was adopted in a popular referendum in December 1993. Though some scholars suggested at the time that the 1993 constitution would be replaced eventually, even by the turn of the century, it remains in place to this day, straining to establish an economic scene that will contain a new Russian democracy (Ahdieh 167; Holmes 126). Just as the constitution endured, so did the scene-act ratio in Yeltsin's discourse.

B. Yeltsin's 1996 Campaign Discourse

More than two years after Russians adopted Yeltsin's constitution, the President's discourse continued to feature the scene-act ratio when he campaigned for re-election in 1996. The candidate who posed the greatest threat to Yeltsin's retention of the presidency was Gennadii Ziuganov, a member of the Communist Party. Yeltsin's discourse sought to neutralize the growing nostalgia for the Soviet era encouraged by Ziuganov's campaign (Janack). To do so, Yeltsin's speeches connected the economic privation of the Soviet era (scene) and the repressive policies of the Communist Party leadership (acts). In February 1996, as Yeltsin announced his bid for a second term in a nationally televised address, he reminded his audience of the economic conditions of the late Soviet period: "how quickly we have forgotten the huge queues for bread, sugar, and other foods in 1991! People queued from the evening through the night and lit bonfires to keep warm. ... Our children and our grandchildren will not know what shortages, ration cards and graft are" ("Yeltsin in Yekaterinburg"). Going hand in hand with the miserable economic situation are the undemocratic acts that occurred in the Soviet Union: "For the first time in many decades, there are no political prisoners in Russia. No one is going into camps. We are not expelling people from the country or depriving them of citizenship for their political, religious, or ideological convictions" ("Yeltsin in Yekaterinburg").

In July of 1996, Yeltsin made a final direct appeal to voters before a run off election between himself and Ziuganov. His discourse continued to feature the scene-act ratio in terms of the economic conditions and political acts. Yeltsin first reminded his audience of the poor economic situation in the Soviet Union when he asked whether "even elderly Russian citizens remember a time when there was plenty of everything in our country?" ("Yeltsin Wraps Up" 2). He then reminded them of the political oppression: compulsory Party meetings, kangaroo courts, and "uniformity of thoughts and words" ("Yeltsin Wraps Up" 2). From Yeltsin's perspective, not only would a market economy enable and encourage the development of democratic acts, but the converse was also true. That is, a centralized economy, such as that in the Soviet period and one that Ziuganov envisioned in his presidential campaign, to some degree, enabled and encouraged the repressive, authoritarian acts of the Soviet era. Despite Yeltsin's image as a democrat and his apparent eagerness to dismantle the Soviet system, his articulation of the relationship between economics and politics was not all that far removed from that of the Marxist philosophy that served as the foundation of that system.

John T. Ishiyama et al. have argued that the early failures of Russian democratic coalitions in the parliamentary elections of 1993 and 1995 were in part due to their tendency to "view political and cultural transformations as the determined effects of material and structural causes," as dialectical materialists tend to do (95). In contrast, they suggest that Yeltsin's victory in the 1996 presidential election was due in part to his rejection of such a materialist perspective (107). However, the predominance of the scene-act ratio in Yeltsin's discourse in 1993 and in his campaign rhetoric in 1996 suggests that he maintained a materialist philosophy throughout his tenure as president, especially during the constitutional drafting process. Though Yeltsin's rhetoric did make efforts to empower the electorate, particularly his slogan "Vote or lose!", as Ishiyama et al suggest, his emphasis on material conditions belies his seeming avoidance of a materialist perspective. However, the combination of empowerment and dialectical materialism is consistent with what James Arnt Aune calls free marketers' "simultaneous celebration and denial of human agency" (147).

IV. Economics and the Russian Constitution

In *Selling the Free Market*, Aune offers a survey and analysis of the rhetoric promoting free market capitalism and suggests that free-market rhetoric deserves much wider public and academic discussion (5). This analysis is one attempt to broaden that discussion and include an international perspective. As he notes, the "market revolution" has seemed to triumph since the fall of the Berlin Wall in 1989, though not without ill effects (1-2). Nowhere are the perceived rewards of the free market greater than in the former Soviet Bloc and other developing nations. Worth noting, however, is that Aune is skeptical of the purported benefits of free market economics. To many in Asia, Africa, Latin and South America, free market capitalism seems to hold the promise of an escape from poverty and emergence from the group of "have-not" nations. In Russia and other former socialist states, some believe the free market promises democracy, human rights, and security, and in Russia's case, a return to its status as superpower. While critics of marketization and globalization have maintained that the World Trade Organization and its free trade policies have subverted democracies around the world, Yeltsin's rhetoric has associated the free market so closely with democratic freedoms that a prospering capitalist economy has become a necessary precondition for personal and political freedoms in Russia. Yeltsin and his administration clearly sought to democratize Russia, though he was often constrained by Soviet era thinking (on his own part and that of his rivals), and institutions, and he occasionally relapsed into authoritarian behavior. Furthermore, as his discourse suggests, Yeltsin and his team firmly believed that a state arrives at democracy by way of economic prosperity. What is more, Yeltsin may be right. Protesting infringements on freedom of expression is far easier when one does not have to worry about the ability to feed one's family. Still, such strict adherence to the scene-act ratio offers the government a justification for anti-democratic acts until the Russian economy dramatically rebounds (by most accounts, a development still a long way off).

From an American perspective, a perspective privileged by 200 years of economic development and (mostly) democratic practices, the Russian constitution seems to contain shortcomings. However, at this early stage of Russia's democratic development, the "flaws" in the constitution have not been fatal. By no means is Russia an ideal democracy. Undoubtedly, atrocities have been committed under the cover of war in Chechnya. The government curtails religious freedom by legally recognizing only a handful of religions. The Russian government still struggles to cope with freedom of expression. Several journalists have been victimized, most recently Grigory Pasko, who has been charged with espionage and treason for passing video of the Russian navy dumping nuclear waste in the Pacific Ocean to a Japanese television company ("Witnesses"). The government supported the takeover in 2001 of Vladimir Gusinsky's media empire (the only nationwide independent media company) by the state dominated natural gas monopoly Gazprom (Wines). Indeed, like Yeltsin's discourse in the 1990s, Vladimir Putin's response to criticism of that takeover featured the scene-act ratio when he stated that "the state has to do everything to guarantee freedom of speech for every citizen and freedom of the press in particular, [but only] when economic conditions that make a free press affordable are created" (qtd. in Tyler). Also discouraging is the fact that Russians themselves question the extent of the protection of human rights. In a 1998 survey, nearly a quarter of Russians polled (24%), when asked "who protected human rights in our country to the greatest extent," responded "nobody" ("A Quarter").

Though problems exist in terms of basic civil rights, there is cause for optimism. As Robert Sharlet has noted, "in a society long accustomed to arbitrary fiat and devoid of real politics... the constitution symbolically conveyed the message that Russia would continue—although probably not without lapses—down the road of government by law" ("New Russian" 6). Sharlet has also noted the emergence of a more "genuinely federalist system" between Russia and its administrative subdivisions since the passage of the constitution, despite the fact that the portion of the constitution devoted to outlining Russia's federalist system was greatly diminished in the final draft ("New Russian" 7). The Constitutional Court, so vulnerable to the whims of the president, has also functioned relatively independently. Its decisions have been largely objective and unhindered by the executive branch. For example, in 1998, the Court ruled that Yeltsin could not run for president a third time ("Yeltsin Cannot"). In 1999, the Court banned the practice of returning criminal cases to prosecutors for further investigation, effectively establishing in practice the presumption of innocence on the part of the accused and encouraging a speedy trial. In the past, if prosecutors lacked evidence or pressed ambiguous charges, courts would routinely return the cases to the prosecutor's office without ruling "guilty" or "not-guilty." The Court ruling determined that such cases must now be dismissed (Badkhen). In his book-length study of constitutional courts in post-communist Europe, Herman Schwartz expressed surprised satisfaction and optimism regarding the Russian Constitutional Court, declaring that it is a "wonder ... that [the Court] has done as well as it has, and that it may still become a vital and significant institution" (110). Though clearly far from perfect, the fledgling Russian democracy is making progress toward viable constitutionalism. Certainly, the problematic legal practices in Russia up to this point are no worse than the missteps in the early days of American democracy, such as the Alien and Sedition Acts of 1798, or the governmental acts of a more mature American democracy, such as the Espionage Act of 1917, the Sedition Act of 1918, the internment of Japanese Americans during World War II, and even, some may argue, the PATRIOT Act of 2001.

Kenneth Burke's dramatistic pentad helps explain the seeming incompatibility among Yeltsin's June 1993 speech, the constitution he offered to Russia, and Hoffmann's concept of viable constitutionalism. Close study of Yeltsin's discourse at key points in Russia's post-Soviet transition reveals a pattern of rhetorical emphasis on the dramatistic term scene and its influence on acts, thus making the composition of the current constitution, despite its authoritarian features, an understandable development. The contradictions between Yeltsin's speech to the Constitutional Conference and his constitutional draft may draw into question just what kind of democrat was Yeltsin? One answer to that question is that Yeltsin was a Russian democrat. He was a late convert to democracy, raised on Marxist-Leninist ideology that maintained that political culture derives from economic conditions. Yeltsin's discourse suggests that one should look to the economy to ensure the separation of powers, protection of civil rights, and other democratic institutions. A prosperous nation does not necessarily have to write such guarantees into its constitution. From the perspective of Yeltsin and his drafters, the constitution may have seemed essentially democratic, despite some potentially significant shortcomings for the legal preservation of democracy, because it explicitly and thoroughly seeks to establish a prosperous market economy. From the prosperity of the economy, democratic acts ought to follow naturally, given the materialist philosophy of the Yeltsin administration, as revealed by the emphasis on scene in the President's discourse. Though guarantees of civil freedom and separation of powers within the text of the constitution may seem inadequate, the economic freedoms would presumably disallow any undemocratic acts.

Finally, a close reading of the discourse and constitution has revealed how Yeltsin can appear as both an authoritarian and a democrat. In American political culture, democracy is the God term, with economic prosperity a close second behind it. Yeltsin's speeches and the constitution reversed the American hierarchy of values, making prosperity the God term, closely followed by democracy. For Yeltsin, material considerations are of primary importance, with democracy an important fringe benefit of free market prosperity. The Russian President's rhetoric offered a set of priorities that may seem "undemocratic" to many Westerners, but a clear (if perverse) extension of Marxist-Leninist ideology. Given these priorities, Yeltsin, as a Russian democrat, voiced greater political reforms than he ended up delivering. Ironically, Yeltsin, who arguably did more than anyone to promote the collapse of the Communist Party, emerged as the democrat, but one who speaks the language of the Communist, as he suggested that all good (and bad) things emerge from the economic conditions of a society. As Aune has noted, radical free-market thought is "like a perverse mirror image of communism" (33). The authoritarian aspects of the Russian constitution would not be contained or restricted by other branches of government (agents), but instead by the economy (scene) which would engender democratic acts and disallow dictatorial acts. Whereas Trotsky held that you cannot get a fully socialist act unless you have a fully socialist scene (Burke, Grammar 14), Yeltsin's rhetoric seemed to suggest that you cannot get a fully democratic act unless you have a fully democratic scene, and in this case, such a scene requires a free market and capitalist prosperity. Though it is too early to know how democratic Russia will remain/become in the long term, rhetorical analysis of Yeltsin's discourse makes clear the complexity and contradictions that emerging democracies can face when they seek to develop free market democracy amid dialectical materialist traditions.

WORKS CITED

Ahdieh, Robert B. *Russia's Constitutional Revolution*. University Park, PA: The Pennsylvania State UP, 1997.

Aune, James Arnt. *Selling the Free Market: The Rhetoric of Economic Correctness*. New York: Guilford, 2001.

Badkhen, Anna. "Constitutional Court Bans 'Do-Over' Cases." *The St. Petersburg Times*. Online. LexisNexis. 30 Apr. 1999.

Birdsell, David S. "Ronald Reagan on Lebanon and Grenada: Flexibility and Interpretation in the Application of Kenneth Burke's Pentad." *Readings in Rhetorical Criticism*. Ed. Carl Burgchardt. State College, PA: Strata, 1995. 227-239.

Brudny, Yitzhak M. "Ruslan Khasbulatov, Aleksandr Rutskoi, and Intraelite Conflict in Post-Communist Russia: 1991-1994." *Patterns of Post-Soviet Leadership*. Eds. Timothy J. Colton and Robert C. Tucker. Boulder: Westview, 1995: 75-101.

Burke, Kenneth. *A Grammar of Motives*. Berkeley: U of California P, 1962.

———. *The Philosophy of Literary Form: Studies in Symbolic Action*, 3rd ed. Berkeley: U of California P, 1973.

"Constitution Watch Russia." *East European Constitutional Review 2, 3* (Fall 1993 and Winter 1994): 17-18.

Ellis, Frank. *From Glasnost to the Internet: Russia's New Infosphere*. New York: St. Martin's, 1999.

Elsner, Alan. "U.S. Sees Yeltsin Pushing On with Democracy." Reuters North American Wire. Online. LexisNexis. 5 Oct. 1993.

Friedman, Milton. *Capitalism and Freedom*. Chicago: U of Chicago P, 1982.

Hoffmann, Erik P. "Challenges to Viable Constitutionalism in Post-Soviet Russia." *The Harriman Review* 7 (November 1994): 19-56.

Holmes, Stephen. "Superpresidentialism and its Problems." *East European Constitutional Review* 2, 3 (Fall 1993 and Winter 1994): 123-126.

Huskey, Eugene. *Presidential Power in Russia*. Armonk, NY: M.E. Sharpe, 1999.

Ishiyama, John T., Michael K. Launer, Irina E. Likhchova, David Cratis Williams, and Marilyn J. Young. "Russian Electoral Politics and the Search for National Identity." *Argumentation and Advocacy* 34 (1997): 90-109.

Janack, James A. "The Future's Foundation in a Contested Past: Nostalgia and Dystalgia in the 1996 Russian Presidential Campaign." *Southern Communication Journal* 65 (1999): 34-48.

Kaplan, Fred. "Yeltsin Acts to Bolster His Powers." *The Boston Globe* (6 Oct. 1993): 1.

Kenny, Robert Wade. "The Rhetoric of Kevorkian's Battle." *Quarterly Journal of Speech*. 86 (2000): 386-401.

Lapidus, Gail W. and Edward W. Walker. "Nationalism, Regionalism, and Federalism: Center-Periphery Relations in Post-Communist Russia." *The New Russia: Troubled Transformations*. Ed. Gail W. Lapidus. Boulder: Westview, 1995: 79-113.

Lester, Jeremy. *Modern Tsars and Princes: The Struggle for Hegemony in Russia*. London: Verso, 1995.

Ling, David A. "A Pentadic Analysis of Senator Edward Kennedy's Address to the People of Massachusetts, July 25, 1969." *Readings in Rhetorical Criticism*. Ed. Carl Burgchardt. State College, PA: Strata, 1995. 221-227.

McFaul, Michael. *Russia's Unfinished Revolution: Political Change from Gorbachev to Putin*. Ithaca, NY: Cornell UP, 2001.

McManus, Doyle and Elizabeth Shogren. "Yeltsin's Defiant Victory." *Los Angeles Times* 22 Aug. 1991: A1+.

Mickiewicz, Ellen. *Changing Channels: Television and the Struggle for Power in Russia*. New York: Oxford UP, 1997.

Monticone, Ronald C. "A Brief Comparative Analysis of the Russian Constitution." *Constitution of the Russian Federation: Special Presidential Edition*. Eds. Vladimir V. Belyakov & Walter J. Raymond. Lawrenceville, VA and Moscow: Brunswick and Novosti, 1994: 7-14.

Moore, Rita. "The Path to the New Russian Constitution: A Comparison of Executive-Legislative Relations in the Major Drafts." *Demokratizatsiya: The Journal of Post-Soviet Democratization* 2 (1995): 44-60.

Nichols, Thomas M. *The Russian Presidency*. New York: St. Martin's, 1999.

"A Quarter of Russians Are Certain that Their Rights Are Being Protected by Nobody." *Novye Izvestia*. Online. LexisNexis. 17 Dec. 1998.

Remnick, David. *Resurrection: The Struggle for a New Russia*. New York: Vintage, 1998.

Rigby, T. H. "Conclusion" Russia in Search of its Future. *Russia in Search of its Future*. Eds. Amin Saikal and William Maley. Cambridge: Cambridge UP, 1995: 207-225.

Sakwa, Richard. *Russian Politics and Society*. 2nd. ed. London: Routledge, 1996.

Schwartz, Herman. *The Struggle for Constitutional Justice in Post-Communist Europe*. Chicago: U of Chicago P, 2000.

Sharlet, Robert. "The New Russian Constitution and Its Political Impact." *Problems of Post-Communism* 42 (Jan./Feb. 1995): 3-7.

"Russian Constitutional Crisis: Law and Politics Under Yel'tsin." *Post-Soviet Affairs* 9 (1993): 314-336.

Tonn, Mari Boor, Valerie A. Endress, and John N. Diamond. "Hunting and Heritage on Trial: A Dramatistic Debate Over Tragedy, Tradition, and Territory." *Quarterly Journal of Speech* 79 (1993): 165-181.

Tucker, Robert C. "Post-Soviet Leadership and Change." *Patterns in Post-Soviet Leadership.* Eds. Timothy J. Colton and Robert C. Tucker. Boulder: Westview, 1995: 5-24.

Tyler, Patrick E. "NTV Takeover Dominates Meeting Between Putin and Schröder." *The New York Times on the Web.* 10 Apr. 2001. Online. 18 Apr. 2001.

Urban, Michael. "December 1993 as a Replication of Late-Soviet Electoral Practices." *Post-Soviet Affairs* 10 (1994): 127-158.

Wines, Michael. "Russian Media Empire is Hit by New Blow." *The New York Times on the Web.* 17 Apr. 2001. Online. 18 Apr. 2001.

"Witnesses Do Not Confirm Spy Charges Against Russian Journalist: Lawyer." Agence France Press. Online. LexisNexis. 23 June 2001.

Yeltsin, Boris. "Obrashchenie Prezidenta Rossiiskoi Federatsii B. N. Yeltsina k grazhdanam Rossii i otvet emu chitatelei Pravdy." *Pravda* (24 March 1993): 1+.

———. "Opening Speech by Yeltsin." British Broadcasting Corporation. Online. Lexis-Nexis. 7 June 1993.

———. "O Rossiiskoi gosudarstvennosti i novoi konstitutsii Rossii: Doklad Prezidenta Rossiiskoi Federatsii B. Yeltsina na otkrytii Konstitutsionnogo soveshchaniia." *Konstitutsionnoe Soveshchanie* August 1993: 12-20.

———. "Text of President Yeltsin's Decree on Constitutional Reform." BBC Summary of World Broadcasts. Online. LexisNexis. 23 Sept. 1993.

———. "Yeltsin's Address to the General Public." Official Kremlin International News Broadcast. Federal Information Systems Corporation. Online. LexisNexis 20 March 1993.

———. "Yeltsin in Yekaterinburg." British Broadcasting Corporation. Online. LexisNexis. 16 Feb. 1996.

———. "Yeltsin Wraps Up Campaign Amid Health Questions." *The Current Digest of the Post-Soviet Press* 48.26 (1996): 1-2.

———. "Yeltsin Cannot Stand for President Again—Constitutional Court." British Broadcasting Corporation. Online. LexisNexis. 5 Nov. 1998.

———. "Yeltsin's Victory Seen as a Boost for Democracy." *The Record* (7 Oct. 1993): A33.

Vladimir Zhirinovsky: The Clown Prince of Russia

*James A. Janack**

Abstract

Vladimir Zhirinovsky, the leader of the Liberal Democratic Party of Russia, achieved remarkable popularity and electoral success in the first five years after the collapse of the Soviet Union. He managed this despite advocating seemingly absurd and contradictory policies and engaging in eccentric and inappropriate behaviors. This essay analyzes the rhetoric and symbolic action of Zhirinovsky in the first half of the 1990s and argues that his outrageous rhetoric and behavior amounted to an enactment of Mikhail Bakhtin's concept of the carnival with its spirit of protest against the dominant socio-political system, thus enhancing his appeal as a protest candidate.

In December, 1993, it appeared that Russia would finally embark upon its journey toward democracy after a thousand years of authoritarian rule. The reform movement in Russia had survived the August, 1991, coup attempt against Mikhail Sergeevich Gorbachev. After almost two years of intractable conflict between President Boris Yeltsin and the more conservative Parliament, it had survived Yeltsin's dissolution of the Parliament and the tank attack on the White House in October, 1993, which had set the stage for the first free elections in post-Soviet Russia. However, instead of serving as a resounding endorsement of democracy and reform, the results of the election shocked much of the international community, as well as the ruling reformists in Russia, when the misleadingly-named Liberal Democratic Party of Russia (LDPR), led by neo-fascist Vladimir Volfovich Zhirinovsky,[1] emerged with the most party list votes of any single party (approximately 25%).[2] This essay seeks to provide a plausible interpretation of Zhirinovsky's rhetoric in the context of his electoral success in 1993.

The Rise of the LDPR

Zhirinovsky founded the LDPR in June, 1990, shortly after the Soviet leaders had repealed the Communist Party of the Soviet Union's (CPSU) constitutionally guaranteed monopoly on power. In 1991, Zhirinovsky ran in the presidential elections for the Soviet Republic of Russia, advocating the forcible preservation of the USSR and even its expansion through the incorporation of Finland, parts of Poland and Alaska. He finished third, collecting six million votes (7.8%) (Yasmann and Teague 35; Tolz, "Russia's" 1; Clark 771).

In the Autumn of 1993, Zhirinovsky published his autobiography and political manifesto, *The Last Bid for the South* (*Poslednii Brosok na Yug*, the title of the English translation is *My Struggle*).[3] Though exact figures regarding the circulation of the book are unavailable, Vladimir Solovyov and Elena Klepikova, in their biography of Zhirinovsky, note that it was "to become the most scandalous of best-sellers in the history of Russian book publishing. The book sold like hotcakes. It couldn't have come out at a better time and worked as a kind of campaign advertisement" (169). In the introduction to a later book by Zhirinovsky, Aleksei Churilov writes that *Brosok* "was read, it seems, even by the illiterate (judging from the stupidity of some interpretations)" (3).

In addition to the book, Zhirinovsky was one of the first Russian politicians to adopt Western style campaign tactics, exploiting the medium of television and establishing name recognition. As Vladimir Kartsev remarks in his biography of Zhirinovsky, the candidate's two-week pre-election campaign was filled from morning to night with radio and television interviews and constant meetings with the people (91). Solovyov and Klepikova note that "his speeches were more visual, theatrical, and original" than the other candidates' (170-171). He spent most of his air time talking directly to the public, dividing his time up into short pieces, giving the impression that he was always on the television screen (Mickiewicz 152-153; Remnick 92-93). His speeches, both on television and at his non-televised appearances, echoed the geo-political content of the book (Remnick 96).

The book suggests that the crucial step to regaining Russia's proper place among the great nations of the world is to first reclaim the territories held by the Imperial Russian Empire (this includes the territory of the former Soviet Union ((FSU)) along with Finland and Alaska), and to make a final "bid" for the South. This bid would secure for Russia access to the Indian Ocean and Mediterranean Sea, bring order to the war-torn areas of that region (Tajikistan and Afghanistan), and divide the world into spheres of influence that would secure worldwide peace. It would also entail the annexation or "dismemberment" of Turkey, Iran and Afghanistan.

Though such a plan probably strikes most Western readers as ultra-radical, absurd, and impossible to actually fulfill (or did before the United States of America invaded Afghanistan in 2001), that is only one of the problems the reader of the book encounters. Contradictions, incompatibilities, inconsistencies and oxymorons within the book have been recognized by both Russian and non-Russian readers. As Vitaly Svintsov wrote in *Nezavisimaia Gazeta* (*Independent Newspaper*), the text "does not reach a middling level of logic, if one understands this [a middling level] as such elementary properties as consistency, non-contradiction, and argumentation" (8).[4]

Zhirinovsky did not limit his irrational discourse to his book. Upon hearing his speeches Natasha Fairweather, a journalist for *The Moscow Times* suggested that "one cannot allow Zhirinovsky simply to speak for himself, for his words are inconsistent and often contradictory." Put simply, Zhirinovsky's discourse at times does not make sense to a rational audience member.

As David Remnick writes in *Resurrection*, his description of the immediate post-Soviet period in Russia:

> to American ears, [Zhirinovsky] committed career-ending gaffes in nearly every sentence, threatening Japan with "more Hiroshimas" and the Baltic states with radiation; he vowed to become a dictator and immediately jail a hundred thousand "offenders"; he promised cheap vodka to all and vowed that "under my regime, no Russian woman will be lonely." (93)

Similarly, Alan J. Koman, in the only other thorough treatment of Zhirinovsky's rhetoric, devotes more than ten pages to "flaws" in the rhetoric of Zhirinovsky's book. Among them, he notes the LDPR leader's inconsistent attitude toward Muslims in general and Iraq in particular, the contradictory claims that Russia's greatest threat results from both chaos and conspiracy in the regions south of Russia, the incompatible suggestions that Muslim lands should be both isolated and acquired by Russia, the lack of a thorough analysis of Russia's situation and the likely international resistance to his "last bid" (Koman 309-319). Solovyov and Klepikova sum up the problems with Zhirinovsky's political positions succinctly:

> Zhirinovsky is both war and peace; he is a tyrant and a dictator but a democrat to the marrow of his bones; he is a national socialist but a liberal democrat; he is for pluralism but also for a

tough regime; he is a strict pragmatic but also a visionary idealist; he advocates law and order but seizes other people's territories and threatens global blackmail; he opposes destroying the state sector and supports 100 percent the private sector; he is against dismantling the collective farms but is for private farmers. No politician with the slightest bit of self-respect could seriously promote all these contradictory positions. It is not a problem for Zhirinovsky, however. (163)

One could explain his appeal by suggesting that Zhirinovsky drew his support mainly from relatively uneducated sectors of the population, as Koman and Specter have claimed. This is true to a certain extent. It was believed that he enjoyed large support from rural voters who would not be as educated as those living in larger cities, and among older, less educated males. However, his hard-core supporters also included relatively well educated young males, between the ages of twenty-five and forty, who live in Russia's larger cities (Tolz, "Russia's" 4; Shokarev 4). More than half of his voters either graduated or at least attended college (Solovyov & Klepikova 18). Ignorance on the part of his supporters does not seem to explain his popularity.

It is also difficult to imagine that people were unaware of his conduct and views. Zhirinovsky was notorious for his absurd behavior and any Russian who watched television regularly would have been aware of his less-than-respectable antics. Shortly before the 1993 Duma elections he marched up to the lingerie counter in Moscow's largest department store, held up a brassiere and announced that if he were elected to parliament, underwear would be cheaper (Seward). More ominously, while in France in the spring of 1994, Zhirinovsky spit at demonstrating Jewish students and then threw a flowerpot and dirt at them (Service 20). Other outrageous behavior, such as bringing cases of beer and vodka with his own picture on the label to Duma sessions and physically attacking a female deputy during a debate in the Duma, was also widely reported in Russia and around the world (Gutterman; Beeston). With his political manifesto rife with ambivalences and incompatibilities and his clownish public behavior, his relatively widespread appeal may have seemed incomprehensible to many observers. The question remains, considering his boorish behavior and the incoherence of his rhetoric, why would anyone, much less almost a quarter of the electorate, vote for him and his party?

Part of his appeal, most certainly, lay in his deft use of television during the campaign and his promises of high wages, cheap vodka, and the restoration of empire (Solovyov & Klepikova 151). Still, one would think it would be difficult to believe his promises and to disregard his obvious inconsistencies, contradictions, and absurd behavior, particularly for the educated portion of his supporters.

This essay will offer yet another explanation for why Zhirinovsky was so popular in 1993. I will argue that his appeal can be attributed at least partly to the themes and images in his book, public statements, appearances, and other symbolic actions, which amounted to an enactment of Mikhail Bakhtin's concept of the carnival and its associated antinomian character (Bakhtin, *Rabelais* 4-13). By striking a carnivalesque pose, Zhirinovsky positioned himself as the incarnation of protest against the prevailing system and conditions, and a vote for him became an expression of the protest inherent in carnival. In assuming a role as conduit of protest, the Zhirinovsky phenomenon may be understood as what Herbert W. Simons has described as a "top-down movement," a "movement-like struggle ... by people in positions of institutional authority on behalf of a cause whose guiding ideas, characteristics modes of action, or organizational structures have not been fully institutionalized" (101). While most protest movements are of a grass-roots nature, Simons notes that an establishment group (such as a political party like Zhirinovsky's LDPR) "may continue to act in movement-like ways either for rhetorical effect or because the group feels it must, given its rhetorical situation" (Simons 99). Lloyd Bitzer defines the rhetorical situation as "a complex of persons, events, objects, and relations presenting an actual or potential exigence which can be completely or partially removed if discourse, introduced into the situation, can so constrain human decision or action as to bring about the significant modification of the exigence" (220). In the case of Russia in the first years after the collapse of the Soviet Union, exigences included dismal economic conditions, the painful and sometimes violent transition from communist dictatorship to market economy and democracy, and the first post-Soviet elections to a newly created legislature. Amid this situation, there was much that could have provoked Russians' dissatisfaction, confusion, and protest. Communism had seemed to fail them and a market democracy was offering little cause for optimism. The dominant institutional systems of their recent experience not only failed to relieve the deprivation and chaos, but seemed to exacerbate it. Into this situation came the clownish Zhirinovsky, railing against the democrats and communists (and their policies) in the most outrageous ways, playing the role of the fool, carnival's representative outside of "carnival season," who carries with him carnival's historic role of symbolic protest (Bakhtin, *Rabelais* 8).

In many ways, the Russian context, both past and present, plays a vital role in Zhirinovsky's rhetoric. Indeed, Russia also has a tradition of holy foolishness. Related to monastic asceticism, the holy fool was a sufferer for Christ and was a familiar figure in Russian towns prior to, and to a lesser extent, after the Bolshevik revolution. Daniel Rancour-Laferriere describes the holy fool as "a sufferer, part of whose masochism was specifically provocative or exhibitionistic in style," and notes that Russians had a special fondness for holy fools (21). A holy fool would "resort to all manner of scandalous behavior in order to provoke aggression: they sat in dung heaps, refused to wash, wore little or no clothing; they would dance about, shout obscenities or make incoherent utterances, smash objects, and so on" (Rancour-Laferriere 21-22). However, there was more to holy fools than masochism for the sake of the Lord's glory. They also offered a form of social protest and prophesies (Rancour-Laferriere 23). Before the Bolshevik revolution, there was supposed to be a village idiot in every community. A Russian proverb claims that Russia has enough fools to last one hundred years and even in the late Soviet period, the phrase "country of fools" often appeared in the press (Rancour-Laferriere 122). As will be demonstrated, the parallels between the holy fool's behavior (both literal and symbolic) and Zhirinovsky's are unmistakable. Both figures fit seamlessly into Bakhtin's description of the carnival.

Zhirinovsky's book is situated in a unique historical period for Russia. In the 1990s, the country experienced a transitional phase of its national identity development, in which political actors of various ideological leanings struggled for dominance in the realm of political and economic policy, and social elites (politicians included) struggled to shape how Russians would conceive of themselves and their nation in the twenty-first century. Simultaneously, economic conditions placed severe burdens on many Russians. Indeed, Rancour-Laferriere associates the Russian tradition of the suffering of the holy fool with another time of transition in Russia, the mid-seventeenth century schism in the Russian Orthodox Church that was related to questions of the growing secularization of Russian culture and challenges to Church traditions and organization (23). It is worth noting the importance of transition, both in Russia and in Bakhtin's thinking, what Bakhtin called "threshold moments" (Bakhtin, "Forms" 248-249).

Russia at the Threshold

For Bakhtin, thresholds, both literal and symbolic, often signify crisis and break in life ("Forms" 248). In Dostoevsky's work, Bakhtin maintains that the author "always represents a person *on the threshold* of a final decision, at a moment of *crisis*, at an unfinalizable—and *unpredeterminable*—turning point for his soul" (emphasis in original) (*Problems* 61). As Bakhtin points out, the threshold, in life and in literature, suggests that the opportunity for a life-changing decision is at hand ("Forms" 248; Morson and Emerson 375).

In the time since the collapse of the USSR (and arguably even before that), Russia has found itself at a national threshold. Mary McAuly, a researcher for the Ford Foundation's Moscow office, maintains that Russia's citizens

> find themselves facing a series of basic issues. The resolving of these lies at the heart of any political community. There is the identification of the community: who *are* its citizens? There is the question of who is to make authoritative decisions and of their implementation. This involves deciding how conflicts are to be resolved and order ensured. There is the question of how interests are defined, and can be defended. These provide an extremely contentious set of issues, and there are no ready-made answers to them (emphasis in original). (1)

Since 1991, the Russian electorate has flirted with political parties of vastly different persuasions. After the reformers' early victories, the December 1993 elections signaled the popularity of Zhirinovsky and his ultra-conservative LDPR, and a backlash against the architects of market reform and privatization (Lapidus 2).[5] The country has also faced a series of political and economic crises, suggesting that Russia is by no means assured of any one particular socio-political trajectory. Russians remain undecided regarding fundamental national issues and their nation's direction of future development remains unfinalized. Such threshold periods of decision become part of what Bakhtin calls the all-embracing chronotope of carnival time ("Forms" 248-249).

Bakhtin's Carnival and the Clown Prince of Russia

Though rhetorical scholars have not hesitated to draw on Mikhail Bakhtin's theories despite his ambivalent attitude toward rhetoric, most have relied mainly on his theories of heteroglossia and polyphony (see Hopkins; Jasinski; Murphy).[6] His theory of the carnival can offer another unique insight into rhetorical texts.

Most fully elaborated in his work *Rabelais and His World*, Bakhtin discusses how the carnival worldview inverts the world. Instead of celebrating the vertical ascent of humanity, it celebrates the horizontal, the corporeal, the sexual, the digestive, the excretory. Carnivalesque novels such as Rabelais' provide vivid imagery of some of the human body's less spectator-friendly acts. Overall, carnival signifies the symbolic destruction of authority and official culture. Bakhtin describes carnival as a liberating escape from official institutions. Carnival "builds its own world versus the official world, its own church versus the official church, its own state versus the official state" (Bakhtin, *Rabelais* 88). In the Middle Ages "carnival celebrated temporary liberation from the prevailing truth and from the established order" (Bakhtin, *Rabelais* 10). Carnival rejected the prevailing truths that were on offer in the everyday world and built a second world and a second life outside officialdom (Bakhtin, *Rabelais* 6). Bakhtin maintains that people have used popular-festive images for thousands of years to "express their criticism, their deep distrust of official truth, and their highest hopes and aspirations" (*Rabelais* 269). Anti-institutionalism is at the essence of carnival. It is a form of criticism aimed at the existing dominant system (Bakhtin, *Problems* 127).

Bakhtin's theory of the carnivalesque, particularly resonant in times of crisis and decision (threshold moments), offers a form of symbolic protest and criticism of the existing ideology and socio-political system. Though Vladimir Zhirinovsky's rhetoric and behavior strike one as irrational and absurd, I contend that irrationality and absurdity, attributes of carnival, in part contributed to his appeal by enhancing his image as the protest candidate. From the vantage point of "normalcy," carnivalistic behavior appears eccentric and inappropriate (Bakhtin, *Problems* 123), as some would describe Zhirinovsky's behavior. The next few sections of this essay will explore in greater detail some of the characteristics of the carnival, including its elimination of hierarchy, its corporeal images, the role of the carnival clown, and its tendency toward the ambivalent, and it will demonstrate how Zhirinovsky's discourse and behavior enacted those characteristics.

Free and Familiar Contact

One defining characteristic of carnival, consistent with its anti-institutional nature, is that it is not only a phenomenon presented for the people, but also presented by the people. During carnival everything resulting from socio-hierarchical inequality or any other form of inequality among people is suspended.

> All distance between people is suspended, and a special carnival category goes into effect: *free and familiar contact among people.* This is a very important aspect of a carnival sense of the world. People who in life are separated by impenetrable hierarchical barriers enter into free familiar contact on the carnival square (emphasis in original). (Bakhtin, *Problems* 122-123)

Carnival, according to Bakhtin, is a purely popular phenomenon, though it can be appropriated by authorities.[7] It is not a performance presented to the people, but a spectacle that does not differentiate between those who perform it and those who view it. "Carnival does not know footlights, in the sense that it does not acknowledge any distinction between actors and spectators. ... Carnival is not a spectacle seen by people; they live in it" (Bakhtin, *Rabelais* 7). In carnival the line between actor and audience member blurs (Bakhtin, *Problems* 122). In a modern political context, this would suggest that there be no distinction between the rulers and the ruled, between government representatives and those they represent.

In exemplifying this aspect of the carnival, Zhirinovsky presented himself as one of the people, no different from the voting masses. He portrayed himself in contrast to those who make up the ruling elite. In his rhetoric he did this both implicitly and explicitly. The style of his book, particularly in Russian, was stunningly simple. For example, in the beginning of the book Zhirinovsky described the night he was born: "I was born on April 25, 1946, in Alma Ata. It was a Thursday, it was evening, eleven o'clock. It was raining. It was the first post-war spring" (*Poslednii* 6). Though his sentence structure became slightly more sophisticated as the book progressed, the writing style and word choice remained relatively simplistic: "The last bid for the South. As I imagine it, Russian soldiers will wash their boots in the warm water of the Indian Ocean and always wear their summer uniforms. Light boots, light pants, soldiers' blouses with short sleeves, no tie, with an open collar, light forage caps" (*Poslednii* 66).

Zhirinovsky also made more explicit attempts to cast himself as one of the common people. Approximately the first third of the book was devoted to a biographical narrative relating his childhood, college years, his time in the army and his first few jobs before entering politics. He provided this narrative partly because he considered it representative: "Being the child of a socialist state, I and my story will seem typical and familiar to the majority of my countrymen" (*My Struggle* 10). As a review in *The Observer* noted, after reading the biographical section, "many a Russian reader will be gripped— recognising his or her own deprived childhood, loving the simple sentences, the 'sincerity'" ("Life and Times").

Zhirinovsky offered a demoralizing tale of a lonely, fatherless childhood. He rarely saw his mother because she worked long hours and he had no true friends: "I was never happy. No one said hello to me. No one hugged me. No one caressed me. My mother never had any time or energy to show affection because of her hard work" (*My Struggle* 14). "Life itself forced me to suffer from the very day, from the moment, from the instant of birth. Society could give me nothing" (*Poslednii* 13). Yet he did not consider his background unique. "My whole life was humiliating and suffering. This, evidently, was the lot of our entire people..."(*Poslednii* 19). Indeed, in Victor Yasmann and Elizabeth Teague's analysis of the 1993 elections, they noted that when many Russians "look at Zhirinovsky they see themselves. ... His exclusion from a place at the table of the rich gives him something in common with ordinary Russian citizens who, like Zhirinovsky, resent the power and privileges of the *nomenklatura* and, even more so, of their pampered children. Throughout his election campaign Zhirinovsky played on the theme 'I am one of you'" (34).

Zhirinovsky's tales of misery seem the Russian equivalent of Kenneth Burke's example of a politician addressing an audience of farmers and stating that "I was a farm boy myself." (xiv). As Burke maintains, "A is not identical with his colleague, B. But insofar as their interests are joined, A is *identified* with B.... And often we must think of rhetoric not in terms of some one particular address, but as a general *body of identifications...*" (emphasis in original) (20, 26). Yet this identification did not only serve persuasion in a Burkean sense, but demonstrated a key characteristic of Bakhtin's carnival.

Zhirinovsky's rhetoric managed to erase the line separating politician and voter, between political spectacle and political spectator. Through his language of the common person Zhirinovsky managed the "temporary suspension, both ideal and real, of hierarchical rank" that allows for "a special type of communication" during carnival time, a type of communication that is not governed by the rules of propriety outside of carnival (Bakhtin, *Rabelais* 10).

The Bodily Element

Another characteristic of carnival that finds expression in Zhirinovsky's discourse is the emphasis on the body in all its messy glory. Bakhtin points out that in Rabelais' work, the prime example of a carnivalized world, "the material bodily principle, that is, images of the human body with its food, drink, defecation, and sexual life, plays a predominant role" (*Rabelais* 18).

In the carnival sense of the world, the bodily images are not a source of humiliation, but a means of inverting top and bottom in any structure. Images of the body offer a means of debasement or casting down and erase the social distinctions enforced by the prevailing order by demanding acknowledgment that everyone eats, defecates, urinates and has sex. Emphasis on the corporeal symbolizes defiance of the dominant culture. As Bakhtin explains, the carnival includes "the slinging of dung, the drenching in urine, the volley of scatological abuse hurled at the old, dying, yet generating world. All these images represent the gay funeral of this old world; they are ... like handfuls of sod gently dropped into the open grave" (*Rabelais* 176).

Coming from someone who has positioned himself as "one of the people," Zhirinovsky's bodily images served to bring down to earth the dominant systems in the average Russian's life up to this point: communism and reform. In one televised address, the leader of the LDPR condemned the single-party nature of the Soviet Union because it "'reminds one of the problem of homosexuality, where there are relationships between representatives of the same sex.' Khrushchev, alone and joyless, is described as a masturbator. And as for Brezhnev, Chernenko, and Gorbachev's periods in power, 'these were times of political impotence. These leaders wanted to perform but could not ... just as in the case of physical impotence'" (qtd. in Fairweather).

His political campaign in 1995 was laden with sexual overtones. In his televised campaign ads various Russian women promised to "do anything" for him. He was spotted in a Moscow nightclub where he was greeted by a stripper wearing only a sequined G-string and brassiere dancing to the words: "Spank me, I want a man who will spank me." He then got up on stage and told the audience that going to vote was like having sex. "The difference between my party and the others is like the difference between a prostitute and a virgin. ... All the others are like a prostitute who has rolled in the mud a thousand times. No matter what they do, they cannot get their virginity back. Only my party is a virgin" (qtd. in Beeston).

Zhirinovsky's retelling of his childhood also offered prevalent bodily images of a grotesque, carnivalistic sort. When describing his experience of growing up in a communal apartment, he noted that "there was always a line for the toilet, there was always a stench, because it always smells bad if there are no air fresheners, and even more so when people go in there one after another in a row. If in the morning ten to eleven people go to the toilet it doesn't smell like any air fresheners. And several of them smoked there, which was also offensive" (*Poslednii* 12). After his mother enrolled him in twenty-four hour daycare he recalled how they used to wake him and the other children to urinate:

> We were put to bed at nine and woken at eleven so that we would urinate into a bucket. Several of us did not hold it at night and urinated in bed. In order to avoid changing and drying the sheets the nurses put into practice the following system: the whole group was woken, two buckets were placed in the middle of the room, and the lights were turned on. The boys went to urinate in one bucket, the girls in another. And maybe, for the first time, at three or four years old, something sexual stirred in me. I saw completely naked girls. We all slept naked, and when we went to urinate under the burning lamps, of course the forms of the body were easy to see. I still did not understand anything, but I was already conscious that we are boys and those are girls, and they have different types of bodies, different organs. (*Poslednii* 14)

The theme of sex continued in his book. After leaving for Moscow to study at the age of eighteen, he recalled how the "Moscow boys at this time had as much of a sex life as they could. But I, a boy from a provincial city, had still only had my first kisses. The first attempts to engage in the act of sex were unsuccessful" (*Poslednii* 34). He related how once while on vacation he asked a girl "to take off her shorts. But what kind of girl takes off her own shorts first thing? I didn't know that I should have done it myself, to help her" (*Poslednii* 34).

In explaining the advantages of a multi-party system, he drew an analogy to sex, claiming it is as natural as having multiple partners:

> Imagine that you have entered into a sexual relationship with a woman you love and that you have renounced all others.... But what if the love is neither deep nor pure, or if it runs dry? What if it becomes one sided? Do you put your life on hold for the sake of your monogamous idea? In fact, the vast majority of men and women have not one, but several sexual partners in a lifetime. (*My Struggle* 84)

Though some may consider his discussions of sexual and excretory practices inappropriate for a work in which he laid out his ambitious geopolitical philosophy and intentions, in the world of carnival, his bodily images are natural and serve to strengthen his position as critic of the ruling class.

In addition to bodily images, the carnivalized world pays particular attention to the role of the clown, fool, or rogue. Clowns unmask life and the established truths; they mock and expose the falseness of the "official." The next section will explore Zhirinovsky's reputation and role as a clown in the Russian political environment.

The Clown and the Right to be "Other" in this World

Bakhtin considers clowns and fools "the constant, accredited representatives of the carnival spirit in everyday life outside of carnival season" (*Rabelais* 8). The frequency with which the media has dubbed Zhirinovsky a clown, rogue, or buffoon is significant.[8] Immediately following his electoral success in 1993 an article in *The Financial Times* claimed that Zhirinovsky "is more than a clown, though he is funny. ... He is like one of Shakespeare's most bitter and diseased jesters with a skinhead retinue" (Lloyd and Boulton). Alexander Yakovlev, then head of Russia's Central Television Network, called Zhirinovsky a "would-be all-Russia clown" after Zhirinovsky verbally attacked him in a press conference.

In Bakhtin's theory of carnival, the figures of the clown, rogue and fool carry with them a vital connection with the carnival atmosphere (Bakhtin, "Forms" 159). These roguish mask-wearers are represented as agents of truthfulness and authenticity, mocking the "official" (Morson and Emerson 352-353). The great privilege bestowed on these characters is "the right to be 'other' in this world, the right not to make common cause with any single one of the existing categories that life makes available; none of these categories quite suits them, they see the underside and the falseness of every situation" (Bakhtin, "Forms" 159). The clown's laughter and behavior act to liberate him from the constraints imposed by the prevailing conditions of class, status, profession or ideology. Clowns and fools enjoy the right to rip off masks and to survive any delimiting condition or narrative (Morson and Emerson 436). The privilege afforded the clown-like Zhirinovsky not only allowed him to engage in his outrageous antics, but also allowed him a niche in the developing political climate in post-Soviet Russia, distinct from both the Communists and the reformers.[9]

Zhirinovsky's rejection of both the Soviet system and Yeltsin's reforms provided an outlet for those who were not satisfied with Communism but were equally disillusioned by their experience with "democracy" and capitalism. His harangues against the Communists and the reformers sought to disrupt the hierarchies that have existed in Russia for eighty years.

The character of the clown suggests what Bakhtin calls the "primary carnivalistic act," the mock crowning and subsequent decrowning of the carnival king (*Problems* 124). Often he who is crowned is the antipode of a real king, such as a slave or a jester. The act of ritual crowning opens and sanctifies the inverted, carnivalesque world (*Problems* 124). Bakhtin considers the dualistic crowning/decrowning act (from the very beginning the act of crowning contains the immanent act of decrowning) the core of the carnival sense of the world. The crowning/decrowning enacts the pathos of shifts and changes and is rich with carnival categories, such as free and familiar contact, the reversal of hierarchy, and playing with the symbols of authority (*Problems* 124-125).

In true carnival spirit, when Zhirinovsky announced his candidacy for the presidency in February, 1996, he did so in a ceremony that reenacted a *khodynka*, the celebration to mark the coronation of Nicholas II, the last tsar of Russia. Zhirinovsky not only staged his own crowning, but, like at Mardi Gras, tossed ruble notes, scarves and cheap costume jewelry into the crowd. Much like a festival banquet, the crowd was drawn there by the promise of free "Zhirinovsky" brand vodka, a splendid public feast, and barrels of beer and champagne. The "feast," however, consisted of standing in line for rolls and pirogi and there was only a "steady trickle" of vodka (Gordon A1; A6). This oxymoronic meager "feast" coincides well with the carnivalistic trait of ambivalence.

The Ethic of the Loophole

Bakhtin maintains that ambivalence is an "indispensable trait" of the grotesque images of the carnival (*Rabelais* 24). He suggests that all images of carnival are dualistic and therefore ambivalent. Carnival rejoices in relativity. At the core of carnival is the impossibility for "thought to stop and congeal in one-sided seriousness or in a stupid fetish for definition or singleness of meaning" (Bakhtin, *Problems* 124-132). An umbrella term for the concept that allows and encourages ambivalence is the "loophole." As Bakhtin explains it:

> a loophole is the retention for oneself of the possibility for altering the ultimate, final meaning of one's own words. ... This potential other meaning, that is, the loophole left open, accompanies the word like a shadow. Judged by its meaning alone, the word with a loophole would be an ultimate word and does present itself as such, but in fact it is only the penultimate word and places after itself only a conditional, not a final period. (*Problems* 233)

The loophole makes statements ambiguous and elusive, even for the speaker, removing any hard and fast meaning from a word.

Zhirinovsky's book was nothing if not ambivalent. He condemned all "violence to, domination by, or discrimination against any particular nation," and contended that his "world view is a global one," that he realized that "we are all citizens of the same planet" (*My Struggle* 36). Yet later in the book, he suggested violence and dominance when he maintained that "nothing would happen to the world if the entire Turkish nation perished" (*Poslednii* 130).

Further, he asserted that "removed from the agenda of the new Russia will be the questions of nationality, with no discrimination because of national origin" (*My Struggle* 119). However, scattered throughout the book were indications, as well as explicit statements, that nationality was very much part of his agenda. In addition to an adamant defense of his own Russian heritage that opened the book, he suggested that in the future, "Russia must remember ... to care for and protect the welfare of her own people" (*My Struggle* 113). He insisted that, for his plan to be successful, Russians "must acquire a national consciousness," and that they must become "nationally aware of [them]selves as Russians first and foremost" (*My Struggle* 124-125). At turns eschewing nationalism and encouraging it, Zhirinovsky acted the part of the carnivalesque clown, clinging to the loophole within the word "nation."

Zhirinovsky also contended that the "last partition ... does not require war or aggression" (*My Struggle* 61). At the same time, in contradiction, he described how "the concentrated presence of Russian troops will press upon the central Asiatic region, leading, in the end, to an opening to the Indian Ocean" (*My Struggle* 53). He further explained that "Russian soldiers will stop this butchery, this violence, this outrage to human culture" (*My Struggle* 68).[10] It leaves one to wonder how Russian soldiers will implement this plan without the threat or use of violence. Why would Afghanistan, a country that viciously fought Soviet soldiers for ten years, passively allow the dismemberment and annexation of its country? Without a doubt, violence would erupt with the first move toward realization of the "last bid" and Zhirinovsky was well aware of that. The inherent characteristics of soldiers and a military build-up are violent, or at least imply and threaten violence.

Another supposedly essential aspect of Zhirinovsky's vision was pluralism. If he had his way, the future Russia "will be a country without the suppression of different ideas and population groups, without any single political dictate, without a monopoly in the economy or culture. Pluralism should exist in everything" (*My Struggle* 91). Nevertheless, the new Russia:

> will have a unifying symbol for the whole country: a black, yellow, and white state flag of Russia that will flutter atop all state institutions, in all regions and villages of our huge Fatherland. There will be a single hymn for the entire country, a state language of inter-ethnic communication—Russian—and a single currency—the ruble. (*My Struggle* 119)

He also envisioned the "last bid" as a means to spread Russian Orthodoxy: "we should turn all the houses of God in Anatolia into Orthodox churches, allowing the bells of Russian Orthodox churches to ring out along the shores of the Indian Ocean and the Mediterranean Sea" (*My Struggle* 54). This all seems particularly disturbing when one considers the huge Fatherland to which he refers presently includes Kazakhstan, Uzbekistan, Tajikistan, and parts of Turkey, Iran and Afghanistan. He repeatedly insisted that the "people will be fused into a single Russian nation by the great Russian language and ruble" (*My Struggle* 55), and that "in this new geopolitical space stretching to the Indian Ocean and consisting of peoples of various faiths—Turkic- and Farsi-speakers, Slavs and Greeks, Kurds and Arabs— everyone will speak Russian" (*My Struggle* 75). It is difficult to imagine imposing a foreign language, currency, and religion upon other people without some degree of suppression of culture.

It probably comes as no surprise that other incompatibilities, ambivalences, and paired opposites surfaced in the book. The end result of his "bid" would be to create a Russia "whose division or dismemberment is impossible" (*My Struggle* 49). Despite his insistence on his own country's unity, he did not hesitate to advocate "the dismemberment of the artificial states of Turkey, Iran, and Afghanistan" (*My Struggle* 53). He asserted that the Turkic-speaking world "seeks to create a Turkic state stretching from Istanbul to the Altai Mountains" and that "no other country on the earth entertains such lofty ambitions" (*My Struggle* 73), but then he stated that Russia would "emerge a stronger nation that stretches from La Mancha to Vladivostok" (*My Struggle* 125-126).

Zhirinovsky's book enacted the ambivalences characteristic of the carnival. Though his discourse wilts under the rigorous standards of rational argument, it offered an entry into a carnival sense of the world where one is free from the prevailing order. Through his discourse and behavior Zhirinovsky personified the carnivalesque, attacking the official through the absurd and irrational. Zhirinovsky represented a way of "casting down" both the hierarchy imposed by Communist rule and the hardships created by the Democratic, free-market reformers.

Not as Much "For" as "Against"

In an interview with the *New York Times* the director of the All-Russian Center for Public Opinion Research, Yuri Levada, stated that "a vote for Zhirinovsky was the most dramatic protest available. In a way, he seemed to be the only truly anti-establishment figure" (qtd. in Teague 5). Such an interpretation of Zhirinovsky would be consistent with the thesis that at least part of Zhirinovsky's appeal was the lure of the carnival. As a representative of the carnivalesque, one would expect his support to have been an expression of dissatisfaction and criticism of the established order. Indeed, that was the explanation that many academics and voters offered after the LDPR's success in December, 1993. In an article entitled "Not as Much 'For' as 'Against'," political scientist Viktor Bondarev examined letters from voters, some who voted for the LDPR and some who did not. One letter suggested that "voters voted not for Zhirinovsky, but against the incompetence of the ruling team to manage reforms" (Bondarev 2).[11] Another writer from Irkutsk rattled off a list, including "theft..., racketeering, public sex, low birth rate, high death rate, growing unemployment..., murder..., the homeless..., against all of this Russians are protesting as they can" (Bondarev 2).[12]

Bondarev himself editorialized that "voting for Zhirinovsky, people in part were protesting against the price of the realization of the course toward a market economy and genuine democracy" (2).[13] Similarly, *Izvestia* published an article naming three "obvious reasons" for Zhirinovsky's success, the first of which was that he received the "ownerless protest votes" (that is, the votes cast merely to oppose the ruling party and not support anyone) (Kondrashov 4).[14] However, as Mikhail Savin and Alexander Smagin of the Institute of Socio-Political Research pointed out, this reason was too simplistic, and any oppositional party builds its platform on the criticism of the ruling party. It did not account for why the other oppositional parties did not receive the same degree of support, or why a greater number of people did not cast their votes against every party (an option on Russian ballots).

Alexander Rahr suggested that Zhirinovsky "received support from many disillusioned voters who, while not wanting a return to the communist past, at the same time rejected Yeltsin's reform policy or wanted to protest against the latter's ability to establish law and order" (33). I suggest the carnival atmosphere that surrounded Zhirinovsky and his discourse and the antinomian character associated with carnival contributed to his appeal. That is, carnival rejects the existing order by creating an absurd, inverted, humorous alternative order. Zhirinovsky's carnivalistic behavior exemplified that alternative order, and a vote for him became a protest against the dominant system. As Sergei Kibalnik notes, to the West, Zhirinovsky seems frightening, but in Russia they laugh at him (16).

Vera Tolz cited an article that appeared in *Obshchaia Gazeta* that argued that Zhirinovsky's success "may have been a vote against the political establishment as a whole, against all the 'respectable' political parties" ("Russia's" 1). This suggests that Zhirinovsky's apparent appeal was not just an expression of protest and criticism of one particular party or policy. Instead, Zhirinovsky and his party seemed to symbolize, somewhat paradoxically, a rejection of the entire prevailing order (though to participate in the elections at all, as candidate or voter, is also a capitulation to that order). Zhirinovsky's carnivalesque behavior and discourse exemplified the anti-establishment spirit of the carnival. At least part of his support derived from the perception that he was a symbol of criticism and protest against the dominant order. As Michael McFaul has noted, "the vote for Zhirinovsky was not simply a protest vote against economic reform but a vote against all within-the-system parties. ...

Zhirinovsky openly espoused antisystemic goals and threatened to employ antisystemic means to achieve them" (276-277). The theme of protest is also at the heart of Bakhtin's concept of carnival. Its emphasis on the elimination of social hierarchies, the grotesque body, and ambivalence has traditionally served as a symbolic criticism of officialdom. Indeed, there was much for Russians to protest in the early 1990s, and Zhirinovsky's carnivalesque rhetoric and behavior reflected that spirit of protest against official culture.

Fortunately, Zhirinovsky's star has faded significantly since his party's electoral success in 1993. He ran for president in 1996 and received less than 6% of the votes cast. After a precipitous decline by the LDPR in the 1999 Duma elections, Zhirinovsky's party rebounded strongly in 2003, gaining 11.6% of the vote, though still much below the 25% won in 1993 (Lavelle).[15] The 2004 presidential election marked the first time that Zhirinovsky did not run (though he has vowed to run in 2008 and beyond). Just as with his initial appeal, there are a multitude of possible reasons for his decline in popularity. Times have changed in Russia since 1993. The wars in Chechnya and the terrorist attacks in Russia have focused attention away from the poor economy and many have rallied around President Vladimir Putin. Nevertheless, he remains in the Duma and even serves as Vice Speaker. However, the fact that Zhirinovsky and his party have lost support seems consistent with Bakhtin's concept of the carnival. Tom Sobshack notes that carnival is only temporary and fails to last. Eventually, carnival ends and the status quo keeps its grip on society. Mikita Hoy reminds us that "it would be unwise to forget that the potential of carnival for radical rebellion is in the end politically limited, since it is, after all, licensed misrule, a contained and officially sanctioned rebellion, after which everybody gets back to work" (291).[16] Though Zhirinovsky's outrageous behavior and rhetoric captured the Russian public's imagination in the early years of its post-Soviet transition, the LDPR's legislative agenda never materialized. McFaul notes that "Zhirinovsky never devoted real resources to developing antisystemic structures and weapons but instead was easily and often bribed into cooperating with the Yeltsin government" (360). Indeed, one could argue that Yeltsin, the Communists, and Putin have all contributed to Zhirinovsky's declining appeal by appropriating some of his language and platform, decreasing the degree of difference between him and other politicians. Russians may have looked elsewhere for politicians who seemed get work done. Sergei Kibalnik offers anecdotal evidence of the public's disillusionment with the LDPR leader's performance when he notes a joke that was circulating in Russia in the mid 1990s:

"Why aren't you getting married?

Well, you know, my boyfriend, Zhirinovsky, is a politician.
He can only promise, he doesn't follow through" (16).

It is perhaps fitting that the clown prince of Russia would be the butt of a joke after he had become a part of the system that he seemed to criticize. The Zhirinovsky phenomenon illustrates the difficulties politicians face as they try to simultaneously offer carnival's anti-institutional rhetoric and seek to maintain a place of privilege in the very institutions they criticize. In the end, he has become the target, rather than the source, of carnival's oppositional humor. Arguably, Zhirinovsky is not the only carnivalesque politician. One can see less extreme carnivalesque traits in the images of some American politicians such as Jesse Ventura and, to a lesser degree, Arnold Schwarzenegger. However, in transitional democracies such outlandish behavior, when paired with extreme ideologies and policies such as Zhirinovsky's, can be far more dangerous than in more established democracies where conditions are less ripe for extremists to accede to power.

Whether in emerging or established democracies, carnivalesque rhetorical strategies within the realm of politics constrain both the public and the politician. The public's protest is limited because in the end, election, even of the most outrageous personality, is an act of acceptance of the official order. Voting, even as an act of protest, is necessarily an agreement to work within the system. The politician is also limited by the strategy. Playing the role of the carnival clown is plausible as long as the candidate is not actually elected. Once the clown serves within officialdom, s/he ceases to be carnival's representative criticizing official institutions and instead becomes a court jester whose powers of criticism are constrained by the fact that s/he has become a member the ruling class and it is no longer in her/his interest to subvert the system.

NOTES

* This study was made possible by a grant from the Kennan Institute at the Woodrow Wilson Center for Scholars. The author would also like to thank Barbara Warnick, Leah Ceccarelli, and James West for their assistance in the development of this essay.

1. There are several accepted systems of transliteration of Russian proper names into the Latin alphabet. *Controversia* employs a transliteration system that results in spelling his name Zhirinovsky, rather than, for instance, Zhirinovskii.

2. The format of the election was a rather complicated affair. Half the seats in the Duma, or lower house of parliament, were contested on the basis of proportional representation according to party. For the

other half of the Duma seats, as well as the upper chamber of parliament (the Council of the Federation), the electorate voted for individual candidates. As a result, the pro-reform bloc, led by Russia's Choice, won the most seats, followed closely by the anti-reform parties, led by the LDPR and the Communist Party of the Russian Federation (CPRF) (Rahr 32; Tolz, "Russia's" 1).

3. *My Struggle* is not an absolutely faithful translation. Though the parts of the original that it does translate are quite accurate, it leaves out sections from the original. When possible, quotations will be taken from the English translation and will be cited from *My Struggle*. When quoting passages that were not translated the citation will be from *Poslednii* and the translation will be my own. Queries to the LDPR and to Barricade Books, the publisher of the English translation, regarding the origin of the Hitlerian English title have not been acknowledged.

4. my translation.

5. The term *nomenklatura* refers to former Communist Party officials and top managers and administrators who went on to become elected regional deputies and from whom most governors were drawn. Over time, this group of elite Party members evolved into a privileged social class of Party functionaries. With the collapse of Soviet power, much of the old *nomenklatura* converted their privileges into material assets and have become quite well off in recent years (Sakwa 159).

6. For a good defense of using Bakhtin's theory despite his own indictments of rhetoric, see Jasinski's article.

7. Thomas B. Farrell has noted that confessionals on the part of politicians can also contain a degree of carnival, as they break down barriers between the politician and the public (252).

8. Entering the key words "Zhirinovsky" and "clown" into LexisNexis for a search between the dates of the 1993 Duma election and the 1996 Russian presidential election turned up thirty-six articles in the field of European News Sources.

9. Though his own and the LDPR's fortunes have declined since 1993 (He finished fifth with only 5.7% of the vote in the 1996 presidential elections (Sakwa 393).), both the Communists and the democrats have appropriated aspects of his style and content. The Communists have taken on a distinctly nationalist demeanor and the Yeltsin government has taken more steps to reassert Russia's "great power" status in significant, if mild, confrontation with the West. It could even be said that Yeltsin initiated his own "push to the South" with the war in Chechnya. Solovyov and Klepikova note what they call "political plagiarism," when they contend that in 1994 "there wasn't a single foreign or domestic policy issue on which the Kremlin did not make a concession in some degree to Zhirinovsky" (216). Bakhtin has noted appropriations of carnival by the establishment, such as royal masquerade balls and feasts (*Rabelais* 9).

10. Zhirinovsky refers here to civil strife in Afghanistan, Tajikistan and Georgia.

11. my translation.

12. my translation.

13. my translation.

14. my translation.

15. The LDPR was denied registration by the Central Election Committee in 1999. As a result, Zhirinovsky and others registered as Zhirinovsky's Bloc.

16. It is worth noting here that the LDPR was the first party registered in the USSR after the Communist Party's constitutionally guaranteed monopoly was repealed. This has led some to speculate that it was encouraged to register in order to "undermine the influence of genuine liberal organizations" (Kagarlitsky 63).

REFERENCES

Bakhtin, Mikhail. "Forms of Time and Chronotope in the Novel." Trans. Caryl Emerson and Michael Holquist. *The Dialogic Imagination*. Ed. Michael Holquist. Austin: U of Texas P, 1981. 84-258.

———. *Problems of Dostoevsky's Poetics*. Trans. and Ed. Caryl Emerson. Minneapolis: U of Minnesota P, 1984.

———. *Rabelais and His World*. Trans. Hélène Iswolsky. Bloomington, IN: Indiana UP, 1984.

Beeston, Richard. "Slav Casanova Woos Voters." *The Times*. 30 Dec. 1993. Online. LexisNexis. 12 Jan. 1999.

Bitzer, Lloyd F. "The Rhetorical Situation." In *Contemporary Rhetorical Theory: A Reader*. Eds. John Louis Lucaites, Celeste Michelle Condit, and Sally Caudill. New York: Guilford, 1999. 217-225.

Bondarev, Viktor. "Ne stol'ko 'za,' skol'ko 'protiv'." *Trud* 4 Feb. 1994: 2.

Burke, Kenneth. *A Rhetoric of Motives*. Berkeley: U of California P, 1950.

Churilov, Aleksei. Introduction. *Poslednii vagon na sever*. By Vladimir Zhirinovsky. Ed. Aleksei Churilov. Moscow: V. Zhirinovsky, 1995. 3.

Clark, Terry D. "The Zhirinovsky Electoral Victory: Antecedent and Aftermath." *Nationalities Papers* 23 (1995): 767-778.

Fairweather, Natasha. "Instant Book, Just Add Zhirinovsky." *The Moscow Times*. 30 Nov. 1994. Online. LexisNexis. 12 Jan. 1999.

Farrell, Thomas B. "The Carnival as Confessional: Re-reading the Figurative Dimension in Nixon's 'Checkers' Speech." *Texts in Context: Critical Dialogues on Significant Episodes in American Political Rhetoric*. Eds. Michael C. Leff and Fred J. Kauffeld. Davis, CA: Hermagoras, 1989. 243-252.

Gordon, Michael R. "Russian Nationalist Woos Voters With Vows and Vodka and Gifts." *New York Times* 12 Feb. 1996, natl. ed.: A1+.

Gutterman, Steven. "Raucous Russian Parliament Shuts Down." *United Press International*. 22 Dec. 1995. Online. LexisNexis. 12 Jan. 1999.

Hopkins, Mary Frances. "The Rhetoric of Heteroglossia in Flannery O'Connor's *Wise Blood*." *Quarterly Journal of Speech* 73 (1989): 198-211.

Hoy, Mikita. "Joyful Mayhem: Bakhtin, Football Songs, and the Carnivalesque." *Text and Performance Quarterly* 14 (1994): 289-304.

Jasinski, James. "Heteroglossia, Polyphony, and *The Federalist Papers*." *Rhetoric Society Quarterly* 27 (1997): 23-46.

Kagarlitsky, Boris. *Restoration in Russia: Why Capitalism Failed*. London: Verso, 1995.

Kartsev, Vladimir. *!Zhirinovsky!*. New York: Columbia UP, 1995.

Kibalnik, Sergei. "Zhirinovsky as a Nationalist 'Kitsch Artist.'" *Kennan Institute Occasional Papers*. Washington, DC: Woodrow Wilson International Center for Scholars, 1996.

Koman, Alan J. "The Last Surge to the South: The New Enemies of Russia in the Rhetoric of Zhirinovsky." *Studies in Conflict and Terrorism* 19 (1996): 279 -327.

Kondrashov, Stanislav. "Tri ochevidnosti v uspekhe zhirinovskogo." *Izvestia* 16 Dec. 1993: 4.

Lapidus, Gail W. Introduction. *The New Russia: Troubled Transformation*. Ed. Gail W. Lapidus. Boulder, CO: Westview, 1995. 1-4.

Lavelle, Peter. "Analysis: The Right Under Putin's Thumb." *United Press International*. 10 Dec. 2003. Online. InfoTrac. 6 Mar. 2005.

"The Life and Times of a Dangerous Clown." *The Observer* 19 Dec. 1993: 11. Online. LexisNexis. 12 Jan. 1999.

Lloyd, John, and Leyla Boulton. "Smile Masks a Scream of Rage: Vladimir Zhirinovsky is Part Clown, Part Victim, Say John Lloyd and Leyla Boulton, but his Contradictions Cause Concern." *The Financial Times* 18 Dec. 1993: 8. Online. LexisNexis. 12 Jan. 1999.

McAuly, Mary. *Russia's Politics of Uncertainty*. Cambridge: Cambridge UP, 1997.

McFaul, Michael. *Russia's Unfinished Revolution: Political Change from Gorbachev to Putin*. Ithaca, NY: Cornell UP, 2001.

Mickiewicz, Ellen. *Changing Channels: Television and the Struggle for Power in Russia*. New York: Oxford UP, 1997.

Morson, Gary Saul, and Caryl Emerson. *Mikhail Bakhtin: Creation of a Prosaics*. Stanford, CA: Stanford UP, 1990.

Murphy, John M. "Inventing Authority: Bill Clinton, Martin Luther King, Jr., and the Orchestration of Rhetorical Traditions." *Quarterly Journal of Speech* 83 (1997): 1-19.

Rahr, Alexander. "The Implications of Russia's Parliamentary Elections." *RFE/RL Research Report* 3.1 (1994): 32-37.

Rancour-Laferriere, Daniel. *The Slave Soul of Russia: Moral Masochism and the Cult of Suffering*. New York: New York UP, 1995.

Remnick, David. *Resurrection: The Struggle for a New Russia*. New York: Vintage, 1998.

Sakwa, Richard. *Russian Politics and Society*. 2nd ed. New York: Routledge, 1996.

Savin, Mikhail, and Alexander Smagin. "LDPR: Slagaemye Pobedy." *Nezavismaia Gazeta* 18 Dec. 1993: 1+.

Service, Robert. "Menace in his Madness." *The Guardian* 13 Apr. 1994: 20. Online. LexisNexis. 12 Jan. 1999.

Seward, Deborah. "Zhirinovsky Captivates with Jokes, Threats and Promise of Strong Russia." *The Associated Press*. 11 Dec. 1993. Online. LexisNexis. 12 Jan. 1999.

Shokarev, Vladimir. "Kto golosoval za LDPR." *Izvestia* 30 Dec. 1993: 4.

Simons, Herbert W. "On the Rhetoric of Social Movements, Historical Movements, and 'Top-Down' Movements: A Commentary." *Communication Studies* 42 (1991): 94-101.

Sobshack, Tom. "Bakhtin's 'Carnivalesque' in 1950s British Comedy." *Journal of Popular Film and Television* 23 (1996): 179-185.

Solovyov, Vladimir, and Elena Klepikova. *Zhirinovsky: Russian Fascism and the Making of a Dictator*. Trans. Catherine A. Fitzpatrick. Reading, MA: Addison-Wesley, 1995.

Specter, Michael. "Russians Ask: Are We Better Off Now Than Years Ago?" *New York Times* 16 June 1996, late ed.: 1, 10.

Svintsov, Vitaly. "Eto est' nash poslednii brosok na yug." *Nezavisimaia gazeta*, 20 Jan. 1994: 8.

Teague, Elizabeth. "Who Voted for Zhirinovsky?" *RFE/RL Research Report* 3.2 (1994): 4-5).

Tolz, Vera. "Russia's Parliamentary Elections: What Happened and Why." *RFE/RL Research Report* 3.2 (1994): 1-8.

Yakovlev, Alexander. "To Zhirinovsky and Other 'Patriots'." *Izvestia* 25 Apr. 1995: 5. *Russian Press Digest*. Online. LexisNexis. 12 Jan. 1999.

Yasmann, Victor, and Teague, Elizabeth. "Who is Vladimir Zhirinovsky?" *RFE/RL Research Report* 3.1 (1994): 34-35.

Zhirinovsky, Vladimir. *My Struggle*. New York: Barricade, 1996.

———. *Poslednii_brosok na yug*. Moscow: Pisatel', 1993.

The Islamic Idiom and the Prospects for Arab World Deliberative Democracy: A Book Review Essay

David M. Cheshier

Abstract

Scholarly inquiries on the role of public deliberation in the Arab world have proliferated since the attacks of September 11, 2001, and the subsequent U.S. attacks on Afghanistan and Iraq. The review essay considers six such inquires.

Dale Eickelman and Jon Anderson (editors), *New Media in the Muslim World: The Emerging Public Sphere*, 2d. Ed. (Bloomington, IN.: Indiana UP, 2003).

John Esposito and François Burgat (editors), *Modernizing Islam: Religion in the Public Sphere in Europe and the Middle East* (New Brunswick, NJ: Rutgers UP, 2003).

Sohail Hashmi (editor), *Islamic Political Ethics: Civil Society, Pluralism, and Conflict* (Princeton, NJ: Princeton UP, 2002).

Miriam Hoexter, Schmuel N. Eisenstadt, and Nehemia Levtzion (editors), *The Public Sphere in Muslim Society* (Albany, NY: SUNY Press, 2002).

Tareq Y. Ismael, *Middle East Politics Today: Government and Civil Society* (Gainesville, FL: UP of Florida, 2001).

Carrie Rosefsky Wickham, *Mobilizing Islam: Religion, Activism, and Political Change in Egypt* (New York: Columbia UP, 2002).

The September 11, 2001 attacks on the symbolic centers of American economic and military power and their devastating consequences have provoked a fierce and sometimes painful public debate over the prospects for open democratic deliberation in the Arab world. In spite of worldwide trends, which have almost everywhere favored democratic transitions, the vast majority of the Arab world population still lives under authoritarianism. Even those countries with emergent and relatively free presses (such as Lebanon, Jordan, and Kuwait) have been charged with fostering pent-up desperations likely to culminate in violence, as their leaders remain relatively unresponsive to the normal give and take of public controversy. That the attackers came from Saudi Arabia and Egypt, two countries governed under especially tight control, has not escaped notice.

In the American academy and elsewhere the legacy of 9/11 still reverberates. Considerable discussion centers on the nature of American public
diplomacy in the Middle East, and the Bush Administration has by now
experimented with everything from the creation of public relations campaigns to television productions aimed at the so-called "Arab street" (the
just launched Al-Hura network has already produced a predictable lack of
enthusiasm in the region). The U.S. Congress, concerned that American
Middle Eastern studies centers have too readily turned a blind eye to regional
terror, is debating the imposition of funding strings on research support. In
late 2002 the Congress held hearings called by New York Senator Charles
Schumer on the extent to which indigenous Middle Eastern media (with
particular attention on the Palestinian National Authority) encourage violence in entertainment and news programming. And a recently published
"expose" of Middle Eastern studies, written by Martin Kramer, has generated considerable attention.[1]

The challenges posed by Islam, especially as manifested in Arab world
nations, transcend the repercussions of September 11. The Arab world is the
last region of the world to fully experience the democratization effects that
followed the end of the Cold War and the collapse of the Soviet regime. Arab
nations are still among the most autocratic on the planet, despite encouraging democratization news in almost every country in the region. And the
Middle East is no small or isolated zone of potential danger. Straddling a
large portion of the world's energy supplies and the scene of repeated military conflict, almost everywhere the region is undergoing explosive population growth rates that (to name only one often cited consequence) are causing painful demographic skews. [2]

Furthermore, the region has suffered from repeated colonizing and its
populations are still mostly economically impoverished. As Tareq Ismael
notes, "between 1948 and 1991, interstate and intrastate conflicts resulted
in over 2.2 million casualties in the region" (a figure which would obviously
have to be revised upwards given the experiences of the last decade).[3] The
cultural reverberations of this long history are much debated but undeni-
able. From American and European support for dictatorships and arbitrary
geographical partition designed to preserve power balances, to the subtler
ways by which such a legacy continues to shape Western discourse about the
region's population and challenges,[4] the Islamic world is still unknown to
most outsiders.

These factors make up a complex and daunting backdrop for scholarly inquiry on the role of public deliberation in the Arab world, which is the subject of the books under review here. In works such as Ismael's 2001 volume, *Middle Eastern Politics Today: Government and Civil Society,* the topic's complexity is given due attention in careful documentation of diverse national experiences and histories. Ismael reveals the full range of governmental activities, media environments, and civil society organizational patterns that pervade the Arab world experience. Ismael's work, which also aims to position contemporary developments in the deeper histories of the region (going back all the way to the dissolution of the Ottoman Empire and before), brings to mind the manner by which the great debates recur again and again.[5] Questions today contemplated by American military occupiers are often no different than those considered decades ago by British and French commanders. And the slogans that today dominate resistance movements throughout the region eerily echo the appeals drafted in the name of the Turks and others. Ibrahim Yaziji's poem, an "Ode to Patriotism," arguably the first regionally widespread call for pan-Arabism, was written in the mid-19th century. The much-reviled Muslim Brotherhood has been in existence for more than three quarters of a century, having gotten its start in Cairo in 1928. And the language of the 1915 Damascus Protocol, which demanded political independence from the Ottomans, contains the seeds of demands still articulated today in the context of anti-Americanism.

The authors of five other books explored here join Ismael in debating three major questions of considerable relevance for scholars and students of public argument. First, although there are democracies whose populations are predominantly Islamic (Turkey and Malaysia are often cited examples), many observers ask whether the general confluence of Islam and autocracy is more than coincidental, and whether cultures where the religion/state connection is so close can be realistically expected to tolerate criticism. Second, the Arab case is isolated frequently as a pessimistic caveat undermining the widespread scholarly optimism that often accompanies civil society formation. What exactly is the relationship between civil society organizing and the prospects for democratization in the Arab world? Finally, what does the Arab experience teach us about the connection of media transformation and information globalization, and its relationship to democratization pressures?

Although much of the commentary on political Islam has tended to group it with the world's other fundamentalisms, most of the authors considered here resist this move, and rightfully so. There are, of course, some structural functional affinities between the contemporary anti-modernism of, say, fundamentalist American militia groups and Arab world terrorist brigades (e.g., both distort the mainstream teachings of their faiths). But the danger is oversimplification.[6]

Can Genuine Deliberation Thrive in an Islamic Context?

The very question of whether the Islamic faith is compatible with public deliberation can be read as a kind of slander, as if implying that thoughtful and principled adherence to one of the world's richest intellectual faith traditions entails a fit of irrationality. One simply cannot generalize about a religious tradition that claims more than a billion followers and spans every continent. Islam has undeniably been a force of world historical transformation as nations from North Africa to Southeast Asia have experienced the pressures of religious resistance, but the nature of system challenge varies widely given local particularities of culture and governance. As John Esposito recently catalogued it, "Islam has inspired revolution in Iran as well as reform, resistance, and opposition movements in countries as diverse as Tunisia, Algeria, Lebanon, Jordan, Egypt, Pakistan, Afghanistan, Kashmir, Malaysia, and Indonesia."[7] Keeping this in mind is an important inoculant against the now-common tendency to see Islamism as socially pathological.

The central contribution of the collection of essays edited by Hoexter, Eisenstadt, and Levtzion is the careful way it refuses to confine analysis of Arab world civil society organizing to the last fifteen or twenty years.[8] The contributed essays address such questions as whether a pre-modern Islamic public sphere can be said to have existed, as well as the broader questions regarding the intersection of strong religious conviction and public sphere organizing. Although the papers were first prepared for a 1997 conference, the themes they address are surprisingly prescient given recent democratization activity, and the editors' insistence on the term *public sphere* prompts readers attuned to that phrase in the usual argumentation studies context to think through the relevance of the idea for non-Western (especially non-European) contexts.[9]

Despite the range of organized state-Islam arrangements (which range from open cooperation to open disdain), the greatest attention in the West is given to manifestations of Islamic revivalism, phenomena variously referred to as *Islamism, political Islam,* or *Islamic fundamentalism.* For understandable reasons decision makers in the industrialized world focus most intently on the violence done by those acting in the name of more radical articulations of Islam. The global sense of unease prompted by the Iranian revolution and subsequent American embassy takeover, along with the assassination of Egyptian president Anwar Sadat, has been emphasized many times since given the global aspirations of Osama bin-Laden and his followers and the unending cycle of attack and reprisal in the Israel-Palestinian context.

Among other changes in the area studies scholarship has been a growing acknowledgement that violent manifestations of political Islam, while not often specifically supported by Muslim electorates, has not suppressed potential electoral support for Islamic movements either. Movements dismissed as electorally marginal in the 1980s and even into the early 1990s are now conceded to have support sufficient to dominate openly contested elections.[10] While the popular press and punditry too often refer to the *Arab Street*, a misnomer that only reproduces an attribution of irrationality to Arab world populations (even if the idea is used by some Arab governments), the parliamentary success of religious opposition in Egyptian and Algerian elections has earned for religiously affiliated political movements a greater respect, and in some cases fear.

The academic argument over Islam is often contextualized in the context of global economic developmental patterns and the widely conceded failure of Middle Eastern populations to benefit from international trade flows, despite oil wealth. As we shall see, this dispute has important implications for anyone interested in the potential for deliberation. One view sees Islam as an anti-modern throwback that galvanizes popular support from populations disillusioned by their exclusion from regional sources of prosperity.[11] Such a view invariably pits Mecca against mechanization (Daniel Lerner's phrase[12]), despite a wealth of evidence that complicates so simple a view (for instance, observers sometime overlook how the most enthusiastic adherents of Islamic conservatism are often from science and engineering backgrounds[13]).

To an increasing extent recent scholarship challenges the idea that Islam is essentially at odds with economic modernization. These dissenting views often start by observing that in the context of the extraordinarily fast economic modernization of the last fifty years,[14] some social force like Islam was bound to arise, if not to pull the wind out of the sails of development then at least to make the whirlwind comprehensible for displaced workers. Bjørn Utvik, adopting this view, sees Islam as actually paving the way for economic development, since it provides a kind of cultural cover for those interested in the quick economic transformation of Muslim societies; a discourse of moral regeneration simultaneously rationalizes economic policy and distinguishes it from Western cultural templates for local audiences predisposed to anti-Western chauvinism.[15] Utvik even discerns this discursive work reflected in calls to enshrine Shariah law; although his claim that demands to make Islamic law the basis of state legitimacy facilitate modernization by connecting religious law with modern legal practice is well defended, it seems hard to reconcile with the more theocratically centered contexts in which such demands usually arise. [16]

Advocates like Bruce Lawrence (of the "Islam is anti-modern" view) can see along with everyone else how even Islamic clerics have tended to favor rapid economic development as a necessary cure for endemic poverty and relative deprivation. And so in nuancing their claims, the effort is made to distinguish between *modernity* and *modernism*. Islamic fundamentalists, argues Lawrence, oppose Enlightenment rationalism (and not modern technology per se) in defense of the Truth claims articulated by the Prophet. This makes their approach potentially hostile to the procedures for open deliberation that are prized by advocates of a fully open society. [17]

Debate on this issue continues. Where Lawrence sees Islam as embodying a renunciation of deliberative norms, Utvik sees even in the more conservative articulations of Islam openness to argumentative claims capable of contestation (which is to say, arguments that go beyond the simple assertion that this or another faith tradition dictates a certain conclusion). Such exchanges typically turn on two questions. The first asks whether Islam's net influence is likely to encourage or disable democratic transitions. The second asks whether Islam is theologically and substantively open to the mechanisms and social protocols that enable deliberative practice. These questions are not redundant, for one can easily imagine reaching the conclusion that Islam is doctrinally open to the rigorous exchange of ideas in contingent political moments, while also concluding Islam is organized institutionally so as to discourage or even repress such deliberative moments from unfolding in assorted national contexts.

As for the first question, it seems hard to deny that Islam simultaneously enables and disables deliberation. While the Islamic tradition rigorously trains its elite leadership for sophisticated argumentative practices, as a political oppositional force Islam is often characterized as inimical to the open exchange of ideas, as when calls for freer public discussion and disagreement are branded as heretical.

Yet, the very fact of Islam's thriving survival as an autonomous public sphere can empower political forces opposed to autocratic governments. In countries where secular opposition is too easily and too readily crushed, no leader would dare silence the mosques or their most esteemed leaders. Apart from participation in Islamic socio-political activity (whether sanctioned by leading clerics or only indirectly reflective of tolerance for Islamic adherence), "the real political forces have no access whatsoever to legal political competition" in many Arab world countries.[18] This sets into motion a dangerous blend. Secular political leaders who wish at all costs to contain Islamic activism impose draconian limits on religious political participation. Meanwhile the politically interested mosques remain as a kind of training ground in pent-up and articulate oppositional activity. The mosques provide both the speaker training and receptive audiences necessary for radicalizing perspectives, but because they often lack the final ability to translate such organizing into electoral victories, explosive social volatility is ever present. Make believe democratization ("for the Yankees to see")[19] simultaneously raises and frustrates grassroots expectations, while violence serves as one of the few remaining outlets for the expression of such suppressed anger. Thus the cycle continues, and the opening for deliberative decision making enabled by the mosques remains always already marginalized.

Such a rendition bears a certain (albeit weak) affinity to Jürgen Habermas' account of how capitalism simultaneously produced the conditions for and then quickly disabled European public spheres and deliberative institutions responsive to relatively open argumentative interaction.[20] In both cases (capitalism and Islamism), powerful socio-political practices operate with double and contradictory effect. In the European context, at least if Habermas is right, the forces (here, European monarchs) most inclined to quash deliberative practice came to realize, if only for an historical instant, how their self-interests were served by allowing effectual debate. The question is whether the kinds of argument galvanized by Islamic opposition will ever be welcomed by secularizing governments, or, relatedly, whether governments organized in fidelity to Islamic law will sustain openness to dissenting perspectives or rigidly interpret cleric law.

Among the sources of insight on the democratization commitments of conservative Islamic organizations is evidence relating to their own internal practices, and this has been of some reassurance to outside observers. In the context of state autocracy, for instance, groups like the Muslim Brothers succeeded, in part, by organizing themselves as meritocracies. The prospect that hard work and passionate commitment to the cause would be more influential in one's ascendancy than family connections or wealth has obvious appeal for students and young underemployed professionals frustrated by patronage politics.[21]

This brings one to the second question (whether Islam is doctrinally friendly to democracy), which on the surface can be more readily addressed than the first if only because the polysemic vastness of so diverse a faith tradition quickly leads one to Islamic interpretive communities open to (even strongly supportive of) political pluralism. The invariably theological context in which such voices are heard gives rise to at least two points of contention, both significant for students of public deliberation:

Does the Islamic adherence to the idea of Absolute Truth as revealed in the Koran and the sunnah (example) of the Prophet peremptorily foreclose openended deliberative exchange and the tolerance for competing worldviews necessary to sustain free discourse communities over time? Islam, of course, does not uniquely assert proprietary ownership of the Truth, and any discourse community is likely to be dominated by those voices passionately motivated by their certain convictions. The Islamic faith tradition arguably poses a unique challenge, though, because of its apparent resistance to the kind of procedural church-state separation codified in the Western legal tradition. That tradition of separation, although regularly challenged, at least theoretically denies any one Possessor of the Truth from freely using mechanisms of coercion to silence Heretics.

Utvik rightly notes that a belief in absolute truth does not foreclose deliberatively rational engagement where outcomes are undetermined and where discussants are genuinely willing to see their views modified by interaction.[22] Even where one takes an emphatic truth claim as the starting point for discussion, space for disagreement is still preserved, if only over how best to translate unchallengeable worldviews into action. Along with others, Utvik sees this space as available in contemporary Islamist economic discourse, where Koranic injunctions (e.g., against riba, or usury, or in favor of self-reliance) are converted into axioms for contemporary policymaking. Yes, Utvik agrees, this context for public deliberation always already imposes a larger and perhaps coercive moralism, which can create a discourse more apologetic than probative, but (he adds) moral discourses can still be rationally pursued and instrumentally beneficial. Referring to the Muslim Brothers, for example, Utvik writes, "Islam is seen as an absolute source of moral injunctions, but not as a provider of an infinite number of particular truths about how to organize society." [23]

All this is reasonable enough. But one still wonders about the prospects for real disagreement when the ends of social policy are taken off the agenda, and where only debate concerning means is allowable. And here the very richness of the Islamic tradition, both as originally established and since interpreted, can become a straightjacket for arguers. It is not as if Islam (or any rich and exclusive faith tradition) simply stipulates vague goals (like happiness or justice) whose ambiguity makes them infinitely generative of contestation. Even conceding the tremendous range of theological debate within the Islamic faith, the worldview it stipulates seems to foreclose the possibility of the very values pluralism often cited as a precondition for democratic governance. [24]

Is Islam's doctrinal toleration of worldview disagreement expansive enough to inculcate effective citizenship practices? However broad or narrow the range of permissible disagreement, a related question is whether the domain of public argument is rich enough to foster social norms which, in time, will produce ever-opening deliberative practices. This question sounds academic but is directly relevant to oppositional practices in the region. To give just one example: the work done in countries like Egypt by Transparency International, a Chamber of Commerce-related initiative designed to encourage civil society and the "rule of law" worldwide, is partly predicated on the idea that the local encouragement of deliberative practices will eventually inoculate citizens against the temptation to concede too readily to the demands of authoritarian power.

The strong tendency in Islamic theology toward relentless self-improvement through struggle (still the dominant regional and religious meaning given to the term jihad) can be read as encouraging precisely the personal behaviors necessary for democratic institution building. In the same way Puritan moralism drove the first European émigrés to America toward a cultural acceptance of surprisingly well enforced thrift and productivity (famously analyzed by Max Weber[25]), one might see in today's Islamic calls for the generation of economic wealth commensurate with the West a similar emphasis on progress-oriented discourses, which may yet in turn fuel political practices open to pragmatic renegotiation. Some measure of this potential is illustrated by the enormous electoral success achieved by Islamically connected political parties even when electoral opportunities have been slight. Time after time, in countries as diverse as Tunisia and Turkey, Iran and Algeria, openings have resulted in outpourings of electoral interest, often driven by grassroots networks first promulgated by civil society organizing. [26]

Must Grassroots Deliberation be Reassessed Given the Arab World Experience?

As these works illustrate, depending on the government and its domestic audiences, Islam can be used for diametrically opposed purposes; either the religion is celebrated in the name of enhancing state legitimacy (where national leaders perform faithfulness as evidence of their right to rule) or (contrarily) the faith is carefully redefined for the purpose of stereotyping regime opponents as anti-modern fundamentalists.[27] In much the same way grassroots, non-governmental organizations (NGO's) are carefully managed by Arab world governments to simultaneously secure legitimacy and vent domestic passions. In a world of close supervision, NGO's are nonetheless growing fast in number and purpose, and explosively so. As Esposito puts it, "across the Muslim world, Islamically oriented political parties, professional associations, social welfare agencies, and educational and financial institutions have proliferated in Egypt, Algeria, Lebanon, Jordan, Palestine, Turkey, Pakistan, India, Bangladesh, Malaysia, and Indonesia."[28]

These facts give rise to very different interpretations of the relationship between democratization and civil society formations in the Arab world context. Admitting that some governments are adept at extending the appearance of democratization (usually by permitting expanded civil society activity) even when the reality is forever deferred, some (including the National Endowment for Democracy's Larry Diamond) insist that once a thirst for democratic participation is activated, an inevitable and forever escalating appetite for freedom is thereby set into motion. In the context of such a perspective, democratic retrenchment is seen as simply a short-term transitional consequence. A more pessimistic alternative view asks whether civil society can lead to real democratization (given clever manipulation by autocrats) or whether such an outcome would even be desirable if elections are only to install strong popularly supported theocracies (a view more commonly articulated by those committed to one or another version of international security realism). Sohail Hashmi's edited volume, *Islamic Political Ethics: Civil Society, Pluralism, and Conflict*, comprehensively surveys these issues.

The recent Iranian experience well illustrates the complications that immediately arise in trying to tell the story of the interrelationship between civil society and democratization. Iran's government provides for a kind of weak secular constitutionalism, although under the structurally stronger control of an Islamically controlled judiciary.[29] After the extraordinary collapse of the Shah's government in the late 1970's, a development which shocked even close observers of the region, the 1997 election of President Mohammed Khatami, who ran on a strongly pro-civil society agenda, and the manner by which his efforts to secularize authority have since been rebuffed, provide ammunition to both sides of the argument. One can either see Khatami's ascendancy to power as the basis for optimism about the eventual opening of Iranian society, or alternatively point to his failure to achieve such secularization (and the recent extent to which even his original supporters are now disillusioned by his leadership) as grounds for pessimism about the Islamic capacity for democratic transformation.

Where does one turn for evidence to definitively settle so stark a disagreement? Fariba Adelkhah points to what she sees as the micro-changes evident in Iranian daily life, and observes how such changes signify a redefinition of the lines of authority and legitimate power. The manner by which funeral rituals have become subtly politicized, she argues, reflects the deep extent to which fundamental democratization impulses now extend all the way down.[30]

In the same vein, Carrie Wickham's remarkable 2002 study of Egyptian political activism, *Mobilizing Islam: Religion, Activism, and Political Change in Egypt*, combines thoughtful appropriation of current social movement theory and research with extended field research in Cairo's diverse neighborhoods. The book begins by noticing the paradox of rising expectations, and their special force in the Egyptian context, where out of a system of free higher education has emerged the most successful location for Islamic recruitment. Drawing on detailed interviews with local activists and government officials, official documents, and the discourses which pervade the state-influenced media, Wickham repeatedly reveals how even closely organized systems of state control are never seamless, and how oppositional practices can be enabled in dozens of quiet ways. Such work can expand our understanding of how social movement mobilization occurs in authoritarian environments and reveals the complex and subtle mechanisms by which well-organized religious conviction can flourish even under secular autocracy.[31]

Considered more broadly, Islam provides at least a double-edged vernacular for advocates of social change. Even in the domain of gender relations, where Islam is often attacked for its unrelenting conservatism, a complicated picture emerges on closer inspection. As Esposito puts it, "in many Muslim societies, women have found Islam offers alternative paths to empowerment and liberation. Many women have become more religiously observant, attend mosque, study and recite the Quran, participate more fully in society, and choose to wear modern forms of Islamic dress as a sign of their modesty and independence." Islamization is thus "both a source of oppression and a source of empowerment."[32]

The civil society context is also complicated. Compared with Western accounts of civil society formation, which largely consider it a secular counterweight to state and market power, Islamic civil society is often explicitly religious and implicitly supportive or supplemental to state forces.[33] The largest Islamic civil society organizations are often welfare organizations that disclaim political interests, or professional associations, which govern accreditation and navigate complex relationships with their governments often requiring support.[34] American democracy promotion assistance, predicated on a conception of civil society organizations that assumes they will function oppositionally, is thus often mandatorily directed at nongovernmental organizations that are not characteristic of the most visible and credible operations. This in turn creates a double bind for recipients of U.S. aid, who will either end up starved of resources (if they turn down outside support) and institutionally puny when they assert their point of view with their own regimes, or discredited if they become reliant on external help.

The historical parallel most commonly cited relates events in the Islamic world today with the Protestant Reformation and the broader trajectories of the European Enlightenment.[35] There is a remarkable irony in the trajectory of such a comparison, since a strong case can be made that it was Arab civilization that sparked the European Renaissance.[36] But today analysts ask whether the Reformation should lead to hopefulness or depression when it comes to the prospects for Arab self-governance. Utvik has noticed the striking parallels between the two, as have many others.[37] Former Secretary of State Henry Kissinger, for example, argues that regional elections held in haste will only install regimes hostile to American interests, and that such haste is unnecessary given the larger sweep of human history. If it took centuries for Enlightenment thinking to break through European religious autocracy, he asks, why should we expect an Islamic Enlightenment to be accomplished with a quick military victory in Iraq?[38]

How relevant is the Reformation analogy? It is true that both Protestant reformers and Islamic clerics operate(d) in an environment where religion provided the only difficult-to-assail ideological vernacular usable by oppositional rhetors. This is especially so in today's globalized and capitalist world, where the competing discourses of pan-Arab nationalism and socialism are simply not viable, at least for now. And optimists also note that unlike their European predecessors, today's Islamic advocates are required to articulate their ideology under tremendous external pro-secularizing pressure, a force that will invariably condition regional democratic articulations.[39]

Does Media Transformation have Predictable Democratization Effects?

The literature relating media processes to the Middle East has tended mainly to focus on Western portrayals of the Islamic Other, in part due to the considerable attention rightly received by Edward Said's now classic works on the topic.[40] The shortage of information in the western media about Middle Eastern topics beyond the issues of war and terror, combined with coverage sometimes bordering on willful distortion, have demonstrably reinforced caricatures about the Islamic faith tradition.[41] Less attention has been paid to media transformations underway in the Arab world, and the way in which indigenous mass communication outlets are potentially transfiguring the prospects for regional deliberation. Beyond attention given by the western media to Al-Jazeera, the Qatar-based television network, it is harder to find references to the burgeoning proliferation of information sources in the region.[42]

To some extent the growing visibility of Muslim populations in western countries, especially the United States, Britain, and France, has begun to transform coverage, although in ways still distorted by patterns of Otherization. Thus, recent debates in France over the appropriateness of the veil in public schools and coverage in America of underground Islamic banking systems have too easily been folded into lingering journalistic frames focused on Islamic exoticism or danger.

Within the region media systems typically remain under tight state control, although there is considerable country-by-country variation. In nations like Egypt, the main newspaper and broadcasting outlets operate with a reasonable degree of official freedom, but self-censor to avoid incurring the wrath of the president and state bureaucracies. Elsewhere, as in Lebanon, a relatively weak government has enabled a surprising degree of press flourishing. Al-Jazeera (the word means "island" or "peninsula") operates in Qatar under the supportive auspices of the emir (Sheikh Hamad bin Khalifa Al-Thani); the network's relative freedom to broadcast has reverberated throughout the region and often trumped western network coverage.

When Egyptian President Hosni Mubarak paid an unofficial visit to the Al-Jazeera production facility in January 2000, he reportedly said off-handedly to his information minister, "All this trouble from a matchbox like this!"[43] The contrast between Qatari press freedom and the almost constantly swinging pendulum of freedom and restriction characterizing Egyptian state media policy is obvious to even the most casual observer. Journalists in Egypt operate within the constraints of an organized press syndicate; although the syndicate often ably advocates the interests of journalistic freedom, it can easily become a target of state ire. State supported programming related to religion well reflects the dynamics of control and articulation. Institutional Islam (which while not political is certainly not oppositional) has ready access to the Egyptian airwaves, whether broadcasting the Mufti of the Republic or the clerics of al-Azhar University, but the louder and more insistently radical voices coming from some of the larger urban mosques rarely if ever receive nationwide exposure.[44]

In this context of tight state control, one fact often noticed is that conservative Islamic groups invariably are willing to exempt communication technology from the list of outside technological instruments seen and shunned as corrupting. Whether it is Osama bin Laden and his followers on cell phones and VHS cassettes, or the followers of the Ayatollah Khomeini who earlier faxed and tape recorded messages of support from Paris into Tehran, "Islamists are extremely adept at utilizing in their organizational work the most modern means of communication and propaganda." [45] Does such openness to new information technologies reflect simply a tactical concession to modernity, or does it signify a deeper receptivity to modern technology?

It would be a mistake to assume that dissenting voices are specifically enabled by the new communication technologies, as influential as they certainly are. Even media considered retrograde, like audiocassettes and books, have a central and continuing significance in regional debates over democratization. Consider the tremendous influence of Muhammad Shahrour's book, which reconsiders Islamic legal theory in light of contemporary practice.[46] Censored by several governments, it has still been widely circulated in the Arab world (by some estimates tens of thousands of copies have been sold). Nonetheless, the long distance broadcast capacity enabled by satellite broadcasting and the internet has had a major regional influence. Governments cannot control dissenting voices as easily when they travel over the World Wide Web and originate in, say, London. Nor can state bureaucrats easily counteract the allure of Arab-language programming, even when they disagree with it, if it comes from another country in the area. Thus is the Qatari network Al-Jazeera able to broadcast debates on controversial topics like gender roles, polygamy, and human rights by way of television shows like "The Opposite Direction." [47]

Eickelman and Anderson's edited volume, *New Media in the Muslim World: The Emerging Public Sphere*, now in its second edition, brings together some of the most prominent scholars of Middle Eastern civil society. Augustus Richard Norton put together the still most commonly cited monographs on Arab world civil society, [48] and writes here about new media issues, focusing especially on how (in the Egyptian context) attempts at government regulation are struggling to remain in charge of public deliberation. [49] The Oxford scholar Walter Armbrust, who has written widely on Middle Eastern media systems (including his books *Mass Media and Modernism in Egypt* in 1996, and his 2000 edited volume, *Mass Mediations: New Approaches to Popular Culture in the Middle East and Beyond*), contributes an essay on how the Egyptian media structures the fantasy world of the country's bourgeois leisure class. [50] A considerable strength of the volume is its repeated attention to how media portrayals provide a shared cultural fantasy that competes for legitimate authority with what Salvatore has called the "theater of the state." [51]

In a context of rapidly expanding mass mediated debates over culture, politics, and religion, it would be easy to conclude optimistically that changes in the media environment will usher in corresponding weakness within authoritarian systems. Here Eickelman's cautionary note is well placed: "An expanding public sphere does not necessarily pose a direct challenge to authoritarianism, nor does it necessarily preclude appeals to violence such as those advocated by al-Qa'ida worldwide, Hamas in occupied Palestine, or the paramilitary Laskar Jihad in Indonesia, disbanded in the wake of the October 2002 terrorist attack in Bali. Authoritarian regimes are compatible with an expanding public sphere.... [52]

Conclusion: Implications for Public Controversy Scholarship

Among the dominant accounts of civil society formation is the view that nongovernmental grassroots organizations mainly have a kind of teaching function. As the argument goes, a woman or man who learns to challenge a neighborhood council when it comes to advocating for a traffic light at the dangerous intersection a block away will end up learning the practices of citizenship necessary to transform cities, and then regions, and then nations. In such an account the prospects for a rich collective democratic life are the equivalent of the sum of lived democratic experiences, and pluralistic cultures thus reproduce themselves based on their success at institutionalizing civic socialization strategies.

In the context of the Arab world, such a view leads one to ask whether such educative functions can be fully achieved under the sway of the often severe constraints of a conservative, non-secular religious worldview, and in an environment where tightly controlled political activity only reluctantly provides an opening for meaningful grassroots participation. And, given such constraints, one is led to wonder whether the practices of democratic life can be induced from the outside.

The normal skepticism regarding these questions, which has already led to a kind of conventional wisdom about the impossibility of "inducing" (or imposing) democracy, must be reconsidered in light of the work reviewed here. It is surely clear that oppressed populations will find ways to articulate their grievances, even when their leaders cling tightly to the instruments of power. And this is so even with respect to institutions directly under the control of autocrats, as the Islamic end-run around state sponsored schooling and centrally directed curricula illustrates. In Egypt, where the educational system is fairly tightly controlled, the minister of education, Dr. Kamal Baha Eddin, has nonetheless described schools as "factories of terrorism."[53] How can this be so when the ministry of education so carefully seeks to regulate everything from curriculum to student dress? Because governmental mandates aimed at driving Islamic influence from the schools has only elicited a backlash vigorous enough to keep the issue alive in public discourse.[54]

We might better understand the potential relationship of democratization and faith by scrutinizing the experience of Muslims who have left the Arab world, and who now live in other more fully democratized societies. Dilwar Hussain, who assesses the experience of expatriated Muslims living on the European continent, sees a not unfamiliar diaspora trajectory unfolding, where Muslim families first focus on guaranteeing basic access to the prerequisites of Islamic life (access to mosques and culturally appropriate schools, *halal* food) and then on finding ways to pass on to their children the core social mores connected with Islamic practice. As such families intergenerationally assimilate, faith practices tend to emphasize cultural fidelity with the faith, while the larger political and economic norms of the new culture are internalized.[55]

The impulse to see the "Islamic problem" as one of simply slowed assimilation should not lead us to underplay the real prospects for regional democratization which may or may not be irreversibly underway. While the grandiose predictions from some Bush Administration officials that victory in Iraq and the overthrow of Saddam Hussein's brutal regime would usher in regional democracy are as yet unfulfilled, longstanding trends (globalization, demographic changes, international democracy formations, modes of oppositional politics enabled by new media, etc.) may have set in motion democratization nonetheless. It remains to be seen whether the region's autocrats will accede to truly open elections and genuinely power- ful parliamentary opposition, but a regional dialogue about such matters is undeniably underway.

NOTES

1. Martin Kramer, *Ivory Towers on Sand: The Failure of Middle Eastern Studies in America* (Washington, D.C.: Washington Institute for Near East Policy, 2001).

2. Many of the same challenges also exist if one reconceptualizes these issues not as Arab world specific but as also intrinsic to nations whose faith traditions are predominantly Islamic. Muslim countries are experiencing rapid population growth—by 2050, some estimate the world will be more Muslim than non-Muslim. Such demographic strains are compounded by the political stresses that come from pres- sures for fidelity to Islamic principles and the related (and understandable) resistance to American power projection. Meanwhile, on three continents—North America, Africa, and Europe—Islam is the fastest- growing faith tradition, a fact that is already causing internal political conflict in countries like France.

3. Tareq Ismael, *Middle Eastern Politics Today: Government and Civil Society* (Gainesville: UP of Florida, 2001), 74. Ismael's estimate comes from Michael Klare.

4. The term "Middle East" is itself a Europeanist term, coined during World War II by British defense planners who had to distinguish theaters of war (where India and Pakistan were in the Far East, and Jordan and others in the "Middle" East). The point is both obvious (from what vantage is Egypt eastern?) and often unnoticed.

5. On the relationship between "the oppressive state and civil society," see Ismael's chapter three (of the same title), *Middle East Politics Today*, 59-106, which provides both a good brief historical review of the important issues and a quick country survey.

6. "What speaking out in an undifferentiated way against 'fundamentalisms' often does is, in fact, to conceal the refusal to take into account more complex situations and claims far more legitimate than their reading through a religious lens may suggest." François Burgat, "Veils and Obscuring Lenses," in *Modernizing Islam: Religion in the Public Sphere in Europe and the Middle East,* edited by John Esposito and François Burgat (New Brunswick, NJ: Rutgers UP, 2003), 24.

7. John Esposito, "Modernizing Islam and Re-Islamization in Global Perspective," in *Modernizing,* 1.

8. Miriam Hoexter, Shmuel N. Eisenstadt, and Nehemia Levtzion (editors), *The Public Sphere in Muslim Societies* (Albany: State University of New York Press, 2002).

9. A *public sphere* is typically conceived as an oppositional space where conversants have relatively equal access to debate on issues of widespread social import, and whose deliberations have a broader political effectivity. In light of such definitional criteria, consider Nimrod Hurvitz's use of the phrase *religious public sphere* in referring to ninth, tenth, and eleventh century Islamic religious practice. In some respects

the terminology seamlessly translates into the context of Islamic deliberative practice—religious discourse, for instance, served as a counterweight to royal power—but in other ways the term seems an unusual fit (it seems odd and inconsistent with Habermas' use of the term, for example, to describe the power struggle between fundamentalist ninth century clerics and dictatorial caliphs as occurring within a discursive public sphere). Nimrod Hurvitz, "The *Mihna* (Inquisition) and the Public Sphere," in *Public Sphere in Muslim Societies*, 17-29.

10. "Within twenty years, religious-based political protest, that is Islamism, became the sole idiom of social protest and of opposition to the incumbent regimes in most of the Muslim Arab world." Basma Kodmany Darwish and May Chartouni DuBarry, *Les Etats arabes face à la contestation islamique* (IFRI, Paris: Armand Colin, 1997), qtd. in François Burgat, "Veils and Obscuring Lenses," in *Modernizing*, 18.

11. Cf., Bruce Lawrence, *Defenders of God: The Fundamentalist Revolt Against the Modern Age* (London: I.B. Tauris, 1990).

12. Daniel Lerner, *The Passing of Traditional Society: Modernizing the Middle East* (New York: Free Press, 1964), 405.

13. As Esposito puts it, "if any one vocation is typical for Islamist, it is that of the engineer." Esposito, *Modernizing*, 5. Such a fact is surprising but not very difficult to explain. A recent *Chronicle of Higher Education* report summarized a series of Arab government reports, which criticize regional universities for their failures in science and technical training. The unusual outcome is that engineers, for example, are both educationally elite and socially disadvantaged by institutional inattention to cutting edge scientific advancement, which means the best and brightest end up often un- or under-employed. This in turn makes technical specialists and scientists a prime demographic recruiting ground for more reactionary strains of Islam. Daniel Del Castillo, "The Arab World's Scientific Desert: Once a Leader in Research, the Region Now Struggles to Keep Up," *Chronicle of Higher Education*, 5 March 2004, p. A36. The sociological implications for this are well described at the Egyptian micro-social level by Carrie Rosefsky Wickham's *Mobilizing Islam: Religion, Activism, and Political Change in Egypt* (New York: Columbia UP, 2002).

14. As recently as the 1940's industrialization had not yet seriously begun even in the larger urban context of Cairo, apart from some textile manufacturing. Bjørn Olav Utvik, "The Modernizing Force of Islam," in *Modernizing*, 45.

15. Utvik, *Modernizing*, 43-67.

16. Baudouin Dupret examines this issue in the Egyptian context, with specific attention to places in Egyptian legal experience where Islam arises. Interested in whether the invocation of Shariah law represents a fundamental effort to impose a new legal model on the Egyptian polity, or whether its use simply provides a legitimate rhetorical cover for other purposes, Dupret finds some evidence supporting both views; that is, Egyptian judges invoke Shariah both to uphold and to challenge secular authority. Dupret, "A Return to the Shariah?: Egyptian Judges and Referring to Islam," in *Modernizing*, 125-143.

17. This summary comes from Utvik, *Modernizing*, 45.

18. Burgat, *Modernizing*, 27.

19. Burgat, *Modernizing*, 27 ("make believe democratization" is his phrase), quoting Nazih Ayubi, *Over-stating the Arab State* (London: I.B. Tauris, 1995) regarding Yankees.

20. Jürgen Habermas, *Structural Transformation of the Public Sphere: An Inquiry into a Category of Bourgeois Society*, translated by Thomas Burger (Cambridge, Mass.: MIT Press, 1989; original work published 1962).

21. This is among Wickham's findings. See Carrie Rosefsky Wickham, *Mobilizing Islam: Religion, Activism, and Political Change in Egypt* (New York: Columbia UP, 2002). Esposito makes a similar point: John Esposito, "Islam and Civil Society," in *Modernizing*, 72-73.

22. Utvik, *Modernizing*, 45 and passim.

23. Utvik, *Modernizing*, 49.

24. Consider the work of John Rawls. It would seem difficult to reconcile even his later minimalist proceduralism with Islam as conservatively articulated. When Rawls explicitly addressed the issue of Islam,
he read the tradition as potentially compatible with his "overlapping consensus" framework, thereby
implicitly acknowledging that his reading did not reflect mainstream Islamic governance. John Rawls,
The Law of Peoples, with 'The Idea of Public Reason Revisited' (Cambridge, Mass.: Harvard UP, 1999),
151n. "The Idea of Public Reason Revisited," which originally appeared in the *University of Chicago
Law Review* 64 (1997): 765-807, is also reprinted in *John Rawls: Collected Papers*, ed. Samuel Freeman
(Cambridge, Mass.: Harvard UP, 1999), 573-615. This reading of Rawls is consistent with those done
by Burton Dreben ("On Rawls and Political Liberalism," 345), T.M. Scanlon ("Rawls on Justification,"
165), and Samuel Freeman ("Introduction," 39), all in *Cambridge Companion to Rawls*, ed. Samuel Freeman (New York: Cambridge UP, 2003). Notably, Rawls' example of a place where liberal Islam coexists
with values pluralism is fictive; he imagines an invented republic of Kazanistan to illustrate the potential coexistence of religion and a government, which accedes to the existence of overlapping consensus.
Rawls, *Law of Peoples*, 75-78.

For elaboration of the basic Rawlsian framework, see his *A Theory of Justice* (Cambridge, Mass.: Harvard
UP, 1971); *Political Liberalism* (New York: Columbia UP, 1993); *Justice as Fairness: A Restatement* (Cambridge, Mass.: Harvard UP, 2001).

25. Max Weber, *The Protestant Ethic and the Spirit of Capitalism*, translated by Talcott Parsons (New York:
Charles Scribner's Sons, 1958, original work published 1904-1905).

26. Esposito reviews this pattern for Tunisia, Algeria, Turkey, Egypt, Iran, and the Gulf. Esposito, *Modernizing*, 78-88.

27. In the first category we might put Saudi Arabia and Iran; in the second Turkey, and to a lesser extent,
Egypt. Western nations, including the United States and the former colonial powers (Britain and France),
have often been complicit in championing crackdowns on the "street" in the name of support for modernization. From the Shah of Iran to President Mubarak and the House of Saud, it has been easy for outside benefactors to look the other way while crackdowns are underway. The paradoxical result, of course,
has been to position industrial democracies against indigenous democratization forces, all accomplished
in the name of modernization and anti-fascism. As Burgat puts it, referring to Western European nations,
"the assistance it provides to regimes lacking popular support directly contributes to the emergence of
this Islamist 'threat' from which, with the legitimate concern for defending both its 'principles' and its
'interests,' it thinks it is thereby protecting itself." Burgat, *Modernizing*, 20. Meanwhile, regional leaders
have quickly mastered the rhetoric: "If you are the Arab leader of a military junta that has mastered the
art of manipulation through terror, you may present yourself as a 'bulwark against fundamentalism.'"
Burgat, *Modernizing*, 25.

28. Esposito, *Modernizing*, 71.

29. Power remains centered in the Supreme Guide, Ali Khameini.

30. Fariba Adelkhah, "Islam and the Common Mortal," in *Modernizing*, 103-123.

31. As an example, Wickham argues that in Egypt "it was precisely the dispersed, informal, and local
character of Islamic institutions that enabled them to evade the watchful eye of authoritarian elites and
hence to serve as 'safe' sites of contact with potential recruits." Wickham, *Mobilizing*, 13. The project also
interestingly problematizes social movement accounts predicated on rational choice models of human
behavior.

32. Esposito, *Modernization*, 9.

33. Such comparisons are immediately suspect for many reasons. Among them, consider the strong advocacy given in American public discourse over the past decade for "faith-based" civil society organizations.
Such attention, eagerly promoted by the Bush Administration, quickly complicates theoretical accounts
contrasting Western/secular to Islamic/religious modes of state oppositional organizing.

34. This is true worldwide, and not just in the Arab world. As Esposito notes, "ABIM in Malaysia, Diwan Dawat al-Islam in Indonesia, the World Assembly of Modern Youth (WAMY) in Saudi Arabia and the Ansar al-Islam in Nigeria reflect the combination of preaching with education, medical, and other social services." Esposito, *Modernizing*, 77.

35. The best recent summary of scholarship exploring this analogy is Michaelle Browers and Charles Kurzman (editors), *An Islamic Reformation?* (Lanham, Md.: Lexington Books, 2004).

36. As Ismael notes, "the works of scholars such as al-Razi (864-940), known in the West as Rhazes, Ibn Sina (980-1037), known in the West as Avicenna, and al-Tusi (1201-74) reached Western Europe during the Renaissance and helped spark the Enlightenment. Indeed, the Islamic preservation of the works of antiquity, as well as substantial scientific endeavors in their own right, played a significant role in the flowering of European culture." Ismael, *Middle East Politics Today*, 49.

37. For example, "in both cases we are talking about middle and lower middle class groups upwardly mobile through education and, to a certain extent, business endeavors." Utvik, *Modernizing*, 51.

38. Kissinger has made this point in a number of his columns, which are distributed by the *Los Angeles Times Syndicate*. For instance, in a March 8, 2004, piece on the transfer of Iraqi sovereignty, Kissinger warned that "the early stages of democratization … tend to fragment the country rather than unify it," and cited the risky histories of Yugoslavia and others. Kissinger, "Common Purpose Based on Common Fear," *The Australian*, 8 March 2004, p. 11. For other examples of this realist orientation regarding democracy in his recent columns, see also Kissinger, "The Custodians of the World?" *San Diego Union-Tribune*, 8 September 2002, p. G2; Kissinger, "Shaping a New World Order," *San Diego Union-Tribune*, 2 December 2001, p. G6; Kissinger, "America's Role: Searching for a Post-Cold War Foreign Policy," *San Diego Union-Tribune*, 30 January 2000, p. G1.

39. A notable detractor from this point of view is Samuel Huntington, who claims this external pressure is most likely to simply reinforce local bellicosity by providing ammunition for nativist opponents of global culture. Samuel P. Huntington, *The Clash of Civilizations and the Remaking of World Order* (New York: Simon and Schuster, 1996), 258 and passim. Huntington specifically sees this as the likely outcome of information globalization (cf., pgs. 129, 254, 274). Huntington's "West vs. the Rest" perspective is rightly criticized, but is fast becoming a self-fulfilling prophesy given the American use of force in Iraq, which may have been justified but has certainly polarized regional views about the United States.

40. Said has documented the distorting effects of the Western worldview in imagining the Orient in a range of literary, socio-political, media, and artistic contexts. Among his other claims, Said argued that Western representations simultaneously portray the East as the scene of danger/degradation and erotic allure. Cf., Edward Said, *Orientalism* (New York: Vintage, 1978), *Culture and Imperialism* (New York: Vintage, 1993), and *Covering Islam: How the Media and the Experts Determine How We See the Rest of the World* (New York: Pantheon, 1991). The basic themes of *Orientalism* are elaborated to a lesser extent in Said's later work. Cf., Gauri Viswanathan, *Power, Politics, and Culture: Interviews with Edward Said* (New York: Pantheon, 2001); Edward Said, *Out of Place: A Memoir* (New York: Knopf, 1999); Edward Said, *Reflections on Exile, and Other Essays* (Cambridge, Mass.: Harvard UP, 2000). For recent overviews of the debates which now center on Said's legacy, cf., Moustafa Bayoumi and Andrew Rubin (editors), "Introduction," in *The Edward Said Reader* (New York: Vintage, 2000), xi-xxxiv; Shelley Walia, *Edward Said and the Writing of History* (Cambridge UK: Totem, 2001); William D. Hart, *Edward Said and the Religious Effects of Culture* (Cambridge: Cambridge UP, 2000); Abdirahman Hussein, *Edward Said: Criticism and Society* (London: Verso, 2002); Valerie Kennedy, *Edward Said: A Critical Introduction* (Cambridge: Polity, 2000); Naseer Aruri and Muhammad Shuraydi (editors), *Revising Culture, Reinventing Peace: The Influence of Edward W. Said* (New York: Olive Branch Press, 2001).

41. Cf. Yahya Kamalipour (editor), *The U.S. Media and the Middle East: Image and Perception* (Westport, Conn.: Praeger, 1997) and Kai Hafez (editor), *Islam and the West in the Mass Media: Fragmented Images in a Globalizing World* (Cresskill, NJ: Hampton Press, 2000).

42. The definitive account of Al-Jazeera's rise to prominence is Mohammed El-Nawawy and Adel Iskander's *Al-Jazeera: The Story of the Network That Is Rattling Governments and Redefining Modern Journalism*,

updated with a new epilogue (Cambridge, Mass.: Westview, 2003). Beyond the Hafez book reviewed here, another interesting summary of broader media developments, though by now slightly dated, is Jamal Al-Suwaidi (editor), *The Information Revolution and the Arab World: Its Impact on State and Society* (Abu Dhabi, UAE: Emirates Center for Strategic Studies and Research, 1998).

43. The story is reported by El-Nawawy and Islander, *Al-Jazeera*, 23.

44. Al-Azhar University's role as keeper of Egypt's mainstream Islamic tradition is, as Burgat notes, complicated. While the mufti might one day issue a fatwa endorsing government financial policy, he is just as likely the next day to issue a statement supporting a Palestinian Hamas suicide bombing. Such support, it must be noticed, would not likely evoke ire from the Mubarak government given its general support for Palestinian resistance. Burgat, *Modernizing*, 29-30.

45. Utvik, *Modernizing*, 45.

46. Muhammad Shahrour, *al-Kitab wa al-Qur'an: Qira'a Mu'asira* (Beirut: Sharikat al-Matbu'at lil-Tawzi' wa al-Nashr, 1992). Shahrour is a Syrian engineer.

47. Dale Eickelman, "Who Speaks for Islam? Inside the Islamic Reformation," in *Islamic Reformation?*, 21.

48. Augustus Richard Norton (editor), *Civil Society in the Middle East*, vols. I and II (New York: E.J. Brill, 1995/1996).

49. Norton, "The New Media, Civic Pluralism, and the Struggle for Political Reform," in *New Media*, 19-32.

50. Walter Armbrust, "Bourgeois Leisure and Egyptian Media Fantasies," in *New Media*, 102-128.

51. Armando Salvatore, "Staging Virtue: The Disembodiment of Self-Correctness and the Making of Islam as a Public Norm," *Yearbook of the Sociology of Islam 1* (1998): 87-119.

52. Eickelman, *Islamic Reformation?*, 24.

53. Qtd. in Esposito, *Modernizing*, 10.

54. The complicated relationship between state sponsored education and popular politics is carefully explored by Wickham, *Mobilizing*, and Herrera, "Islam and Education in Egypt," *Modernizing*, 167-189. Another high quality source on this topic is Gregory Starrett, *Putting Islam to Work: Education, Politics and Religious Transformation in Egypt* (Berkeley: University of California Press, 1998). For a more general overview, see A. E. Mazawi, "The Contested Terrain of Education in the Arab States: An Appraisal of Major Research Trends," *Comparative Education Review* 43:3 (1999): 332-352.

55. Dilwar Hussain, "The Holy Grail of Muslims in Western Europe: Representation and Relationship With the State," in *Modernizing*, 215-250. Obviously such an account presumes a fuller optimism than that provided when attention centers on mosques which have organized more radical political activity, such as those which received heavy state scrutiny in London and New York City. Burgat sees the same assimilationist trajectory at work, and relies on it to explain why apparently trivial symbolic issues become so inflamed. Controversy in France over whether young girls should be allowed to wear the veil in public schools (France recently voted lopsidedly to outlaw the veil) acquires mythic force for diaspora communities who may feel they have nothing left of their home culture but the remnants of faithful religious observance. Burgat, *Modernizing*, 34.

Notes on contributors

Georgeta Bradatan is head of the English Department at the Petru Rares National College in Suceava, Romania. She was one of four Romanian teachers chosen to participate in the Fulbright Teacher Exchange program in 1994-1995, spending a year teaching middle school in California. She is working on her MA in Public Relations and Communication at Stefan cel Mare University in Suceava, Romania.

M. Lane Bruner is associate professor of rhetoric and politics at Georgia State University in Atlanta, Georgia. He is author of *Strategies of Remembrance: The Rhetorical Dimensions of National Identity Construction* (The University of South Carolina Press, 2002) and *Democracy's Debt: The Historical Tensions between Economic and Political Liberty* (Humanity Books, 2009); the edited volume, *Market Democracy in Post-Communist Russia* (Wisdom House Academic Publishers, 2005); and over two dozen scholarly essays and book chapters on rhetoric, identity, and political economy.

David Cheshier is associate professor and chair of the Department of Communication Studies at Georgia State University. His research focuses on rhetorical theory and criticism, argumentation studies, civil society and globalization, democracy transitions in the Arab World, and rhetoric and political philosophy. He is former director of debate at Georgia State.

Dejan Colev (Cirilo & Metodije School, Serbia) is a debate educator and community leader who participated in the 2005 Southeast European Youth Leadership Institute at Wake Forest University in Winston-Salem, North Carolina.

Frans H. van Eemeren is professor of speech communication, argumentation theory, and rhetoric in the University of Amsterdam and director of the research program Argumentation in Discourse. Among the books he has co-authored with Rob Grootendorst are *Speech Acts in Argumentative Discussions* (1984), *Argumentation, Communication, and Fallacies* (1992), *Reconstructing Argumentative Discourse* (with Sally Jackson and Scott Jacobs, 1993), *Studies in Pragma-Dialectics* (eds. 1994), *Fundamentals of Argumentation Theory* (with Francisca Snoeck Henkemans and an international group of argumentation scholars, 1996), the textbook *Argumentation* (with Snoeck Henkemans, 2002), and *A Systematic Theory of Argumentation* (2004). Several of these books are translated into Chinese, Dutch, French, Italian, Russian, and Spanish. Among Professor van Eemeren's most recent books are *Argumentative Indicators in Discourse* (with Peter Houtlosser and Snoeck Henkemans, 2007), *Controversy and Confrontation* (with Bart Garssen, eds., 2009), *Pondering on Problems of Argumentation* (with Garssen, eds., 2009), *Examining Argumentation in Context* (ed., 2009) and *Fallacies and Reasonableness Judgments* (with Garssen and Bert Meuffels, 2009).

James A. Janack is associate professor of communication at Eckerd College. His research explores the relationship between political rhetoric and democratic principles, both in post-Soviet Russia and in the United States. In addition to *Controversia*, his scholarship has appeared in the *Southern Communication Journal, Communication Studies,* and *Social Semiotics.*

Tsvetelina Manolova (Alexander Language School, Bulgaria) is a debate educator and community leader who participated in the 2005 Southeast European Youth Leadership Institute at Wake Forest University in Winston-Salem, North Carolina.

Gordon R. Mitchell is an associate professor and director of the William Pitt Debating Union in the Department of Communication at the University of Pittsburgh. His academic work focuses on rhetoric of science, public argument, social movements, and argumentation pedagogy. Mitchell is author of the award-winning book, *Strategic Deception: Rhetoric, Science and Politics in Missile Defense Advocacy* (Michigan State University Press, 2000) and co-editor of *Hitting First: Preventive Force in U.S. Security Strategy* (University of Pittsburgh Press, 2006). His work has appeared in journals such as *The Bulletin of Atomic Scientists, The Fletcher Forum of World Affairs, Rhetoric & Public Affairs, Philosophy & Rhetoric, Social Epistemology, Argumentation &*

Advocacy, and *The Quarterly Journal of Speech*. As director of debate at the University of Pittsburgh and associate director of debate at Northwestern University, Mitchell led teams to two national championships and moderated some 65 public debates.

Gligor Mitkovski (Independent scholar, Macedonia) is a debate educator and community leader who participated in the 2005 Southeast European Youth Leadership Institute at Wake Forest University in Winston-Salem, North Carolina.

Robert P. Newman is *emeritus* professor of communication and former director of the William Pitt Debating Union, University of Pittsburgh. He is author of some 75 articles and several books, including *The Cold War Romance of Lillian Hellman and John Melby* (1990; winner of the Outstanding Book on Human Rights Award from the Gustavus Myers Center), *Owen Lattimore and the Loss of China* (1993; winner of the National Communication Association Winans-Wichelns Award for Distinguished Scholarship; nominated for both the Pulitzer Prize and the National Book Award; finalist in the *Los Angeles Times* Book Prize Competition), and *Truman and the Hiroshima Cult* (1997; winner of the National Communication Association Diamond Anniversary Book Award). Newman received the International Society for the Study of Argumentation Distinguished Research Award in 1994 and the National Communication Association Distinguished Scholar Award in 2000.

Ivanichka Nostorova is a senior lecturer in the Department of Foreign Languages (Faculty of Philology) at Southwestern University in Blagoevgrad, Bulgaria. Her teaching focuses on British and American culture, English phonetics and phonology, English-Bulgarian translation, and public debate. From 1996-2004, she served as head of the English Section at Southwestern University, supervising teacher training and administering the department. She has also served as a council member of the Bulgarian English Teachers Association.

Damien Pfister is assistant professor in the Department of Communication at the University of Nebraska. As a critic and theorist of public culture and deliberation, he focuses on analysis of democratic practice in the Internet-worked societies. He has presented research at the Alta Argumentation Conference, the American Studies Association Conference, and the National

Communication Association Convention. As an undergraduate debater for the University of Alabama, Pfister reached the elimination rounds of major national tournaments, including an appearance in the semi-finals of the 2000 Cross Examination Debate Association National Tournament. Before beginning his graduate studies at the University of Pittsburgh (Ph.D., 2009), he worked for two years as assistant program manager of the New York Urban Debate League. Pfister served as acting director of debate at the University of Pittsburgh in Fall 2004.

William Rehg is associate professor of philosophy at Saint Louis University. He is the author of *Cogent Science in Context: The Science Wars, Argumentation Theory, and Habermas* (MIT Press, 2009) and *Insight and Solidarity: The Discourse Ethics of Jürgen Habermas* (University of California Press, 1994); the translator of Habermas's *Between Facts and Norms* (MIT Press, 1996); and co-editor (with James Bohman) of *Deliberative Democracy* (MIT Press, 1997) and *Pluralism and the Pragmatic Turn* (MIT Press, 2001).

Milena Ristic (Economic-Trade School, Kosovo) is a debate educator and community leader who participated in the 2005 Southeast European Youth Leadership Institute at Wake Forest University in Winston-Salem, North Carolina.

Gentiana Sheshi (Educational Directorate, Albania) is a debate educator and community leader who participated in the 2005 Southeast European Youth Leadership Institute at Wake Forest University in Winston-Salem, North Carolina.

Gordon Stables (Ph.D., University of Georgia, '02) is the director of debate for the Annenberg School for Communication, University of Southern California. His research explores the nature of representations of military conflict in mass media and the examination of public diplomacy campaigns. An example can be seen in the Summer 2003 issue of *Critical Studies in Media Communication*, titled "Justifying Kosovo: Representations of Gendered Violence and U.S. Military Intervention." His current research projects involve examining the 1993 military operation in Somalia and campaigns targeted at world public opinion during the current war in Iraq.

Christopher W. Tindale is professor of philosophy and chair of ancient history and classics at Trent University. He is the co-author of *Good Reasoning*

Matters! (3rd ed. Oxford, 2004), and the author of *Rhetorical Argumentation* (Sage, 2004), and *Acts of Arguing* (SUNY, 1999), as well as many papers in argumentation and related subjects. Early drafts of the current paper were written while a fellow of the conflict resolution project (2001-02) at the Center for Interdisciplinary Research, Bielefeld, Germany.

David Cratis Williams is associate professor of public communication and director of graduate studies in the School of Communication and Multimedia Studies at Florida Atlantic University. Author of several articles on rhetoric, argumentation, and criticism, including articles on Russian democratization and cultures of democratic communication, Williams has edited six books, including *Ongoing Conversations: New Writings By and About Kenneth Burke* (with Greig Henderson, 2001), *Argumentation Theory and the Rhetoric of Assent* (with Michael D. Hazen, 1990), *Contemporary Perspectives on Argumentation: Views from the Venice Argumentation Conference* (with Michael David Hazen, Frans van Eemeren, and Peter Houtlosser, 2006), and *Understanding Argumentation. Work in Progress* (with Frans van Eemeren and Igor Zagar, 2008). A former director of debate at Wake Forest University, Williams is also co-director of the Biennial Wake Forest University Argumentation Conference. He is co-editor of *Controversia: An International Journal of Debate and Democratic Renewal.*

Carol Winkler (Ph.D., University of Maryland, 1987) is professor of communication studies and associate dean for the humanities in the College of Arts and Sciences at Georgia State University. Winkler's research interests include presidential foreign policy rhetoric, argumentation and debate pedagogy, and visual communication. Her book, *In the Name of Terrorism* (SUNY 2005), traces the behind-the-scenes development of the leadership's public communication strategies since the Vietnam War in response to terrorism. Her research appears in the *Quarterly Journal of Speech, Rhetoric and Public Affairs, Argumentation, Controversia, Argumentation and Advocacy, Political Communication and Persuasion,* and *Terrorism.* She has won the National Communication Association's Political Communication Division's Outstanding Book Award for her terrorism monograph, as well as the Visual Communication Commission's Award for Excellence in Research for her work on linkages between visual images and ideology. As co-executive director of the National Debate Project, she is expanding access to the benefits of debate training into traditionally underserved populations. Dr. Winkler is past president of the American Forensics Association.

Marilyn J. Young is the Wayne C. Minnick Professor of Communication Emerita at The Florida State University. In addition to authoring many scholarly articles, she is the author of *Coaching Debate* (Springboards, Inc., 1977), co-author (with Michael K. Launer) of *Flights of Fancy, Flight of Doom: KAL 007 and Soviet-American Rhetoric* (University Press of America, 1989), and co-editor (with David Marples) of *Nuclear Energy and Security in the Former Soviet Union* (Westview, 1999). Professor Young is past president of the Southern States Communication Association and a former chair of the Committee on International Discussion and Debate of the National Communication Association (USA). Her current research interests include democratization and the development of a political lexicon in Russia. She is co-editor of *Controversia: An International Journal of Debate and Democratic Renewal.*

Citations of Original Publication of Articles

M. Lane Bruner, "The Rhetorical *Phrominos:* Political Wisdom in Postmodernity" first appeared in *Controversia: An International Journal of Debate and Democratic Renewal* 2.1 (2003): 82-102.

David M. Cheshier, "The Islamic Idiom and the Prospects for Arab World Deliberative Democracy: A Book Review Essay" first appeared in *Controversia: An International Journal of Debate and Democratic Renewal* 3.1 (2004): 74-93.

Frans H. van Eemeren, "Democracy and Argumentation" first appeared in *Controversia: An International Journal of Debate and Democratic Renewal* 1.1 (2002): 69-84.

James A. Janack, "Vladimir Zhirinovskii: The Clown Prince of Russia" first appeared in *Controversia: An International Journal of Debate and Democratic Renewal* 3.2 (2005): 13-34.

James A. Janack, "We'll Guarantee Freedom When We Can Afford It: The Free Market, the Russian Constitution, and the Rhetoric of Boris Yeltsin" first appeared in *Controversia: An International Journal of Debate and Democratic Renewal* 1.2 (2002): 57-74.

Gordon R. Mitchell, Damien Pfister, Georgeta Bradatan, Dejan Colev, Tsvetelina Manolova, Gligor Mitkovski, Iva Nestoro, Milena Ristic, and Gentiana Sheshi, "Navigating Dangerous Deliberative Waters: Shallow Argument Pools, Group Polarization and Public Debate Pedagogy in Southeast Europe" first appeared in *Controversia: An International Journal of Debate and Democratic Renewal* 4.1-2 (2006): 69-84. An earlier version of this essay appeared in *Engaging Argument. Selected Papers from the 2005 NCA/AFA Summer Conference on Argumentation.* Patricia Riley, Ed. Washington, D.C.: National Communication Association, 2005: 104-113.

Robert P. Newman, "Hypocrisy and Hatred" first appeared in *Controversia: An International Journal of Debate and Democratic Renewal* 2.1 (2003): 12-39.

William Rehg, "The Argumentation Theorist in Deliberative Democracy" first appeared in *Controversia: An International Journal of Debate and Democratic Renewal* 1.1 (2002): 18-42.

Gordon Stables, "Between The Arab Street and the Arab Basement: Dimensions of Civility & Civil Society in American Public Diplomacy" first appeared in *Controversia: An International Journal of Debate and Democratic Renewal* 2.2 (2003): 53-73.

Christopher W. Tindale, "Power and Force in Argumentation: A Dialogic Response" first appeared in *Controversia: An International Journal of Debate and Democratic Renewal* 3.2 (2005): 63-90.

David Cratis Williams and Marilyn J. Young, "Introducing *Controversia*" first appeared in *Controversia: An International Journal of Debate and Democratic Renewal* 1.1 (2002): 8-13.

Carol Winkler, "Manifest Destiny on a Global Scale: The U.S. War on Terrorism" first appeared in *Controversia: An International Journal of Debate and Democratic Renewal* 1.1 (2002): 85-105.